THE BUSINESS OF INVESTMENT BANKING

THE BUSINESS OF INVESTMENT BANKING

K. THOMAS LIAW

John Wiley & Sons, Inc.
New York · Chichester · Weinheim · Brisbane · Singapore · Toronto

Copyright © 1999 by John Wiley & Sons, Inc. All rights reserved.

Published simultaneously in Canada.

This publication is designed to provide accurate and authoritative information in regard to the subject matter covered. It is sold with the understanding that the publisher is not engaged in rendering legal, accounting, or other professional services. If legal advice or other expert assistance is required, the services of a competent professional person should be sought.

Library of Congress Cataloging-in-Publication Data:

Liaw, K. Thomas.
  The business of investment banking / K. Thomas Liaw.
   p. cm
  Includes index.
  ISBN 0-471-29305-9 (cloth : alk. paper)
  1. Investment banking. I. Title.
 HG4534 I.528 1999
  332.66—dc21   98-11841
                     CIP

Printed in the United States of America.
10 9 8 7 6 5 4

Contents

Preface

*T*he *Business of Investment Banking* provides a comprehensive description of major activities in investment banking and the trend towards one-stop shopping and globalization. In particular, this book goes beyond the subjects and contents covered in traditional investment banking books. This book provides a comprehensive coverage on subjects that are an integral part of the business but are missing in most other books in the field, such as foreign listing on Wall Street, emerging markets, proprietary trading, repurchase transactions, operations, and money management. This book presents an investment banker's perspective on what the environment is and how to best manage it. It is written to provide information that improves a reader's intuition and background similar to what can be gained through an internship at an investment bank.

The book is designed for use as a professional reference and academic text suitable for business professionals and upper-level undergraduate or graduate investment banking and capital market courses. For practitioners, it demonstrates how decisions in one area affect performance and opportunities in other areas of financial services and thus provides a comprehensive view of managing the investment bank. The objective is to provide professionals relevant and in-depth information in order to compete in the investment banking business. For someone new to the global capital markets, the text describes the full range of investment banking activities and the strategic decision-making process.

The Business of Investment Banking begins in the first chapter with an overview of the investment banking business, not just underwriting and mergers and acquisitions but also proprietary trading, global presence, and money management. The subsequent chapters can be divided into four parts: basic business, global perspective, trading and risk management, and special topics.

Part One (Chapters 2 to 6) introduces the basic business areas. The book first describes in detail the process of venture capital investment and mergers and acquisitions. The process includes sourcing, investigation, negotiation, valuation, letter of intent, merger agreement, legal opinions, and regulatory filings. Investment bankers' fees and venture capital exit strategies are also analyzed. On the subject of underwriting, the mechanics, process, pricing, distribution, and underwriting risks are described. Aftermarket trading is an integral part of underwriting. In discussing the government securities market, it is essential to discuss the primary dealer's responsibility, hedging, and regulation. The primary dealer's bidding strategy at the auction goes beyond the standard fixed-income valuation principle. The intricacy of Treasury coupon rolls and the when-issued transactions are also described. On the subject of municipal bond markets, the coverage offers insights on investment bankers' municipal financing techniques and regulatory compliance. The rules on financial contribution to elected officials, the so-called pay-to-play, and the disclosure requirements in both the primary and secondary markets have significantly affected the evolution of the $1.3 trillion municipal securities markets. Asset securitization is a growing trend. The ability to design new structures and bring in new asset types is the key to success.

Part Two (Chapters 7 to 10) presents the global perspective. A key feature of this book is the detailed coverage on how foreign firms list on Wall Street. This book discusses the foreign issuer's motivation to listing shares in the United States. The legal requirements of listing and the valuation and trading of depositary receipts are also examined. Euromarkets and emerging markets are naturally in the investment banking arena. Doing business in Japan and major European financial centers is part of the global presence. This book thoroughly covers the investment banking business in those markets, ranging from trading, underwriting, currency and liquidity risk, to settlements. The complexity of economic, political, and social environments in these markets poses a big challenge for investment banks. The inclusion of emerging markets and extensive coverage of the global markets in an investment banking text is new.

Part Three (Chapters 11 to 14) covers trading, fund management, and risk management. Another special feature of this book is the extensive coverage of proprietary trading and repurchase agreements markets. The contribution of proprietary trading at times accounts for as much as one-third or more of an investment bank's net income. This book offers an insider's perspective on the various approaches to trading. In addition, the repos and reverses markets are at the core of a dealer's business. Part Three also documents the development of these markets in the United States, Europe, and Japan. The current market practices and the use of these markets by the Fed, dealers, banks, and investors are described. Brokering, matched-book operations, and mismatched trading are examined. The emerging equity repo markets present an alternative financing source and a trading opportunity. Financial engineering has played a significant role in the business of investment banking. The emphasis here is on the examination of innovation process with a risk management perspective. In addition, Wall Street firms have added fund business as part of their one-stop shopping strategy. Today major investment banks are among the largest money managers.

Part Four (Chapters 15 to 17) focuses on special topics. Covered first is clearing and operations, a subject that is essential but frequently ignored. Understanding this aspect of the business is crucial to the prevention of failure and to ultimate success. Next comes a comprehensive coverage of securities regulation and ethics. Compliance with securities regulation is an essential part of the business. In ethics, company codes and traditions are usually the guide. It is important to maintain a high professional standard in areas such as confidentiality, firewalls, disclosure, due diligence, inside information, and self-dealing. Finally, commercial banks may engage in securities underwriting and dealing through Section 20 subsidiaries. The ratio of revenue from such ineligible activities has risen to 25% of the total revenue of the Section 20 company, and it is likely that the Glass–Steagall Act will eventually be repealed. What is the impact on the investment banking industry? What is the future trend in investment banking?

In summary, this book provides a comprehensive description of the investment banking business in an increasingly competitive global marketplace. In particular, the book describes in detail the current market practices in all relevant business segments. The objective is to provide an intuitive and rigorous analysis both for practicing professionals seeking to advance their professional development and for students interested in a career in capital markets.

Acknowledgments

Writing this book has been a wonderful experience. I would like to express my heartfelt thanks to those who helped me. To my family, Evergreen, Christine and Kevin, I very much appreciate their encouragement and understanding. I owe thanks to Thomas E. Christman on many ventures. I thank Herb Evers, former president and CEO of HSBC Markets, for assignments in various capacities at the firm during my sabbatical. Angela Burt-Murray provided valuable suggestions in structuring the book coverage. I benefited also from helpful discussions with and valuable comments by a number of other individuals:

Andrew Amstutz, Morgan Stanley Dean Witter
Patricia Brigantic, The Bond Market Association
Chun-Hao Chang, Florida International University
K.C. Chen, California State University
Krishnan Dandapani, Florida International University
Jim Gibbs, Northwestern University and Hines Hospital
Francis A. Lees, St. John's University
Lily Wang, Merrill Lynch
K. Wong, Latham & Watkins
Paula Worthington, Federal Reserve Bank-Chicago

Investment Banking in Global Capital Markets

T he business of investment banking is intensely competitive and is trending toward one-stop shopping and globalization. The scope of investment banking operations has increased to include all major capital market activities, such as underwriting, private placement, mergers and acquisitions, venture capital, market making, proprietary trading, financial engineering, clearing and settlement, and financing and money management. The securities business has also been consolidating. This introductory chapter describes the market environment on Wall Street and briefly outlines the coverage of each chapter.

THE BUSINESS OF INVESTMENT BANKING

Wall Street firms get their net revenues from a variety of sources. Investment banks no longer engage in investment banking operations only; they have ventured into other areas of financial services to meet clients' demands for one-stop shopping. On the other end of the financial services spectrum, commercial banks are taking advantage of the opportunities granted through Section 20 of the Glass–Steagall Act to manage clients' investment banking requirements. As global capital markets have become more integrated, Wall Street firms have moved to establish a local presence in major financial markets around the world and to enhance this presence with broad cross-border capabilities.

Sources of Income

Investment banking, principal transactions (trading and investment), commissions, asset management, and advisory fees are the main contributors to Wall Street's net revenues. For example, Morgan Stanley Dean Witter & Co., the largest Wall Street house in terms of capital, earned 23% of its revenue from investment banking, 31% from principal transactions, 17% from commissions, and 21% from asset management in 1997. Merrill Lynch, the largest if ranked by number of brokers, derived 18% from investment banking, 24% from trading and investment, 30% from commissions, and 18% from asset management during the same year. Even smaller investment banking boutiques such as Hambrecht & Quist, which does lots of technology underwriting, has diversified its income sources: 27% from investment banking, 35% from principal transactions, 13% from commissions, and 16% from advisory fees. The 1996 results

TABLE 1.1   Income Statements for Morgan Stanley Dean Witter (MSDW) and Merrill Lynch ($ Million)

	MSDW 1997	MSDW 1996	Merrill 1997	Merrill 1996
Investment banking	2,694 (23)	2,186 (24)	2,749 (18)	1,945 (15)
Principal transactions	3,654 (31)	2,745 (30)	3,769 (24)	3,454 (26)
Commissions	2,059 (17)	1,768 (19)	4,667 (30)	3,786 (29)
Asset management & services	2,505 (21)	1,717 (19)	2,789 (18)	2,261 (17)
Interest and dividends	10,455	8,580	17,087	12,899
Other	132	125	670	666
TOTAL REVENUES	**21,499**	**17,121**	**31,731**	**25,011**
Interest expense	9,633	7,909	16,062	11,895
NET REVENUES	**11,866**	**9,212**	**15,669**	**13,116**
Compensation and benefits	5,475 (46)	4,569 (50)	7,962 (51)	6,704 (51)
Occupancy and equipment	462	432	1,160	1,067
Brokerage, clearing, & exchange fees	448	316	505	413
Information processing & communications (depreciation & amortization)	602	512	446	411
Marketing and business development	393	296	597	514
Professional services	378	280	813	582
Other	511	390	1,136	859
Total noninterest expense	8,269	6,795	12,619	10,550
Income before income tax	3,597	2,417	3,050	2,566
Income tax expense	1,416	875	1,097	947
Dividends from subsidiaries			47	
NET INCOME	**2,181**	**1,542**	**1,906**	**1,619**

Source: Adapted from *1997 Annual Report.* Morgan Stanley Dean Witter Discover and Merrill Lynch.
Note: Number in parenthesis is percentage relative to net revenues.

were similar. Table 1.1 lists income statements of Morgan Stanley Dean Witter and Merrill Lynch for fiscal years 1996–1997.

Merrill Lynch earned a higher proportion of income from commissions. It has aggressively bought into fund business; assets under management grew to $446 billion at year-end 1997, up from $212 billion in 1996. Income from asset management increased from $1.717 billion in 1996 to $2.505 billion by 1997 at Morgan Stanley Dean Witter, with assets under management soaring from $58 billion to $338 billion. Two additional observations are worth noting: Interest expense is the largest expense item, signifying the high leverage on Wall Street, and employee compensation takes away almost half of the net revenues. This is necessary because the company's success depends on highly specialized and skilled individuals, and competition for key personnel has been increasing. Most firms retain employees with incentives, such as a bonus plan and stock options.

Income components for other major investment banks and boutiques are listed in Table 1.2. Bear Stearns, Lehman Brothers, Donaldson Lufkin Jenrette (DLJ), and Hambrecht & Quist did not derive significant earnings from asset management. Investment banking boutique Hambrecht & Quist earned a higher percentage of net revenues from investment banking. Friedman Billings is the only firm that still has most of its eggs in one basket. It earned 81% of net revenues from investment banking in 1997.

TABLE 1.2 Major Income Components and Compensation Expenses for Investment Banks (as percent of net revenues)

	Bear Stearns		Lehman Brothers		DLJ		Paine Webber		J.P. Morgan		Hambrecht & Quist		Frieman Billings	
	1997	1996	1997	1996	1997	1996	1997	1996	1997	1996	1997	1996	1997	1996
Investment banking	19	20	34	29	24	26	11	11	16	13	27	40	81	61
Principal transactions	45	42	37	46	18	22	26	27	36	39	35	26		
Commissions	21	23	11	11	21	21	35	37	9	9	13	10	12	31
Corporate finance fees					22	17					16	10		
Asset management							12	12	10	10			8	7
Compensation and benefits	49	49	51	51	57	56	59	59	42	42	52	51	62	57

Source: Adapted from Company Annual Reports, 10-Ks, and earnings reports.

The Blurring of Commercial and Investment Banking

A growing number of clients prefer to deal with a single financial advisor for all capital needs. Thus, many investment and commercial banks see the need to combine talents. On March 6, 1997, the Federal Reserve Board raised the amount of revenue that a bank's Section 20 subsidiary can earn from underwriting and dealing in securities to 25% of its total revenue. The new ceiling set off a flurry of deal making. Recent headline deals include Bankers Trust's acquisition of Alex. Brown, NationsBank's marriage with Montgomery Securities, BankAmerica's acquisition of Robertson Stephens, First Union's linkup with Wheat First Butcher Singer Securities, and U.S. Bancorp's takeover of Piper Jaffray.

Another reason that banks want to operate securities activities is that they are profitable. Wall Street earned an estimated $12.4 billion of pretax profits in 1997, up from the 1996 record level of $11.3 billion. Returns on equity (ROE) have been in the range of 20–30%, except in 1994, when the industry recorded a 3.3% ROE. Table 1.3 lists Wall Street profits and ROEs from 1992 to 1997.

TABLE 1.3 Wall Street Profits

Year	Pre-tax profits ($ billion)	% Return on Equity
1992	6.2	22.8
1993	8.6	27.1
1994	1.1	3.3
1995	7.4	20.9
1996	11.3	29.1
1997	12.4	29.3

Source: Adapted from *SIA 1997 Annual Report.*

Globalization

Rapid advances in information technology and greater cooperation among financial regulators have led to closer links in the international capital markets. Larger sums of money are moving across borders, and more countries have access to international finance. To serve clients better, major securities firms have gone global. The *Big Three*—Morgan Stanley Dean Witter, Merrill Lynch, and Goldman Sachs—have operations in almost all countries with significant capital market activities. Many other Wall Street firms have also pursued a globalization strategy. For example, Salomon Brothers linked up with Smith Barney to better position itself as a global player.

With all major Wall Street firms operating in at least one overseas market, international securities activities have grown sharply in importance for Wall Street, and U.S.-based investment banks have dominated global investment banking activities. Major firms earn between one-quarter and one-half of their revenues from overseas. At the same time, foreign financial institutions are expanding investment banking operations in the United States. Major foreign firms with operations in the United States include Deutsche Morgan Grenfell, SBC Warburg Dillon Read, Union Bank of Switzerland, HSBC Capital Markets, Credit Suisse First Boston, CIBC Oppenheimer, NatWest Markets, Daiwa, and Nomura.

SCOPE OF THIS BOOK

The Business of Investment Banking covers the major activities essential to investment banking, including venture capital, mergers and acquisition, underwriting, financing, asset securitization, trading, financial engineering, fund management, emerging markets, and international markets. Successful bankers need to understand the changing regulatory environment and the back-office functions, as well.

Venture Capital and Acquisitions

Investment banks are involved with venture capital investments. This includes venture capital fund management, taking the portfolio companies public, or selling out to other businesses. Most investment banks have venture capital operations. Venture capital typically provides capital and strategic guidance to companies that may be recently formed and rapidly growing, but not yet large enough to access the public equity markets. Venture investing includes startups, growth stage, buyouts, and consolidation and company turnaround. Chapter 2, "Venture Capital Markets," describes venture capital operations, investment agreements, and exit strategies. Mergers and acquisitions (M&As) are an integral part of investment banking business. Investment bankers take in billions of dollars in fees each year. U.S. M&As set a record in 1996 at $626 billion. Volume in 1997 continued the upward trend, with $919 billion in value of deals. Chapter 3, "Mergers and Acquisitions," covers strategic planning, valuation, financing, closing, and legal considerations. Top advisors in the United States include Merrill Lynch, Goldman Sachs, Morgan Stanley Dean Witter, Salomon Smith Barney, Lehman Brothers, Lazard Freres, Credit Suisse First Boston, J. P. Morgan, Bear Stearns, and DLJ.

Securities Underwriting

Most Wall Street firms offer a full range of capital raising and corporate finance service, from initial public offerings (IPOs) and secondary equity offerings, to debt financing, to private placements. Chapter 4, "Stock Underwriting," describes the process of bringing securities to the public. The volume of IPOs climbed to $37.62 billion in 1997, from $35.86 billion in 1996. Secondary equity offerings recorded a volume of $46.84 billion in 1997, versus the 1996 level of $56.97 billion. Top underwriters include Goldman Sachs, Merrill Lynch, Morgan Stanley Dean Witter, Credit Suisse First Boston, and J.P. Morgan.

Corporate nonconvertible bond issuance surged to $564 billion in 1997, a 58% surge from the full year 1996 total of $356.2 billion. Major Wall Street firms are all active in fixed-income underwriting. Donaldson Lufkin Jenrette, Merrill Lynch, and Morgan Stanley Dean Witter claimed the top three positions in underwriting high-yield debt in 1997.

Investment banks, through their primary dealerships, actively participate in the government securities market. The annual issuance volume is huge—$2 trillion to $2.5 trillion in recent years. The government securities market is the largest and most liquid of all markets. Other fixed-income securities, such as agency issues, amount to additional hundreds of billions of dollars. Those markets for fixed-income securities are included in Chapter 5, "Underwriting Fixed-Income Securities."

Asset Securitization

Asset securitization (Chapter 6) is the selling of securities backed by the cash flows from a pool of financial assets. It has revolutionized the way businesses are financed. It provides businesses with access to new sources of capital at lower costs, even after factoring in upfront analysis, structuring, and credit enhancement costs. The revolutionary process first began with mortgage pass-throughs and then moved to other asset types. Chapter 6 discusses the benefits and costs and the basic structure. One of the largest asset-backed markets is the mortgage securities market, with $1.8 trillion outstanding. The discussion covers prepayment risk, valuation, trading, and settlement. Other asset-backed issuances reached $180 billion in 1997. Collateralized bond obligations, which convert junk bonds to investment-grade investments, are recent additions to the asset-backed innovations.

Foreign Listing on Wall Street

Foreign companies seek U.S. listing to raise capital and gain liquidity. U.S. investors want to take advantage of new capital growth opportunities and diversify their portfolios by buying international securities. Chapter 7, "Foreign Listing on Wall Street," describes the listing process, the types of programs, and SEC regulations. The chapter provides a detailed explanation of sponsored American Depositary Receipts (ADRs), Rule 144A ADRs, and Global Depositary Receipts (GDRs). The last part of the chapter describes how to evaluate ADRs and the unique characteristics of trading ADRs.

International Capital Markets and Emerging Markets

The integration of the world's capital markets has accelerated dramatically over the last few years. Merrill Lynch is most aggressive in pursuing the global presence, with offices in Latin America, Australia, India, Singapore, and Korea, to name only a few. This book covers Japanese securities markets, Euromarkets and major European markets, and emerging markets.

Chapter 8, "Euromarkets and European Markets," covers the Euromarkets and the three largest capital markets in Europe: London, Frankfurt, and Paris. Euromarkets are global, trading around the clock in all major financial centers throughout the world. The first part of Chapter 8 examines the roles played by investment bankers in eurobonds, floating rate notes, euro commercial paper, and euro medium-term notes. The subsequent sections focus on the three largest European markets. The discussion provides a roadmap on how to participate in the London, Frankfurt, and Paris markets. The implications of the 1999 European Monetary Union (EMU) are also examined.

Chapter 9, "Japanese Securities Markets," provides an overview of the Japanese capital markets and explores the opportunities for Wall Street firms when Japan begins implementation of the *Big Bang* in 1998. Investment banking, brokerage, and money management are attractive areas of business for U.S. firms.

Emerging markets are an integral part of the global capital markets and are one of the fastest growing destinations for global investors. Chapter 10, "Emerging Markets," describes the complex process involved in doing business in emerging markets. The risk factors include liquidity risk, political instability, insufficient legal infrastructure, currency risk, and contagion effects. This chapter also studies the Brady bond markets, clearing and settlement, and emerging market derivatives.

Trading

Many investment banks put up a substantial amount of capital for proprietary trading (Chapter 11) as part of the firm's principal transactions. Such activities may involve a significant exposure to market, credit, and liquidity risks. Most investment banks earn a significant proportion of revenue from trading and investment. Outstanding players in trading include many of the best-known investment banking houses and hedge funds. Scientific-approach-based trading and arbitrage plays are high-stakes games. Directional strategies anticipate changes in absolute rate and price levels, while relative-value strategies anticipate changes in relationships between markets and classes of instruments. Day trading requires the trader's feel of the market. To succeed, day traders must understand that they are competing with the sharpest minds and have to handle it as a serious intellectual pursuit.

Repurchase Agreements

Repurchase agreements (repos) are extensively used in dealer financing, customer funding, and matched-book trading. In addition, understanding the market is essential to assessing value in the securities markets. The repo market has grown rapidly over the past several years, with the average daily amount outstanding topping $2 trillion. The market is expected to continue to grow, fueled by the increase in demand for funding and innovations in the marketplace. The relaxation of Regulation T will further benefit the fixed-income repo market and will, together with the National Securities Markets Improvement Act of 1996, help foster the equity repo market. Chapter 12, "Repurchase Transactions," provides a comprehensive coverage of the repo markets.

Financial Engineering

Chapter 13, "Financial Engineering," explains how competition among investment banking professionals to meet the needs of borrowers and investors—such as hedging, funding, arbitrage, yield enhancement, and tax purposes—drives the explosive growth in the structured and derivatives markets (rapidly approaching the $30 trillion mark). The junk bond and asset-backed markets provide borrowers with additional funding sources at lower costs. Structured notes add another dimension in the funding and investment spectrum. Transactions in repurchase agreements provide borrowers with lower funding costs and give lenders legal title to the collateral. Through swap contracting, borrowers and investors obtain a high degree of flexibility in asset–liability management at better terms. Credit derivatives are the new trend with widespread applications, but new products emerge all the time.

Money Management

Money management is an important segment of the capital markets and is becoming an integral part of the investment banking business. Chapter 14, "Money Management," explains why. For investment banking houses, fund business is not a question of whether to enter, but whether to "buy" or to "build." Wall Street firms are buying into fund management operations for obvious reasons. First of all, it is one of the most attractive segments of the financial services industry. It expands the scope of products and services that investment banks offer to clients. Furthermore, the income stream is less volatile than trading, underwriting, or mergers and acquisition. The affiliated funds also provide synergy to the bank's underwriting business.

Clearing and Settlement

Chapter 15, "Clearing and Settlement," describes the process of clearing and settlement for various types of securities. Clearing is processing a trade and establishing what the parties to the trade owe each other. Settlement is the transfer of cash and securities between the parties so the transaction can be completed. Clearing and settlement are usually referred to as the back-office operations. The first step in the clearing and settlement process is to convey the details of the trade from traders to the back office. The second step is to compare and match between the purchaser and the seller to ensure that they agree on what is to be traded and on what terms. The final phase is to deliver what has been promised in the trade.

Securities Regulation and Ethics

The main objectives of securities regulation (Chapter 16) are facilitating capital formation and protecting the interests of the investing public. Registration of new securities ensures full and accurate disclosure of material information. Exemptions of registration are available when the securities are sold to certain qualified institutional investors or the amount of issuance is limited. Active secondary-market trading is key to successful primary-market capital-raising activities. Hence, regulating sales and trading in the secondary markets is to ensure fairness and maintain public trust. Professional investment management has become an essential part of the capital markets. Regulation of invest-

ment companies and investment advisors is in the public interest and for the protection of investors. Furthermore, integrity and professionalism are basic to success on
Wall Street.

Major Trends and Section 20 Subsidiaries

The final chapter (Chapter 17—"Investment Banking Trends and Section 20") outlines
the major trends in the business of investment banking. Increasingly, the biggest profits
are concentrated among a few industry titans and a handful of small, specialized boutiques. This is mainly driven by the trend of globalization and one-stop shopping. The
crumbling Glass–Steagall Act permits large commercial banks to engage in securities
underwriting and dealing, which might eventually threaten top investment banks. In
addition to the analysis of the implications of Section 20 subsidiaries, this chapter also
describes the process and requirements for the application of a Section 20 subsidiary.

SELECT BIBLIOGRAPHY

Bloch, E. *Inside Investment Banking*. Burr Ridge, IL: Irwin Professional Publishing,
    1989.
Carroll, M. "Goldman's public deliberations." *Institutional Investor* (July 1998) pp.
    11–18.
Celarier, M. "Chipping at the firewalls." *Euromoney* (December 1996): pp. 52–55.
Friedman, Billings, Ramsey Group, Inc. *IPO Prospectus*. December 22, 1997.
Hayes, S. L., and P. M. Hubbard. *Investment Banking*. Boston: Harvard Business School
    Press, 1990.
Johnson, H. J. *The Banker's Guide to Investment Banking*. Chicago, IL: Irwin
    Professional Publishing, 1996.
Kuhn, R. L. *Investment Banking*. New York: Harper & Row, 1990.
Mester, L. J. "Repealing Glass–Steagall: The past points the way to the future." *Business
    Review*, Federal Reserve Bank of Philadelphia, 1997.
Securities Industry Association. *1997 Annual Reports*.
Wall Street Journal. *Guide to Who's Who and What's What on Wall Street*. NY:
    Ballantine Books, 1998.

2

Venture Capital Markets

Investment banks are involved with venture capital investments, from raising capital for the funds to taking the portfolio companies public or selling out to other businesses. An investment bank may simply raise money for external venture capital funds. An investment bank, alternatively, can manage the fund itself as part of its merchant banking operations. Even though many venture investments turn sour, the successful ones are so profitable that the overall annual returns have exceeded 40% in recent years. The goal of this chapter is to provide a complete discussion on how to succeed in venture capital investing. To achieve this objective we examine issues such as venture capital fundraising, sourcing, due diligence, investing, risk factors, management fees, profit–loss allocations, exit strategies, and tax and legal issues.

VENTURE CAPITAL INVESTING

Venture capital (VC) firms make equity investment in entreprencurial companies. The financiers recoup their investments when the portfolio companies either go public or sell out to other corporations. The VC market includes the merchant banking subsidiaries of large institutions such as investment banks, bank holding companies, industrial companies, and insurance companies. The VC industry also has many specialized investment entities formed principally to make VC or private equity investments. A private VC fund typically raises its capital from a limited number of sophisticated investors in a private placement, and has a life of about 10 to 12 years. The investor base consists of wealthy individuals, pension plans, endowments, insurance companies, bank holding companies, and foreign investors. VC firms receive income from two sources, the annual management fee and profit allocation of the fund. The fund's main source of income is a capital gain from sale of stock of the portfolio companies (the companies in which the fund has invested). The general partner (venture capitalist) typically receives 20% of the profits and the limited partners (capital providers) receive 80%.

A VC fund passes through four stages in its life. The first stage is fundraising. It takes the general partner usually 6 months to 1 year to obtain capital commitment from VC investors. The second stage is to carry out investment. After sourcing a perspective deal, satisfactory due diligence leads to an investment, and the company then becomes a *portfolio company*. This phase typically lasts for about 3 to 7 years. The next stage, which lasts until the closing of the fund, is to help portfolio companies

9

grow. The final stage in the life of a VC fund is its closing. The VC firm should have liquidated its position in all of its portfolio companies by the expiration date of the fund. Liquidation takes one of the three forms: an initial public offering, a sale of the company, or bankruptcy.

Venture capital investing has several unique features. The first unique feature is the venture capitalist's active involvement in sourcing portfolio company candidates, negotiating and structuring the transaction, and monitoring the portfolio company. Often the VC professionals will serve as board members and/or financial advisors to the portfolio company.

Second, VC investing is generally intended for a period of several years, typically 3 to 7 years, with the expectation of high returns when the portfolio company is successful and its securities soar in value. Venture capitalists generally invest in common stock, stock plus debt unit, convertible debt, stock warrant, and preferred stock. They typically expect returns in the 20% to 50% range. Empirically, annual returns on VC investments are quite volatile. The annual rate of returns soared to 40% in 1983, and then plunged to single digits for the remainder of the decade. Helped by the bull markets, the returns in 1995 were greater than 50%, and professional VC firms posted greater than 40% returns in 1996 and 1997.

The third difference from other types of investing is that the securities purchased are generally privately held whether the venture is a new business or an existing company. If the venture fund makes an investment in a buyout of a public company, the company is typically privately held after the buyout. Even in the rare cases when venture capitalists invest in public companies, they generally hold nonpublic securities.

Another important aspect is that VC funds will take interest in a target only if the company has superior management. Weak management means that it will be necessary after the investment to seek management replacements, which risks significant business disruption. Also, it means that the VC professionals will have to invest a significant amount of time while they seek new management for the portfolio company. Thus, it diverts them from other portfolio companies.

Finally, venture capitalists frequently seek board-level control or representation. They do not necessarily demand a majority on the board seats. It depends on how mature the business is and what fraction of the business they own. Regardless of whether venture capitalists demand a majority, they seldom are silent investors. Frequently, VC professionals and the management of the portfolio company work in partnership. Venture capitalist's judgment and contacts are helpful as the portfolio company grows. This is because VC professionals do not view the investment as supplying capital alone, but, rather, as also providing advice on strategic and financial planning and management oversight in order to enhance value.

MARKET OVERVIEW AND A BRIEF HISTORY

The United States has a well-developed VC market. Venture capitalists funded 1,686 young companies in 1996, for a total of $10.1 billion. The number of new businesses that received VC money in 1997 increased by 162 to 1,848, with a record $11.4 billion investment money. Most of the new investments are in information technology and health care companies. Active VCs include New Enterprise Associates (Baltimore), Kleiner Perkins Caufield & Byers (Menlo Park, California), Institutional Venture Partners

(Menlo Park), Oak Investment Partners (Westport, Connecticut), Accel Partners (San Francisco), and Norwest Venture Capital (Minneapolis).

Venture capital specialists set up partnerships pooling funds from a variety of investors. They seek out fledgling companies to invest in and work with these companies as they expand and grow to become publicly traded companies. By way of going public or selling out to other businesses, VC realizes its returns. For VC-backed companies, they use venture capital for broad purposes such as seed capital, working capital, and acquisition capital. Seed capital is used to cover expenses during the setting up, development, and testing stages of a new product, process, or business. Working capital is raised to pay for outlays during the finalization of the development stage when the product is near market potential. Acquisition capital is to fund the purchase of a business.

Seed-stage venture capital and leveraged buyouts are two investment strategies that can be viewed as the two end points of a continuous investment spectrum in VC investing. It is common to view the private equity market as a broad umbrella consisting of seed, startup, growth, mezzanine, buyout, turn-around, and industry consolidation investing. The shift from one strategy to the next is subtle. It is a natural step to move from seed to start-up and then to expansion financing. At some point during the growth phase, an add-on acquisition is likely to present itself. Turn-around investors belong to the private equity market as well. Turnaround investing is called for when a business has run into operational or financial difficulties. Furthermore, consolidating a fragmented industry is another opportunity for VC investing.

Historical Development

Private equity investing has existed in one form or another in every society in which there was significant commercial activity. One interesting historical example was documented by Levin (1994). It involved the financing of a private fire department by Marcus Licinius Crassus in Julius Caesar's Rome. His business agents and firefighters would rush to the site when a building caught fire. If they believed the building was worth saving, the agents would offer to buy it for cash at a substantial discount. If the owner of the property turned down the offer, they would leave without rescuing the building. If accepted, Crassus' firefighters would then attempt to save and repair the building. Crassus made substantial profits.

With the Industrial Revolution in the nineteenth century, banks became the main source of business financing. Venture capitalists shifted to funding the type of companies that lacked access to bank financing. They frequently provided equity capital as the necessary underpinning for a bank loan. The players were mostly amateur venture capitalists, such as wealthy individuals and entrepreneur's friends. However, as the scale of business and the capital needs escalated, VC became more institutionalized. In England, merchants had emerged as the principal providers of the private risk capital. English merchant banks helped finance the U.S. Industrial Revolution and provided a model for U.S. merchant banking development.

The development of professional venture investing in the United States began in the 1940s. The VC market was given a big burst when the Small Business Investment Act was enacted in 1958. Under the act, the small business investment companies (SBICs, licensed by the Small Business Administration) were armed with tax-advantaged status and government lending leverage. The act also permitted banks to invest in SBICs. The entry of banks into the VC business in the late 1950s and the growth through the 1960s and 1970s was a key link in the formation and development of a professional and institutionalized VC industry today.

The VC industry first developed on a large scale in the 1970s. In the early 1970s, many VC funds had a capitalization of $10 million to $20 million, raised from wealthy individuals, endowments, and foundations. These venture groups targeted small and often early-stage technology companies. In the late 1970s, several factors added new sources of capital to the VC industry. First, the Labor Department clarified that invest- ment in a VC fund could be prudent for a private pension plan. Secondly, insurance companies began to provide a significant portion of VC funding. During the same period, the traditional investors remained active.

By the 1980s there was an enormous increase in funding the private equity mar- ket. The major driving force behind the serge was the hot initial public offering (IPO) market. Many VC-backed companies went public and returned investors many times over the money invested just several years back. This allure of high returns attracted many new investors. VC investment reached a peak in 1987. After 1987, money flow- ing into VC funds declined, due to a combination of factors. Since the early 1970s, as more money flooded into the VC market, the number of venture firms had exploded. Some of the VC professionals did not have the fundamental skills to succeed. Furthermore, there was too much money chasing too few good deals. The failure of VC to provide investors returns comparable to that in the early 1980s resulted in a decline in VC funding in the late 1980s.

In the early 1990s, the amount of money raised by VC funds each year was signifi- cantly lower than the 1987 peak. However, the IPO market in 1991–1992 again improved returns for many funds and hence improved fundraising aspects. VC was making a comeback by the end of 1992. The amount of money raised by venture capi- talists surpassed the 1987 peak in 1995–1997. Table 2.1 lists the annual VC commit- ments from 1986 to 1997. The renewed investor interest in VC investing is clearly due to the bull market on Wall Street in recent years.

TABLE 2.1   Venture Capital Commitments

Year	Amount (in $ billions)
1986	3.3
1987	4.2
1988	2.9
1989	2.4
1990	1.8
1991	1.3
1992	2.5
1993	2.5
1994	3.8
1995	6.6
1996	10.1
1997	11.4

Sources: Adapted from *Statistical Abstract of the U.S.*, 1996; *Wall Street Journal* (February 5, 1997, B2, and February 2, 1998, B2); *Pratt's Guide to Venture Capital Sources*, 1995.

Information Sources of Venture Capital

The best sources of VC funding are the established boutiques and venture arms of most major investment or commercial banks. *Platt's Guide to Venture Capital Sources* is a comprehensive directory that lists the addresses and telephone numbers of VCs. The National Venture Capital Association is another source.[1] The *Directory of Venture Capital Clubs* is an excellent information source for first stage venture capital.[2] The American Venture Capital Exchange is a national database listing companies for sale and financing sources.[3]

SETTING UP VENTURE CAPITAL OPERATIONS

Frequently, professionals experienced in private equity investing, such as former executives of venture capital operations, will set up their own shops. They often raise money from a limited number of sophisticated investors, including pension plans, endowment funds, wealthy individuals, foreign investors, bank holding companies, investment banks, and insurance companies. The life of the fund is typically in the range of 10 to 12 years.

A VC fund is generally set up in partnership form, mainly because of tax advantages granted to a "flow-through" entity. A partnership is entitled to the flow-through tax status if it meets the test of the Kintner regulations; that is, the partnership has to satisfy at least two of the following four tests:

1. Unlimited liability test
2. No centralized management test
3. No free transferability of interest test
4. Limited life test

In addition, the general partner must contribute 1% of partnership capital and have at least 1% interest in partnership income and deductions. Then the partnership format avoids federal income tax at the fund level. Each partner is required to report on his or her own federal tax return, if applicable, such partner's distributive share of the partnership's income, gains, losses, deductions and credits for the tax year. There is no tax at partner level for a tax-exempt organization, provided that the investments producing long-term capital loss are not debt financed and that the VC fund is only engaged in a passive investment activity rather than an active business. For a foreign person, there is no tax at the partner level, as long as the capital gains are not effectively connected to an active U.S. business. Under a partnership form, it is permitted to pass through the loss in early years of the fund's life, when management fees exceed income.[4] Also a corporate partner is entitled to an 80% dividends-received deduction with respect to the allocable share of the VC fund's dividend income.

Alternatively, but not as common, a VC fund may be structured in corporate form. As a corporate entity, the fund is entitled to a 100% dividend deduction if it is an SBIC (otherwise, the deduction is 80%). A corporate form provides partners protection against liability for the fund's debt. This liability protection is also obtainable through a partnership structure by compliance with Revised Uniform Limited Partnership Act of 1976 or 1985 (as the case may be), or the formation of corporate intermediaries.

As noted, most VC funds are formed as partnerships. However, they might begin to form or switch to limited liability companies if more states adopt the Limited Liability Company statues.

Profit and Loss Allocations

A VC fund splits profits on a prenegotiated basis. A fund's profits are generally split, with 20% of net profits going to the fund's general partner as a *carried interest* and the remaining 80% going to the limited partners in proportion to their contributed capital. A less common alternative for profit allocation is that partners receive all profits based on contributed capital until the fund has achieved a specified rate of return or a *hurdle rate*. Profits in excess of the hurdle rate are then distributed, 20% as a carried interest and 80% according to capital contributed. In yet another alternative, all profits exceeding the specified returns are distributed to the general partner as a carried interest until the general partner catches up and thereafter the allocation is 20–80.

For loss allocation, the industry practice is that losses are allocated in the same manner as profits were previously allocated until such losses have offset all prior allocated profits and general partner's capital contribution. Then losses exceeding this amount (*excess losses*) are allocated 100% to limited partners, but subsequent profits are allocated to the limited partners until the excess losses are recovered. A less common alternative is to exclude the general partner's capital contribution in calculating the excess losses. Any further losses are allocated proportional to capital contribution, but subsequent profits thereafter are allocated first to restore losses.

Distributions are subject to heavy negotiations. The pro-investor view is to have a full payout in which all capital providers receive distributions according to capital contributions, except for distributions to the general partner to cover his tax liability on the 20% carried interest. Alternatively, a pro-general-partner approach is to make distributions equal to the 20–80 allocations. Distributions in excess of net profits or return of capital are in proportion to capital contributions. Under this approach, the limited partners generally would seek a back-end giveback that would apply if later losses cause the general partner to have received more than a 20% carried interest. As a practical matter, most VC partnership agreements are in the middle ground. The general partner frequently has a certain degree of discretion on the timing of distributions. The partners therefore may be required to pay income tax on partnership income without receiving any cash.

Management Fees

The current industry standard is equal to 1.5% to 2.5% of capital commitments per year, payable to the general partner every quarter. In the 1980s, it was common to set the management fee in the range of 1.5% to 3.0% of asset fair value plus uncalled capital commitments. Obviously, this approach created a conflict of interest in asset valuation and the timing of distributions.

Sometimes the agreement calls for stopping management fees or paying on a declining schedule after a specified period. For example, the management fee declines 10% each year after 6 years. When a venture fund is specializing in buyouts, the regular management fee is payable for a period of typically 4 to 6 years, then a lower monitoring fee is payable thereafter.

Other Issues

Limited partners are the passive investors contributing the major share of capital, but they have no direct involvement in running the fund. All limited partners must be individually indemnified against liabilities arising from the venture operations. The partnership agreement also provides for admission of additional partners and specifies the new allocation of profits and losses based on the contributed capital or other yardsticks.

The partnership agreement provides for a definite life of the partnership, generally 10 to 12 years. It also contains provisions that stipulate the dissolution date. A majority vote by all partners can reset the date to a later period. Additionally, provisions must be set for raising additional capital as business grows. Ideally, further equity investment will be spread proportionally among all partners. In practice, however, only several partners share the responsibility for generating new equity as needed. As new equity comes in, ownership percentages and allocations must be revised.

INVESTING STRATEGY

Venture capital is high-risk, high-return investing. In pursuit of high returns while managing risk, VC professionals need to understand that many deals fail due to poor strategic planning and a lack of vision. Too often, VC fund managers get bogged down in details, ignoring the big picture. Venture capitalists need to define their goals and source the myriad of prospects in order to find a good match with the best financial and strategic edge, before engaging in a costly and time-consuming evaluation process. Once this phase is completed, most VC firms evaluate potential investments based on four fundamental criteria: management, marketing, products, and financial opportunity.

Venture Capital Investing Evaluations

Management experience is a major consideration in evaluating financing prospects. Venture capitalists generally will not take interest in a company unless it has superior management. A strong management team comprises individuals who have successful track records in relevant industries and have gained a superior understanding of their market. The team will work well together and will have extraordinary drive to grow the company. An "A Team" with a "B Product" is more likely to get VC financing than a "B Team" with an "A Product."

The ideal market is one that is growing rapidly and has the potential to become enormous. Popular industries include biotechnology, telecommunications, computer, Internet, and other specialty niche areas. The management of the portfolio company needs to understand and establish relationships with key distribution channels. One effective approach is a direct sales force and close relationships with resellers and original equipment manufacturers.

The ideal product has many proprietary features that differentiate it from others offered by competing companies. A *commodity* product has no unique features, can be manufactured by new entrants easily, and hence is not attractive. In addition, the product should achieve above-average gross margins, offer repeat sales opportunities, and demand a limited amount of additional capital. Because the fate of the company should not be riding on a single product, plans for a full product line are important.

Once the VC fund managers identify a company that has superior management, an attractive market opportunity, and an excellent product, they seek to acquire stakes at as low a price as possible. An entrepreneur, on the other hand, wants to have a price as high as possible. The price of the deal is the outcome of a complex negotiation process. Liquidity is the final goal. Thus, an assessment of likely exit opportunities is made before money is invested.

Risk Factors

Venture capital investing is subject to a high degree of risk. The evaluations criteria outlined are to assess value as well as the risk involved. First, an early-stage company has a limited history of revenue-producing activities. Its operations are subject to the difficulties frequently associated with the growth of a new business and the competitive environment in which the company operates. Furthermore, the new business generally needs strong strategic alliance partners. In addition to other benefits, strategic alliance will also help create name recognition that is an important factor in marketing any product or service. Without such partners, the growth of the company may not proceed as planned.

New products and technological changes present a big uncertainty. This is especially true when investing in a high-tech company. The market evolves with the rapid and frequent changes in technology and customer preferences. The company's growth and future financial performance will depend on its ability to develop and introduce new products. Failure to anticipate or respond to the changing market environment will adversely affect the company's potential. There is no assurance that any new products will be successfully developed or achieve market acceptance, or that competitors will not develop and market products that render obsolete the company's products.

A new startup's success is critically dependent upon a few key personnel. Retention and recruitment of a quality team is essential. Long-term employment contracts that defer a portion of the compensation over time and contain noncompete provisions, stock options, phantom stock, and other profit-sharing schemes have been used with a certain degree of success. The company must attract additional talented individuals to carry out its business plans.

Before long, the company may need additional financing. The required additional investment will have substantial dilution effect. Venture capitalists usually accept the dilution, because there is no public market for the company's securities yet. Typically, the share certificates acquired by a venture capitalist will bear a legend on the back referring to sell restrictions:

> *The shares represented by this certificate have not been registered under the Securities Act of 1933, as amended, and may not be sold or transferred in the absence of an effective registration statement under the said Act, or an available exemption thereunder and under applicable state securities laws.*

Also, stop-transfer instructions will be noted in the company's records with respect to these shares. Venture capitalists need to be prepared to accept the liquidity risk.

VENTURE CAPITAL TRANSACTIONS

Venture capital investing covers a wide range of the investment spectrum. Seed money is provided to the entrepreneur to establish the feasibility of the "innovative concept or product." The next step is the startup financing, which involves financing for product development and the initial phase of marketing. Then comes first-stage financing. At this stage of corporate development, the firm has developed a prototype that appears marketable. The firm begins its growth through second-stage financing. During the growth stage, funds are provided for working capital to finance goods in process, inventories, shipping, and so on. The company is growing and the hopes for profitable operations are reflected in the progressively lower losses. Gradually, this development process leads directly to the third-stage financing. In this phase funds are needed for major expansion, when sales begin to take off and the company is moving from "in the red" to "in the black." At a certain point in the process of corporate development, the company will be ready to go public or will become a target for acquisition. This marks the exit of the VC financing cycle.

Venture capital funds are also frequently involved with buyout, troubled-company, and special-situation investing. The following section groups the private-equity investment spectrum into startup phase, growth stage, buyout financing, and special-purpose investing. The exit strategies will be covered in a later section.

Startup Phase Transactions

An entrepreneur with a new invention or an improvement on an existing product or a marketing process might wish to start a business. The concept may require substantial research or other activities before the actual sales take place. So the entrepreneur approaches a venture capitalist seeking financing for the proposed new business. Suppose the entrepreneur has convinced the venture capitalist that this is a solid and realistic business plan, that the entrepreneur is an extraordinarily able manager, and that the business will prosper. Both parties will begin to negotiate and structure the transaction.

A typical transaction involves the entrepreneur contributing services, ideas, and a small amount of capital, while the venture capitalist contributes a relatively large amount of money. Both parties on a negotiated basis would share the corporate ownership. The venture capitalist would probably insist on investing most of the funds in the form of convertible debt and/or preferred stock and only a small amount in common stock, and would ask the entrepreneur to put up a good faith amount of money. Venture capitalists prefer to invest in convertible instruments, they want to recover most of their invested capital and want only the profits to be shared. The arrangement enables them to receive most of the residual value if the business is not successful. On the upside, if a company is successful, venture capitalists recoup their invested capital and share only profits with the entrepreneur. In addition, the interest expense will be tax-deductible to the portfolio company.

Entrepreneurs are frequently asked to make a good-faith investment in their project. To ensure that the entrepreneur will stay and make best efforts to the business, some shares will *time vest* based solely on the entrepreneur's continued employment and some will *performance vest* based on achieving specified goals.

Control of the board can be split according to proportional equity ownership, or they can agree on allocation of directors different from the equity split. This can be accomplished through the use of a voting agreement, a voting trust, or voting and non-voting common or preferred stock. The venture capitalist will also seek provisions in a shareholder's agreement that sets forth certain parameters for a sale of the company or going public after a stated time period.

The issuance of securities to the venture capitalist, entrepreneur, or any others requires registration with the SEC under the Securities Act of 1933, unless the issuance fits within an exemption. Because of the time and expense required of a registration, it is desirable to seek exemption. The company may be able to comply with the private placement exemption either by meeting the "safe harbor" contained in Regulation D or by the statutory exemption[5] contained in the Securities Act of 1933. The offering must also comply with each applicable state blue-sky laws. It should be noted that the SEC regulation is aimed at full disclosure of information, while some state securities laws go further to regulate the merit issue.

Growth-Stage Transactions

Sometimes the company is successful and needs more money to expand its business. Other times, the need arises for shareholders to redeem shares for the purpose of estate planning and/or liquidity (this is a *recapitalization*). At this stage the business is not ready for a public offering. Hence, the company approaches venture capitalists for growth-stage financing. A venture capitalist makes the investment because it believes that the value will quickly rise once the company has the necessary funds for expansion. The infusion of new capital provides additional needed money that will further enhance the existing borrowing base.

The growth-stage investing is more complex than the early-stage startups. There are several major differences. In a growth-equity transaction, the venture capitalist must negotiate with more shareholders with divergent interests. The company would have far more assets, contingent liabilities, and operating history. A substantial due diligence research and a more extensive investment agreement are required.

In preparation for the investment, the venture capitalist should conduct legal and business due diligence. The investigation examines contingent liabilities, material contracts, debt agreements, insurance, prior acquisition agreements and joint ventures, capital structure, outstanding securities, and so on. A fair value is estimated after the due diligence examinations. The ownership percentage for the VC financing is negotiated and determined. The venture capitalist would want some fixed securities and would want the management shareholders to own a larger percentage than they currently own so they have a greater incentive to perform. In order to achieve these goals, the venture capitalist will propose to engage in a front-end rearrangement of shareholdings. After the rearrangement, the passive nonmanagement shareholders will own a smaller share, the management will own a larger share of common stock, and the venture capitalist will control a larger percentage of equity. There are several methods to achieve this rearrangement of stockholdings. One is a preferred stock recapitalization with the passive shareholders. A second approach is to make redemption from the preferred shareholders for subordinated debt. Alternatively, the company could make a pro rata dividend of preferred stock to all stockholders combined with issuance of shares or options to the management. Why would the passive investors go along with the plan? The first incentive is the higher current yield on the new fixed security. There is less downside risk. And it is better to have a smaller equity percentage with happy management and adequate capital than the old structure.

As discussed, the recapitalization approach calls for the passive shareholders to swap at least some of their old common stock for new preferred stock to raise the management and venture capitalist's equity ownership. The passive shareholder's exchange qualifies as a tax-free recapitalization. The passive shareholders take a basis equal to the basis in the old common stock and postpone the long-term capital gains tax until the new preferred stock is sold. They are responsible for paying taxes on the amortized *phantom dividend income* each year to the extent that the preferred stock's redemption price is above the issuing price.

Under the second alternative, the passive shareholders exchange at least some of their old common stock for new subordinated notes. The swap satisfies the installment-method tax reporting if it meets the following three conditions:

- Both the common stock surrendered and the new notes received are not publicly traded.
- The new notes satisfy other installment conditions, such as not payable on demand or not secured by cash.
- The passive shareholders surrender enough old common shares so the redemption would not be treated as a dividend.

The exchanging shareholders do not recognize capital gains at the time of the exchange. Thereafter, they recognize a proportionate part of the deferred long-term capital gains upon receiving principal payments on the notes.

Finally, the last approach calls for a pro rata distribution of preferred stock and issuing cheap common stock or options to the active management executives. In general, the preferred holders will recognize the imputed dividend income over the life of the preferred, based on the extent at the time of distribution the preferred has a fair value below the redemption price.

Venture Capital Investing in a Buyout

There are three types of buyout targets: a corporate subsidiary, a private company, or a public company. In either case VC fund managers need to be convinced that with additional capital and necessary improvements at the company, the target will rise geometrically in value.

The key acquisition issues involving buyout of a corporate subsidiary include purchase price, debt financing, and equity financing. The purchase price is the outcome of a lengthy negotiation process. The currency used could be cash, subordinated notes, or preferred stock. The acquirer will seek representations and warranties from the target for several reasons. They can be used to call off the deal prior to closing if the target fails to conform to the representations and warranties. They are also used to recover money or to rescind the transaction if the representations and warranties turn out to be incorrect. The venture capitalist will typically seek the right to terminate the transaction if any of the closing conditions such as successful completion of financing, satisfactory completion of due diligence, Hart–Scott–Rodino Antitrust Act clearance, or necessary third-party consent, is not satisfied.

Buyout of a private company is, in many respects, similar to that of a corporate subsidiary, except that an individual or a group now owns the target. There are several ways a private company can be acquired:

- Targeted shareholders can sell stock to the acquirer.
- In a reverse subsidiary merger, the acquirer transitory subsidiary can merge into the target.
- The acquirer can merge into the target in another type of reverse merger.

- It is possible to use a forward or forward subsidiary merger, with the target merging into the acquirer or acquirer's subsidiary.
- The buyout may be structured such that the target sells assets to the acquirer.

Buyout of a public company is more complex. One key issue is how to approach the target: Make a firm offer fully backed by financing commitments, or simply express an interest to minimize target's disclosure obligations? The venture capitalist generally will seek protection against competing bids, and might seek to be compensated if another bidder ultimately triumphs. Typical protective devices include no-shop clauses, break-up fees, lock options to buy unissued target's shares, and crown-jewel options to buy a key asset. Ideally, these protective devices should be negotiated and signed before announcement. Another complexity involving a public company buyout is the federal and state securities laws. The general materiality standard under SEC Rule 10b-5 requires the target to make a public announcement at appropriate timing. The so-called antifraud provisions of SEC Rule 10b-5 under the 1934 Act prohibit trading on material nonpublic information. The offer to purchase the company should follow the tender offer provisions of the Williams Act. In addition, caution should be exercised regarding state regulations such as fiduciary duty of target board and state takeover status.

Special-Purpose Investing

Venture capitalists frequently invest in industry consolidation and company turn-around. When a venture capitalist identifies a fragmented industry in which there are many small firms and no or few market leaders, it will recruit top-notch management to establish a leadership presence in the industry. Or when the venture capitalist identifies a company experiencing significant problems, it will seek to arrange an infusion of new turn-around capital as part of the shared-pain debt restructuring or workout for the troubled company.

Investing for the purpose of industry consolidation can be accomplished in several ways. One is to acquire strategically located players through a series of buyouts. Venture capitalists can also start new business in markets where there is no ideal target or the existing targets are overpriced. The investment can be structured as one of the following:

- A holding corporation is formed to do buyouts and startups, each a subsidiary under the holding company.
- A partnership is formed to do buyouts and startups, each a subsidiary under partnership.
- A partnership holding company is formed to do buyouts and startups, each structured as a partnership.
- All buyouts and startups are together under one single corporate structure.
- All buyouts and startups are together under one single partnership.
- The venture capitalists and other shareholders structure each investment as a direct share ownership.
- Each interest is structured as a partnership and owned by venture capitalists and others.

Under a turn-around investment situation, the troubled company plans to renegotiate its old debt by stretching out principal maturities, reducing interest rates, delaying interest payments, and also canceling a portion of its debt. To induce creditors to participate in the restructuring, the company needs to issue shares to the old creditors. Venture capitalist would want to invest new turn-around capital, provided that they believe the business is basically sound and that the old creditors accept the restructuring. They would intend to simultaneously bring in new management.

Other than this shared-pain restructuring, there are alternative debt-workout transactions, such as partial payments to creditors in cash and new debt, or partial payments in cash, new debt, and common stock. Tax issues are complex in the restructuring in the sense that the amount of debt cancellation—equal to the adjusted issue price of the old debt cancelled less the consideration issued in cancellation of such old debt—could constitute taxable income for the troubled company. In addition, because the debt restructuring or workout involves issuance of stock or new debt instruments, the SEC and other disclosure rules should be followed unless the company can find an applicable exemption.

LEGAL DOCUMENTATION

Venture capital investing is a long-term commitment of support to the portfolio company. A key element in building a successful relationship between the business enterprise and the venture capitalists is the careful crafting of the legal structure of the transaction. The legal documentation represents a charter of legal rights of the parties. Therefore, the legal documentation sets the tone of the relationship between the business entrepreneur and the private equity investors. The documents also serve as a platform for resolution of their differing interests. The legal documents must foresee the changing requirements during the evolution of the business, from a startup to a public company or an acquisition candidate.

Each transaction is unique. There is no "one size fits all" perfect model. Each set of legal documents is tailored to reflect the unique combination of interests involved. However, most legal documents cover the term sheet, investment agreement, stockholder agreements, employee stock options, employee confidentiality and property rights agreements, and legal opinion.

The Term Sheet

The *term sheet* contains a summary of the agreed-on financial and legal terms of the transaction. It may be used to impose enforceable legal obligations upon the parties, such as requiring the payment of expenses in the event the transaction does not close. Although the letter of intent generally does not bind the parties to complete the transaction, as a practical matter, both parties often consider it sufficient evidence of their mutual commitment to warrant the advance of "bridge financing" by the VC funds. Bridge loans are used to fund the expenses during the interim period when the lead VC investor completes the assembly of the investing syndicate or during the time necessary for the preparation of definite legal documents.

Bridge financing typically takes the form of debt due on demand or convertible to the security to be issued for the deal. Bridge financing often includes an *equity kicker* in the form of a warrant to purchase equity securities at substantial discounts. The size of the warrant is tied to the length of time the bridge financing is in place.

The Investment Agreement

The *investment agreement* sets forth the detailed substantive terms of the transaction. It serves as the basic disclosure document. It presents a *stop action* paragraph that must exist at time of closing. It also defines the business parameters within which the enterprise must operate in the future. The legal effect of the investment agreement is similar to most commercial contracts. The most common consequence of a breach of the investment agreement is the ability of the venture capitalist to cancel the transaction because of the company's failure to satisfy certain conditions or a significant misrepresentation by the company.

The investment agreement will include a description of the securities being purchased, the purchase price, and a requirement that the securities be properly authorized. Ancillary agreements such as the stockholder agreement and employee confidentiality and property rights agreements are frequently attached as exhibits. If more than one venture capitalist participates in the transaction, each may be listed in an exhibit to the agreement. In some cases, the portfolio company executes separate investment agreements with other VC funds.

The *representations and warranties* are not intended to screen the company for suitability of investment, but rather, are intended to provide full disclosure of the company's operations. Examples of typical items are organization and authority, capitalization, government approvals, litigation matters, ownership of assets, insurance, taxes, environmental protection, financial information, compliance with securities laws, related-party transactions, disclosure, Employee Retirement Income Security Act of 1974 (ERISA), registration rights, and so on.[6] An affirmative declaration or affirmation of compliance, subject to stated exceptions, prefaces each category.

The *covenants and undertakings* section contains several affirmative and negative covenants relating to the future conduct of the company. Affirmative covenants are actions or results the company promises to undertake or achieve. Negative covenants are actions or positions the company promises to avoid. If the VC fund acquires a significant ownership that grants it control of the board of directors, the covenants are often kept to a minimum. The VC firm will typically rely on the board control to influence the development, and will not impose extensive contractual restrictions on strict covenants. If the inside management continues to control the board, the covenants are frequently extensive.

Most affirmative and negative covenants are designed to end upon a specific date, upon completion of an IPO, or because of some other factor. Typical affirmative covenants in a VC investment agreement are payment of taxes and claims, property and liability insurance, legal compliance, access to premises, maintenance of corporate existence, compliance with key agreements, life insurance, Rule 144A information, environmental matters, financial and operating statements, indemnification, and so on. In contrast, the negative covenants serve to prevent the company from taking actions it otherwise might be inclined to take. Typically, these negative covenants relate to matters that would affect the fundamental nature of the business. The negative covenants commonly included in the VC investment agreement are sale or purchase of assets, dealings with related parties, charter amendments, change in business, distribution and redemption, security issuance, employee compensation, and so on.

In addition, this section customarily includes registration rights, rights to participate in future financing, and indemnification. Registration of their securities under Securities Act of 1933 for public sale is key for venture capitalists to achieve liquidity and realize the investment return. Venture capitalists often insist on a right to partici-pate in future financing by the company, through such provisions as rights of first refusal, preemptive rights to maintain same percentage ownership, or rights of prior negotiations before the company's offer of such opportunity to others. Venture capital-ists may require founders or top management to share personal responsibility for the representations and warranties in the investment agreement and to indemnify them for any breaches thereof.

Closing conditions are used for two main purposes: (1) to guarantee that certain fundamentals relating to the securities invested and the transaction are in place, and (2) to change or affect the financial or business operations of the company such as the contemporaneous execution of a bank loan agreement. Typical closing conditions seen in venture investing include legal opinion, execution of ancillary agreements, and exe-cution of compliance certificates by senior management.

Investment Securities

The securities commonly used in venture investing include common stock, stock plus debt unit, convertible debt, stock warrant, and preferred stock. The simplest, but not necessarily the best, way is to invest in common stock. Most venture capitalists would prefer to invest in a senior security that carries the rights to purchase common stock. In a stock-plus-debt structure, the debt component provides modest interest, reason-ably long term, and minimum or no principal amortization. In a convertible debt trans-action, the debt can be converted into equity at a predetermined conversion ratio. A preferred stock transaction is typically tailored to contain a variety of debt and equity features. Corporate holders may prefer preferred stock to debt because of its tax-advan-taged status. Purchase of a stock warrant is generally made in combination with some other security. A package of straight debt plus a warrant is similar to a convertible debt. However, this type of combination might be more flexible than convertible debt, because the debt and warrant can be traded separately.

Although the terms of convertible debt may be structured to resemble preferred stock, there are several fundamental differences. First, debt securities do not automati-cally carry voting rights. So investors must resort to voting agreements or covenants contained in the investment agreement. But the status as a creditor of the company in any bankruptcy proceedings may be affected (subordinated to other creditors) by the exercise of such equity-like control. Second, the creditor's right to receive interests is more secure than preferred stockholder's to receive dividends.

Ancillary Agreements and Documents

The first ancillary agreement is the stockholders agreement. It is designed to control the transfer and voting of the equity security by major stockholders so stable owner-ship and management may be maintained during the term of the investment. This is accomplished by restrictions on the sale of stock by insiders, which is important in maintaining a balanced composition of the board of directors.

Employee stock purchase agreements are typically included for the purpose of attracting, retaining, and motivating key employees. The benefits of a correctly im-plemented employee stock option program are obvious. Both the entrepreneur and VC professionals are willing to accept the dilution of their respective equity owner-ship to better motivate employees. Establishment of appropriate employee stock plans is frequently a condition of closing on the investment. Incentive objectives and tax considerations play a significant role in determining the terms of an employee equity program.

Employee confidentiality and property rights agreements are used to secure the company's claim to its valuable proprietary and business rights. Such agreements often entail employee's commitment to cooperate with the company to perfect the company's ownership of the inventions. Founding stockholders may also agree to noncompete covenants.

A favorable legal opinion is a classic example of closing conditions. The legal opinion of company counsel generally covers the legality of securities, compliance with state and federal securities laws, and related matters. A common error is to confuse the opinion of legal counsel with due diligence. Counsel is not a surety for business uncertainty, and the opinion of counsel is not a substitute for business analysis.

COMPLIANCE WITH REGULATIONS

Venture capital funds must comply with regulations imposed by the Department of Labor (DOL) Plan Asset Regulations, the Investment Company Act of 1940, and the Investment Advisors Act of 1940. State regulations are also important, since many VC investors are pension plans regulated by state laws as well. State plans usually have their own specific issues related to state laws or requirements.

Under the DOL rules, a VC fund that has an ERISA plan[7] as a limited partner is subject to ERISA fiduciary requirements. An exemption is granted if it meets one of the four exceptions:

- ERISA-type entities hold no more than 25% of the limited partnership interests.
- The fund is a venture capital operating company.[8]
- The limited partnership interests are publicly traded.
- The fund was formed before March 13, 1987, and no ERISA-type plan acquires an interest thereafter.

A VC fund is also subject to the regulatory provisions of the Investment Company Act of 1940 because its primary activity is investing in securities of its portfolio companies. However, the fund qualifies for an exemption from the definition of an investment company if it meets certain requirements and has not made and does not plan to make a public offering of its securities.

The general partner is an investment advisor under the Investment Advisors Act of 1940. An investment advisor is required to register[9] under the act unless an exemption is available. The registration exemption is available where the investment advisor has fewer than 15 clients, is not held out generally to the public as an investment advisor, and does not act as an investment advisor to registered investment companies during the preceding 12 months.

EXIT STRATEGIES

The exit strategies are planned when the venture capitalists are making the front-end investments. This is important because the actual exit strategy executed may require cooperation from some shareholders who do not agree with the pricing or timing. Therefore, it is important for venture capitalists to have obtained certain contractual rights to control their exit. For this purpose, they want to insist at the front end that the portfolio company and its other shareholders sign an agreement that gives them control over issues such as the timing of IPO, selection of underwriter, and right to demand additional SEC registrations subsequent to the IPO. When the venture capitalist is the majority shareholder, it will insist on *drag-along agreements* that give it the right to find buyers for all or part of the portfolio company's stock. However, if the venture capitalist is a minority investor, it will often want *take-along* rights to sell with management and other shareholders.

Venture capitalists' exit strategies include taking the portfolio company public or selling the portfolio company to another company. The IPO approach could further involve a post-IPO registered offering or SEC Rule 144. Selling out to another company can be structured as exchange for the acquirer's stock, cash, or for a combination of cash and debt instruments.

If the exit is through a public offering, there are several methods for reselling the restricted securities. Restricted securities can be sold via a subsequent private sale or a public offering registered with SEC. After the IPO, the portfolio company is a 1934-Act reporting company and hence, may qualify for short-form registration statements that allow the portfolio company or its holders to sell securities with less delay and less expense than a full-blown S-1 registration statement. Once the portfolio company has completed its IPO, venture capitalists and other holders can sell their restricted securities without filing an SEC registration statement if all SEC Rule 144 requirements (such as volume limitation, holding period, and SEC notification) are met. Effective April 29, 1997, the holding period requirements for the resale of a limited amount of restricted securities are one year.[10] Rule 144 previously required a two-year holding period. In addition, under amended Rule 144(k), nonaffiliates of an issuer may sell unlimited numbers of restricted securities if at least two years have elapsed since the acquisition of such securities from the issuer or an affiliate of the issuer. Rule 144(k) previously required a three-year holding period.

Alternatively, venture capitalists could sell the portfolio company to, or merge with another firm for acquirer's stock, notes, and/or cash. If the acquirer's stock is paid to venture capitalists and other holders as principal consideration, the transaction can be regarded as a tax-free reorganization. In addition, under the post-reorganization continuity-of-interest doctrine, venture capitalists and other shareholders of the portfolio company as a group must intend to hold the new securities for long term. Hence, from a tax standpoint, none of them is free to sell all of the new shares received in a tax-free reorganization. When debt instruments are used as part of the consideration to venture capitalists and other holders of the portfolio company, the IRS installment rules allow tax deferral on a pro rata portion of their gains until the debt instruments are paid.

SUMMARY

Venture capital investing, buyouts, mergers and acquisitions are interrelated. They are an integral part of the investment banking business. Investment bank's VC investing will benefit other operations as well, such as underwriting and financial advisory. This chapter discusses the essential issues investment bankers in venture capital business should know, such as how to form a VC fund, how to make a successful VC investment, the regulations to comply with, the tax issues, the legal documentation, and the exit strategies. The next chapter will focus on mergers and acquisitions.

SELECT BIBLIOGRAPHY

Blackman, I. L. *Valuing Your Privately Held Business*. Revised edition. Burr Ridge, IL: Irwin Professional Publishing, 1995.

Gompers, P. A. "Venture capital fundraising, firm performance, and the capital gains tax." Working paper, Harvard Business School, 1997.

Halloran, M. J. et al. eds. *Venture Capital & Public Offering Negotiation*. New York: Aspen Law & Business, 1996.

Journal of Private Equity. Various issues.

Levin, J. S. *Structuring Venture Capital, Private Equity, and Entrepreneurial Transactions*. Chicago, IL: CCH Inc., 1994.

Lim, Y., and T. Weissberg, ed. *Pratt's Guide to Venture Capital Sources*. New York: Venture Economics, 1995.

Lipman, F. D. *Venture Capital and Junk Bond Financing*. Philadelphia, PA: American Law Institute-American Bar Association, 1996.

Pratt, S. P., R. F. Reilly, and R. P. Schweihs. *Valuing Small Businesses and Professional Practices*. Second edition. Homewood, IL: Irwin, 1993.

Sullivan, M. K. "Segmenting the informal venture capital market: economic, hedonistic, and altruistic investors." *Journal of Business Research* 36 (May 1996): pp. 25–35.

Todd, K. M. "The institutional investor's view: effect on venture capital and private equity funds." In *The New Era of Investment Banking*. Raymond H. Rupert. ed. Chicago: Probus Publishing, 1993.

Tuller, L. W. *The Complete Book of Raising Capital*. New York: McGraw-Hill, 1994.

Venture Capital Journal. Various issues.

3

Mergers and Acquisitions

Takeover activities, including mergers and acquisitions (M&As) and leveraged buyouts (LBOs), are an important part of investment banking business. The volume of transactions in the 1980s totaled $1.719 trillion, and investment banks took in billions of dollars in fees. The volumes have increased to record highs in the mid-1990s. The M&As in the U.S. set another record at $626 billion in 1996. Volume in 1997 continues the upward trend, with $919 billion in value of deals. The activities in M&As and buyouts will continue to generate significant fee income for Wall Street and help build up merchant banking operations. Successful M&A bankers need to understand client business and objectives and respect the confidence of clients. Bankers should also examine options to overcome the effect of the proposed bill in Congress that would prohibit selling subsidiaries on a tax-free basis under the *Morris Trust* structure. This chapter discusses the motivations, negotiation process, valuation techniques, M&A banker's fees, regulatory issues, closing, legal risks, and risk arbitrage.

MARKET OVERVIEW

The M&A[1] market has been a part of the continued evolution of the U.S. business. The forces that drive the market are from the strategic buyers, the financial buyers, and the consolidators. The strategic buyers are seeking to extend their geographic reach, expand their customer base, boost market share, and fill out product lines to be more competitive. The financial buyers play a significant role in increased M&A activity. Financial buyers are formed from various sources including buyout funds, wealthy individuals, and investment arms of financial institutions. Another type of buyer is the consolidator. Consolidators are to roll up or consolidate businesses in industries that were previously characterized by a large number of mom-and-pop type shops.

Investment banks frequently act as a finder and/or a financial advisor. Bankers are knowledgeable in finding a seller or a buyer, terms of recent transactions, financing structure, arranging or providing bridge loans, fairness opinion, negotiations, and conducting divesture auction.

The M&A transactions totaled $1.719 trillion in the 1980s. Investment bankers took in billions of fee income. Wall Street is obsessed with M&As, because win, lose, or draw, they produce fees: fees for advising, fees for lending money, and fees for divesting unwanted assets. The activities in the early 1990s were below the 1988 peak, but were still significant and generated substantial income for Wall Street. By the mid-1990s, the M&A market revitalized and the dollar volumes in annual deals set record highs. The

TABLE 3.1   Value of M&A Deals
1980–1997

Year	Deals	Value ($ billion)
1980	79	12
1981	1,030	75
1982	1,928	56
1983	3,385	96
1984	3,618	169
1985	2,255	204
1986	3,148	228
1987	3,317	224
1988	3,915	352
1989	5,451	303
1990	5,650	183
1991	5,260	138
1992	5,503	150
1993	6,309	234
1994	7,570	340
1995	9,122	510
1996	10,330	651
1997	NA	919

Source: Adapted from Securities Data Co. and *The Wall Street Journal*, various issues.

M&As in the U.S. announced in 1996 totaled $626 billion, a significant increase from the record $510 billion in 1995.[2] Value of deals in 1997 has swelled to $919 billion. The value of U.S. M&A transactions from 1980 to 1997 is listed in Table 3.1.

The size of the largest mergers and acquisitions keeps increasing. Multibillion-dollar deals are now common. The largest deal so far is the proposed merger of Travelers Insurance and Citicorp, announced in April 1998 ($72 billion). A partial list of other large transactions include the linking of British Petroleum and Amoco in 1998 ($49 billion), KKR's purchase of RJR Nabisco in 1989 ($25 billion), the merger of Bell Atlantic and Nynex announced in 1996 ($22 billion), AT&T and McCaw Cellular in 1994 ($18.9 billion), SBC Communications and Pacific Telesis in 1997 ($16 billion), Lockheed and Martin Marietta in 1995 ($10 billion), Disney and Capital City/ABC in 1995 ($19 billion), Chase Manhattan and Chemical Bank in 1996 ($10 billion), and Salomon and Smith Barney in 1997 ($9 billion).

During this period, insider trading gained front-page attention. Insider trading is governed by Rule 10b-5, which bars corporate insiders or their affiliates from trading on knowledge of material information before it is made public. A number of prosecutions under Rule 10b-5 stemmed from trading on pending M&As prior to public announcements. Well-known defendants include Dennis Levine of Drexel Burnham Lambert, arbitrageur Ivan Boesky, and Martin Siegel of Kidder Peabody.

MOTIVATIONS

Corporate acquisitions are capital investments. The decision to acquire is determined by whether it makes a net contribution to shareholder wealth. The sources of gains include synergies, strategic planning, tax considerations, undervalued shares, agency problems, and diversification. From the seller's perspective, the decision to sell involves reasons such as founder's retirement, estate planning, eliminating personal liabilities, divesture, and venture capital exit strategies.

Buyers' Motivations

The most common argument put forth by acquirers in the merger market has been *synergies*. Cost-saving synergy[3] is most frequently mentioned. The merger of Chemical Banking and Manufacturer Hanover, and then with Chase Manhattan, was successful because of overlapping operations and other cost-saving synergies that enhanced shareholder wealth. There are sometimes revenue synergies, which are the additional sales the two would not have made if they were operating independently. Revenue synergies were part of the expected benefits when AT&T purchased Teleport for $11 billion in January 1998. Another related potential benefit is financial synergy.[4] The cost of capital might be lowered as a result of merger. If the streams of cash flows of the two companies are not perfectly correlated, a merger that reduces the instability of revenue streams can reduce the potential costs of financial stress. In addition, there might be economies of scale in flotation and transactions costs.

M&As could be part of corporate *strategic planning* in a changing market environment as well. One aspect is to increase market power so that the firm has the ability to set prices or to compete more aggressively. Furthermore, the combined company could be better positioned to take advantage of further industry consolidation or marketing channels. For example, the 1995 combination of Lockheed Corp. and Martin Marietta Corp. to form Lockheed Martin Corp. positioned itself to take advantage of further consolidation in the defense industry by acquiring Loral's defense operations in 1996 and merging with Northrop Grumman in 1997. As another example, a major plus in Gillette's 1996 merger with Duracell is the potential for Gillette to use its distribution clout to increase Duracell sales abroad, where the battery maker is not as strong as in the United States.

Unused tax shields are another benefit. As an example, Penn Central, subsequent to its bankruptcy and reorganization, had billions of unused tax-loss carry forwards. To take advantage of this, Penn Central purchased several taxpaying companies. It should be noted that the IRS might challenge the use of tax-loss carry-forwards if a company acquired another firm and then quickly liquidated its assets.

Another argument for acquisition is *undervalued shares*. This refers to the revaluation of shares because of new information generated during the merger negotiations or the tender offer process. There are three aspects to this argument. One is the kick-in-the-pants explanation, in which management is stimulated to adopt a higher-valued operating strategy. The second is the sitting-on-a-gold-mine hypothesis; the market revalues previously undervalued shares because of the dissemination of new information or the perception that bidders have superior information. The third aspect is related to inflation. The inflation of the 1970s deflated stock prices and increased replacement costs. This resulted in a decline in the q ratio, defined as the ratio of a company's market value to its replacement costs of assets. If a firm seeks expansion and if other firms in its target business segment have a q ratio of less than one, it is efficient to expand by purchase.

Agency problems are a result of the separation of ownership and management. If compensation to management is a function of firm size, then the managers are motivated to expand regardless of returns to shareholders. Alternatively, if a profitable firm is in a mature industry but lacks attractive investment opportunities, the firm should distribute the surplus cash to stockholders by raising dividends or share repurchase. However, managers sometimes prefer to use it for acquisition or to retain the surplus cash; in the latter case, the firm often finds itself a takeover target.

Diversification for shareholders or reducing systematic risk has been regarded as a dubious reason for mergers. However, the perception is not necessarily correct, and it has been proven that it is possible to reduce risk for shareholders through mergers.[5] For horizontal mergers, the risk can be lowered if the market is imperfectly competitive. In the case of conglomerate mergers, the risk will be reduced if economies of scope exist.

Sellers' Motivations

Turning to the selling business, owners and managers reach a decision to sell for many reasons. One major motivation is that founders and other individual owners sell as part of their retirement and estate planning, or as a strategy to other business ambitions. Another reason for sale is the recurring need for expansion capital when the public markets are either not desirable or not available. For a private company, another powerful stimulant is the elimination of personal liabilities such as personal guarantees of corporate debt. Such guarantees may risk a family's entire wealth. Eliminating personal guarantees and liabilities is an appropriate motive.

Large companies sometimes divest businesses that do not fit into their strategic plans. Some business sales are forced by venture capitalists as an exit strategy. Also, some sales are caused by financial distress.

Personal Issues

In practice, ego and pride (such as who gets to run the show) affect many merger deals. These social issues are among the most difficult aspects of negotiating multibillion-dollar deals. Often, a big factor in the success of a merger negotiation is an aging chief executive. Many megadeals tend to take place when one chief executive is nearing retirement and looking to go out with a bang. Cases include the union of Bell Atlantic and Nynex, Ciba-Geigy AG and Sandoz AG, and Lockheed and Martin Marietta. Bell Atlantic's chairman and CEO, Raymond Smith, was 58 and nearing retirement, while Nynex chairman and CEO, Ivan Seidenberg, was 49. In the case of Novartis, Ciba's chairman Alex Krauer was 65 and Sandoz's top executive Daniel Vasella was 43. The Lockheed Martin case was helped by the fact that Daniel Tellep was 62 and Martin Marietta's chief, Norman Augustine, was 58.

Another practical issue involving the sale of private companies is related to nonfinancial concerns. By way of example, a seller entrepreneur's continuing involvement in the business may be a condition of sale. The nonfinancial factors frequently involve the employees, as well. It is also important for the seller entrepreneur to feel comfortable with the new management and owners.

STRATEGIC PLANNING AND INTERMEDIARY

Growth is vital to the well being of a business. Acquisitions are but one of the many alternatives, and each should be evaluated carefully. The incentive to acquire exists when acquisition is more beneficial than other alternatives. The alternatives include joint ventures, strategic alliance, minority investment, venture capital, licensing, technology sharing, franchising, and marketing and distribution agreements.

If an acquisition is determined to be the optimal path, a team consisting of internal and external professionals[6] will plan and implement strategies during the acquisition process. The company could rely on in-house analysis or hire investment bankers to complete the acquisition. Lower expenses,[7] reasons of confidentiality, staff transaction experience, and speed frequently motivate completing transactions in house. On the other hand, the advantages of negotiating through third parties are that bankers can tap into information flow in sales and trading and thus can obtain better terms regarding the pricing of securities and company assets. As an example, targets with bankers from 1993 to September 1996 received a median premium of 31.6 percent, while those without bankers received a 26.1 percent premium. For acquirers, those who used bankers paid a median premium of 30.3 percent, compared to a 32.3 percent premium for acquirers without bankers. Additionally, if the deal falls apart, the working relationships would not be jeopardized.

A successful acquisition program must be an integral part of a company's overall strategic plan. The strategic needs and preferences of the management determine the initial selection criterion of targets. One way of finding the candidates is to hire an intermediary, broker, or finder. There are several published sources for finding an M&A intermediary. Two such sources are *Buyouts: Directory of Intermediaries* and *The Corporate Finance Sourcebook*. Another method of discovering acquisition candidates is through networking. *World M&A Network* is a quarterly publication that lists companies for sale, merger candidates, and willing buyers. Other electronic directories can also be used to screen for acquisition candidates.

Each selected candidate should be evaluated. The key to evaluating an acquisition candidate is first to understand the acquirer's business strategy and reactions to the deal among shareholders. Then the evaluation process proceeds to performing a segmentation analysis to determine the segments in which the target operates. The competitive position and operating strategies of the target should be analyzed. In the due diligence process, the following information about the acquiree is often required: market environment, market position, market structure, products, customers, suppliers, operations, financial measures, and legal and regulatory issues.

Investment Banking Fees and Agreements

Fees are usually negotiable and contingent upon the success of a deal. The most usual fee scale is the Lehman 5–4–3–2–1 formula. Under this formula, 5 percent is paid on the first $1 million of sale price, 4 percent on the next $1 million, 3 percent on the next $1 million, 2 percent on the next $1 million, and 1 percent on the amount in excess of $4 million. In a small transaction, the fee may range between 5 percent and 10 percent of the sale. For a large transaction, the fees are less than 1 percent of the deal's value.[8] In yet another turn in the compensation schedule, AT&T's Chairman M. Armstrong instructed his advisers in the Teleport deal that their compensation would be based on how well the company was able to realize the scenario put forward. Many investment bankers seek an up-front retainer before they begin M&A work with a company, especially a private company where owners have been known to change their minds halfway through the process. Regardless of the transaction outcome, out-of-pocket expenses are always billed to the client.

The M&A banker should be paid commission in full at the time of closing if the sale price is payable in a lump sum or in installments. When a portion of the sale price is determined on an *earn-out basis*, in which the payments are contingent on operations after closing, the intermediary is to be paid out of these payments when made to the seller.

Fees in tax-free transactions—such as stock-for-stock exchange—are also paid in cash, despite the fact that the seller has not received cash. There are ways of accomplishing this without affecting the tax-free aspect of the sale. The fee can be paid by the surviving entity. When the transaction is stock-for-assets exchange and the seller must pay the intermediary, two methods can be used. In one approach, the seller pays the fee prior to the exchange and then exchanges only its remaining assets for the buyer's stock. A second technique is to have the purchaser assume the selling company's obligation to pay the fee.

Another important contract is the *confidentiality agreement*. The basic function of the agreement is to protect sellers against the misuse of confidential information provided to potential buyers. The agreement typically contains (1) confidentiality provisions to protect the seller against the business risks of disclosure or misuse of information by competitors, and (2) standstill provisions (corporate peace treaties) to protect the seller against unsolicited takeover attempts by bidders. Other goals of the agreement might include complying with securities law, preventing bidders from forcing unfair offers on the target, governing the sale process, blocking the raiding of target personnel, and timing the announcements.

The types of information that bidders often require include financial, technical, and human resource materials. At times, potential buyers may request that confidential technical information be excluded from the material provided to avoid any possible future claim that it has misused the target's proprietary information. Also, it is a good practice to require that all personnel contacts be made through the target's investment banker and that they are properly briefed.

The agreement may prohibit the disclosure of negotiations by either buyer or seller. The selling company will try to control a bidder's ability to discuss the possible transaction with other potential acquirers. If the target is a public company, the contract typically contains *standstill provisions* setting the terms under which the bidder may acquire, vote, or dispose of target stock. A potential buyer with separate trading and investment functions, such as a securities dealer, may request that some of its units be permitted to continue trading in target stock without violating the standstill, provided that trading and merchant banking divisions are separated by the so-called *Chinese wall*.

The target may, through its investment banker and legal counsel hired by the special committee of the board of directors, provide bidding guidelines governing the substance, timing, and manner of submission of acquisition offers. The restrictions on proposals are most effective when coupled with a provision in which the bidder agrees not to request any waivers or amendments of the standstill. Typically, there is a term to which the bidder is subject to the restrictions of the standstill and non-solicitation provisions. Other provisions—such as technological know-how—may be perpetual or may expire after a stated number of years or a stated event. The acquiree may or may not accept the request of *most favored nation* status by bidders, giving the bidder the right to get the same concessions granted to any other potential buyers.

VALUATION AND FINANCING

The valuation process involves a self-evaluation by the acquiring firm and the valuation of the acquisition candidate. The self-evaluation phase estimates the value of the acquiring firm and examines how it is affected by each of the various scenarios. Self-evaluation takes on special significance in the exchange-of-shares acquisition. Valuing the purchase price at market might induce overpayment if the company's shares are undervalued, or might obscure the opportunity to offer the seller additional shares while still achieving the acceptable return if the shares are currently overpriced.

The valuation of a merger candidate takes place after a suitable candidate has been identified. This is made to determine what price should be offered to the shareholders of the target company. It is important to recognize that the valuation techniques, as discussed shortly, are used only in determining the price range reference for the target company. Each acquirer should be guided by the technique that fits its objective. Equally important, a risk analysis (such as scenario analysis or sensitivity analysis) should be performed. The valuation is not complete until the impact of the acquisition on the acquirer is also carefully examined.

Estimating the Value of a Business

Several techniques are available to estimate the value of a business. They include discounted cash flow, comparable transactions, comparable company, breakup valuation, target stock price history, M&A multiples, LBO analysis, leveraged recapitalization, gross revenue multiplier, book value, multiple of earnings, and liquidation analysis.

The *Discounted Cash Flow* (DCF) technique is widely used in evaluating internal growth investments and external acquisitions. The DCF method determines the value by evaluating the cash flow projections of the target and discounting those projections to the present value. The DCF approach is future oriented. It begins with a projection of sales and operating profit, based on the assessment of historical performance as well as certain assumptions regarding the future. Obviously, the usefulness of this technique depends on the accuracy of the assumptions. These assumptions include estimations of how those sales will affect the company's other areas of business, how much additional working or fixed capital will be required, and what will be the discount rate and residual value. The value of the DCF should be estimated under different scenarios, using projection periods of varying lengths.

Comparable transaction analysis is used to analyze transactions involving companies in the target's industry or similar industries over the last several years. Acquisition multiples are calculated for the universe of the comparable transactions. These multiples are then applied to the target's financial results to estimate the value at which the target would likely trade. This technique is most effective when data on truly comparable transactions are available.

The *comparable company* approach makes assessment of how the value of the potential acquisition candidate compares with the market prices of publicly traded companies with similar characteristics. This method is similar to the comparable transaction approach in that it identifies a pricing relationship and applies it to the candidate's earnings, cash flow, or book value. A change-of-control premium should be added to the value identified by this method to arrive at the estimated valuation range for the target. One weakness of this technique is that it works well only when there are good comparable companies for the target. Another weakness is that accounting policies can differ substantially from one company to another, which could result in material differences in reported earnings or balance-sheet amounts.

The *breakup valuation* technique involves analyzing each of the target's business lines and summing these individual values to arrive at a value for the entire company. Breakup analysis is best conducted from the perspective of a raider. The process is first to determine the value of each piece of the target and then compute the total value. Then the acquisition cost is estimated. If value exceeds cost, the raider computes the rate of return. This technique provides the required guidance under a hostile bid.

Target stock price history analysis examines the stock trading range of the target over some time frame. The target stock price performance is analyzed against a broad market index and comparable company stock performances. The offering price is based on the price index plus some premium. Similar analysis is performed on the acquiring firm if the transaction is a stock-for-stock exchange. The purpose is to determine the exchange ratio. This approach fails to account for future prospects of the company. Nevertheless, it does provide historical information many find useful in framing valuation thoughts.

The *M&A multiples* technique analyzes the current and past broad acquisition multiples and the change-of-control premium. This technique is used when comparable transactions or comparable companies are not available. The limitation is that a broad market average may be inapplicable to a single transaction.

Leveraged buyout (LBO) analysis is performed when the target is a potential candidate for LBO.[9] The objective is to determine the highest price an LBO group would pay. This is often the floor price for the target. On the other hand, it may set the upper value for the target company if a corporate buyer cannot be located. The LBO analysis typically includes cash-flow projections, rates of returns to capital providers, and tax effects. The primary difference between the LBO analysis and DCF technique is that the LBO approach incorporates financing for the LBO. The availability of financing depends on the timing of cash flows, particularly in the first two years after the deal is completed. As is clear, the value derived by the LBO approach can be materially affected by temporary changes in financing conditions.

Leveraged recapitalization method is aimed at identifying the maximum value that a public company can deliver to its shareholders today. In general, the analysis is performed in the context of a probable or pending hostile offer for the target. The value in a recapitalization is delivered to the shareholders through stock repurchase, cash dividends, and a continuing equity interest in a highly leveraged company. This technique focuses on the target's capital structure, and is largely affected by the availability of debt financing at a particular time.

A *gross revenue multiplier* is the so-called price-to-sales ratio. The basic concept is that the value is some multiple of the sales the target generates. The method implicitly assumes that there is some relatively consistent relationship between sales and profits for the business. Obviously, the usefulness of the technique depends on the revenue–profit relationship. In practice, this method may be quite useful when acquiring a private company where gross sales are the only reliable data available.

The *book value* approach is an accounting-based concept and may not represent the earnings power. Generally accepted accounting principles permit the use of alternative depreciation and/or inventory methods. Also, the value of intangible assets may not be reflected in the balance sheet. However, it will help provide an initial estimate of goodwill in a transaction.

The *multiple of earnings per share* method involves taking the past or future income per share and multiplying that figure by an earnings multiplier, derived from publicly traded companies in the same industry. One difficulty is that the known multipliers do not reflect control premiums, as evidenced by the rise in the multiplier in the event of an acquisition. Another problem is that income does not necessarily represent cash flow from operations.

Liquidation analysis could be used to establish a floor for valuation. This approach is relevant if a business is being acquired for its underlying assets rather than for its going-concern value.

Financing

Financing is often left as a final detail in structuring an M&A. In structuring acquisition financing, financial positions and expectations of both parties must be considered simultaneously. The flexibility available through various means of payment (currency) and the ability to balance the requirements of both parties involved are among the key ingredients of the negotiated outcomes. Taxable or tax-free transactions are important considerations in the choice of financing methods as well; buyers are more willing to pay a higher premium in tax-free transactions (pooling-of-interests). For example, buyers between 1993 and September 1996 paid a median premium of 30 percent in tax-free acquisitions, compared to a 21.5 percent premium when pooling was not used.[10] The forms of payments include cash, common stock, preferred stock or debt, convertible securities, and contingent payments. *Pooling of interests* is the most popular method companies use for big stock mergers. Poolings let companies simply combine their assets, which does not create goodwill charges. Companies currently can write off goodwill for as long as 40 years. A new FASB proposal would force companies to break down goodwill into its component assets, calculate the average useful life for the goodwill, and write it off over that period.

All-cash transactions can be closed faster than those made with any other currency.[11] All-cash deals allow the acquirer the greatest flexibility from a tax standpoint, although the transaction is clearly a taxable event to the selling shareholders. The acquirer has certain tax elections that may produce greater cash flows than the target enjoyed before the acquisition. Much of the tax benefit comes from writing up the tax basis of the assets in order to create larger noncash depreciation or amortization expenses that reduce taxable earnings. Under generally accepted accounting principles (GAAP), all acquired assets and liabilities must be recorded at market values, whether the cash is used to purchase assets or stock.

Common stock transaction is another possibility. The most common appeal is that it substitutes stock for a large outlay of cash or a heavy accumulation of debt. The exchange of shares is a tax-free transaction. The recipients do not pay taxes on the stock received until they sell the stock. There is, however, a potentially negative consequence of dilution. Another factor is that a company cannot intend to repurchase treasury shares and at the same time select to use pooling accounting in an acquisition. For example, the SEC took action forcing U.S. Office Products and Corporate Express to account for their stock financed acquisitions as if they had been cash purchases instead, because both companies announced hefty stock buybacks within six months of closing those deals.

Preferred stock or debt is often issued when the deal is so large that the required acquisition financing is difficult to obtain or the earning power precludes sufficient financing by alternative modes. The preference of deferring tax liability of the selling entity is another reason. It is possible to structure a note so that the sellers are not taxed until the principal payments are made. This method is easier to structure and is frequently used in the sales of closely held companies. Structuring this type of financing is more difficult with public companies that have large and diverse shareholder groups. Deals with this type of financing will be treated as purchases. The buyers are required to substract from their future earnings the premium of the takeover price over the book value of the target.

Payment by issuing convertible securities offers a means of issuing common stock in an M&A without immediate dilution. This also effectively allows the acquirer to issue fewer shares than if financed entirely with common stock, because the conversion price is typically set at a level higher than the current market value. It does require payment of interest or preferred dividends for a period of time. In practice, convertible preferred stock is most frequently used because it is possible to structure the transaction so the seller receives new securities tax free, until the securities are sold. The transaction will be accounted for as a purchase for bookkeeping purposes.

Earnout-contingent payments are typically structured so that part of the purchase price is contingent on the target's post-acquisition achievement of certain goals. The contingent formula for additional compensation is often based on financial performance. Experienced M&A bankers representing a private-company seller would typically recommend an operating-based contingency instead of a profit-based one, since the profit picture can be manipulated by the new owner. This approach helps bridge the gap when there is a large difference between the bid price and the asking price in a private transaction. It also provides a means to keep and motivate the former owners of a business subsequent to an acquisition. From an accounting perspective, one of the most difficult aspects is that all contingent payments generally accrue to goodwill. There is no tax benefit. This method of payment precludes the use of pooling of interest accounting.

Securitization[12] has rapidly become a method for generating funds to finance M&A transactions. This type of financing has several benefits, including off-balance-sheet treatment and lower interests costs. The savings in interest payments for non–investment-grade companies could be hundreds of basis points. Typically, the time required is about 8 to 12 weeks. When an acquirer has an existing securitization program in place, the process will go a lot faster.

Bridge loans were common elements in M&As during the 1980s. However, they are rarely used in the 1990s because of the loss experience. The use of a bridge loan is to secure closing a deal. Junk bond issues were commonly used to pay off bridge loans in the 1980s in highly leveraged transactions. Bridge loans are more expensive than other credit products. Structuring and underwriting fees can range from 1 percent to 5 percent. Closing fees and interest rates are higher than the borrower would normally incur. Bridge loans might also involve escalating interest costs, an equity kicker, or a penalty fee if such a loan is not refinanced by a set date.

CLOSING AND REGULATORY ISSUES

Most deals begin with preliminary negotiations. The buyer wants to find out as much as possible about the seller. By contrast, the seller walks a thin line between disclosing enough so the buyer won't have future recourse, but not too much negative information to cause the buyer to walk away. The characteristics of the deal will certainly affect the negotiations. The first significant characteristic is whether the target is privately or publicly owned. The currency or form of payments is another matter subject to heated negotiations. If these preliminary negotiations are successful and both parties agree in principle on the basic points, they sign a letter of intent. A press release may be issued concurrently.

Although the letter of intent generally is not legally binding, it does represent a moral obligation that is normally taken seriously by both parties. The letter of intent can form the basis of filing under the Hart–Scott–Rodino Antitrust Improvement Act. However, there are good reasons not to have a letter of intent. The parties might not wish to make a public announcement that is not required of privately held companies. The selling company might also be negotiating with other potential acquirers and might want to avoid disclosure that could weaken its bargaining position.

The letter of intent is in the form of a letter addressed to the seller or seller's stockholders. It is signed by the acquirer and countersigned by the seller or seller's stockholders. It covers the following areas: form of transaction, currency, protective provisions for purchaser, special arrangements, brokerage or finder's fees, and break fees.

The Acquisition or Merger Agreement

When negotiations reach a point of agreement, the lawyers from both sides face an elaborate process of document drafting to reflect the terms of the transaction. Whether the transaction takes the form of merger, stock purchase, asset purchase, or other variations, the fundamental document is the *acquisition* or *merger agreement*. The acquisition agreement is often accompanied or followed by a variety of documents required by federal and state laws regulating acquisitions, and also a variety of documents pertaining to the acquisition agreement itself.

There are four most critical features in the agreement: representations and warranties, covenants, closing conditions, and indemnification.

Representations and warranties serve three important purposes:

1. *Informational.* They provide the means through which the purchaser is able to learn as much as possible about the selling company.
2. *Protective.* They provide a mechanism for the purchaser to be relieved of its obligations if adverse facts are discovered between signing and closing.
3. *Framing.* Representations and warranties provide a framework for the seller's indemnification of the acquirer following the closing.

The seller's representations and warranties normally account for the largest part of the acquisition agreement. They include financial statements, assets, taxes, contracts, employee matters, environmental protection, product liability, litigation and compliance, corporate organizations and capitalization, and existing restrictions. The acquirer typically performs the definite investigation of the seller's business after the execution of the agreement, although an earlier preliminary investigation is usually made. Standard conditions for closing is that the seller's representations be true both at the signing of the agreement, as well as at the time of closing. The information about the seller and its business is frequently generated by the so-called disclosure schedule. The parties can agree on the length of time that certain representations survive the closing. Environmental issues and product liability generally survive longer than other commercial representations and warranties. The seller will raise the issues of materiality and knowledge qualification. That is, the seller will want to limit disclosure to material items and only to items of which it has knowledge.

Covenants cover the period between signing and closing, including negative covenants and affirmative covenants. Negative covenants restrict the seller from taking certain actions without purchaser's consent. They are intended to protect the purchaser against the seller's actions that might change the nature of what the purchaser expects to acquire at the closing. For example, the acquirer does not want the seller to take cash out of its business, increase debt, or change accounting methods. Affirmative covenants typically obligate both parties to the transaction to take certain actions prior to the closing. Typical affirmative covenants provide for (1) purchaser's full access to the seller's books and records for the purpose of evaluation and investigation, (2) calling and holding stockholder meetings to obtain approval, and (3) making required filings with government agencies and obtain necessary approvals. Some covenants contain both absolute obligations and reasonable-efforts qualification.

Conditions of closing must be met. The first condition in every agreement is that the representations and warranties are true and all of the covenants and agreements required to be performed at or prior to closing have been performed in all material respects. The condition is confirmed by each party's delivering to the other a certificate to this effect. Other common conditions include expiration of the waiting period under the Hart–Scott–Rodino Act, approval of regulatory authorities, receipt of third-party consent, receipt of favorable tax rulings, settlement of litigation, signing of employment and noncompete agreements by key employees, registration of officers and directors, satisfactory results of investigations, and any other conditions deemed important. If the acquisition involves a non–U.S. citizen, the conditions for closing would need to include compliance with the Exon–Florio Amendment relating to national security concerns. Written notification of the proposed transaction must be sent to the Committee on Foreign Investment in the United States (CFIUS). The committee has 30 days to decide whether an investigation is necessary, the investigation must be completed in 45 days, and a final decision must be announced within 15 days thereafter. The final issue is the date of the closing. A good approach is to set a target date and then provide that if a condition is not met, the party unable to meet the condition may postpone the closing, but not later than a specified date.

Indemnification provisions are crucial in an acquisition agreement. Indemnification is used to protect the purchaser because of the potentially high costs of certain liabilities such as taxes, environmental matters, and litigation. The provisions normally cover damages incurred by the purchaser resulting from (1) a breach of a covenant or a misrepresentation that is discovered after closing, or (2) an allocation of responsibilities between the buyer and seller in the acquisition agreement. These provisions are the subject of heavy negotiations. The seller may seek a basket provision that provides purchaser indemnification only if the damages exceed a certain amount. The seller may want to include a cutoff date beyond which the purchaser cannot assert claims. Also, it is not uncommon to see an upper limit on liability in the provisions.

Regulatory Issues

Legal considerations often affect the timing and structure of an acquisition, especially for a publicly held target. The legal counsel should examine the antitrust concerns, SEC regulation, state laws, IRS rulings, ERISA filings, and other regulatory filings.

An important consideration in any acquisition is the potential constraint posed by federal antitrust laws. The Hart–Scott–Rodino Antitrust Improvements Act requires parties to certain acquisition transactions to provide the Federal Trade Commission (FTC) and the Antitrust Division of the Department of Justice (DOJ) with a Premerger Form detailing the businesses involved and the proposed deal. The act requires an initial waiting period of 30 days after the Premerger Form is filed before the transaction can be consummated (only 15 days in the case of a cash tender offer). The purpose is to help the government enforce antitrust laws. Responsibility for enforcing federal antitrust laws is shared by the DOJ and the FTC. For vertical mergers, portions of the DOJ 1984 merger guidelines provide a framework for analysis. Few, if any, such deals have been challenged in recent years.[13] For horizontal mergers, the 1992 Horizontal Merger Guidelines, issued jointly by DOJ and FTC, outline the framework that the federal agencies will apply in investigating the proposed transactions. The guidelines employ the Hirfindahl–Hirschman Index (HHI) as a measure of market concentration. Proposed transactions are likely to be challenged if the post-merger market is highly concentrated. If a deal is challenged, the new rules (adopted in September 1996) require FTC administrative law judges to file their final decisions within a year. Those decisions could be appealed to the five-member commission. In merger cases, companies could opt for a fast-track program that guarantees a decision by the commission within 13 months. Before the new rules were adopted, it took an average of three to five years for a final approval or rejection. As an example, R.R. Donnelley & Sons Co.'s $536.5 million acquisition of Meredith/Burda Co. was challenged in October 1990. An administrative law judge did not issue a decision until January 1994. Donnelley appealed and won the approval in August 1995.

Another important legal process involves SEC filings. When an acquiring company is issuing securities to finance the purchase, registration must be filed with the SEC (under the Securities Act of 1933) unless the private placement or intrastate offering exemption is available. If the target's securities are registered under the Securities Exchange Act of 1934, it must use a proxy statement or information statement that complies with SEC Regulation 14A. An exception is when the acquisition is via an exchange of securities directly with the target's shareholders. If a target company proxy statement is used, a Form S4 registration statement is generally filed. Within 10 days after purchasing 5% of any class of equity securities, the acquirer must make public disclosure of the purchase by filing with SEC[14] a Schedule 13D and delivering it to the target. In addition, if the method adopted is tender offer, the purchaser must file with the SEC and deliver it to the target a Schedule 14D-1 (Williams Act of 1968). A tender offer commences at the time the offer is first published, sent, or given to stockholders. If the acquirer publicly announces the tender offer, it must file its 14D-1 within 5 days. A tender offer must be open to all holders of a class of securities that the offer is made, and must remain open for at least 20 business days. The offer must remain open for at least 10 days after any amendment.

State securities laws filings can be lengthy and complicated. When an acquisition takes the form of a statutory merger, the agreement of merger must be filed in each state where the company is incorporated. Some states may require tax clearances.

A favorable tax ruling by the Internal Revenue Service (IRS) is frequently among the conditions of closing. The most typical request is that the IRS rules the transaction tax free. The request requires an extensive document describing the transaction in detail. It usually takes several months for the IRS ruling. A recent development worth special attention involves the proposed bill in Congress to eliminate the popular

Morris Trust structure used to sell subsidiaries on a tax-free basis. Although stock-for-stock mergers of entire companies are often tax free, division sales are taxable if paid with cash. But under the Morris Trust structure, a buyer can pay with its own stock and assume debt of the seller. If the bill is passed and becomes law, many corporations may choose other options such as straight spinoff, rather than selling the business for cash and paying taxes.

The Employee Retirement Income Security Act of 1974 (ERISA) is intended to protect the interest of employee benefit plan participants and their beneficiaries. A report must be filed with the Pension Benefit Guaranty Corp. Reports are required when the acquisition changes the plan employer, completely or partially terminates the plan, or results in merger of plans. In certain circumstances, filings must be made to the IRS as well.

Legal opinions are standard features of an acquisition agreement. Counsel renders legal opinions for both buyer and seller on behalf of their respective clients. Legal opinions affirm that the acquisition agreement has been duly authorized, executed, and delivered; that the agreement is binding on both parties; and that it does not violate the corporate charter, bylaws, or agreements of which the counsel have knowledge.

When an acquisition is in a regulated business such as banking, transportation, or communications, additional filing with Federal Reserve Board, Interstate Commerce Commission, or Federal Communications Commission is required. Furthermore, several states require their environmental agencies to be notified if there is a change in company ownership and to conduct environmental audits. For example, New Jersey's Environmental Cleanup Responsibility Act requires the target's hazardous wastes be cleaned up when there is a change in corporate control. This may materially increase the costs of acquiring a target with manufacturing facilities in New Jersey.

Closing Summary

Closing is governed by the acquisition contract. The objective is to permit buyers, sellers, lenders, and others to complete the transactions in a coordinated manner. Some of the commonly used closing documents include:

- Certificates of incorporation
- Bylaws
- Letter evidencing the passage of Hart–Scott–Rodino waiting period
- SEC order declaring registration statement effective (if applicable)
- Letter evidencing listing of securities (if applicable)
- Approval or clearance by other government agencies
- Tax rulings from IRS or state tax agencies
- Comfort letters from accountants
- Legal and fairness opinions
- Instructions for securities and/or funds transfer
- Escrow agreements

Before and during the closing, other important activities may be taking place and must be coordinated with closing. These activities include:

- Audit of seller's financial condition
- Registration of securities with the SEC

- Compliance with state securities laws and regulations
- Stock exchange listing and rules
- Tax ruling from IRS
- Antitrust clearance
- Escrow agreements

These important activities are completed before the deal is closed. The closing documents are carefully reviewed and signed. When everyone is satisfied with the documents, they are exchanged and funds or securities (sometimes both) are transferred in payment. The deal is closed.

TAKEOVER DEFENSES

Takeover defenses, or *shark repellents*, generally fall into three classifications. The first involves corporate charter and bylaw amendments, which require shareholder approval. Another involves financial techniques that can be installed by directors without shareholder approval. Also, structural and strategic actions have been occasionally used to fend off unwanted takeover attempts.

Charter and bylaw amendments were used frequently in the 1980s, but were rarely tried in the 1990s because of opposition by institutional investors. If used, the menu includes the following. One is the staggered board, in which directors serve a term of three years and only one-third of the board is up for election every year. The aim is to prevent a hostile acquirer from taking control of the board in one blow. The company may set a minimum acceptable price or a supermajority vote in an event of a takeover. Another possibility is to adopt the McDonald's amendment, allowing directors to make decisions on a wide range of issues beyond the purchase price. Anti-greenmail was common practice in the 1980s in fending off raiders. Also, some companies reincorporate in a state with stiff anti-takeover laws.

Certain financial techniques or changes in capitalization are measures costly to the raiders. A *poison pill* is a shareholder right that allows them to buy additional shares when triggered by certain events. Similarly, poison securities take on a deterring character when the company is under siege. Poison shares are preferred stock with supervoting right, triggered by an unwanted takeover attack. Poison puts are attachments to debt securities, puttable if the control of the company changes hands—which effectively increases the amount of debt, making it less attractive for a takeover. Capitalization changes include multiple classes of common stocks, with one class superior to the other in voting rights. Also, financial engineering techniques may produce temporary changes in capital structure. The techniques include leveraged recapitalization, self tenders (large-scale repurchase), employee stock ownership plans (ESOP), pension parachutes, and severance parachutes (golden parachutes).

Strategic and structural defenses involve a wide range of initiatives. One common technique is to seek a *white knight*, a more compatible buyer that will pay a higher price than the hostile bidder. A management buyout, in which management becomes its own white knight, is another tactic. Another defense is for the target to sell its "crown jewel" to keep a hostile acquirer away. At the other end of the spectrum, the besieged company can use acquisitions as defensive tactics, either by purchasing a poor-performing company to make itself look worse or by buying a business that competes with the acquirer to set up a possible antitrust conflict. The most extreme of this type of defense is the *Pacman strategy*, the counterattack by the target to tender the acquirer's shares.

LEGAL CONSIDERATION IN BUYING PUBLIC TARGETS

The important legal issues facing acquirers and investment bankers are break fees and lock-up options, deal poaching, the role of controlling shareholders at a target, just-say-no defense, and conflicts of interests.

Break fees are paid by the target to the first accepted bidder if it is beaten out. *Lock-up options* for target stock or selected assets are triggered by a successful competing bid. These two are at times combined, and sometimes given mutually by the acquirer and the seller. Break fees and lock-up options are among the most intensely negotiated items in public deals. The acquirer almost always asks for a large break fee or lock-up option for the risk of providing a floor value for the target. The target usually argues for lower fees or smaller options in order to retain flexibility to consider better offers. The break fees are currently in the 1% to 3% range, while the lock-up options to buy shares usually involve between 10% to 20% of target stock. For example, the break fees for the proposed merger between British Telecom and MCI were $450 million—if either company canceled the deal, it would have had to pay that much to the other.[15] A target's board may grant break fees and lock-up options without breaching fiduciary duty, provided that the terms are reasonable.

Another issue is *deal poaching*. There are several examples. One is Medtronic's acquisition of Electromedics in 1994 for $95.1 million in stock, beating out a previously accepted bid of $92 million by St. Jude Medical. Another is Moorco's $150 million bid accepted by Fisher & Porter and later upset by Elsag Bailey Process NV's bid of $156.5 million in 1994. Also, NBC acquired Outlet Communications in 1996 for $395.9 million. Outlet Communications originally had agreed to sell to Renaissance Communications for $350.5 million. The bidders were willing to absorb the break fees and lock-up options because the amounts were not high enough to deter them.

A *controlling shareholder* has the right, with certain exceptions, to decide whether, when, and on what terms to sell its shares. However, it is also a fundamental legal principle that a company's board of directors owes a fiduciary duty to all shareholders, not just some subgroup, even if that group has a controlling position. If the controlling shareholder wants to sell its entire position and the buyer wants to buy the whole company, the deal gets done only if the price offered to the minority is the best available. The legal outcome becomes uncertain if the target's financial advisor determines that terms of the offer are inadequate. Under Delaware case law, dissenter's rights are normally the exclusive remedies for minority shareholders cashed out by the controlling party. Additional remedies are available if there has been fraud or unfair dealing.

A target board can decide not to sell the company—*just say no*, even in the face of a premium or fair bid. The 1989 Time Warner case reaffirmed the target board's flexibility in dealing with hostile bids. The court permitted Time Inc. and Warner Communications Inc. to proceed with a strategic alliance in the face of a hostile bid for Time by Paramount Communications. This ruling is in contrast to a corporate principle in which a target board cannot take unilateral steps to absolutely preclude a takeover proposal or proxy contest. Therefore, what can or cannot be done in this area will continue to be a battleground.

Next, a transaction is most legally vulnerable if one or more parties has an actual or potential conflict of interest. When there is a suspicion of conflict, many jurisdictions shift the burden of proof to the contracting parties to demonstrate fairness if challenged. Companies often set up special committees of independent directors to deal with conflict situations. Another area for conflict of interest involves fairness opinion fee arrangements. It is a common practice that the target of public deals receives a fairness opinion from a reputable financial advisor. Fairness opinion fees typically range between $75,000 and $200,000. Usually the financial advisor also provides advice and assistance in deal structure and negotiations, receiving a fee based on the deal value and contingent on closing. The overall transaction fees to a financial advisor often are in the range of 0.5% to 1%. The size of the deal fee and its dependence on closing certainly create pressures on a financial advisor to give fairness opinions in close calls. To date, courts generally have not barred reliance on fairness opinions, despite the potential conflict of interest imbedded in the fee structure. An increasing number of boards have either insisted on receiving a second fairness opinion from another advisor or assigned deal advice and fairness opinion to different advisors.

POSTACQUISITION INTEGRATION

The period shortly after closing is the time when critical steps are taken to integrate the acquired business with the buyer organization. During the same period, a variety of steps—legal, accounting, tax, insurance, employee benefits, and others—should be taken to ensure a successful transition.

Many acquirers form transition teams composed of executives of both companies to coordinate the postmerger integration process. This includes developing recommendations for combining a wide range of functions and proposing the configuration of the new organization. It is better to organize a small team of results-oriented experts around postmerger projects, in order to stabilize the organization and build early momentum. The poor transition in the 1989 merger of SmithKline Beekman Inc. and Beecham PLC illustrates the importance of a small, efficient transition team. The company saw its operating costs and interest expenses rise and its R & D synergy falter while it stumbled through a hierarchy of 250 transition teams.

Early management placement is a critical factor in stabilizing the company and positioning it for quick gains. The crucial task is in deciding whom to retain, whom to redeploy, whom to dismiss, and at what price. A striking point frequently is that the compensation schedule at the acquired company is out of line with acquirer's policies. Also, competing organizations often attempt to lure away the best and brightest managers and technical stuff immediately after the acquisition. The acquiring company often has to offer "stay bonuses" to retain these employees.

The changes in benefits, particularly changes in pensions, have highly complex ramifications. Important items in benefits are pensions, health insurance, life insurance and disability plans, and labor agreements. The administration of qualified retirement plans is guided by many tax and labor laws, as well as by numerous accounting guidelines. Health insurance costs are among the major cost items for a company. The buyer must analyze current life insurance and disability plans to determine whether they match the buyer's objectives.

Collectively bargained labor agreements present a unique set of issues. In addition, postacquisition discrimination tests must be applied to ensure continued compliance with applicable legislation. When acquiring a target's stock, the acquirer assumes all of the target's obligations.

Manufacturing units and back-office operations are to be integrated after the merger. This might take several months, at least. Another related issue is that every attempt should be made to prevent the rise of such feelings as "us versus them" or "winners versus losers."

In addition to these important areas of integration, there are several other crucial steps. A partial checklist of important items is as follows:

- File Form 8-K with the SEC.
- File affidavit with the IRS.
- File Forms BE-13 with the DOC.
- Obtain issuance of formal title insurance policies.
- Record assets at stepped-up values for tax and accounting purposes.
- Arrange for seller's employees to read and sign corporate code of conduct.
- Obtain recorded originals of deeds.
- Monitor sales of shares covered by any shelf registration.
- Comply with Rule 10-b.
- Change corporate name and signatories on seller's bank accounts.

Another post-closing project is to identify and obtain evidence of the seller's historical insurance coverage. Many courts interpret statutory time limits on the right to sue as running from the date the claimant allegedly discovered the damage or injury, and the claims might be covered by policies written years ago. A determined effort should be made before or right after closing to obtain old liability policies and related records.

RISK ARBITRAGE

Risk arbitrage is an important part of the M&A market. The arbitrageurs (arbs) help make the M&A market liquid and provide shareholders a way to sell stock at a price near the tender price right after the announcement. The arbs are, in essence, taking over shareholder risk and hence, they expect a high return.

A transaction can involve a cash exchange, an exchange of securities, or a combination of both. First consider the case of a cash offer. Suppose an acquirer is offering to buy the target's stock at a price of $50 per share at a time when it is traded at $40 per share, a 25% premium. The target's stock can be expected to rise to about $50. There is a chance that the acquirer might withdraw or change the offer, however, so the target's stock might rise to, say, $46 rather than $50. An arbitrageur purchasing the target at $46 will realize a profit of $4 per share if the acquisition takes place at $50. The arb will lose $6 or more per share if the deal does not go through and the target's share falls back to $40 or lower. As the deal becomes more of a certainty, the stock price will be bid up to almost $50. Late-entering arbs will face less risk—and lower possible returns.

A classic example of the risk associated with this type of risk arbitrage is the various buyout attempts of UAL Corp. in 1989 and 1990. In September 1989, a group consisting of pilots and management of United Airlines proposed a $300-per-share bid for UAL's stock. The board approved the transaction and the stock reached $296. However, the group could not obtain financing to close the deal, and subsequently the stock fell by almost 50% in just a few days. In January 1990, the union proposed a bid of $201 per share. The stock plunged again because of financing problems. It has been estimated that the arbs lost more than $1 billion resulting from these failed takeover attempts.

When the transaction involves an exchange of securities, the arb would *long* the securities of the target, expecting them to rise in price, and *short* the securities of the acquiring company, expecting them to decline. There are two risks involved: Either the acquisition would not be consummated, or the length of time would be longer than anticipated. As an example, assume that the stock of an acquirer is trading at $50 per share. The company offers to exchange one share of its stock for one share of the target, which is traded at $40. The transaction is expected to be complete in three months. Suppose that the arb offers the target stock $46 per share. The target's shareholders can immediately take a $6 profit from the proposed deal by selling now to the arb. Or these shareholders can wait three months and receive one share of the acquirer's stock. This gives an extra $4 per share profit, but only if the acquisition is completed and only if the shares of the acquirer are still traded at $50 per share.

Suppose the target's shareholder decides to sell to the arb and take a profit of $6 per share. The arb will have a profit of $4 per share if the deal is closed as proposed. The same outcome remains even if the shares of the acquirer are traded at a level lower than $50. For example, the acquirer's shares are traded at $48, instead of $50. The arb has a $2 profit from the short position (acquirer) and another $2 profit from the long position (target).

As an example of such profitable risk-arbitrage business, consider the 1988 Hoffman–LaRoche's hostile bid of $72 per share for Sterling Drug. Sterling rejected the offer and Hoffman–LaRoche sweetened the offer to $76 and again to $81. The bidding war ended when Sterling agreed to be bought by Eastman Kodak for $89.50 per share. The arbs had hit the jackpot.

The primary risk is that the deal will not go through and the prices of both companies will go back to their levels before the announcement. The arb will lose $6 per share. The secondary risk is that the time horizon involved might be longer than anticipated.

The level of complexity in risk arbitrage varies depending on the structure of the transaction. A more complicated transaction is the two-tiered offer, in which cash is offered for an initial given percentage of stock, while securities are offered for the remainder. Another still more complex transaction offers cash and combination of securities for stock. To reduce risk, the arbs must perform comprehensive research to examine the likelihood of the proposed transaction and the structure of the deal.

The relentless pursuit of information by the arbs in M&A markets is vital to their success. However, occasionally arbs have violated insider-trading regulations. Several prosecutions were cited earlier in this chapter. Among them, Ivan Boesky reportedly made $50 million on the acquisition of Getty by Texaco, $65 million on the marriage of Chevron and Gulf, and $150 million in the failed Ted Turner's CBS takeover attempt. On the other hand, he reportedly lost $40 to $70 million when Phillips Petroleum bought off T. Boone Pickens.

SUMMARY

Mergers and acquisitions are one of the major areas of investment banking business. Investment banks provide important services to this market, including intermediary, negotiation, pricing, advisory, and financing. An understanding of the dynamics in

M&As and buyouts provides the foundation for playing a successful role as an M&A banker.

SELECT BIBLIOGRAPHY

Asquith, P., R. F. Bruner, and D. W. Mullins, Jr. "The gains to bidding firms from mergers." *Journal of Financial Economics* 12 (1983): pp. 121–139.

Burrough, B., and J. Helgar. *Barbarians at the Gate*. New York: Harper Perennial, 1990.

Dennis, D. K., and J. J. McConnell. "Corporate mergers and security returns," *Journal of Financial Economics*, (15) 1986, pp. 143–187.

Ernst & Young. *Mergers and Acquisitions*. New York: Wiley, 1994.

Halperin, M., and S. J. Bell. *Research Guide to Corporate Acquisitions, Mergers, and Other Restructuring*. Westport, CT: Greenwood Press, 1992.

Jensen, M.C., and R.S. Ruback. "The market for corporate control." *Journal of Financial Economics* 12 (1983): pp. 5–50.

Jones, G. E., and D. Van Dyke. *The Business of Business Valuation*. New York: McGraw-Hill, 1998.

Lane, S. J., and M. A. Schary. "Motivations for mergers: The effects of sample selection criteria." In D. K. Ghosh and S. Khaksari. eds. *New Directions in Finance*. London: Routledge, 1995, pp. 63–89.

Lee, C. F., and K. T. Liaw. "Mergers can reduce systematic risk." *Advances in Financial Planning and Forecasting* 6 (November 1994): pp. 347–353.

Lipin, S. "Takeover premiums lose some luster." *Wall Street Journal* (December 31, 1996), pp. 13–14.

Lipin, S. "Closing loophole puts a chill in tax-free deals." *Wall Street Journal* (April 21, 1997), pp. A3 + A13.

Marren, J. H. *Mergers & Acquisitions: A Valuation Handbook*. Homewood, IL: Business One Irwin, 1993.

Mergers and Acquisitions. Various issues.

Pratt, S. P., R. F. Reilly, and R. P. Schweihs. *Valuing Small Business and Professional Practices*. Homewood, IL: Business One Irwin, 1993.

Rock, M. L., R. H. Rock, and M. Sikora. eds. *The Mergers and Acquisitions Handbook*. New York: McGraw Hill, 1994.

Wasserstein, B. *Big Deal: The Battle for Control of America's Leading Corporations*. New York: Warner Books, 1998.

4

Stock Underwriting

The investment bank that wins the mandate to run an issue of new securities is referred to as the lead manager or the bookrunner. Other houses could participate as members of the underwriting syndicate or the selling group. Investment banks earn billions of dollars each year through underwriting initial public offerings and secondary offerings. Increased competition certainly pressures underwriters for lower fees. Successful investment bankers must have a keen awareness of market condition and a strong perception of client capabilities and financial position. This chapter covers the major aspects in underwriting equities, including the mechanics and process, pricing, underwriter risks and compensation, aftermarket trading, and equity takedowns. The chapter also covers expenses associated with an offering, alternative types of offerings, and the new SEC "aircraft carrier" proposals.

MARKET OVERVIEW

The market includes initial public offerings (IPOs) and secondary offerings. The IPO underwriting spreads in the 1990s average slightly above 6%, compared with about 4% for the secondary offerings.[1] The underwriting fees for IPOs each year from 1991 to 1997 are $1.6 billion, $2.4 billion, $3.5 billion, $2.1 billion, $1.9 billion, $3.0 billion, and $2.6 billion, respectively. Over the same period, Wall Street earned between $1 billion and $2 billion each year in underwriting secondary offerings. Major houses engaged in equities underwriting include the *Big Three* (Morgan Stanley Dean Witter, Merrill Lynch, and Goldman Sachs), Credit Suisse First Boston, Lehman Brothers, J.P. Morgan, Salomon Smith Barney, Chase Securities, Donaldson Lufkin Jenrette, BT Alex. Brown, SBC Warburg Dillon Read, NationsBank Montgomery, and BancAmerica Robertson Stephens. There are also many boutique houses such as Hambrecht & Quist (technology) and Friedman Billings (financial-services firms and mortgage REITs). It should be noted that commercial banks are permitted to engage in investment banking activities through their Section 20 subsidiaries, but revenues from such ineligible activities are capped at 25% of total revenue of the securities affiliate.

In a public offering, the Securities Act of 1933 requires the lead manager to conduct *due-diligence* research. The lead manager must prepare a *registration statement* to begin the SEC registration process. This is done in close coordination with the company, accountant, and counsel. Supporting documents such as the underwriting agreement, legal documents, and financial data are made available to the public at SEC offices. The day the investment bank turns in the registration statement with the SEC is known as the *filing date*. The amendments to the registration statement, if so required, are submitted to the SEC again. If there are no further changes, registration becomes effective. In addition, if certain conditions are met, the issuer may file for *Shelf Registration* (Rule 415). Rule 415 permits issuers—with as little as 24-hour notice to the SEC—to register securities they expect to sell within two years.

There are two types of agreements between the issuing company and the investment bank. The first type is the *firm commitment*, in which the investment bank agrees to purchase the entire issue and reoffer to the general public. The second type is known as a *best efforts* agreement. With this type of agreement, the investment bank agrees to sell the securities but does not guarantee the price.

Other steps also take place during the registration process.[2] The *red herring* is printed and distributed. The stock certificates are printed, and the listing exchange and the transfer agent are selected. The lead manager forms the underwriting group and promotes the issue in a *roadshow*. These terms will be explained later in this chapter.

After the issue goes public, the lead manager assures sufficient liquidity in the aftermarket by making market after the underwriting period. A public company is subject to the SEC disclosure requirements, including regular filings of financial data and timely disclosure of material information. The company is also required to send quarterly and annual financial statements to shareholders.

The basic process just described is applicable to both IPOs and secondary offerings. Therefore, the following discussion focuses on IPOs. There are, however, some basic differences between IPOs and secondary offerings. First of all, the motivations are often quite different. Second, IPOs are typically smaller but more lucrative for underwriters. The stock market responses are more dramatic for IPOs. Share price in an IPO generally surges, while in a secondary offering the price remains flat or declines. In addition, the process for a secondary offering is faster because the management team, listing exchange, and transfer agent are already in place.

The SEC is drafting proposals to simplify and modernize securities offerings. The SEC is considering whether to allow public companies to sell securities without having to file a registration statement for each transaction, other than a short written notification, for all small and mid-sized transactions. Companies selling big blocks of securities or selling stock in IPOs are still subject to the registration process. Thus, many small and mid-sized public companies could bypass underwriters and sell securities directly to investors or in private-placement transactions. Because of their significance, these proposals are known as *the aircraft carrier*.

MOTIVATIONS OF ISSUERS

Financing needs by an emerging firm are often the results of the firm's success. Alternatives for satisfying the needs include a public offering, private placement, venture capital, and debt financing. The entrepreneur must evaluate each alternative carefully when searching for new capital. Theoretically, successful business people consider sharing their businesses with others because the firm is unable to obtain enough financing through other alternatives. In practice, there are many reasons motivating the decision to go public.

Advantages of an Initial Public Offering

An important reason for issuing an IPO is to raise capital as a source for ongoing financing, which will enhance the company's chance for successful growth and thereby increase stock value. If needed, a public company with a broader equity base has more access to the capital markets for future financing. Another advantage is greater public exposure and the improvement of corporate image. There is also a higher degree of public confidence because of disclosures required of public companies. This allows for a greater borrowing capability.

Beyond the gain to the company coffers, the greatest financial advantage of going public falls to the founders of the company. The benefits are distributed to the founder–manager, passive founding investors, and members of the management team who have received shares. An IPO provides founding insiders with opportunity to diversify their wealth and facilitates the exit of founding entrepreneurs from the business. With shares traded in the market by way of an IPO, it provides for liquidity as well as better estate planning flexibility for insiders. In addition, if the founding stockholder wishes to take a personal loan from a financial institution, the marketable shares offer a more acceptable form of collateral.

There are also added benefits for management and employees working for a public company. In a public company, stock options plans provide an attractive employment inducement. The plans make it easier to recruit quality employees, and often lead to improvement in productivity and long-term loyalty by the employee–shareholders. These enhancements in company value certainly result in a higher share price.

Disadvantages of Going Public

Prospective issuers should carefully examine the costs, risks, restrictions, and duties associated with going public. First of all, there is a lack of operating confidentiality resulting from the filing of the registration statement and meeting the subsequent reporting requirements. Some particularly sensitive areas of disclosure are remuneration packages (for the top five employees) and extensive company financial information.

Once the company becomes publicly owned, the management is under constant pressure to enhance short-term performance. The requirement that the board of directors or shareholders approve certain management decisions could cause delays or missed opportunities. As a public company, shareholders may demand that the company establish a dividend policy. Furthermore, if a substantial portion of shares is sold to the public, the original owners could lose control of the company.

Another area of concern is the possible change in accounting practices and reduction in management perquisites. Owner–managers are typically more concerned with tax savings than with earnings per share. Further, the company's financial statements may not have been audited. Certain compensation packages and related-party transactions that might be acceptable for a private company might appear imprudent in a public company. A company considering an IPO must be prepared to meet these additional burdens.

One important but frequently ignored negative effect is the possible damage to the thriving entrepreneurial culture as a result of tighter legal constraints or public exposure. Furthermore, the diffusion of corporate ownership could increase the possibility of a hostile takeover.

Finally, the process of going public is expensive and time consuming. The expenses include underwriting discount, counsel fees, printing costs, and other incidental costs. Preparation of the registration document and financial statements is a complicated process that demands a substantial amount of time from management. After going public, the company is subject to the SEC's reporting requirements and the disclosure of material information. These add significantly to the cost of operations.

ASSEMBLING THE IPO TEAM

Once the decision to go public is made, the next step is to assemble the IPO team. The team consists of the management and company's legal counsel, underwriter and its legal counsel, independent accountants, and financial consultants and advisors, and in some cases a financial public relations firm.

The quality of the management team is one of the most important factors in a successful offering. A quality management team should be able to foster growth and establish a leadership position in the market. Underwriters are especially pleased if some members in the management have experience in an IPO. It adds credibility to the management's role. A good board of directors with highly regarded business people who could be objective is a big plus in an offering.

The selection of an underwriter is important because the investment bankers are responsible for selling the securities. Management should begin building an underwriter relationship long before the offering. Usually a company selects one investment bank as the *lead underwriter* or *syndicate manager.* The underwriter will typically form a syndicate to underwrite and distribute the issue. When selecting an underwriter, consideration is paid to reputation, experience, market-making capabilities, fees, and after offering services. The underwriter will perform a preliminary investigation of the company to decide whether to undertake the offering. If satisfied, the investment banker and the company will discuss the type of security to be offered, firm commitment or best-efforts underwriting, the range of offering price, and the number of shares to be offered. Then the investment bank issues the letter of intent to formalize the arrangement, which will later lead to the *underwriting agreement.* One important note here is that the letter of intent signals the beginning of the *quiet period* (or silence period), during which the company is subject to SEC guidelines on publication of information outside of the prospectus.

Accountants are a key figure in this process. Much of the financial information contained in the registration statement is obtained from the audited financial statements. SEC regulations require the independent public accountant to certify the financial statements and examine other information included in the registration statement. The accountants also assist in responding to SEC comments on accounting issues and are required to sign the comfort letter stating that the financial statements conform to GAAP.

A consultant or advisor is sometimes retained on a dedicated basis for a specific task. A knowledgeable consultant can be very helpful in starting a company off on the right foot in the offering process. A knowledgeable consultant or advisor can also help in finding a suitable underwriter, making timely proper filings to the SEC, and several steps in between. The best advisors are those who have had years of experience in the area.

Attorneys are retained to advise on compliance with the securities laws during and after the registration process. In addition, attorneys usually conduct due-diligence matters, such as reviewing minutes of the board and shareholder meetings, articles of incorporation, contracts and leases, and the ownership status of major assets. They also coordinate the efforts of other members, resolve any question arising from SEC comments, and file necessary amendments. The attorney's competence and experience with the registration process are critical to the timely and effective coordination of the complex process. Top IPO legal counsels include Wilson, Sonsini & Goodrich; Brobeck, Phleger & Harrison; Testa, Hurwitz & Thibeault; Hale & Dorr; Fenwick & West; Skadden, Arps, Slade, Meagher & Flom; Latham & Walkins; Cravath, Swaine & Moore; Davis, Polk & Wardwell; Sullivan & Cromwell; and Shearman & Sterling; among others.

Another important member is the financial printer, who is responsible for printing the registration statement according to the SEC format and guidelines. Bankers, attorneys, or accountants are able to recommend financial printers. For example, Manhattan-based Browne & Co. is a leading financial printer.

Sometimes an IPO company might use the services of a financial public relations firm. A PR firm experienced in SEC registrations can often guide the company through the restrictions of the quiet (silence) period and help prepare materials for roadshows. A good PR firm can also help in developing the list of analysts and business press editors who follow the industry and providing them with news releases and information about the company. Furthermore, a transfer agent should be selected. The transfer agent provides services beyond simply transferring stock and recording the transaction. The transfer agent must report to IRS when dividends are paid. The transfer agent also provides a complete mailing service for sending out reports, proxy statements, and meeting notice to shareholders.

MECHANICS AND PROCESS

It usually takes at least several months to complete the offering process. The length of time needed depends on the readiness of the company, the availability of information required in the registration statement, and market conditions. The silence period typically begins once the company reaches a preliminary understanding with the underwriter and ends 25 days after the offering becomes effective if the security is listed on an exchange or is quoted on Nasdaq, otherwise it ends 90 days after the effective date. The steps in the process include filing registration statement, SEC letter of comments, preparing the amended registration statement, preparing the red herring or preliminary prospectus, conducting roadshows, performing due-diligence research, negotiating price amendment and signing the underwriting agreement, and closing.

Registration Statement

The commonly used forms[3] for SEC registration are Form S-1 and Form SB-2. There is no limitation on the amount of offering using SEC Form S-1 or SB-2. In general, the same things must be disclosed in SB-2 as in S-1, but the required degree of detail is substantially reduced in SB-2.

Form S-1 requires the most extensive disclosure, and hence it will be illustrated here. Major items required in Part I and Part II of Form S-1 are as follows:

Part I
1. Forepart of the Registration Statement and Outside Front Cover Page of Prospectus
2. Inside Front and Outside Back Cover Pages of Prospectus
3. Summary Information, Risk Factors, and Ratio of Earnings to Fixed Charges
4. Use of Proceeds
5. Determination of Offering Price
6. Dilution
7. Selling Security Holders
8. Plan of Distribution
9. Description of Securities to Be Registered
10. Interest of Named Experts and Counsel
11. Information with Respect to the Registrant
12. Disclosure of Commission Position on Indemnification for Securities Act Liabilities

Part II
1. Other Expense of Issuance of Distribution
2. Indemnification of Directors and Officers
3. Recent Sales of Unregistered Securities
4. Exhibits and Financial Statement Schedules
5. Undertakings

Part I is usually distributed as a separate booklet to prospective investors. The prospectus also must contain any additional data to make it meaningful and not misleading. Part II contains additional information such as the signatures of company officers, directors, consent of counsel and experts, and the financial schedules called for by Section 12 of Regulation S-X. Part II is made available for public inspection at SEC headquarters in Washington or can be accessed online through Electronic Data Gathering, Analysis, and Retrieval (EDGAR).

In general, disclosed in the registration statement are various kinds of important information for investors when making investment decisions. Not all the items just listed will appear in every registration statement. Some information may be incorporated by reference to another statement filed with the SEC and need not be duplicated in the Form S-1 filing.

Part of the data includes information about the company's business, officers, directors, and principal shareholders and their compensation. The company must also disclose the size of the offering, the price range, the intended use of the funds, the audited financial statements, and the risk factors. Additional disclosures include the selling shareholders (if any), underwriting syndicate, type of underwriting, dividend policy, dilution, capitalization, related party transactions, and certain legal opinions. A key portion in Form S-1 filing is the management's discussion that examines the company's financial condition and results of its operations and the business plan.

Before a filing, there are often prefiling conferences with the SEC staff. The purpose is to discuss and make certain adequate disclosure and compliance with relevant regulations. The SEC staff is adept at pinpointing potential problem areas that may arise during the process of assembling information for the registration statement. For example, the company may wish to know how to handle a legal or accounting problem or how to deal with questionable regulation compliance in a filing.

Once the registration statement has been filed with the SEC, the *waiting period* (cooling off) begins. During the cooling-off period, the issue is considered *in registration*, and there are restrictions on the activities the company or the underwriter may undertake. During the waiting period, the underwriting syndicate begins soliciting *indications of interest* from potential purchasers, but no actual sales can be made until after the registration statement becomes *effective*. The effective date is usually the date when the issue is offered to the public for a firm commitment, or the date when selling begins for a best-efforts underwriting.

SEC Review and Comments

SEC staff specialists, consisting of an attorney, an accountant, and a financial analyst, review the IPO registration statement. The review group may also include other staff experts familiar with a particular industry. The staff reviews the documents to determine full and fair disclosure, particularly any misstatements or omissions of material facts that might prevent investors from making a fully informed investment decision. The SEC does not pass judgment on or evaluate the quality of a proposed offering, which is made by the marketplace.

After reviewing the registration statement, the SEC typically sends the company's legal counsel a letter of comments concerning deficiencies and suggestions. There are four basic types of SEC reviews, all aimed at the accuracy and adequacy of disclosure in the registration statement. A *deferred review* is when the initial registration statement is poorly put together, and is notified by a "bedbug letter" advising the registrant to withdraw. A *cursory review*, not often used, indicates that the staff has not found any glowing deficiencies. Similar to cursory review, the *summary review* is not often used. It includes a few comments based on limited review. The most preferred review is the *customary review*, which is a full review by the SEC staff accompanied by a detailed comment letter.

Amended Registration Statement

Each comment in the SEC letter of comments must be addressed and resolved. Common amendments include *delaying amendment, substantive amendment*, and *price amendment*.

A delaying amendment is used to request a new effective date if the company has not been able to reply or to make up the deficiencies. Failure to do so can result in a defective registration or SEC's stop order against the company.

A substantive amendment is typically used to correct the deficiencies in a registration statement. It could be either a reply to the SEC comment or an update of significant interim developments subsequent to the filing. The registration statement must be correct and current when it becomes effective.

A price amendment is commonly used when the price and the size of the offering are not determined until the day of or the day prior to the offering. This amendment supplies the last-minute information.

The Preliminary Prospectus or Red Herring

After the filing, a preliminary prospectus is distributed to brokers and prospective purchasers. The purpose is to gather an indication of interest from investors. This is the main document the underwriting syndicate uses to sell the stock. However, as required by the SEC, the cover page must bear the caption "Preliminary Prospectus" in red ink (hence the term *red herring*) and the following statement:

> *Information contained herein is subject to completion or amendment. A registration statement relating to these securities has been filed with the Securities and Exchange Commission but has not become effective. These securities may not be sold nor may offers to buy be accepted prior to the time the registration statement becomes effective.*

Under SEC rules, the offering price, underwriting discounts, or other matters dependent on the offering price may be omitted in the preliminary prospectus. Once the effective date arrives, the offering price and the effective date will be added to the prospectus. Then the *final prospectus* is issued. A sample of the prospectus cover page and summary is provided in the appendix. The company in the sample prospectus, Friedman Billings Ramsey, is an investment bank that recently went public. Friedman Billings Ramsey itself was the lead underwriter. The issuing price was $20 per share and the underwriting discount was $1.40 per share.

Each state has its own securities laws, called blue-sky laws. However, as part of the efforts to reduce regulatory burdens on issuers, the National Securities Markets Improvement Act of 1996 exempts listed securities or securities sold to qualified purchasers from state registration requirements. It preserves state antifraud authority.

The Roadshow

The roadshow is the key marketing event that precedes the IPO by several weeks. It is arranged to meet with financial analysts and brokers in order for potential purchasers to learn more about the company, which hopefully will improve price performance in the *aftermarket*. The management team has to explain what their market position is, describe how the company will execute its business plan, and show off the quality of the management team. Many analysts consider top management to be among the most important aspects of any company. Investors frequently base their purchasing decision on their perception of the management. The roadshow is also a kind of public opinion trial for the issuer's business plan. By the end of the roadshow, the lead manager should have a good idea of the investor's interest, which assists in determining the final price and size of the IPO. An effective roadshow is crucial to the success of the offering.

Due Diligence

Before the registration statement becomes effective, the underwriter will hold a due-diligence meeting attended by members of the IPO team.[4] The purpose is to list, gather, and authenticate matters such as articles of incorporation, bylaws, patents, completeness and correctness of minutes, and verification of corporate existence.[5]

Due-diligence meetings are held to reduce the risk of liability associated with filing by ensuring that all material matters have been fully and fairly disclosed in the registration statement. This is an important safeguard. Part of the due diligence activity of legal counsel is to make formal visits to the company's offices and plant sites. Legal counsel typically maintains a due-diligence file.

Price Amendment and Underwriting Agreement

The negotiation and final determination of offering size and price are influenced by a number of factors, including financial performance of the company, stock market conditions, prices of comparable companies, market perceptions of the company, and anticipated aftermarket share value. The underwriting agreement is signed when the registration statement is about to become effective. Also at this time the final amendment to the registration statement is filed. The price amendment includes the agreed price, underwriter discount, and the net proceeds to the company. The underwriter will typically request that the offering be declared effective immediately (requesting acceleration) if the staff of the SEC Division of Corporate Finance has no important reservations. The underwriter may then proceed with the sales of the securities if the acceleration is granted.

There are three primary underwriting contracts: *Agreement Among Underwriters, Dealer Agreement*, and the *Underwriting Agreement*. The agreement among underwriters establishes the relationship among the underwriters. It designates the syndicate manager to act on their behalf. The dealer agreement or selling agreement is the agreement in which securities dealers who are not part of the syndicate are contracted to distribute the securities. These other dealers help move the issue to the marketplace. The dealer agreement will allow these dealers to purchase the securities at a discount from the offering price. The underwriting agreement establishes the contractual relationship between the corporate issuer and the syndicate.

The underwriting agreement generally contains introductions, warranties, terms of offering, conditions, covenants, indemnification, and cancellation. The *Introduction* section identifies the parties to the underwriting syndicate, the size and security type to be offered. The *Representations and Warranties* provisions cover the guarantee by the company. It also includes the warranty that the company is properly incorporated and accredited. Additionally, the *Terms of the Offering* include the underwriter's pledge to buy and pay for the securities, the timing, and any green shoe provisions. *Covenants* spell out the rights and obligations of all parties. *Conditions* in the underwriting agreement include the completeness and accuracy of company's representations, and that neither party can sell shares until the effective date. The *Indemnification* provisions excuse the underwriter's liability for material misstatements or omissions in the registration statement on the part of the issuer. Finally, the *Cancellation* section contains a clause that allows the underwriter to cancel the offering after the effective date but prior to the closing date, provided that the underwriter can show cause and justification.

Closing

The closing date is sometime after the effective date but the actual date depends on the type of underwriting. The closing meeting includes all key players and is usually held in the conference room of the escrow institution. At the closing date, various documents as well as the updated comfort letter are exchanged. The company delivers the registered securities to the underwriter and receives payment for the issue. Closing differs considerably between small offerings on a best-efforts basis and larger offerings on firm commitments.

For small, best-efforts offering, the closing takes place after the selling period has been completed. The selling period is usually 60 to 120 days after the effective date, with extension allowance of 60 to 90 days by mutual consent. For a firm commitment, closing is usually a week or two after the effective date.

Tombstones

Tombstone ad is considered an essential ingredient of the process. This is more in the nature of announcement than advertisement. A *tombstone* is a boxed-in ad that appears in financial sections of newspapers and magazines that announces the particulars of the issue. It contains the name of the company, the issuing price and size, the lead underwriter, and other members of the underwriting group. A disclaimer also appears at the top:

> *This announcement is neither an offer to sell nor a solicitation of an offer to buy any of these securities. The offering is made only by the Prospectus.*

The tombstone ads are a good means to introduce the company to the public and to pique the public's interest. But management must make every effort to put together effective due-diligence meetings and roadshows, using all the help it can get from its PR firm and the underwriter. These meetings are presented to a largely critical audience of brokers and analysts who need convincing. The outcomes of these shows often spell the difference between the success and failure of an offering.

TIMETABLE SUMMARY

The share-issuing process is complex and requires team efforts. The following illustration serves to initiate the reader to the registration details and mechanics. Included in the illustration is a listing of some of the major events that must take place, an indication of the individuals involved, and the illustrative timetable.

1. (Day 1) The management selects counsel, underwriter, printer and signs the letter of intent. The quiet period begins.
2. (Day 3) Board of directors authorizes issuing shares, preparing registration statement, and negotiating underwriting agreement.
3. (Day 6) The IPO team in the initial organization meeting determines the type and structure of the offering, and selects the form of the registration statement.
4. (Day 8) The underwriter and its counsel commence due-diligence review.
5. (Day 10) The management, counsel, and independent accountant begin gathering necessary information and financial statements for the registration statement.
6. (Day 15) The management, underwriter, and respective counsels meet to prepare a draft of the underwriting agreement, agreement among underwriters, and power of attorney.
7. (Day 20) The management, its counsel, and underwriter's counsel distribute questionnaires to directors, officers, and selling shareholders related to the registration statement.
8. (Day 25) The management and its counsel complete the corporate cleanup.
9. (Day 30) All members of the IPO team meet to review the first draft of textual portion of the registration statement.

10. (Day 35) The management and independent accountant complete a draft of financial statements for inclusion in the registration statement.

11. (Day 45) Members of the IPO team hold a prefiling conference with SEC staff. All members meet again to review and comment on the draft registration statement, including financial statements.

12. (Day 50) The management sends first draft of registration statement to the financial printer. The management at this stage also needs to appoint a stock transfer agent and registrar and arrange for preparation of stock certificates. Separately, the management, underwriter, and independent accountant discuss comfort letter requirements and procedures.

13. (Day 70) The board of directors approves and signs the registration statement and prospectus.

14. (Day 71) The company files the registration statement. The underwriter distributes the preliminary prospectus.

15. (Day 80) The management, PR firm, and underwriter begin the roadshows.

16. (Day 100) The SEC comment letter arrives.

17. (Day 101) The IPO team prepares amendments to the registration statement and sends draft to the printer.

18. (Day 105) The team reviews printer's proof of amendments. The company files amendments to the registration statement covering SEC comments and updating any material development. Notification is also sent to SEC that a final price amendment will be held on Day 110 and that the company requests acceleration, so that the registration may become effective on Day 110.

19. (Day 106) The management, its counsel, and independent accountants resolve any final comments and changes with SEC by telephone.

20. (Day 107) In the due-diligence meeting, the team determines whether any additional events should be disclosed in the registration statement and if all parties are satisfied that the registration statement is not misleading.

21. (Day 108) The management and underwriter finalize the offering price.

22. (Day 110) This is the offering date. The independent accountant delivers the first comfort letter to underwriter. Management, underwriter, and respective counsel sign underwriting agreement. The company files price amendment to registration statement, and notifies stock exchange and NASD of effectiveness.

23. (Day 111) The tombstone advertisement appears in newspapers.

24. (Day 112) Managing underwriter provides registrar with names in which the certificates are to be registered, and packages certificates for delivery.

25. (Day 120) This is the closing date. The independent accountant delivers a second comfort letter to the underwriter. The company completes settlement with the underwriter, issue stock, and collect proceeds from offering. The management and underwriter sign all final documents.

VALUATION AND PRICING

The issuer often believes the stock is worth much more than the suggested price. But the underwriter wants to create a demand for the new issue, and to sell it quickly. The best way to do that is to offer the stock at a price attractive enough to encourage prospective purchasers to buy it. In this area, investment bankers need to make the entrepreneur realize that his or her interests are not in conflict with the investors.

When the share does well, the entrepreneur also realizes a huge profit. This is the big difference between being acquired and going public. When a company is acquired, the entrepreneur is giving up a claim to the stream of future profits that the company will bring. In a public issue, the entrepreneur retains a big portion of ownership. What has been sold to the public is just a fraction of the entrepreneur's potential wealth.

Valuation and pricing are related, but they deal with different issues. Valuation is estimating the value of the company. The underwriter typically conducts a survey of comparable public companies, which will help provide a preliminary valuation. The underwriter also looks into the following factors: efficiency, leverage, profit margins, use of proceeds, operating history, operating base, management, and product differentiation. Furthermore, it is important for the underwriter to take into account whether this is a single-product or a multiple-product company. The use of proceeds is a key variable to the underwriter and to the investors. Many underwriters would be deterred or would only engage in best efforts if they perceive that the prime purpose of the issue is for the selling shareholders to bailout.

Pricing refers to setting the offering price. The main concern is how much the market will bear. Most underwriters follow historical traditions in pricing a new issue. The price should not be too high or too low in order to appeal to potential investors. For example, a price of $5 or less might be considered too risky, and a price of $20 or more might be considered too high unless for a prestigious company. It is common to see an IPO priced from $10 to $20 per share.

One formula underwriters often use is the method of discounting. Underwriters like to price a new issue a certain percentage below what they consider a fair value. This creates an incentive for investors to put money into the new issue. This discounting practice is clearly evidenced by the observations that a new issue typically traded at a much higher price in the aftermarket, averaged at 16%.

Timing is also critical. The offering price is adjusted upward when the underwriter has received a higher over-subscription in indications of interest. The offering price needs to be lowered or the issue may be postponed if indications of interest are weak. Certainly the overall market environment in part influences investor's interest.

Another pricing reference is the price/earnings ratio, especially for the secondary offerings. In an IPO, this yardstick is not as crucial. The size of the offering also plays a role. Underwriters typically want to see broad distribution and provide liquidity in the aftermarket. The SEC rules require disclosure for owners of 5% or more of shares. Institutional investors usually purchase blocks of securities. The SEC rules might prevent institutional investors that want to avoid disclosure from participating in an IPO if the offering size is small. This could negatively affect the demand and the price of the security.

UNDERWRITING RISK AND COMPENSATION

It is customary for the lead underwriter to form a distribution syndicate consisting of the *underwriting syndicate* and a *selling group.* Each member in the underwriting syndicate is committed to buying a portion of the IPO shares, while members of the selling group accept no risk. The lead underwriter's decision to distribute shares outside of its own organization has its positives and negatives. The lead underwriter benefits because each underwriter shares a portion of the underwriting risk. Second, the syndicate manager has the responsibility to ensure liquidity in the aftermarket. A broad participation by the street provides incentives for other firms to make a market in the stock and regularly research it. On the other hand, the lead manager has to make some economic concessions in sharing the underwriting spread. Another risk is that one of the syndicate members might outshine the lead manager and hence gain an edge in competing for future offerings.[6] In general, the selection of underwriting syndicate and the selling group should be based on a solid distribution of shares and the ability of market making.

Underwriting Risks

In underwriting, investment bankers "sell" risk services to the issuers by assuming at least part of the floating risk when they underwrite an offering by firm commitment. A firm commitment becomes absolutely firm only on the offering day or the night before, when the underwriting agreement is signed. The signing typically occurs just before the issue goes effective. By then, all the marketing has been done, the roadshows have been conducted, and the underwriter knows the "indication of interests." The risk or uncertainty can occur when the market shifts after a firm commitment on price has been made.

Floating risk consists of waiting risk, pricing risk, and marketing risk. During the period after the filing of the registration statement, but before it is declared effective by the SEC, changes in market environment often affect the offering price. Such waiting risk is mainly borne by the issuer, and has been minimized by the introduction of Rule 415 Shelf Registration. However, the pricing risk and marketing risk are exclusively borne by the underwriters. The pricing risk occurs when the market conditions worsen after the underwriting agreement is signed. Marketing reduces flotation risk by building a "book of interest" before the effective date and by aftermarket trading. Forming a syndicate in which each member is taking only a portion of the total risk also lessens the risk. Institutional sales help bankers place large pieces of new issues.

The risks cannot be underestimated. Underwriters for even the highest quality issues have suffered big losses. In October 1979 IBM's $1 billion issue was priced just prior to the weekend in which the Fed shifted policy (known as the Saturday night massacre). The underwriters took heavy losses. Another example is the 1987 British Petroleum stock issue on Thursday, October 15, 1987 (days before the October 19 market crash). The four underwriters of that issue took a total loss of $283 million.[7]

Compensation

The underwriting spread is the difference between the price to the public printed on the prospectus and the price the corporate issuer receives. The amount of the spread is determined through negotiation between the managing underwriter and the corporate issuer. All members of the syndicate are paid out of the spread. The varying amount of risk accepted by the members of the distribution syndicate is reflected in the compensation schedule. The *manager's fee* is compensation to the managing underwriter for preparing the offering. Participating in a thorough due-diligence review and putting the deal together are the primary basis for the compensation.

The *underwriting* or *syndicate allowance* covers expenses incurred by the underwriting syndicate, including advertising, legal expenses, and other out-of-pocket expenses. Finally, the selling concession is allocated among all firms based on the amount of securities they accept to sell. Therefore, the syndicate manager will have all three, the manager's fee, the underwriting allowance, and the selling concession. The underwriting dealers will get the underwriting allowance and the selling commission. The selling group is allocated a portion of the total selling concession.

THE PRICE OF GOING PUBLIC

The costs of a public offering are substantial. There are no hard and fast numbers. Total costs vary, depending on the size of the offering and the company's ability to market the offering smoothly and efficiently. As an example, for an issue around $150 million, the total costs can be as high as 10%. It also demands a great deal of time from top management, resulting in internal costs that may be difficult to quantify. Furthermore, there are costs of "underpricing."

Direct Costs

Direct costs include direct expenses plus the underwriting spread. The company pays the direct expenses whether or not the offering is completed. The underwriter's commission is contingent on the completion. The first big item is the gross spread. This is generally negotiable, and depends on factors such as the size of the offering, the type of underwriting commitment, and the type of security offered. There is also reimbursement for some of the banker's direct expenses. Additional compensation is in the form of warrants, stock issued to the underwriter before the public offering at a price below the offering, or a right of first refusal for future offerings.

Legal fees are usually the second largest item of expenses. They vary depending on the complexity of the company, the orderliness of its records, and the amount of time necessary to draft and file the registration statement.

Accounting fees are substantial as well. The accountant reviews and verifies the data in the registration statement and issues the comfort letter. These fees do not include audits of the financial statements, which vary depending on the size of the company and the number of years audited.

Printing costs are determined by the length, number of changes made to the registration statement, and the number of photographs. Registration fees, registrar and transfer agent fees, and miscellaneous fees are not insignificant. The SEC registration fee is 0.0278% of the dollar amount of the securities being registered (gradually reduced to 0.0067% by year 2007). The NASD filing fee is $100 plus 0.01% of the maximum dollar amount. Additionally, there are exchange listing fees.

Underpricing Costs

A public offering is costly in yet another way. Since the offering price is typically less than the aftermarket value, investors who bought the issue get a bargain at the expense of the firm's original shareholders, to a certain degree. The original shareholders typically retain a large portion of the company's shares on which they made enormous profits. Furthermore, the public would be eager to subscribe to subsequent offerings.

When a company goes public, it is very difficult for the underwriter to judge how much investors will be willing to pay for the stock. Hence, underpricing is a means of soliciting investor interest. According to a study by Ibbotson, Sindelar, and Ritter

(1994), the average underpricing is about 16%. IPOs in 1996 and 1997 showed an average first day gain of 17% and 15%, respectively.

Underpricing helps the underwriter. It reduces the risk of underwriting and gains them the gratitude of investors who buy the IPO issues. The true cost of underpricing is difficult to judge. If the business is sufficiently competitive, underwriters will probably take all these hidden benefits into account when negotiating the spread.

Hidden and Future Costs

During the lengthy process of preparing the first listing of the company, unanticipated costs will crop up. These include extra transportation costs to and from consultants, counsels, accountants, and underwriter; meals and entertainment; postage; phone calls, faxes, and messenger deliveries. Another important item is promotions. Thousands of dollars may be required to make the brokerage community and investors aware of the company. Another cost worth mentioning is directors' and officers' liability insurance, which is not only difficult to obtain for small companies, but also costly.

Although management has considerable control over the amount and extent of some of these hidden costs, the costs invariably exceed what is anticipated. In addition, the one cost that is difficult to put a dollar value on is the management time it takes to complete the offering.

A further consequence is the expense of being a public company. First, the SEC requires the company to file periodic reports, including annual Form 10-K, quarterly Form 10-Q, Form 8-K for report of significant events, and proxy and information statements. Significant costs and executive time are incurred in preparing and filing these reports. The financial printing business is about $800 million per year. The SEC required that all corporate documents be filed with it electronically by May 1996 through the introduction of Electronic Data Gathering, Analysis, and Retrieval (EDGAR). However, filing expenses have not declined as expected initially.

SEC REGULATIONS AND EXCHANGE LISTING

The SEC requires that a company planning an IPO follow the communications guidelines concerning the quiet period, preliminary prospectus, trading practices rules, offering, and postoffering communications.

Rule 134 of the Securities Act of 1933 sets forth the specific information that can be released to the public during the quiet period. During this period, the prospectus is the most important marketing document for the offering. The investment bank may not provide any other information to its clients other than what is contained in the red herring. They cannot provide research reports, recommendations, sales literature, or anything from any other firm about the company. Usual ongoing disclosures of factual information are permitted. The SEC also requires that communications only proceed at the level that was in effect before the preparations for the offering began. Therefore, it is in the company's interest to establish a fairly high level of public awareness well in advance of the offering.

After the registration statement is filed, SEC regulations prohibit distribution of any written sales literature about the offering other than the preliminary prospectus and the tombstone ads. Until the quiet period is over, cooperation by the company or its underwriter in the preparation of news stories on the pending offering is not permitted.

The trading practices rules (Regulation M) are aimed at preventing manipulative trading in securities during an offering. The rules govern the activities of underwriters, issuers, selling security holders, and others in connection with offerings of securities. The rules prohibit persons subject to the regulation from bidding, purchasing, or inducing others to bid for or purchase a *covered security* during the applicable *restricted period*. A covered security is any security that is the subject of a distribution or any security into which or for which such a distribution may be converted. For any security with an average daily trading volume (ADTV) of $100,000 or more and having a public float of $25 million or more, the restricted period begins on the latter of (a) the business day prior to the determination of the offering price or (b) the time a person becomes a distribution participant, and it ends when the participation of distribution is completed. For all other securities, the restricted period begins on the latter of five business days prior to pricing or the time that person becomes a distribution participant, and it ends upon completion of such person's participation of distribution. Certain transactions and securities are exempt from the trading restrictions. The exempt transactions cover stabilizing, exercises of securities, basket transactions, transactions among distribution participants, and transactions in Rule 144A. Exempt securities include actively traded securities (ADTV of $1 million and $150 million public float), investment grade nonconvertibles, asset-backed securities, and securities exempted from registration requirements.

Once the registration statement is declared effective, the pricing information is added to the prospectus. The SEC also permits news releases, press conferences, tombstone ads, and one-on-one meetings. However, the quiet period will remain in effect for another 25 days, unless the security is not listed on an exchange or quoted on Nasdaq, in which case the period is 90 days. The content of these communications must conform to information contained in the prospectus.

After the closing of the offering, the issuer becomes a public company and is subject to the disclosure requirements. The company must file quarterly and annual reports. The company must also provide timely disclosure of material information.

The choice of exchange listing is part of the IPO process. The main securities trading markets are the New York Stock Exchange (NYSE), the American Stock Exchange (AMEX), the regional markets, and the over-the-counter markets (OTC). What follows is a brief description of the listing requirements.

The listing requirements on the NYSE are extensive. The form for listing is similar to a full S-1 registration statement. The minimum listing requirements are: 2,000 shareholders, 1 million publicly held shares, market value of public shares of $40 million, and net tangible assets of $40 million. Detailed listing requirements are documented in Table 4.1.

The AMEX is the second largest exchange. The minimum requirements are as follows. There are at least 800 shareholders. Publicly held shares should be at least 300,000 shares and these shares have a market value of $3 million. Income before taxes must be $750,000 annually for the latest fiscal year or for two of the last three years. The stockholder's equity is at $4 million or more. The bid of the stock is at least $3. Table 4.2 lists the details.

The National Association of Securities Dealers Automated Quotations (Nasdaq) is a computer-based quotation/trading system with terminals in broker/dealer offices all over the country. Table 4.3 lists the requirements for national market. The minimum listing requirements for smallcaps (companies with small market capitalizations) are: 300 shareholders, 1 million shares of public float valued at $5 million, a bid price of $4, and three market makers (see Table 4.4).

TABLE 4.1   NYSE Listing Requirements

Round-lot holders	2,000 U.S.
OR,	
Total shareholders AND	2,200 U.S.
Average monthly trading volume for most recent 6 months	100,000 shares
OR,	
Total shareholders AND	500
Average monthly trading volume for the most recent 12 months	1,000,000
Public shares	1,100,000 U.S.
Market value of public shares	$40,000,000
Net tangible assets	$40,000,000
Pretax income	
Most recent year	$2,500,000
Each of 2 preceding years	$2,000,000
OR,	
Aggregate for the 3 years	$6,500,000
Minimum in most recent year	$4,500,000
Or,	
For companies with not less than $500 million market capitalization and $200 million in revenues in the most recent year	
Aggregate for the 3 years	$25,000,000

Source: Adapted from New York Stock Exchange, *Domestic Listing Standards and Procedures,* current as of July 7, 1997.

AFTERMARKET TRADING

Aftermarket trading begins after the new issue has been sold to the original buyers, who purchased the shares at the issuing price. Aftermarket trading is handled differently in a small, best-efforts IPO and in a larger firm commitment underwriting.

In a large firm commitment issue, the underwriters typically want to stabilize the stock if its price does not perform as anticipated. The underwriter will support the

TABLE 4.2   AMEX Listing Requirements

Pretax income, latest year or 2 of the most recent 3 years	$750,000
Market value of public float	$3,000,000
Price	$3
Stockholder's equity	$4,000,000
Alternative Financial Guidelines:	
Market value of public float	$15,000,000
Price	$3
Operating history	3 years
Stockholder's equity	$4,000,000

Source: Adapted from American Stock Exchange. *Listing Guidelines for U.S. Companies,* 1997.

TABLE 4.3   Nasdaq National Market Listing Requirements

Net tangible assets	$6 million	$18 million	N/A
Market capitalization	N/A	N/A	$75 million
OR,			
Total assets	N/A	N/A	$75 million
OR,			
Total revenues	N/A	N/A	$75 million
Pretax income in latest year or 2 of recent 3 years	$1 million	N/A	N/A
Public float	$1.1 million	$1.1 million	$1.1 million
Operating history	N/A	2 years	N/A
Market value of public float	$8 million	$18 million	$20 million
Minimum bid price	$5	$5	$5
Round lot shareholders	400	400	400
Market makers	3	3	4
Corporate governance	Yes	Yes	Yes

Source: Adapted from Nasdaq Stock Market, August 25, 1997.

market price of a new issue in order to keep it from becoming a broken deal or falling below the initial offering price when trading of the stock goes into the aftermarket. If the new issue price goes down on the first aftermarket trading, the underwriters could be negatively branded for months. Underwriters want to avoid that. Furthermore, declining new issue prices point to poor judgment on the part of the lead underwriter and the analysts of the selling group.

The SEC requires detailed reports if stabilization is used. The stock purchased for stabilization cannot be resold at a higher price. It must be resold at or below the purchase price. Losses are shared pro rata by the selling syndicate. If price continues to

TABLE 4.4   Nasdaq Smallcap Market Initial Listing Requirements

Net tangible assets	$4 million
OR,	
Market capitalization	$50 million
OR,	
Net income in latest fiscal year or 2 of the last 3 years	$750,000
Public float	$1 million
Market value of public float	$5 million
Minimum bid price	$4
Market makers	3
Shareholders (round lot holders)	300
Operating history	1 year
OR,	
Market capitalization	$50 million
Corporate governance	Yes

Source: Adapted from Nasdaq Stock Market, August 25, 1997.

fall, the underwriters may withdraw support at their discretion without notice. Underwriters will make every attempt to place stock in strong hands among the syndicate members to avoid the necessity for stabilization. Weak members might have reduced participation in future offerings or might even be eliminated as a player in the syndicate.

On the other hand, a hot new issue will require underwriters to exercise the over-allotment or *green shoe* option. The name comes from the first company to ever use it, Green Shoe Company. The purpose of over-allotment, like stabilization, is to ensure an orderly aftermarket. It allows underwriters to sell up to 15% more of the stock. The additional funds raised by the green shoe go to the company, less commissions.

When the underwriter anticipates either over-allotment or a possibility of stabilization, the fact must be disclosed on the front cover of the prospectus as follows:

> *In connection with this offering, the underwriters may over-allot or effect transactions which stabilize or maintain the market price of the common stock of the company at a level above that which might otherwise prevail in the open market. Such stabilizing, if commenced, may be disconnected at any time.*

For smaller best-efforts offerings, stabilization is not used. The best that can be hoped for is that the primary market makers purchase the stock for their own inventory. If the market goes down, it is often that a weak syndicate member is cutting losses rather than an indication of the market reception of the issue. Typically, a minimum/maximum offering is used. The underwriter may get an indication of the range of interest from syndicate members to determine the minimum and maximum of the offering size.

Generally, during the first several weeks or so, a high degree of volatility in the trading price and volume can be seen. The issuing company is still subject to the 25-day quiet period during which the company cannot begin any publicity efforts. The company can only depend on the support of the underwriters and the selling group to maintain its stock at a reasonable trading level. Hence, it is important for the company to maintain a strong relationship with brokers during the selling period.

DIRECT OFFERINGS, SHELLS, AND EQUITY TAKEDOWNS

The conventional process of issuing equities is quite complex and expensive. Some entrepreneurs are looking for ways to avoid the complexities and expenses. On the other hand, for investment banking firms lacking strong client relationship, it is difficult to compete. Direct Internet offerings, shells, and equity takedowns are the possible alternatives.

Direct Offerings

The expenses associated with raising capital in the equity market are very high. Now Internet offering (or direct offering) is available, through which the issuing company bypasses the underwriters and brokerages. The 1996 IPOs of Spring Street Brewery and Logos Research Systems are the first of the so-called do-it-yourself initial public offerings. On November 14, 1997, The Green Bay Packers, Inc. offered the sale of 400,000 shares of its common stock at a price of $200 per share online. On the fixed-income side, General Motors Acceptance Corp. started marketing $500 million medium-term notes through Chicago Corp. on September 27, 1996.

Entrepreneurs plan to launch virtual stock exchanges and online investment banks that they believe will reach retail and institutional investors more efficiently and cheaply. Ben Ezra, Weinstein & Co. developed software to help companies draft their own prospectuses. Hambrecht & Quist set up a new brokerless electronic division that uses the Internet to sell stocks, mutual funds, and IPOs at the same rates given to its institutional clients. ETrade, Direct Stock Market, and Wit Capital are all working to build an Internet stock exchange. However, the Web's uses will be limited until the legal and regulatory issues are resolved.

Major Wall Street firms think that most corporations still need investment banks to do the bulk of their financing. They have the ability to provide liquidity by market making in the secondary market.

Shells

A public *shell* is the other alternative that entrepreneurs can consider in their quest for going public. A shell is an inactive public company with securities traded in the marketplace. It can be used as a backdoor way of becoming a public company.

The easiest way to become a public company is to merge into the public shell. One big advantage is the time and money saved. There is no need to obtain the SEC approval of the registration statement. The entrepreneurs pay little to "acquire" the shell. The entrepreneurs essentially purchase control of the shell by buying stocks from the existing controlling shareholders. The price of acquiring a shell ranges from $20,000 to $100,000 or more, depending on factors such as the amount of control, board seats, and reporting status. After completing the acquisition, the company could meet the objective of raising money in the capital markets by issuing stock.

Shells have been around for a long time. Many of the new shells were first set up in Utah, which has been a continuing source of supply. Shell brokers have negotiable fees and often retain some of the stock. This approach is legal. However, there have been abuses. In the late 1950s, the SEC prosecuted Alexander Guterman and Lowell Burrell, who manipulated stocks by spreading rumors to push up share prices and then unloaded their stock. Such operators are still around today. These con artists target small private company with alluring line of business, and promise its founders financial assistance. They convince the entrepreneurs to merge that private company with the public shell, getting public listing with minimum disclosure. The next step is to dress up the company by pumping in money and in some cases also acquiring other ventures. Meanwhile, the scheme operators take control of the board. The purpose is to authorize issuing millions of shares and to register them through SEC loopholes, such as Form S-8 and Regulation S. Form S-8 allows company to register shares with a short filing with minimum disclosure. It pertains mainly to employees and consultants. Another loophole involves SEC Regulation S. It permits companies to sell shares to foreign investors without detailed registration statement, and the shares need to be held for only 40 days before the foreigners can trade them back to the U.S. market.[8] The SEC has proposed to lengthen the holding period requirement for such securities.

This type of fraud is difficult to detect and prosecute. In contrast, another type of fraud is about dubious initial public offerings. Investors are lured into a penny stock (usually, stock at less than $5 per share, in a company without a track record) by hard-sell tactics, bait tactics (which wins investor confidence with opener stock), and wooden tickets (unauthorized trades). In October 1996, the NASD accused Sterling Foster and 15 of its officers and brokers of making $51 million of illicit profits in nine months by using manipulative trading, high-pressure sales tactics, and wooden tickets. This is the largest disciplinary case alleging stock manipulation ever brought by the NASD.

Equity Takedowns

Equity takedowns, or super block trades, are aggressive tactics taken by investment banking firms in which the investment banker commits to buy stock at a discount from the issuing company after the market closes, and then seeks to redistribute these shares to clients before the market opens the next day. Until the stock is resold, the investment banking firm has its own capital at risk. These are used primarily in the secondary offerings, known as *spot secondary offerings*. As long as the markets remain robust, spot secondaries are likely to grow in frequency.

The approach is unlike a typical stock underwriting. There is no roadshow nor a lengthy premarketing period during which underwriters seek to build a book of interest from prospective purchasers. This method could undercut the old-line investment banking relationships the Wall Street firms have cultivated with corporate clients. There are significant advantages for the issuing corporation. The stock price is not hurt in the days preceding the offering, as is common in underwritten deals. Speed is another benefit. There is no marketing process, and within a few hours the transaction is completed.

EXEMPT OFFERINGS

The market environment and the company's ability to accept the responsibilities and pressures of being a public company are among the determining factors of going public or using exempt offerings (private placement). There are several basic types of exempt offerings: Regulation D offerings, Regulation A offerings, intrastate offerings, and blank check offerings.

Regulation D Offerings

Regulation D establishes the parameters of limited offering exemptions, which allow companies in need of capital to sell securities under an exempt offering and avoid the complexity and expenses of going public.

Rule 504 allows the sale of securities up to $1 million over a 12-month period. The number of investors is not limited and the offering circular is not required. Rule 504 permits unregistered offering by a nonreporting company without an offering statement if the issuer supplies material information to the purchaser at a reasonable time prior to the sale. Related to Rule 504, there is a Small Corporate Offering Registration (SCOR). SCOR offers small businesses a low-cost alternative. SCOR allows businesses to raise up to $1 million in equity capital annually for business startup, development, or growth. Companies who wish to take advantage of the SCOR program are required to file two forms: Form D and SCOR Form U-7. The Form U-7 is filed with states. It is uniform for all states. A Form D is filed with the SEC under Rule 504. This simplified process reduces a company's legal and accounting fees by up to 75%.

Rule 505 allows sale of securities up to $5 million over a 12-month period. Except for a maximum of 35 nonaccredited investors, all other investors must meet the SEC's definition of *accredited investor.* An accredited investor is an individual or institution that is knowledgeable and has a net worth adequate to make such investments.

Rule 506 permits sale of unlimited amount of securities. The requirement is that all nonaccredited investors (maximum of 35) must qualify as sophisticated investors, who are capable of evaluating the merit of the investments.

Regulation A Offerings

The second type of exempt offering is under Regulation A. It allows a company to raise capital through public offering of up to $5 million per year, including no more than $1.5 million in secondary offerings. Unless the offering is less than $100,000, Regulation A requires the use of an offering circular, similar to a prospectus, which contains financial and other information. Companies are required to notify the SEC and file other information. Audited financial statements are generally not required. The procedures are similar to a regular registration, but the disclosures are not as extensive. The filings are made to and reviewed by the regional offices of the SEC. A notice of no further comments from a regional office indicates the Regulation A offering is effective.

Intrastate Offerings

This is the third type of exempt offerings. There are no limits on the amount of capital to be raised or the number of individuals to whom securities are offered. The qualifications are as follows:

- Be incorporated in the state of offering
- Maintain the principal offices in the state
- Hold 80% of assets in the state
- Derive 80% of revenues from sources in the state
- Offer only to investors with principal residence in the state

It should be noted that securities purchased via this exemption may not be resold to a nonresident of the state within nine months after the offering.

Blank Check Offerings

A blank check offering is the sale of penny stock by a *blank check company.* A blank check company is defined as a company that is devoting all its efforts to establishing a new business, that is issuing penny stock, and has no business plan or has indicated its business plan is to engage in a merger or acquisition with an unspecified business entity. Rule 419 requires funds received from a blank check offering to be placed in an escrow account and must be held for the sole benefit of the purchasers. Once a blank check company agrees to an acquisition or acquisitions that meet certain criteria (one of the criteria is that the acquisition represents at least 80% of the offering), a posteffective amendment must be filed. Notification of the acquisition must be sent to the purchasers. A purchaser would have no less than 20 and no more than 45 business days to either confirm an intent to invest or request a refund.

SUMMARY

Underwriting is a key business for investment banking firms. Investment banks raise a significant amount of capital for companies through IPOs and secondary offerings. Compared with secondary offerings, IPO underwriting spreads are higher, but they involve a higher risk. This chapter covers all major areas in stock underwriting. The coverage includes the investment banker's role as an advisor as well as an underwriter. The mechanics and process of a public offering are discussed in detail. Special focus has been on pricing, SEC regulations, and several capital-raising alternatives. The next chapter will cover fixed-income underwriting.

SELECT BIBLIOGRAPHY

Arkerbauer, J. B. *The Entrepreneur's Guide to Going Public*. New Hampshire: Upstart Publishing Company, Inc., 1994.

Blackman, I. L. *Valuing Your Privately Held Business*. Burr Ridge, IL: Irwin, 1995.

Block, E. *Inside Investment Banking*. Burr Ridge, IL: Irwin, 1989.

Cooper and Lybrand. *Financing Source Guide*. New York, 1992.

Geczi, M. L. "Managing initial public offering communications." In R. H. Rupert. ed. *The New Era of Investment Banking*. Chicago, IL: Probus Publishing Company, 1993.

Going Public: The IPO Reporter. Various issues.

Ibbotson, R. G., J. L. Sindelar, and J. R. Ritter. "The market's problem with the pricing of initial public offerings." *Journal of Finance* (Spring 1994): pp. 66–74.

Kuhn, R. L. *Investment Banking*. New York: Harper & Row, 1990.

Papaioannou, G. J. "Floatation costs and pricing of initial public offerings." *Corporate Finance Review* (November/December 1996): pp. 17–24.

Perlmuth, L. "Behind those falling fees." *Institutional Investor* (August 1995): pp. 25–26.

Raghavan, A. "Salomon's stock deals raise ire." *Wall Street Journal*, October 24, 1996, C1.

Schneider, C. W., J. M. Manko, and R. S. Kant. *Going Public: Practice, Procedure and Consequences*. New York: Browne & Co., 1996.

Schroeder, M. "Caveat entrepreneur." *Business Week* (October 14, 1996): pp. 114–120.

Siconolfi, M., and D. Lohse. "Inside a dubious IPO: sponsor, it appears, held all the cards." *Wall Street Journal* (Nov. 5, 1996), A1 and A16.

Taylor, J. "Arrests highlight rise in small-stock schemes." *Wall Street Journal* (October 14, 1996), C1 and C18.

Zeune, G. D. "Floating a stock offering: New buoyancy from the SEC." *Corporate Cashflow* 14 (August 1993): pp. 38–42.

FBR
11,000,000 Shares
FRIEDMAN, BILLINGS, RAMSEY GROUP, INC.
Class A Common Stock

Of the 11,000,000 shares of Class A Common Stock, par value $0.01 per shares ("Class A Common Stock"), of Friedman, Billings, Ramsey Group, Inc., a Virginia corporation ("FBR" or the "Company"), offered hereby (the "Offering"), 10,000,000 are being issued and sold by the Company and 1,000,000 are being sold by certain shareholders (the "Selling Shareholders") of the Company. The Company will not receive any of the proceeds of the sale of shares by the Selling Shareholders. Prior to the Offering, there has been no public market for the Class A Common Stock. The initial public offering price is $20.00 per share. The initial public offering price was determined by agreement among the Company, the Selling Shareholders and the Underwriters (as defined herein) in accordance with the recommendation of a "qualified independent underwriter" as required by Rule 2720 of the Conduct Rules of the National Association of Securities Dealers, Inc. (the "NASD"). See "Underwriting" for a discussion of the factors considered in determining the initial public offering price. In addition to the shares of Common Stock (as defined herein) offered hereby, PNC Bank Corp. has agreed to acquire a number of shares of Class A Common Stock equal to 4.9% of the outstanding Common Stock upon the losing of the Offering (which, without giving effect to the exercise of the Over-allotment Option (as defined herein) will total 2,451,421 shares of Class A Common Stock) at a price equal to the initial public offering price less a 4% discount. The Company has been approved for the listing of the Class A Common Stock on the New York Stock Exchange, Inc. ("NYSE") under the symbol "FBG."

The Company has two classes of stock outstanding: Class A Common Stock and Class B Common Stock, par value $0.01 per share ("Class B Common Stock" and together with Class A Common Stock, "Common Stock"). Class A Common Stock and Class B Common Stock have identical dividend and other rights, except that Class A Common Stock has one vote per share and Class B Common Stock has three votes per share. Class B Common Stock is converted into Class A Common Stock at the option of the Company in certain circumstances, including (i) upon a sale or other transfer, (ii) at the time the holder of such shares of Class B Common Stock ceases to be affiliated with the Company, and (iii) upon the sale of such shares in a registered public offering. See "Description of Capital Stock—Common Stock."

Up to 1,000,000 shares of Class A Common Stock are being reserved for sale to certain Existing Shareholders (as defined herein), other employees and directors of the Company, and their family members at the initial public offering price less underwriting discount. See "Direct Offering." On December 15, 1997, the Company declared a dividend of $54 million to Existing Shareholders (the "S Corporation Distribution"). The Company intends to make the S Corporation Distribution on or before February 2, 1998. See "Certain Transactions Occurring Prior to the Offering—S Corporation Distribution and Termination of S Corporation Status." A portion of the proceeds of the Offering may be used to fund the S Corporation Distribution.

The Shares offered hereby involve a high degree of risk. See "Risk Factors" at page 9.

THESE SECURITIES HAVE NOT BEEN APPROVED OR DISAPPROVED BY THE SECURITIES AND EXCHANGE COMMISSION OR ANY STATE SECURITIES COMMISSION NOR HAS THE SECURITIES AND EXCHANGE COMMISSION OR ANY STATE SECURITIES COMMISSION PASSED UPON THE ACCURACY OR ADEQUACY OF THIS PROSPECTUS. ANY REPRESENTATION TO THE CONTRARY IS A CRIMINAL OFFENSE.

	Price to Public	Underwriting Discount(1)	Proceeds to Company(2)	Proceeds to Selling Shareholders(2)
Per Share	$20.00	$1.40	$18.60	$18.60
Total (3)	$220,000,000	$15,400,000	$186,000,000	$18,600,000

(1) See "Underwriting" for indemnification arrangements with the several Underwriters (as defined herein).
(2) Not including expenses payable by the Company, estimated at $1,853,000.
(3) The Company and the Selling Shareholders have granted the Underwriters a 30-day option to purchase up to 1,650,000 additional shares of Class A Common Stock solely to cover over-allotments, if any (the "Over-allotment Option"). If such option is exercised in full, the total Price to Public, Underwriting Discount, Proceeds to the Company and Proceeds to the Selling Shareholders will be $253,000,000, $17,710,000, $213,900,000 and $21,390,000, respectively. See "Underwriting."

The shares of Class A Common Stock are offered by the several Underwriters subject to prior sale, receipt and acceptance by them and subject to the right of the Underwriters to reject any order in

(continues)

whole or in part and certain other conditions. It is expected that certificates for such shares will be available for delivery on or about December 29, 1997 at the office of Friedman, Billings, Ramsey & Co., Inc. in Arlington, Virginia.

> FRIEDMAN, BILLINGS, RAMSEY & CO., INC.
> BEAR, STEARNS & CO. INC.
> CREDIT SUISSE FIRST BOSTON
> LAZARD FRERES & CO. LLC
> SALOMON SMITH BARNEY
> December 22, 1997

No dealer, salesperson or other person has been authorized to give any information or to make any representations other than those contained in this Prospectus and, if given or made, such information or representations must not be relied upon as having been authorized by the Company or the Underwriters. This Prospectus does not constitute an offer to sell or a solicitation of an offer to buy to any person in any jurisdiction in which such offer or solicitation would be unlawful or to any person to whom it is unlawful to make such offer or solicitation. Neither the delivery of this prospectus nor any offer or sale made hereunder shall, under any circumstances, create any implication that there has been no change in the affairs of the Company or that the information contained herein is correct as of any time subsequent to the date hereof.

TABLE OF CONTENTS

Until January 16, 1998 (25 days after the date of this Prospectus), all dealers effecting transactions in Class A Common Stock, whether or not participating in this distribution, may be required to deliver a Prospectus. This is in addition to the obligation of dealers to deliver a

Prospectus when acting as Underwriters and with respect to their unsold allotments or subscriptions.

11,000,000 Shares

FBR
FRIEDMAN, BILLINGS,
RAMSEY GROUP, INC.

Class A Common Stock

PROSPECTUS

FRIEDMAN, BILLINGS, RAMSEY & CO.,
INC.

BEAR, STEARNS & CO. INC.

CREDIT SUISSE FIRST BOSTON

LAZARD FRERES & CO.

SALOMON SMITH BARNEY

December 22, 1997

5

Underwriting Fixed-Income Securities

The combination of a stable interest rate environment and a non-inflationary economic growth has contributed to the record-breaking levels of activity in the fixed-income markets in recent years. The U.S. Treasury issued a record $2.48 trillion in 1996. Corporate bond issuance reached a record of $448 billion and municipal issues added an additional $227 billion in the same year. In 1997, Treasury issuance declined on strength in tax revenues, but other fixed-income sectors recorded new highs. This chapter first covers the activities in the government securities market, including the auction process, dealer bidding strategies, trading, short squeeze, rolls, and market practices. The discussion of corporate fixed income focuses on the underwriting process, shelf registration, underwriting spreads, and underwriting risk management. The subsequent section is on the rapidly growing 144A market. The last section covers the $1.3 trillion municipal debt market. Important issues in the municipal securities market include competitive bids and negotiated deals, yield burning, regulation, insurance, and market conventions.

GOVERNMENT SECURITIES

As a means of financing the federal government, the Treasury's *Bureau of Public Debt* (BPD) issues three types of marketable securities: *bills, notes,* and *bonds*. Treasury bills are short-term securities with a maturity period of 13 weeks, 26 weeks, or 52 weeks. Treasury notes are medium-term securities with a maturity period of 2 years, 3 years, 5 years, or 10 years.[1] Treasury bonds are long-term securities with a maturity period of 30 years. These securities are sold through regularly scheduled auctions. The auction frequency is summarized in Table 5.1.

The 10-year inflation-indexed notes (Treasury Inflation-Protected Securities, TIPS) were first issued in January 1997. Treasury plans to issue these securities quarterly (i.e., in April, July, October and January). In July 1997, a 5-year maturity bond was also issued. The securities have a nominal return linked to the Consumer Price Index for All Urban Consumers (CPI-U). The principal amount of the security will adjust daily for changes in the level of inflation. However, the inflation adjustment will not be

TABLE 5.1 Auction Frequency[1]

Term	Auction Frequency
13-week bill	Weekly
26-week bill	Weekly
52 week bill	Every four weeks
2-year note	Monthly
5-year note	Quarterly
10-year note	February, May, July, August, October, November
Inflation-indexed 10-year notes	January, April, July, October
30-year bond	February, August, November

[1] After May 1998, the 3-year notes are no longer issued, and the 5-year notes are auctioned quarterly.

Source: Adapted from Federal Reserve Bank of New York, 1998.

payable until maturity. Although deflation could cause the principal to decline, at maturity Treasury will pay an amount that is no less than the par amount at the date of the issuance. Semiannual interest payments will be made on the inflation-adjusted principal amount as of the interest-payment date based on the coupon rate determined at auction.

Since February 1985, all new bonds and 10-year notes are eligible for *Separate Trading of Registered Interest and Principal of Securities* (STRIPS). Creation of STRIPS program ended the origination of trademarks and generic receipts, such as *Merrill's Treasury Income Growth Receipts* (TIGRs) and Sallie's *Certificates of Accrual on Treasury Securities* (CATS). The profit potential for a government dealer who stripped a coupon security initially was the arbitrage resulting from the coupon stripping, because the total value of the stripped components was greater than the value of the underlying security.

Government Securities Markets

Operating a primary dealership of government securities is a prestigious and significant investment banking activity. Issuance of U.S. Treasury securities has surged in recent years. The U.S. Treasury securities issuance of $2.48 trillion in 1996 was a 6.6% increase from 1995's issuance of $2.33 trillion.[2] From 1990 to 1994 the issuance each year was $1.530 trillion, $1.699 trillion, $1.990 trillion, $2.066 trillion, and $2.111 trillion, respectively. Supply declined in 1997 to $2.168 trillion. In addition, the average daily trading volume of Treasury securities by primary dealers was $204 billion in 1996 and rose to $212 billion in 1997. The proportion of dealer-to-dealer transactions consistently accounts for more than half of the total trading activity (57% in 1997).

The outstanding government securities have steadily increased over the years. The total amount of treasuries outstanding was more than $1 trillion in 1983, more than $2 trillion in 1990, and $3 trillion by year-end 1994. The totals in 1996 and 1997 were about $3.4 trillion. In recent years, much of the increase is due to the need to pay off maturing debt, as opposed to net cash requirements. The Treasury Department raised $173.6 billion in 1995 and $133.2 billion net cash in 1996, but did not raise any net cash in 1997. The issuance and the net cash raised will be on a downward trend as the government cuts its deficit or even runs a surplus.

Trading Government Securities

Trading is mainly over-the-counter in which dealers, brokers, and other investors make trades over the phone. Some dealers have recently provided online trading systems. The most active trading is in the most recently issued securities, called *on-the-run* issues. Coupon treasuries trade on a price basis. The tick size is 1/32, but quotes can be as fine as 1/256. Typical transaction size is $1 million to $100 million. Coupon treasuries generally settle on the next market day; however, cash and skip-day, as well as corporate settlements, can be arranged. The invoice price of a coupon security consists of the quoted price and the accrued interest. The accrued interest is calculated on actual/actual basis. Treasury bills trade on a basis of discount rate and typically settle same day.

Dealers each morning distribute to traders information on issue measures such as price, yield, dollar value of a basis point or dollar value of an 01 (DV01), the yield value of a thirty-second, modified duration, and gain from convexity. The DV01 is the change in the price of a bond resulting from a basis point change in its yield. Frequently the DV01 is expressed in dollars per million. The yield value of a thirty-second is estimated by calculating the yield to maturity if the bond price changes by 1/32. Then the difference between the initial yield and the new yield is the yield value of a thirty-second. For example, you might see that the 7.5s 11/15/24 long bond trades at 95:28 and yields 7.859%. This means that the 7.5% bond maturing Nov. 15, 2024, is trading at $95\,{}^{28}/_{32}$, with a yield to maturity of 7.859%. The DV01 is $1,108.1 per million. The yield value is 0.282 basis point. In the bills market, the DV01 for a 13-week bill is $25.

Dealer profits are generated from one or more of the sources:

1. *Bid–ask spread*—the price spread varies from 1/128 to 4/32, depending on liquidity, volatility, and remaining maturity
2. *Favorable market movements*, such as appreciation in the securities long and depreciation in the securities short
3. *Carry*—the difference between the interest earned on the securities held in inventories and the financing costs

Dealers borrow huge sums of short-term funds to finance their positions each day, and often they find that the least expensive way to do so is in the repurchase agreement (repo) market. A positive carry is a source of profit, while a negative carry is a loss.

Dealers trade with each other frequently through government interdealer brokers because of the speed and efficiency brokers provide. Dealers give bids and offers to brokers, who display the highest bid and lowest offer in a computer network linked to each trading desk. Traders responding to a bid or offer by "hitting" or "taking" pay a commission to the broker. Brokers keep the names of dealers confidential. Major interdealer brokers include Cantor Fitzgerald, Garban, Liberty, RMJ, Tullett and Tokyo, and Hilliard Farber (Treasury bills only). The quotes provided by the brokers represent prices in the inside or interdealer market. Table 5.2 provides an example of a composite page by Liberty Brokerage. The quotations listed represent the best bid and offer at that time. A "+" after the price quote indicates half of a tick. A number of 2 or 6 after the price quote represents 2/8 or 6/8 of a tick. WI (when issued) trades in yield before the coupon rate is set after the auction. ROLL is the yield differential between the new issue and the outstanding issue.

TABLE 5.2　Liberty Interdealer Screen

3MO	4/24	5.02–02	5×5	$7^3/_4$	11/99	104.02+–042	1×1
6MO	7/24	5.11–105	100×5	6	10/99	99.262–276	×1
1YR	1/08	5.29–29 TAK	×5	$6^3/_8$	1/00	100.20+–23	1×1
				$7^3/_4$	1/00	104.086–10	
$5^5/_8$	8/97	100.006–01		$5^3/_4$	10/00	98.112–122	
$5^1/_4$	12/97	99.202–21	1×1	$5^5/_8$	11/00	97.276–286	
$6^1/_4$	7/98	100.15–15+	1×	$6^3/_8$	3/01	100.092–102	
6	9/98	100.02–03	1×1	$6^3/_8$	9/01	100.05+–07	
$8^7/_8$	11/98	104.28+–292	×1	$6^1/_4$	10/01	99.212–22+	
$5^5/_8$	11/98	99.12–122	2×1	$5^7/_8$	11/01	98.032–04+	1×1
$5^3/_4$	12/98	99.186–19	13×1	5 YEAR		99.04+–05	14×2
2 year		99.232–23+	1×11	W.I. 5 YR		6.33–326	1×5
				5 YEAR ROLL		+002/–00	130×185
$6^1/_2$	4/99	100.30+–312	1×1				
$6^3/_8$	5/99	100.20–21	1×1	$5^7/_8$	11/05	95.182–186	
6	8/99	99.236–246	1×1	$6^7/_8$	5/06	102.052–056	
3 year		99.102–106	1×4	7	7/06	103.002–006	
				10 YEAR		99.19–19+	×2
				W.I. TIPS		3.405–395	1×1
				$6^3/_4$	8/26	98.202–212	
				30 YEAR		95.266–28	

Source: Adapted from Liberty Brokerage, Thursday, January 23, 1997 at 13:21:04.

Eleven firms provide institutional investors and broker-dealers electronic trading platforms for fixed income securities (Table 5.3). BondNet is exclusively for corporate bond trading, MuniAuction system trades municipal securities, and Fuji trades Treasury securities only. The other eight electronic trading systems offer capabilities for Treasury securities and some other fixed-income securities. The delivery media of these trading systems include Bloomberg, Internet, Telerate, and proprietary network.

Primary Dealers

Primary dealers are banks and securities broker-dealers that trade in U.S. Government securities with the Federal Reserve Bank of New York. New York Fed's open market desk engages in the trades in order to implement monetary policy.

New York Fed established the primary dealer system in 1960, with 18 primary dealers. The number of primary dealers peaked at 46 in 1988, and then declined to 38 in 1992 and dropped to 36 in 1995. There are currently 37 primary dealers, as listed in Table 5.4. A firm that wants to become a primary dealer must notify the New York Federal Reserve (the Fed) in writing. The New York Fed then consults with the applicant's principal regulator to verify that the firm complies with relevant capital standards. Applicants must be commercial banking organizations that are subject to official supervision by U.S. federal bank supervisors or broker-dealers registered with the SEC. They may be foreign-owned.

According to the New York Fed's current criteria, bank-related primary dealers must be in compliance with Tier I and Tier II capital standards under the *Basle Capital Accord*, with at least $100 million of Tier I capital. Registered broker-dealers must have

TABLE 5.3 Electronic Trading Systems for Fixed Income Securities

Firm/System	Agency	CD	CP	Corp.	MBS	Muni	Repo	Treasury	Delivery Medium
BondNet				X					Bloomberg, proprietary network
CS First Boston	X	X	X				X	X	Bloomberg
Daiwa/Odd Lot Machine	X							X	Internet, Telerate, Proprietary network
Deutsche Morgan Grenfell/ Autobahn					X			X	Bloomberg
Fuji Sec.								X	Bloomberg
InterVest				X		X	X	X	Bloomberg, Proprietary network
Merrill/LMS	X		X		X	X	X	X	Bloomberg, Proprietary network
Morgan Stanley/MS Zeros							X	X	Bloomberg
MuniAuction						X			Internet
Regen Mackenzie/ Auto Execution	X							X	Bloomberg
Trade Web	X							X	Internet

Source: The Bond Market Association, "A review of electronic trading system in the U.S. fixed income securities markets," October 1997.

at least $50 million in Tier II capital and total capital in excess of the regulatory "warning levels" set by the SEC and the Treasury. Plus, the Fed requires primary dealers to make reasonably good markets in their trading relationships with the Fed's trading desk, to participate meaningfully in Treasury auctions, and to offer market information and analysis to the Fed's trading desk that are helpful in the formulation and implementation of monetary policy.

Dealers report weekly on their trading activities, as well as on cash, futures, and financing positions in Treasury and other securities. Such reports supply additional information important to surveillance efforts. Primary dealers' trading volume in government securities averaged about $200 billion per day, according to data released by New York Fed.

TABLE 5.4   Primary Dealers

Aubrey G. Lanston & Co. Inc.
BankAmerica Robertson Stephens
Bear, Stearns & Co., Inc.
BT Alex. Brown Incorporated
BZW Securities Inc.
Chase Securities Inc.
CIBC Oppenheimer Corp.
Citicorp Securities, Inc.
Credit Suisse CS First Boston Corporation
Daiwa Securities America Inc.
Dean Witter Reynolds Inc.
Deutsche Morgan Grenfell/C.J. Lawrence Inc.
Donaldson, Lufkin & Jenrette Securities
  Corporation
Dresdner Kleinwort Benson North American
  LLC
Eastbridge Capital Inc.
First Chicago Capital Markets, Inc.
Fuji Securities Inc.
Goldman, Sachs & Co.
Greenwich Capital Markets, Inc.
HSBC Securities, Inc.
J.P. Morgan Securities, Inc.
Lehman Brothers Inc.
Merrill Lynch Government Securities Inc.
Morgan Stanley & Co. Incorporated
NationsBanc Montgomery Securities, Inc.
Nesbitt Burns Securities Inc.
The Nikko Securities Co. International, Inc.
Nomura Securities International, Inc.
Paine Webber Incorporated
Paribas Corporation
Prudential Securities Incorporated
Salomon Brothers Inc.
Sanwa Securities (USA) Co., L.P.
SBC Warburg Dillon Read Inc.
Smith Barney Inc.
UBS Securities LLC
Zions First National Bank

Source: Adapted from New York Fed, December 4, 1997, effective date.

TREASURY AUCTION AND FEDWIRE

The U.S. debt grew from $909 billion in 1980 to the current $5 trillion. Approximately $3.5 trillion of that debt is held in government securities. The Treasury Department sells these securities at auctions. Most treasuries are bought at auction by the primary dealers, which are financial institutions active in trading government securities that have established business relationships with the New York Fed. Individual investors purchase on a much smaller scale.

The auction process begins with a public announcement by the Treasury. Bids are accepted up to 30 days before the auction, and may be submitted electronically via the *Treasury Automated Auction Processing System* (TAAPS), by mail, or in person. Two types of bids can be submitted: competitive and noncompetitive.[3] Small investors and individuals generally submit noncompetitive bids, capped at $1 million for bills and $5 million for notes and bonds. Primary dealers for their accounts, or on behalf of customers, usually submit competitive bids. Bids are submitted in discount rate for bills (yield for notes and bonds), stated in two decimal places for bills and three decimal places for coupon issues. These bids are accepted until 1:00 P.M. EST on the day of the auction. Primary dealers submit their competitive bids through TAAPS at the last possible moment, sometimes literally seconds before the 1:00 P.M. deadline.

Competitive bidders are permitted to submit more than one bid. But each bidder is restricted to receiving no more than 35% of the total amount of the security being sold. Specifically, under the 35% rule, the bidder's net long position in the auction at any yield inclusive of futures, forwards and WI (when issued) markets may not exceed 35% of the amount of the security in the auction. When the issue is reopened, the net long position will include any position in the outstanding security as well. Once the bidding is completed, the 35% rule is lifted.

The bids submitted through TAAPS are consolidated at the Federal Reserves in New York, Chicago, and San Francisco. Immediately after 1:00 P.M. EST, these bids are reviewed and processed in these locations to assure compliance under the Treasury's *Uniform Offering Circular*. These bids are then sorted and reviewed electronically by the Treasury in Washington. The Treasury nets out the noncompetitive bids and allocates the balance to the highest bidders among the competitive bidders. All lower competitive bids are rejected. The coupon rate is set at the highest bid yield below the quantity-weighted average yield in the auction, rounded off to the nearest one-eighth.

The Treasury currently uses two different techniques for auctioning its marketable securities: discriminary (multiple) price auction and uniform (single) price auction. Up until September 1992, coupon Treasury securities were issued periodically through discriminary price auction. Single-price auction, or *Dutch auction*, was introduced in 1992 following Salomon's Treasury note bid-rigging scandal in 1991. It is used for the 2- and 5-year notes and the 10-year TIPS. Under this system dealers submit sealed bids and both competitive and noncompetitive bidders are awarded securities at the price that results from the highest yield—market-clearing yield—at which competitive bids are accepted. It is argued that a dealer's ability to get the same market-clearing yield irrespective of the dealer's bid will result in two important benefits. First, it will significantly minimize the possibility of short squeezes. Second, it will eliminate the problem of winner's curse (winners generally over pay) and will therefore promote more aggressive bidding and active participation in the auction.

Multiple-price auctions are used for all other marketable securities; securities are awarded at the price established by each of the accepted bids. The average of the accepted bids in the competitive tender on a quantity-weighted basis is then applied to the noncompetitive tender. In this regard, noncompetitive bidders face no quantity uncertainty but are unsure of the prices at which their orders will be filled.

The highest yield that is accepted at the auction is called the *stop-out yield* or simply *stop yield*. The ratio of the bids received to the amount awarded is known as the *bid-to-cover ratio*. The higher the ratio the stronger the auction is. Another measure known as the *tail* of the auction is the difference between the average yield of all accepted bids and the stop yield. Traders use the tail as a measure of success of the auction to form trading strategies after the auction. A long tail signals strength, and hence traders will trade more aggressively. A short tail indicates weakness in market demand, and hence traders will be cautious on the downside. The auction results are released to the public within two hours of the auction, frequently by 1:30 P.M. or 2:00 P.M. EST. Primary dealers dominate the competitive awards; they receive more than 70% of all awards.[4]

When-Issued (WI) Trading

One major feature of the Treasury auction is the "when, as, and if issued" trading, known as *WI trading*. The when-issued trading begins right after the announcement and until the issue date. Prior to the scheduled auction, dealers and investors actively participate in the WI market. Dealers and investors may either take a long position or a short position in the security for a future settlement on the issue date. Thus, WIs are forward contracts with a settlement date equal to the issue date.

Before the auction, WI trading is in terms of yields. The Treasury announces the coupon after the auction. After the coupon is announced, the WI trades on a price basis rather than yield basis. Generally the securities are issued several days to a week after the auction. Furthermore, as positions in the WI market need not be financed, fairly large positions can be taken and offset in a manner similar to the futures markets. Additionally, there is no accrued interest in the WI transactions, which implies a zero carry, where *carry* is the difference between interest income and interest expense.

WI trading ends when the new security settles. After that, settlement is typically the next market day, one day after the trade day. The process of issuance is depicted in Figure 5.1.

WI Trading and Bidding Strategy

WI trading affects the strategy bidders use in the auctions because it affects bidders' positions going into the auction. Bidders who bought the security in the when-issued market before the auction go into the auction with long positions and those who have sold go into the auction with short positions. WI markets also serve a price discovery role. Participating in WI trading provides vital information on the strength of demand for the security and on the disparity of bidder's view about the market. Such information is useful in preparing bids. On the other hand, dealers who believe they have very valuable private information such as future interest rates might refrain from WI trading so they can use the information in their bids.

FIGURE 5.1   Treasury Issuance Process

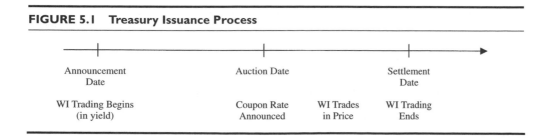

Short Squeeze

All trades in the WI market are settled for delivery and payment on the scheduled issue date. Dealers typically enter the auction with significant short positions. The average short position is 38% of the auction awards, particularly significant for 2- and 5-year notes at more than 45%.[5] This presents significant risks to the dealers. A dealer who is short and unable to get sufficient quantity of the security at the auction must cover the short position before the issue date by buying in the WI after the auction. Or alternatively, the dealer must reverse in the security in the repo market on the issue date to make good delivery. But in such a reverse, the dealer is still short in the security and is exposed to the possibility of a short squeeze.

As already indicated, dealers typically enter the auction with significant short positions. Even if one or two dealers are relatively more aggressive in the auctions, there could be significant imbalances in dealer awards relative to their short positions coming into the auction. This has important implications for both the cash market and the repo market. In a short squeeze, the repo rates are much lower than general collateral rates (called *special*) and the prices tend to be correspondingly higher.

Salomon Squeeze

Salomon Brothers admitted to having controlled 94% of the 2-year notes auctioned on May 22, 1991, which is in violation of the Treasury regulation that the bidder's long position may not exceed 35% of the issue in any single auction. Salomon acquired 44% of the notes at the auction, plus the alleged so-called prearranged trades with big investors, which gave Salomon such a dominant position in the security.

The 2-year note is generally in high demand because it is the shortest-maturing coupon Treasury security. Many investors worldwide buy it at the auction and hold it to maturity. But the price sometimes declines modestly right after the auction, when interest in the note sale fades. Traders and arbitrageurs would short ahead of the auction and cover the short after the price declines. But the price of this particular 2-year note jumped sharply after the auction. The 2-year notes became so scarce that the collateral-specific repo rates were about 75 to 200 basis points special.

The scandal cost Salomon its top management and it was fined nearly $300 million. The firm lost its credibility in the marketplace and might not have survived if not for Warren Buffet's capital infusion and astute management to restore credibility. More importantly, in response to these problems, the Treasury introduced major changes in the Treasury markets, including the right to reopen an issue and the experimentation of uniform price auctions in the 2-year and 5-year notes.

Coupon Rolls[6]

A *roll* arises when a dealer purchases from a customer an on-the-run[7] Treasury security for next-day settlement and simultaneously sells to that customer the same amount of the recently announced new security for forward settlement. A *reverse roll* arises when a dealer sells an outstanding issue and buys a new security. The forward in a roll trade, WI sale, settles on the new issue settlement date. The "roll" is the spread between the yield on the new security and that on the outstanding issue. A *give* in rolls indicates that the WI security provides a higher yield than the outstanding issue. A *take* in rolls implies the opposite—that the new issue has a lower yield.

Dealers use rolls to accommodate customers who have a strong preference for liquidity and tend to trade rolls to maintain positions in the current issues. Dealers also use rolls to position themselves for bidding at the upcoming auction. Dealers will seek to execute a roll if they are short the outstanding issue, because they anticipate a market decline, and/or because they have to accommodate customers. By executing a roll, a dealer closes the short position on the outstanding issue and creates shorts on the new security. Similar to a situation when the dealer is short in the WI market, the dealer executing a roll has an incentive to bid more aggressively at the upcoming auction.

As an example, on October 18, 1995, the Treasury announced the auction dates for the 2-year note (October 24, 1995). The issue settled on October 31, 1995. Trading of the 2-year roll began after the announcement. These 2-year notes follow a monthly issuance cycle. The coupon on the new issue is usually set after the Treasury has received all bids at a level that prices the security at or slightly below par. A give (take) of five basis points in the 2-year roll means the dealer is proposing to purchase the outstanding issue at the then-market yield of 5.654% against selling the new issue at a yield of five basis points higher (lower).

By executing a 2-year roll, the dealer acquires the outstanding 2-year note for next-day settlement against selling to the same customer the same amount of the new note for forward delivery and payment on October 31, 1995. The investor is, in effect, "rolling" over the investment from the outstanding 2-year note to the new 2-year issue, with a month extension in maturity. The investor can invest the funds received the next day until the new issue settles at a term repo rate. On the other hand, the investor gives up the accrued interest by selling the outstanding 2-year note.

Book-Entry and Fedwire

The Treasury offers new securities only in book-entry form. The Treasury began offering new bills exclusively in book-entry form in 1979. In August 1986, the Treasury began marketing all new coupon securities only in book-entry form. The book-entry program has largely replaced physical government and agency securities with computer entries at Federal Reserve Banks. All treasuries held in physical form by depository institutions are eligible for conversion to book entry and for transfer by wire.

The government securities are cleared through Fedwire. Fedwire allows depository institutions to transfer securities and funds for their own accounts and for accounts of customers directly to one another and to depository institutions throughout the United States. Most international transactions are settled through the *Clearing House Interbank Payment System* (CHIPS).

Every Treasury security issue is represented by an entry on a Federal Reserve Bank's computer. The Fed keeps track of which bank holds what amount of a particular issue. At maturity, the Fed transfers funds to the bank. In essence the Fed acts as custodian of the Treasury security for various depository institutions.

For a trade in government securities, two transactions take place simultaneously when the securities are transferred over the Fedwire. The movement of the security takes place by decreasing the seller clearing bank's book-entry securities account at the Federal Reserve Bank and by increasing the buyer clearing bank's account the same amount. Funds movement is opposite to the securities movement just described. The market practice is *delivery versus payment,* so funds and securities are transferred at the same time. The Fedwire operating hours for book-entry securities are 8:30 A.M. to

TABLE 5.5   Fedwire Fee Schedule

Wire Transfer of Funds	Fee	
Basic origination or receipt	$0.45	
Off-line origination surcharge	$10.00	
Telephone advice surcharge	$10.00	
Net Settlement [1]		
Settlement entry	$1.00	
Surcharge per off-line settlement	$10.00	
Telephone advice surcharge	$10.00	
Book-Entry Securities	**Treasury**	**Agency**
On-line transfer: origination	$2.25	$2.25
Off-line transfer: origination or receipt[2]	$10.00	$10.00
On-line transaction reversal receipt	$2.25	$2.25
Off-line transaction reversal receipt	$10.00	$10.00
Monthly account maintenance		
Per account	N/A	$15.00
Per issue, per account	N/A	$0.45

[1] Special settlement fees may be charged if net settlements result in higher operating costs than those for standard arrangements.

[2] Account switch transfers, moving securities between accounts of the same institution, are only accessed one fee for the withdrawal of the securities from one of the institution's accounts. No separated fee for the deposit of securities into the institution's other accounts.

Source: Adapted from Federal Reserve Bank of New York, 1997.

3:15 P.M. for transfer origination. The closing time for transfer reversals is 3:30 P.M. The Fed charges a fee for providing the service. The fee schedule is presented in Table 5.5.

AGENCY ISSUES

There are two types of federal agencies: federally related financial institutions (FRFIs) and federally sponsored agencies (FSAs). FRFIs are branches of the federal government that offer subsidized financing to selected sectors. Through securities issuance, the Federal Financing Bank raises all funds distributed by the FRFIs. FRFIs include Commodity Credit Corporation, Export–Import Bank, Farmers Home Administration, General Services Administration, Government National Mortgage Association (Ginnie Mae), Maritime Administration, Private Export Funding Corporation, Rural Electrification Administration, Rural Telephone Bank, Small Business Administration, Tennessee Valley Authority, and Washington Metropolitan Area Transit Authority. A significant portion of activities in the agency market, agency mortgage-backed securities, will be covered in detail in the next chapter, *Asset Securitization*. Here we only provide a very brief description of the agency market.

FSAs are privately owned, but are perceived as carrying an implicit government guarantee. Each FSA issues its own securities. There are eight FSAs:

- Federal Farm Credit System
- Farm Credit Financial Assistance Corporation

- Federal Home Loan Bank
- Financing Corporation
- Resolution Trust Corporation
- Student Loan Marketing Association (Sallie Mae)
- Federal Home Loan Mortgage Corporation (Freddie Mac)
- Federal National Mortgage Association (Fannie Mae)

FSA securities are pass-throughs, backed by pools of loans issued by each agency. All cash flows, net of processing fees, paid on the pool of underlying loans are passed through to the security holders periodically.

Increased issuance activities by federal and federally sponsored agencies result in substantial growth in agency debt. The outstanding agency debt reached $925.8 billion in 1996 and $983.6 billion in 1997. Major issuers include Federal Home Loan Bank System (FHLB), Fannie Mae, Freddie Mac, and Sallie Mae.

An interesting feature of the agency issues is that a large portion of them is callable. These issues are priced relative to a government security of similar maturity. All agency issues are regarded virtually free from credit risk. They are rated AAA. When they are not rated, they are assumed to be of highest quality. The risk premium of an agency issue is the yield spread that investors demand over comparable treasuries in order to hold these securities. The risk premiums vary over time, but the spread over treasuries increases as the maturity is extended.

CORPORATE DEBT UNDERWRITING

Corporate bond issuance recorded a new high of $687.3 billion in 1997. Issuance reached $427.5 billion[8] in 1996, a big increase over the $332.9 billion sold in 1995, and surpassed the prior record of $416 billion in 1993. As a result of the strong growth in new issuance, the volume of corporate debt outstanding has reached $2.3 trillion in 1997. The record corporate debt supply has been met with strong demand, as evidenced by the declining corporate-to-treasury spread. For example, the spread of the AAA 10-year corporate (industrials) over treasury has declined to about 40 basis points.

As the yield spread has hovered at historically low levels, investors are willing to consider new products that offer additional yield. Hence, all major houses have tried to create new debt structures to pitch to customers. Examples of such recent innovation include pass-through asset trust security (PATS), step-down preferred, and 100-year and 1,000-year bonds. PATS separates a put option from the rest of the bond and sells it in the derivatives markets. Step-down preferred structures a REIT to issue debt security and takes advantage of the special tax status for REITs. The step-down preferred allows issuers to sell preferred stock without paying taxes on dividends. The low interest rates and record M&A deals have made billion-dollar corporate debt offerings commonplace. In May 1997, Norfolk Southern pulled off the largest investment-grade corporate bond issue in U.S. history, $4.3 billion, to finance its joint acquisition with CSX Corp of Conrail. Table 5.6 lists the largest investment-grade bond issues.

Investment grade, Rule 144A, and high-yield sectors have experienced dramatic growth. Nonconvertible investment-grade issuance soared to $563.5 billion in 1997, a 58% increase from the full-year 1996 total of $356.2 billion, which was a big jump over 1995's $288.1 billion. High-yield issuance also set records in 1997. High-yield debt totaled $123.8 billion in 1997, representing a 74% increase over the $71.3 billion sold

TABLE 5.6   The Largest Investment-Grade Bond Deals

Issuer	Date	Size ($ billions)	Book Runner
Norfolk Southern Corp.	5/14/97	4.3	J.P. Morgan, Merrill Lynch
U S West	1/16/97	4.1	Merrill Lynch
Lockheed Martin Corp.	5/16/96	3.5	Goldman Sachs
Raytheon Co.	8/7/97	3.0	Morgan Stanley Dean Witter
JC Penney Co.	4/9/97	2.5	Credit Suisse First Boston
CSX Corp.	5/1/97	2.5	Salomon Brothers
WorldCom	3/26/97	2.0	Salomon Brothers
American Home Products Corp.	2/16/95	2.0	Goldman Sachs

Source: Institutional Investor, February 1998, p. 25.

in 1996, and surpassing the 1993's record level of $72.5 billion. Also, issuers offered $164.8 billion of Rule 144A in 1997, more than double the $74.8 billion sold in 1996. The 144A market has grown rapidly in recent years, due to the simplified registration process and the speed the issuers can bring transactions to market.

Corporate Debt Market

Corporate debt instruments include commercial paper (CP), median term notes (MTN), and corporate bonds. CP is an important source of short-term credit for large, high-quality borrowers and is typically unsecured. Maturities are limited to 270 days or less, but are typically in the range of 35 to 45 days. The largest CP issuers tend to place their securities directly to investors; such corporations are known as direct issuers. Other issuers sell CP through dealers. Major CP dealers are Goldman Sachs, Merrill Lynch, Lehman Brothers, and Credit Suisse First Boston. For highly rated companies, the access to the CP market is a big advantage, as they are able to borrow at rates below LIBOR or at sub-LIBOR. Most issuers in this market enjoy a rating of P-2/A-2 or better.

An MTN is a corporate debt instrument to fill the funding gap between CP and long-term bonds. MTNs are registered with SEC under Rule 415, which gives a corporation the maximum flexibility for issuing securities on a continuing basis. GMAC first used MTN in 1972 to fund automobile loans with a maximum maturity of five years. A corporation wanting an MTN program will file a shelf registration with the SEC for the offering of the securities. The registration will include a list of investment banking houses, usually two to four, that act as agents to distribute the MTNs. The issuer then posts rates as a spread over a comparable treasury over a range of maturities. The agents will then make the offering rate schedule available to their clients. An investor interested in the offering will determine maturity and then contact the agent, who, in turn, contacts the issuer to confirm the terms of the transaction. The process clearly indicates MTNs are underwritten on a best-efforts basis (bought as sold), and it reflects investor's discretion in choosing among an entire program of maturities and structures.

Median term notes combined with derivatives can be used to create structured notes. The most common derivative instrument used in creating structured notes is a swap. By using derivatives in combination with an offering, the borrower is able to offer customized investment vehicles to satisfy institutional investor's objectives, but are not permitted to invest in swaps for hedging. This also allows institutional investors who are restricted to investment-grade debt the opportunity to participate in other asset classes. For example, an MTN coupon rate could be tied to an equity index to provide participation of the equity market without owning common stock. Alternatively, the coupon rate could be tied to a foreign exchange, a foreign stock market index, or a commodity price index. Creating the structured notes enables the borrowers to lower their funding costs by 10 to 15 basis points.

Corporate bonds are debt securities that generally pay periodical coupon and principal at maturity. The maturities are generally in the range of 10 to 20 years. The market has seen 100-year bonds, even though the government challenged its debt status. The issuer of corporate bonds must comply with the registration requirements of the SEC, unless an exemption is available. In addition, corporate debt securities also come under the *Trust Indenture Act of 1939*; a trustee must be appointed to represent the bondholders. All the contractual provisions between the issuer and the trustee must be presented in the indenture provisions and be filed along with the registration documents. Risk premiums are measured as spread over comparable treasuries, determined in part by credit ratings. An important segment of the corporate debt market is the high-yield or junk bond market, which will be covered in detail in Chapter 13. In contrast to investment-grade debt issues, most junk bonds contain call provisions.

Shelf Registration (Rule 415)

The underwriter's waiting period was shortened from the previous three to four weeks to just days or even hours after Rule 415 took effect in 1982. Rule 415 permits certain issuers to file a single registration document indicating that it intends to sell a certain amount of a certain class of securities at one or more times within the next two years. In essence, securities can be viewed as sitting on a shelf and can be taken off that shelf and sold to the public quickly.

Once the issuer's nonprice terms are decided and the issue's effectiveness nears its close, the issue could be placed on the market immediately or overnight. The price risk of a firm offer now shifts to the underwriter and the syndicate. Lead underwriters step up to bid to retain the prestige associated with being a leader firm in the syndicate game. In effect, the shortened new issue process has helped the issuers not only to reduce risk but also to shift a significant share of the waiting risk forward from the issuing company to the investment banking firms, not to mention the increased due-diligence risks. This also leads to, at least in part, the shift of long-term professional relationships between a corporation and a specific investment banker to transactional finance—whoever offers better terms gets the business.

The lead manager runs the book while the red-herring prospectus is outstanding and during the actual selling period of the new issue. Prior to the final price setting, the lead manager keeps a record of "indication of interests." Once the issue is declared effective the lead manager maintains a record of actual sales by members of the syndicate and by the selling group. If a portion of the issue remains unsold because of rising interest rates, the syndicate manager can stabilize the market by offering to buy at or above the offering price. The price stabilization may be continued for a time or stopped.

The greatest risks are encountered when the inventory of unsold bonds grows due to unfavorable interest rate movement. On top of that, the financing costs move up with the rise in rates. The risk-adjusted returns of new underwriting would now be less even if the underwriting spreads did not change. Underwriters cannot hedge perfectly against market vagaries over the shortened process by using financial satellite markets, because asymmetries of flotation agreement prohibit this. As long as the syndicate agreement is in force, no sales to the public may be made at a price higher than that set on the prospectus.

Underwriting Spreads

The *underwriting spread* or gross spread is the difference between the price paid by the buyers and the proceeds to the company. The gross spread is generally less than 1% for high-quality issues. The underwriting spreads on junk bonds are as much as 3%. To that sum the underwriter adds some out-of-pocket expenses for legal fees, due diligence meetings, and so on.

Out of the gross spread, the lead underwriter typically collects a management fee of 20%. Syndicate members and dealers selling directly to the public then get the remaining 80% of the gross spread. Dealers who are not syndicate members but are part of the selling group get the selling commission of about 50% to 55% of the gross spread. As an example, the management fee comes to $200,000 for a $100 million bond issue at 1% spread. The underwriter discount for syndicate members is a quarter of the gross spread, $250,000, and the sales commission amounts to $550,000 for the issue. The lead underwriter collects the management fee, splits proportionally the underwriter discount with the syndicate members, and also receives sales commission for his own share of the distribution. The selling group does not commit its own capital to risk taking. If the bond price drops, the losses from stabilization and the added expenses will be shared on the pre–agreed-on ratio between the lead underwriter and the underwriting syndicate.

Members of the syndicate or the selling group receives *reallowance* if their sales of bonds are over and above those acquired from the manager. A *reallowance* is paid the firm that actually makes the sale, but the member who agreed to release the bonds retains the balance of the spread. As a final point, the manager is the ultimate and final payer of all these amounts, because he runs the book.

Risk Management

If the issue rises in price after it is priced but before the syndicate's distribution is complete, the syndicate members will be able to sell out their share of the commitment more quickly but they cannot make sales at prices higher than the price stated on the prospectus. If the manager took a short position before the unanticipated price surge, he has to cover the short either at a higher market price, resulting in a loss, or by exercising the green shoe option.

On the other hand, the issue price might move down during this period. The flotation process now slows down. The syndicate members now face a greater inventory price risk on larger inventory. Furthermore, investment bankers incur a higher financing cost due to the rising interest rates. Therefore, it is vital for investment bankers to correctly price the issue such that the issuer receives correct valuation and the downside risk is minimized.

PRIVATE PLACEMENTS

Private placements differ structurally from the registered public deals because, among other reasons, they are highly negotiated in covenants and pricing and they do not go through the SEC registration process. Private placements offer distinct cost advantages over a public issue. A private issue can save substantial amounts of legal and registration expenses against a comparable public issue. These expenses amount to several hundred thousand dollars prior to underwriter discount and commissions.

There are two major developments that are purported to make the private placement option increasingly attractive. First, SEC Rule 144A of 1990 allows the trading of privately placed securities among QIBs (qualified insititutional buyers) without the holding period restriction. Second, the holding periods have been cut by half after 1997 for restricted securities to one year in trading limited quantity and to two years in trading unlimited amount. The liquidity of issues has improved since Rule 144A became effective, and investment-banking firms have committed capital and trading personnel to making markets for 144As.

The private placement of debt market is rapidly growing and accounts for a significant portion of the debt market. Private placement volume jumped to $201 billion in 1996, up 50% over 1995. Privately placed bonds boomed again in 1997. The most dramatic growth has come from Rule 144A deals. Rule 144As soared to $164.8 billion in 1997, more than double the $74.8 billion sold in 1996. Unlike traditional private placements, Rule 144As are not registered with SEC. Rule 144A deals generally are $100 million or more in size to provide liquidity for resale. Rule 144As look like public offerings, but can only be sold to QIBs. These deals are usually underwritten and have two credit ratings.

Most 144A issues carry registration rights. That means that noninvestment-grade borrowers can rush out 144A deals quickly and reap the benefits of hitting a strong market and go through the hoops of SEC registration later. Once SEC reporting requirements are satistifed, the 144As are upgraded.

Privately placed debt tends to have a shorter maturity. Insurance companies, pension funds, and finance companies are big lenders in this market. Regulatory pressures to improve capital position force some insurers seeking new mechanisms to raise capital or shed assets. Seeking higher yields, pension funds are best positioned to fill the void left by the insurers.

In a private placement, the term sheet accompanying the memorandum summarizes the offering. Included are the securities being offered, size of the offering, maturity, interest rate, conversion features, redemption or sinking fund schedule, and affirmative and negative covenants.

Term Sheet

The term sheet covers a description of the issuer, the offering, the interest rate, the takedown, use of proceeds, nature of the offering, and risk factors. The first key area is the repayment of principal. Repayments typically take the form of sinking fund payment or bullet maturity. The proposed repayment schedule should be consistent with the projected cash flows. Optional prepayment by the issuer is generally limited to an overall percentage of the total debt outstanding. Frequently the optional prepayments are allowed at an amount up to the required prepayment, known as a *double-up provision*. The term sheet will next summarize the call protection offered to the purchasers. Once callable, the debt may be redeemed at a predetermined standard call premium or the make-whole premium.

Covenants are an essential part of the private placement transactions. They are aimed at providing lenders with a means of monitoring their investments. The successful negotiation of covenants protects the purchaser's investment interest, and on the other hand, it is not to unduly restrict an issuer so that it cannot operate successfully. Affirmative covenants outline the general ground rules by which both parties agree to borrow and lend money. Negative covenants are drafted specifically according to the issuer's financial status. There are two principal types of debt covenants: (1) those limiting the percentage of long-term debt to total capitalization and (2) those restricting the short-term debt. To protect the lender, a *clean-up provision* requiring the borrower to be free of additional debt for a stated period of time may be added. Finally, restricted payment covenants are generally intended to limit a borrower's ability to make payment or distribution, while ancillary covenants cover restricted investment. Other negative covenants include permitted liens, merger and consolidation, and sale of assets.

Timetable

The private placement process begins when the investment banker receives a mandate to proceed and ends when the issuer receives money. The required time for this process varies with market conditions and the readiness of the issuing company. Typical time frame is in the range of 12 to 15 weeks.

Future Trends

Securitized transactions form an investment class that will continue to expand. Privates secured by pools or portfolios of assets are highly rated and well diversified, and they offer attractive yields. For foreign issuers, the U.S. private markets are seen as one of the few sources of long-term committed finance. It is quite clear that given the low interest rates in the United States and the pent-up demand for privates, domestic and foreign issuers will find the private markets increasingly attractive.

MUNICIPAL BOND MARKET

The $1.3 trillion municipal debt market has attracted much attention. Issuance of municipal debt set a record in 1993 with $339.6 billion supply. The municipal borrowing rebounded in 1996 to a volume of $225.7 billion and to $267.4 billion in 1997. Table 5.7 lists the municipal issuance from 1990 to 1997. As is clear from Table 5.7,

TABLE 5.7   The Municipal Market ($ billions)

Year	Short-Term	Long-Term	Total Issuance	Outstanding Level
1990	34.8	127.8	162.6	1,184.4
1991	44.8	172.6	217.4	1,272.2
1992	42.9	234.7	277.6	1,302.8
1993	47.4	292.2	339.6	1,377.5
1994	40.2	164.9	205.1	1,341.7
1995	38.0	160.1	198.0	1,293.5
1996	41.5	184.2	225.7	1,294.8
1997	45.9	221.5	267.4	1,339.8

Source: Adapted from PSA and Securities Data Company, 1998.

most of the municipal borrowing is long-term. Short-term municipal issuance accounts for about 20% of the total.

According to the PSA, the default rate for municipal securities is extremely low. During the period 1940–1994, of the 403,152 issues sold only 0.5% experienced default. Details are listed in Table 5.8. The most notable and largest municipal bond default case is the WPPSS default. It took until 1995 to settle all of the resulting lawsuits. Still, demand for better quality leads to a significant portion of the municipal issuance that is insured. For example, the insured rate is 43% in 1995 and 46.3% in 1996. The insured ratio continued to rise in the first 9 months of 1997, to 50.9% (compared to 47.2% for the same period in 1996). Insured volume reached $78.7 billion in 1997:Q3, only slightly behind the full-year 1996 total of $85.7 billion. Major municipal insurance companies are AMBAC Indemnity Corp. (AMBAC), Capital Markets Assurance Corp. (CapMAC), MBIA Insurance Corp. (MBIA), Financial Security Assurance, Inc. (FSA), and Financial Guarantee Assurance Corp. (FGIC).

Municipal Securities

There are two basic types of municipal security structures: general obligation bonds (GOs) and revenue bonds. A GO is typically secured by the issuer's taxing power. Furthermore, additional fees, grants, and special charges secure certain GOs. These GOs are known as *double-barreled*. Revenue bonds are issued for either project or enterprise financing and are backed by the revenues generated by the operating projects financed. There are numerous revenue bonds, including airport bonds, college and university bonds, hospital bonds, single-family mortgage bonds, multifamily bonds, industrial bonds, seaport bonds, toll road and gas tax bonds, and resource recovery bonds. Additionally, there are tax anticipation notes, grant anticipation notes, revenue anticipation notes, and bond anticipation notes. Notes are usually issued for a period of 12 months or less for temporary borrowings.

In recent years, a number of municipal derivative securities have been created. The ability of investment bankers to create these derivatives has been enhanced by the development of the municipal swap markets. A common type is one in which floater and inverse floater are created from a fixed rate bond. The coupon on the floater is reset based on the results of periodic auctions. The inverse floater receives the residual interest. Typically, a minimum interest rate is established as a floor (0%) on the inverse floater. As a result, a cap is imposed on the floater. The sum of the interest paid on the floater and inverse floater equals the fixed rate.

TABLE 5.8 Municipal Bond Default

Period	Number of Defaulted Issues	Total Number of Long-Term Issues	Default Rate
1940–49	79	40,907	0.2%
1950–59	112	74,592	0.2
1960–69	294	79,941	0.4
1970–79	202	77,620	0.3
1980–94	1,333	130,092	1.0
Total	2,020	403,152	0.5

Source: Adapted from PSA Research, 1997.

Underwriting Process

The selling of municipal securities is usually carried out through a syndicate of banks and securities dealers. The issuance of municipals is either by competitive bidding among several syndicates or negotiated with a dealer or syndicate. Most revenue bond issuance are negotiated, while GO issues are roughly divided. When the underwriting is competitive, potential underwriters do not meet with the issuers first to suggest structure or terms of the issue, as is the case in corporate issues. Instead, the issuers publish a notice of sale in recognized financial publication such as *Bond Buyer* that includes the size, maturity, and conditions that may apply. The security is awarded to the bidder submitting the best bid.

According to a PSA study, there is no clear evidence whether competitive bidding or negotiated deals bring in more money or lower yield for municipalities. For Wall Street, negotiated deals are more lucrative, with a gross underwriting spread of $7.81 in 1996 compared to $7.57 for competitive bids. The gross spread was down from $8.23 in 1995 for negotiated deals but up from 1995's $6.85 a bond for a competitive deal. The spreads have declined since 1980s, when the spread was nearly $24 in 1981. The trend of declining spreads may be attributed to (1) increased competition among firms and fee cutting, (2) the change in the nature of the buy side, (3) issuers' concern about the fees they pay bond dealers, and (4) the overall reduction in risk and expense in underwriting municipal securities. Among these factors, the institutional nature of the buy side is an important element in the new environment. In the early 1980s when mutual funds just got started, bonds were sold in smaller blocks to a broader base of buyers. Now one sale could move a big block of bonds.

However, recent scandals involving financial contributions of underwriters to elected officials, the so-called pay-to-play, have pressured some municipalities to require competitive bidding for all bond issuance. The scandals led to the SEC's adoption of Rule G-37, which places restrictions on municipal bond dealer donations to local elected officials. Underwriters welcome the G-37 restrictions because it has lifted pressures to make political contributions that were almost overwhelming in the past.

Municipal issues are exempt from the SEC registration requirements. Rule 15c2–12 of the Securities Exchange Act of 1934 requires an underwriter of municipal securities to deliver an *official statement* in connection with the issue. An official statement describes the issue, the issuer, and the legal opinions. The legal opinions are essential for two purposes. First, the bond counsel determines if the municipality is legally able to issue the security. Second, the bond counsel verifies that the issuer has properly prepared for the bond sale.

Underwriter Responsibility

Municipal underwriter disclosure responsibility is governed by the *Disclosure Guidelines for State and Local Government Securities*. After the failure of the WPPSS bond issues, the SEC adopted Rule 15c2–12. The rule requires all municipal underwriters to obtain and distribute to investors official statements. Such official statements are required for all bond issues that exceed $1 million.

Exemptions are available if the municipal bonds are in denominations of $100,000 or more, and satisfy any of the following three conditions:

- A maximum of 35 accredited investors
- A maximum maturity of nine months

- Investors given the option to tender to the issuer at least as frequently as every nine months

In addition, American Banker, Bond Buyer, JJ Kenny, and Bloomberg have been designated as Nationally Recognized Municipal Securities Information Repositories (NRMSIRs). Many municipal bond underwriters supply an official statement to an NRMSIR because doing so reduces the length of time that a bond underwriter must supply the official statement. Underwriters can reduce the time period from 90 days from the underwriting period to the date the official statement is made available to an NRMSIR. But this period cannot be less than 25 days.

Also, the MSRB Rule G-32 provides that no dealer shall sell any new-issue municipal securities to a customer unless such dealer delivers to the customer information regarding the initial offering price for each maturity in the new issue (the "Offering Price Disclosure Provision"). The rule also requires that managing underwriters and other dealers that sell new municipal securities to purchasing dealers furnish copies of the official statement to such purchasing dealers. If the deal is negotiated, such information must be disclosed in the final official statement. The underwriting spread, amount of fees paid to the dealer, and the initial offering price must be included as well.

Furthermore, the MSRB Rule G-8 governs books and records to be made by brokers, dealers, and municipal securities dealers in regard to syndicate practices. Rule G-11 provides for regulation on sales of new-issue municipal securities during the underwriting period and Rule G-12 on uniform practice. These rules require the managing underwriter to:

1. Maintain a record of all issuer syndicate requirements.
2. Complete the allocation of securities within 24 hours of the sending of the commitment wire.
3. Disclose to syndicate members all available designation information within 10 business days following the date of sale and all information with the sending of the designation checks.
4. Disclose to members of the syndicate the amount of any portion of the takedown that is directed to each member of the syndicate by the issuer.

The MSRB has also filed for amendment to shorten the deadline for payment of designations from 30 business days following delivery of the securities to the customer to 30 calendar days after the issuer delivers the securities to the syndicate.

Trading

The municipal market is criticized for a lack of consistent on-going disclosure. Even though municipals are publicly traded, municipalities are not required to prepare the equivalent of an 8-K or 10-K. Hence, the market operates with a general lack of public information throughout the life of an issue, this is an important issue in trading. For most issues a trader must contact a broker-dealer for quotation. Two different dealers can result in two significantly different quotations. One objective source of pricing information is the Standard & Poor's *Blue List*. The listings represent municipal dealer's holdings available for sale. The price shown is the dealer's asking price, not the actual prices at which bonds have been traded. In addition, Kenny Drake, the largest interdealer of municipals, provides a comprehensive source of real-time municipal market data.

In the secondary market trading, an odd lot is $25,000 or less in par value for retail. For institutions, anything less than $100,000 is considered an odd lot. Dealer spreads vary, depending on factors such as liquidity, volatility, and market conditions. The retail spreads range from a quarter of a point for large blocks to four points for odd-lot sales of an inactive issue. For institutional investors, the spreads are no more than half of a point.

Yield Burning

New municipal securities are often created to refinance previously issued debt. Often the municipality receives the proceeds of the new issue before the old issue matures or is called. During this waiting period federal law restricts the interest that can be earned on the escrow account to be no more than the interest paid on the new issue. This is to prevent the municipality from engaging in a tax arbitrage.

Since tax-exempt municipal rates are lower than most other yields, financial institutions managing the escrow account must make sure that the escrow account earns a below-market rate. To keep the earnings low, the Treasury issues a special low-interest security called *State and Local Government Series* (SLUGS). By investing in SLUGS and Treasury bills, the interest yield is kept artificially low.

Alternatively, some dealers devised another way to keep the yield in the municipal escrow account low. They sell Treasury securities to the escrow account at inflated prices, thereby lowering yield. This is referred to as *yield burning*, which is the subject of intense government investigation recently.

SUMMARY

The outstanding bond market debt climbed to $12.1 trillion in 1997. The tremendous levels of activity in the fixed-income markets present a great opportunity to bankers. This chapter first covers the auction process, trading, short squeeze, coupon rolls, and market practices in the government securities markets. The discussion of corporate fixed-income focuses on the underwriting process, shelf registration, underwriting spreads, and underwriting risk management. A section is devoted to the rapidly growing 144A market. The last section covers the $1.3 trillion municipal debt market. Recent scandals on dealer donations to local elected officials and yield burning are discussed. Other fixed-income securities such as asset backeds and junk bonds are covered in details later.

SELECT BIBLIOGRAPHY

The Bond Market Association. "Another record year for the U.S. bond markets in 1997." *Research Quarterly*. New York: The Bond Market Association, February 1998.

Carey, M. S., S. D. Prowse, S. D. Rea, and G. F. Udell. "Recent development in the market for privately placed debt." *Federal Reserve Bulletin* 79(2), (1993): pp. 77–92.

Campbell, C. J. "Private security placements and resales to the public under SEC Rule 144." *Corporate Finance Review* 2, (July/August 1997): pp. 11–16.

Fabozzi, F. J. *Bond Markets, Analysis and Strategies*, 3d ed. Upper Saddle River, NJ: Prentice Hall, 1996.

Federal Reserve Bank of New York. *Basic Information on Treasury Securities*. 1997.

Federal Reserve Bank of New York. *Fee Schedule 1997*. 1997.

Government Bond Outlines, 9th ed. New York: J.P. Morgan Securities, April 1996.

Jegadeesh, N. "Treasury auction bids and the Salomon squeeze." *Journal of Finance* 48 (September 1993): pp. 1403–1419.

Johnson, H. J. *The Banker's Guide to Investment Banking*. Chicago, IL: Irwin Professional Publishing, 1996.

Kuhn, R. L. *Investment Banking*. New York: Harper & Row, 1990.

Liaw, T. "Pricing Treasury coupon rolls." *Corporate Finance Review* (March/April 1997): pp. 12–16.

Mester, L. "There's more than one way to sell a security: the Treasury's auction experiment," *Business Review* (July-August 1997), Federal Reserve Bank of Philadelphia, pp. 1–10.

Nevler, J. "A crash course in structured notes." *Global Finance* (October 1993): 43–47.

PSA. *Review of Studies of Competitive and Negotiated Financing of Municipal and Corporate Securities*. New York: Public Securities Association, March 1994.

Sundaresan, S. *Fixed Income Markets and Their Derivatives*. Cincinnati, OH: South-Western College Publishing, 1997.

6

Asset Securitization

Asset securitization is a process of packaging illiquid individual loans and other debt instruments into liquid securities with credit enhancements to further their sale in the capital markets. Investment bankers' creativity has been the driving force behind the powerful revolution in a new era of structured finance. Securitized financing is one of the ways the global marketplace has grown, and has played an important role in the development of the derivatives market. Securitization generates fee income for bankers and provides them additional trading opportunities. Asset types used in securitization include mortgages, auto loans, credit card receivables, equipment leases, junk bonds, and tax liens. This chapter first describes the development of the market, which highlights how Wall Street responded to the challenges with incredible innovative thinking. Subsequent sections cover the major types of asset-backed securities. FASITs (financial asset securitization investment trusts) became effective on September 1, 1997, and are likely to be one of the dominant vehicles in asset securitization. An understanding of FASIT is required of bankers.

MARKET OVERVIEW

Asset securitization—the selling of securities backed by the cash flows from a pool of financial assets—has revolutionized the way businesses are financed. It provides businesses with access to new sources of capital at lower costs, even when upfront analysis, structuring, and credit enhancement costs are factored in. Also, securitization provides a crucial source of funding for companies with limited access to other forms of credit because asset-backed securities (ABS) are rated on their own merit, independent of the issuing company's financial standing. The revolutionary process first began with mortgage pass-throughs. Issuance of agency mortgage securities increased from $269.2 billion in 1995 to $370.5 billion in 1996. Issuance of agency MBS recorded a slight decline to $368.0 billion in 1997. Other asset-backed securities totaled $185.1 billion in 1997 and $151.3 billion in 1996, up from the $107.9 billion issued in 1995. The upward trend is expected to continue. At yearend 1996, the outstanding volume of agency mortgage-backed securities (by GNMA, FNMA, and FHLMC) totaled $1.740 trillion and the total amount outstanding for major types of credit was at $398 billion. By yearend 1997, the outstanding agency mortgage securities increased to $1.83 trillion, and the amount for major types of credit reached $490.0 billion. Table 6.1 presents outstanding volume for both from 1990 to 1997.

TABLE 6.1   Outstanding Volumes, 1990–1997

Year	GNMA	FNMA	FHLMC	Total
1990	403.6	299.8	321.0	1,024.4
1991	425.3	372.0	363.2	1,160.5
1992	419.3	445.0	409.2	1,273.5
1993	414.0	495.5	440.1	1,349.6
1994	450.9	530.3	460.7	1,441.9
1995	472.3	583.0	515.1	1,570.4
1996	510.1	650.7	554.3	1,715.1
1997	538.0	709.6	579.4	1,827.0
Year	Auto Loans	Revolving	Business Loans	Total
1990	24.6	45.6	5.8	102.2
1991	28.6	63.3	8.8	133.6
1992	33.9	74.9	9.7	156.9
1993	39.6	80.2	19.5	179.0
1994	36.4	96.1	23.7	205.0
1995	44.4	147.9	29.6	297.9
1996	51.1	189.1	37.7	390.5
1997	53.0	208.0	33.0	490.0

Source: Adapted from The Bond Market Association, 1998.

An Interesting Concept and Its Development

Bank of America issued the first triple-A-rated mortgaged-backed pass-through security in 1977. How to deal with the tax treatment of the first pass-throughs required creative thinking. John Quisenberry of Brown and Wood came up with the solution that relied on a flow-through of the tax attributes. The issue was a failure because at that time only 15 states accepted these AAA pass-throughs as a legal investment. The blue-sky laws offered no standing for a security of this type. Also, many institutional investors had self-imposed prohibitions on investing in these securities. For example, New York State Retirement System required that all mortgages be at least $1 million in size to qualify for their investment. These securities did not qualify as legal investment because each mortgage in the pool was not $1 million a piece.

In the late 1970s, the banking industry experienced escalating disintermediation. Funds left depository institutions in pursuit of higher rates, since the regulated savings rates (Regulation Q) were not competitive with the free-market interest rates. On top of that, the yield curve inverted, which eroded thrifts' net worth resulting from borrowing short and lending long. The need for alternative sources of funding increased. Wall Street sought securitization, and Freddie Mac, as a federal agency, stepped in to overcome the roadblocks to securitizing mortgages. The status of a federal agency provided the solution to the state and regulatory problems, since it is exempt from the state blue-sky laws and legal investment statutes. Securitization enabled Wall Street to repackage and sell a conventional loan product to public investors nationally. The mortgage pass-through market took off.

Still there were problems. One problem was that, at that time, only 30-year securities could be issued. In the capital markets there are a limited number of investors looking for 30-year securities. It was evident that there was a need to broaden the investment appeal by offering a wider range of maturity choices. Another problem was pricing. These pass-throughs had a maturity of up to 30 years, but consisted of underlying mortgages that could prepay or default at any time. The simple Ginnie Mae formula, which assumes that no mortgages prepay for the first 12 years and that every loan is paid off in full at par on the first day of the thirteenth year, was used as a convention for Wall Street to compute prices and yields. Additionally, these pass-throughs were monthly pay securities and all other bonds were semiannual. Wall Street needed a more efficient back-office operation to overcome the bookkeeping inconvenience.

This led to the development of CMOs (collateralized mortgage obligations). The CMO approach recognizes the mortgage pool as a series of unique annual cash flows for each of the next 30 years. Separate tranches were created, with a whole range of maturities. Each tranche is then priced off comparable treasuries with the similar maturity. Freddie Mac issued the first CMOs, a big success. The Treasury, however, permitted the use of the grantor trusts concept in mortgage-backed securities, but restricted the CMOs to three tranches only.

Wall Street then worked on a legislative route to push for permission for the capital markets to meet the nation's mortgage financing needs more efficiently and effectively. The efforts led to the passage of the Secondary Mortgage Market Enhancement Act of 1984 (SMMEA) and Real Estate Mortgage Investment Conduits (REMICs) as part of the Tax Reform Act of 1986. SMMEA solved the legal investment problems and REMICs gave a favorable provision in the tax code. Now it was possible to issue multi-tranche CMOs, strip mortgage cash flows into IOs (interests only) and POs (principals only), PAC (planned amortization class), TAC (targeted amortization class), and VDAM (very accurately defined maturity).

The securitization concept was then applied to other asset types such as credit card receivables, auto loans, mobile homes, and commercial property mortgage loans. In addition, several municipalities such as New York City, Jersey City, and New Haven, have moved to securitize tax liens. Other innovative structures are securities backed by future royalties from record sales, receivables from utility bills, and junk bonds.

An additional favorable development is the Financial Asset Securitization Investment Trust (FASIT) created by the Small Business Job Protection Act of 1996. FASIT took effect on September 1, 1997, providing an explicit statutory framework for transactions of a type currently structured as "master trusts" under common-law tax principles. This is an important improvement given the growing size and importance of asset-backed securities to the capital markets. Because of the flexibility and certainty of tax treatment, FASITs are likely to become one of the dominant vehicles in structured finance transactions.

Lessons from Failures

Several failures were made in the development process. One major failure was the securitization of second mortgages. Bankers succeeded in securitizing the second mortgages and achieving an investment-grade rating through the use of private mortgage insurance. At first, it appeared to be successful. The business grew, especially through loans from California—until the real estate market took a downturn. These homeowners were faced with declining property values and were unable to sell their homes at expected prices. However, they learned that a lender would make them a sufficiently large second mortgage to protect the first mortgage if they could get a high enough appraisal. The loans were then sold to Wall Street to securitize, which was left with the consequences of the scam.

Mobile home financing was another mistake, due to bankers' failure to recognize two basic facts about mobile home financing. The first was that security for a loan must include both the shelter unit and the lot. Unfortunately, as Lewis S. Ranieri described at Northwestern University's 1994 Colloquium on Securitization, "sometimes our collateral went down the highway, never to be seen again." Second, unlike single-family houses, mobile homes tend to depreciate rather than appreciate. Wall Street suffered large losses from the early mobile home program.

The third fumble was the graduated payment mortgage (GPM). The idea behind GPM was the belief that inflation would enable workers to receive annual wage increases of 6% or more each year so they could afford to make the step-up payment schedule. The GPM product failed simply because pay raises did not keep up with the rising payments. Securities backed by GPMs experienced higher default rates.

BENEFITS AND COSTS

Securitization provides borrowers several advantages. The issuer is able to tap into new sources of funding at a lower all-in cost of capital,[1] because the resulting securities represent a better credit risk than the sponsoring entity itself. To the extent that the issuer services the underlying assets, a steady stream of servicing fees is generated. Liquidity is much enhanced, because mortgages and receivables can be sold in the liquid secondary markets, despite the fact that the underlying assets individually are highly illiquid. Securitization also reduces interest rate risk; the issuer's risk exposure is reduced as assets are taken off the book and credit enhancements are added. As is also evident, it permits these institutions to remove certain assets from their balance sheets for financial or regulatory purposes and thereby frees up equity capital that otherwise would be used to support these assets on the balance sheets. Another benefit that is obtainable only through securitization is the pricing efficiency and transparency resulting from the underwriting process and secondary market trading. Without securitization there is at best infrequent and subjective valuation on the underlying assets. Moreover, by packaging individually illiquid loans into marketable securities, the selling financial institution increases the liquidity of its assets. The value added through securitization can be summarized in Table 6.2.

The securitization process benefits Wall Street as well. It is a new product line and has great potential for innovation and market expansion. The securities created generate profits to bankers. The spreads and potential proprietary trading profits appeal to brokers and investors. More importantly, the process produces a continuous flow of underwriting income.

There are costs to issuers for securitizing assets. These include investment-banking fees, filing fees with the SEC and NASD, fees to rating agencies, fees associated with the trustee of the asset pool, and credit enhancement costs. The actual costs depend on the size and type of assets, as well. The following factors are also important considerations.

- The degree of certainty of the cash flows from the underlying assets
- Maturity of the underlying assets

TABLE 6.2   Value Added Through Securitization

Individual Loans	Asset-Backed Securities
Illiquid	Liquid, active secondary markets for most
Periodical valuation	Pricing efficiency and transparency
Originator assesses risk	Rating agencies and credit enhancers assess risk
Local investor base	National/global markets
Higher cost of funding	Lower costs
No servicing fee generated	Additional fee income if act as servicer
Assets remain on balance sheet, additional loan origination requires additional capital	Assets off balance sheets, additional funds available to support more loan origination

- The historical default rates of the underlying assets
- Homogeneity of the assets
- Credit enhancements

The average cost to issuer is on the order of about 1%.

STRUCTURE AND BASIC ELEMENTS

A successful securitization program requires solid "infrastructures." First, a standardized contract gives all participants confidence that the collateral exists in a form that provides a well-defined and legally enforceable manner to meet contractual obligations. The second ingredient is the banker's due-diligence research that provides interested parties the nature of risk and a proper valuation. Of course, a database of historical statistics enables participants to determine how the securities would perform under various scenarios. Another essential infrastructure is the standardization of applicable laws. Recall that the first Bank of America's triple-A-rated mortgage-backed pass-through security was not successful because it did not meet the legal investment standards across all states. Standards specifying the quality of servicers are critical to successful securitization, as well. The bankruptcy of the servicer or the sale of servicing rights cannot expose investors to loss. The sixth element is a reliable supply of quality credit enhancements. Finally, as is true for other securities in modern finance, computer modeling to track cash flows and transactions data is fundamental to volume growth.

Additionally, the process of securitization involves several key elements. The loan originator makes the loan to the borrower and may service the new securities as well. The trust structure permits the originator to treat the transaction as a loan sale and is exempt from taxes. Ratings are an important element for all nonagency issues. Credit enhancements, in the form of a bank letter of credit or insurance guaranty, are used to assure that the cash flows from the pool are of sufficient quality to meet the scheduled payments. Investment banks underwrite and market the securities to investors. Investors play a vital role in the success of the process. The securities offered must meet their objectives. The basic structure of asset securitization is depicted in Figure 6.1.

FIGURE 6.1   Securitization Structure

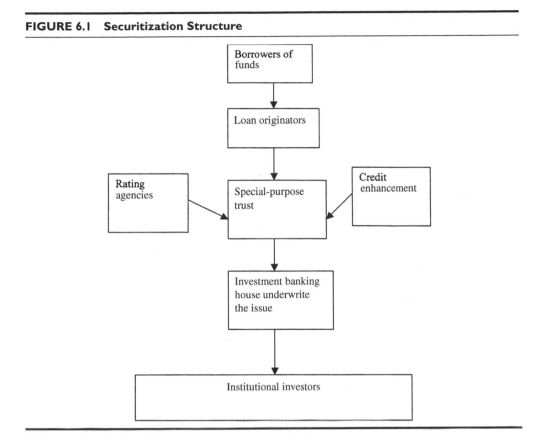

Originator

The loan originators make the loans and create the assets that will become the under-lying collateral. The entities that originate these assets include commercial banks, S&Ls, finance companies, credit card issuers, and securities firms. Mortgages, credit card receivables, lease receivables, auto loans, junk bonds, and municipal bonds are among the assets that have been successfully securitized. The originator generally transfers assets to the pool through a true sale or a transfer of title. The creditworthi-ness of the originator is a concern, although an originator's bankruptcy affects an asset-backed security in ways not directly related to credit. It is the quality of service for the collateral that might be compromised if the originator goes belly up.

Servicer

Servicing includes the collection of payments and other steps necessary to ensure that the borrower meets his obligations and the rights of investors are protected. Thus, most transactions in asset-backed securities have direct credit exposure in connection with the servicer (frequently the originator), because the servicer holds the funds that will be distributed to investors. The degree of the credit exposure is determined by the payment frequency when the servicer passes along payments from pool assets to the investors.

Depending on the nature of the assets, servicers may have considerable discretion in managing the assets. For example, transactions involving multifamily and commercial mortgages typically grant servicers considerable discretion in loan restructuring and foreclosures.

Trust and Issuer

The trust is a special purpose entity created solely to purchase the loans and issue asset-backed securities. The trust structure is employed for tax-exemption purpose. The trust also controls the collateral assets and administers the collection and payment of cash flows. The trust is often a subsidiary of the originator or of the investment bank that underwrites the issue. In some cases an issue will include assets of several originators when individual originators do not have sufficient assets to create a pool.

Credit Enhancement

Credit enhancements are added to the issue either through the guarantee of highly rated credit enhancers or over-collateralization. A bank letter of credit or a guarantee policy from a monoline insurance company is one method of enhancement. Often a bank letter of credit or private insurance guarantees only for the anticipated loss or the maximum tolerable loss of the asset pool. The credit enhancement may step-down for assets that are amortizing as the unpaid balance declines.

A *reserve account* is another technique. A reserve account is established to protect the cash flows of the underlying assets in event of defaults. In some cases a reserve account is established in lieu of a bank letter of credit or a collateral loan. Similarly, a *spread account* is another enhancement device that is widely employed in the securitization of credit card receivables. As an example, suppose Chase wants to securitize its credit card receivables. Assume cardholders are paying 18% on loan balances. Chase has to meet a 6% in funding cost, 5% in default losses, 2% in servicing, and 1% for the securitization program. This leaves a 5% net spread. The excess cash flow can be placed with the trustee and used as a credit enhancement against above average losses on the pool. Any unused funds in the spread account will be returned to Chase.

The senior-subordinated structure is another way of providing credit protection. For example, the issuer places $50 million of mortgages into a trust and issue $45 million worth of senior securities and $5 million of first-loss subordinated securities. The overcollateralized senior securities are protected, as the entire pool can experience a $5 million reduction in value without a dollar of loss to the senior piece. The subordinated security can be sold to investors willing to take on a higher risk for a greater yield or can be retained by the issuer.

Rating

Through information collection, research, and analysis, rating agencies protect investors against unknowingly taking credit risk. The issuer of the securities pays for the services of the rating agencies. The track record for agencies as a group has been very good, particularly in the asset-backed area. Even though many thrifts that issued these securities failed, there have been no defaults in the highly rated securities issued by these thrifts.

The ratings set a defined credit standard that investors understand and accept. Without ratings, the complex asset-backed securities might not sell. With ratings, investment decision can now move to consideration of market risk and duration. This is very important, since there is very little time in the trading process to permit individual analysis of each security.

Issuers seek ratings because they make the securities more marketable at lower interest costs. As investors gain confidence in the rating system, they require a lower yield on an investment. Many regulated investors are not allowed to purchase securities below investment grades, not to mention the unrated issues. Security rating broadens investor base, creating additional demand for the securities. The savings to the issuer can be substantial.

MORTGAGE-BACKED SECURITIES

The mortgage-backed market has gone through several stages of development. The first stage began with the simple pass-throughs. The monthly mortgage payments, net of servicing and insurance fees, are passed along to investors. Faced with the inflexibility of 30-year maturity and prepayment uncertainty, Wall Street devised CMOs to better suit investor's objectives. Since the generic CMOs were introduced, several derivative mortgage products have been developed. As noted in Table 6.1, the total outstanding volume of agency mortgage-backed securities (MBS) is about $1.827 trillion. The daily trading volume has been on an upward trend, soaring to $47 billion in 1997 (Table 6.3). In recent years, transactions of primary dealers with customers have dominated daily trading.

Mortgage Pass-Throughs

There are agency pass-throughs and private-label pass-throughs. The pass-through coupon rate is less than the mortgage rates by an amount paid for servicing and other expenses. Payments are made to security holders each month. The timing of the cash

TABLE 6.3   Average Daily Trading Volume of Agency MBS ($ billions)

Year	Broker/Dealer Transactions	Customer Transactions	Total
1991	6.059	6.786	12.827
1992	7.598	9.435	17.033
1993	9.491	12.617	22.108
1994	11.979	18.432	30.411
1995	10.322	19.071	29.393
1996	13.669	24.479	38.148
1997	15.171	31.905	47.076

Source: Adapted from The Bond Market Association, February 1998.

flow is also different from the underlying mortgages, mortgage payments typically due on the first day of the month, but there is a delay in the corresponding payments to investors. The length of delay varies by the type of pass-throughs.

The market does not call for a rating for an agency pass-through security. An agency can provide two types of guarantees. One type is the timely payment of both interest and principal, referred to as *fully modified pass-throughs*. The second type guarantees the timely payment of interest, but only guarantees that the scheduled principal repayment will be made no later than a specified date. Agency pass-throughs of this type are called *modified pass-throughs*.

There are three major types of agency pass-throughs: Ginnie Mae, Freddie Mac, and Fannie Mae. The full faith and credit of the U.S. government guarantee Ginnie Mae pass-throughs. All Ginnie Mae pass-throughs are fully modified pass-throughs. The second agency pass-through is the *participation certificate* (PC) issued by Freddie Mac. Freddie Mac has two programs: the cash program and guarantor/swap program. Most issues under both programs are modified pass-throughs. In the fall of 1990, Freddie Mac introduced its *Gold* PC that has stronger guarantees. All Gold PCs are fully modified pass-throughs. Fannie Mae mortgage-backed securities consist of four programs. Three of them have pools backed by fixed-rate, level-payment mortgages. The fourth one is collateralized by adjustable-rate mortgages (ARMs). These ARMs are adjusted to one-year Treasury index with a 2% annual adjustment cap and a 6% lifetime adjustment cap. Fannie Mae also issues the so-called boutique securities, which are indexed to the FHLB's eleventh district Cost of Funds if backed by ARMs.

Private-level pass-throughs are issued by private institutions such as commercial banks and private conduits. Private conduits purchase nonconforming mortgages to back the pass-throughs. Unlike the agency securities, private-levels must be registered with the SEC. Most carry credit enhancements and a rating of AA or AAA. Private credit enhancement has been the key to the development of this market. There are two types of credit enhancements, external and internal. External credit enhancements include a letter of credit, pool insurance, and bond insurance.[2] The most common forms of internal credit enhancements are excess servicing spread accounts, senior-subordinated structures, and reserve funds.

Prices of pass-throughs are quoted in the same way as Treasury coupon securities. In addition, a pool prefix and a pool number identify pass-throughs. The prefix indicates the type of pass-through. The pool number indicates the specific mortgage collateral and the issuer. A TBA trade does not specify the pool information. On a TBA trade, the investor could receive up to three pools, with pool numbers being announced shortly before the settlement date. The option of what pools to deliver is left to the seller, as long as they satisfy PSA's guidelines for standards of delivery and settlement for MBS. TBA trades give yet another advantage to the seller. The Bond Market Association delivery variance permits an under- or over-delivery tolerance of 0.01%.

Prepayment

In the mortgage market, the homeowner has the option to pay off the principal outstanding and not make any more mortgage payments. That is, the homeowner owns the option with strike equal to the amount of principal outstanding. The difficulty in valuing mortgage pass-throughs is due to the uncertainty about when the borrower will exercise the call option. Projecting the cash flows from a pass-through requires making assumptions about future prepayments. Several conventions have been used as a benchmark for prepayment rate, including conditional prepayment rate (CPR) and the PSA prepayment benchmark.[3]

The CPR is an annual prepayment rate and is based on the characteristics of the pool and the current and expected future economic environment. To estimate monthly prepayment, the CPR rate must be converted into a monthly rate, known as *single-monthly mortality rate* (SMM). The formula for conversion is

$$SMM = 1 - (1 - CPR)^{1/12}.$$

As an example, suppose the CPR is 5%. The corresponding SMM is

$$SMM = 1 - (1 - 0.05)^{1/12} = 0.00427.$$

A 0.427% SMM means that approximately 0.427% of the remaining mortgage balance, less the scheduled principal payment for the month, will prepay this month. To continue this example, suppose the remaining balance is $60 million and the scheduled principal payment is $1 million. The estimated prepayment for the month will be $25,193 ($0.00427 \times (\$60m - \$1m)$).

The PSA prepayment benchmark assumes that prepayment rates are low for newly originated mortgages and then will speed up as they become seasoned. Specifically, the PSA benchmark assumes that for a 30-year mortgage a CPR of 0.2% for the first month, increased by 0.2% each month for the first 30 months when it reaches 6% per year, and remains at 6% for the remaining years. This is referred to as "100% PSA" or "100 PSA." Slower or faster prepayment rates are then referred to as some percentage of PSA. For example, a 60 PSA means 60% of the PSA benchmark prepayment rate; a 200 PSA indicates twice the benchmark prepayment rate.

The CPR under the PSA approach can be converted to SMM using the conversion formula, where t is time, measured in months:

For months $1 \leq t \leq 30$, $SMM = 1 - [1 - 6\% \times (t/30)]^{1/12}$,
For months $t > 30$, $SMM = 1 - [1 - 6\%]^{1/12} = 0.00514$.

Securities companies frequently use the PSA benchmark as a frame of reference only. Most securities companies rely on their own proprietary prepayment projections. Factors affecting prepayment behavior include the prevailing mortgage rate, seasonal factors, and economic environment.

The prevailing mortgage rate affects prepayment in several ways. The spread between the current rate and the rate homeowners are paying affects the refinancing decisions. The greater the spread, the greater the incentive to refinance. The homeowner is motivated to pay the bank the outstanding balance because the value of the mortgage's future cash flows exceeds the principal outstanding. Historical observations indicate that refinancing increases when the mortgage rate falls by more than 200 basis points. However, the speed should pick up at a much lower spread, because of the creative mortgage designs and advances in information technology in recent years. The path that mortgage rates take to get to the current level is another factor affecting prepayment behavior. The first time the rate drops to an attractive refinancing level, prepayment will speed up. If the rates are volatile, the next time the mortgage rates move down again, prepayment will not surge (refinancing *burnout*).

Seasonal factors are related to the pattern that home buying increases in the spring and summer and declines in the fall and winter. Prepayments mirror this pattern as home buyers sell their existing homes (pay off existing mortgages) and buy new ones (take on new mortgages).

Economic activity affects housing turnover and hence influences the prepayment behavior. This is where the link is. A growing economy provides a higher income and more job opportunities. This increases family mobility and hence housing turnover, which speeds up prepayments. Prepayments slow down in a weak economy.

Valuation of MBS is critically dependent upon prepayment forecast, which, in turn, is determined by the interest rate paths. The procedure used in most valuation modeling of MBS first specifies the interest rate process, which is used in Monte Carlo simulation procedures to simulate interest rate paths. The cash flows each month along each path are projected based on the empirical model of prepayment behavior. The total cash flows along each path are discounted at the appropriate *spot rates*. This process is repeated for numerous paths, and for each path the present value is determined. The average present value on all interest rate paths is the theoretical value. If the average present value is greater (or smaller) than the market price, the security is under-priced (or over-priced). In order to make the model generate a value equal to the market price, a spread is added to all spot rates to raise the discount factor. The spread is referred to as the option-adjusted spread (OAS). Specifically, the OAS is calculated by solving:

$$P = \sum_{t=1}^{T} \frac{CF_t}{\left(1 + \dfrac{R_t + OAS}{n}\right)^t},$$

where P is the MBS market price, t is the time period in months, CF is the expected cash flow, R is the spot rate, and n is the number of cash flows per year. A positive OAS indicates that the security is cheap. Conversely, if the OAS is negative, then the security is rich.

Prepayments also affect MBS valuation through reducing both the duration and convexity of the MBS. This increases the likelihood that the MBS will have negative duration and convexity. Negative duration implies that price decreases as the interest rate declines. This will occur when mortgages are paid off at a fast enough rate—the amount of interest payment will drop rapidly. Negative convexity will result in price compression when the rate declines. As the interest rate declines, the price increases, but at a slower pace than price decreases as rate increases.

Collateralized Mortgage Obligations (CMO)

A CMO is a security backed by a pool of mortgages or mortgage-backed securities. A CMO structure redistributes the cash flows from the pool of collateral to various investor tranches. The principal payments from the underlying collateral are used to retire the classes of bonds on a priority basis. It does not eliminate the prepayment concern, but instead, it transfers this risk among different tranches. This broadens the appeal of the security to various traditional fixed-income investors. For agency CMOs, the total issuance peaked in 1993 with $311.3 billion. The volume dropped to $25.4 billion in 1995, then recovered to $167.0 billion by 1997. The outstanding volume has

TABLE 6.4   Issuance and Outstanding Volumes of Agency CMOs ($ billions)

Year	Issuance	Outstanding
1991	173.8	336.3
1992	286.1	494.0
1993	311.3	587.6
1994	132.6	578.7
1995	25.4	540.9
1996	70.2	521.0
1997	167.0	562.2

Source: Adapted from The Bond Market Association, 1998.

been in the range of $500 billion to $600 billion during 1991–1997. The annual issuance and outstanding volume are listed in Table 6.4.

There are two basic types of CMO tranches: sequential structure and planned amortization class structure (PAC). A typical sequential structure has four tranches. Terms of the bonds dictate how the cash flows from the collateral are allocated to each tranche investor. The first three tranches receive principal and interests. Until the first tranche is fully paid off, no principal payments are made to the other tranches. In other words, each tranche successively receives prepayments as soon as its immediate predecessor is retired. The last tranche is called *Z bond (accrual tranche)* that receives no cash until all earlier tranches are fully retired.

PAC structure separates the collateral's principal into PAC bonds and the *companion*. The amortization schedule for the PAC bonds remains fixed within a certain range of PSA prepayment speeds. The companion bonds absorb prepayment risk for the PAC bonds. The structure leads to stable average lives for the PAC bonds. The companion bonds, on the other hand, have much less stable lives than otherwise similar sequential bonds. As a result, PAC bonds are priced much tighter to comparable treasuries. Bonds in the companion group are priced at much wider spreads relative to treasuries. Similar to a PAC structure, the targeted amortization classes (TACs) are scheduled to receive a specified monthly prepayment. Any excess prepayment is distributed to non-TAC classes. When prepayments are not sufficient to support the TAC classes with the scheduled principal repayment, TAC's average maturity lengthens.

Due to the complexity of the CMO structures, each tranche must be evaluated individually. Recently, Fitch has developed V-Ratings to analyze the potential effect of interest rate changes on individual tranches. The five V-Ratings are as follows:

- V1 exhibits stable returns in all interest-rate scenarios used in the model.
- V2 exhibits relatively small changes in returns and cash flows.
- V3 exhibits relatively larger changes in total return and cash flows, but the changes are less than agency certificates.
- V4 exhibits greater changes than the agency certificates.
- V5 exhibits substantial volatility; negative total returns may result under stressful interest rate scenarios.

Stripped Mortgage-Backed Securities

Stripped mortgage-backed securities are a pass-through that divides the cash flow from the underlying collateral on a pro rata basis across the security holders. There are discount strips and premium strips. A *discount strip* receives a rate well below the current mortgage rates, while a *premium strip* receives all that is left over after paying the discount strip. In another stripped MBS, all the interest is allocated to IO class (interest-only derivatives) and the entire principal to the PO class (principal-only derivatives). The PO security trades at a discount. The yield an investor will realize depends on the prepayment behavior. The faster the prepayment, the higher the yield. When a mortgage prepays, it is redeemed in full at par. When mortgage rates decline, prepayments will speed up, accelerating payments to the PO investors. The unanticipated larger amount of cash flow will now be discounted at a lower interest rate. The result is that the price of a PO rises with declining mortgage rate. When mortgage rate rises, prepayments will slow down, resulting in a lower cash flow. Coupled with a higher discount rate, the price of a PO falls with rising mortgage rates.

In contrast, IO holders receive only interest on the amount of principal outstanding. If the mortgage rate declines, prepayments are expected to accelerate. The smaller amount of principal outstanding results in a decline of income for IO. Although the cash flow will be discounted at a lower rate, the net effect is typically a lower price for IO. On a reverse interest rate trend, the expected cash flow improves, but the cash flow is discounted at a higher rate. The net effect may be either a rise or a fall in IO, depending on the magnitude of the change.

What is the motivation behind the stripping? Same as in the case of Treasury strips, it is the arbitrage profits. Here is one example.[4] In late January 1987, the FNMA Trust 1 pass-through was traded at 102.19% of par. After the stripping of interest and principal in February, the IO traded at 58.16% and PO at a level of 48.00% of par. The stripping created an arbitrage return of almost 4% on the $750 million FNMA pass-throughs.

ASSET-BACKED SECURITIES

The market refers to asset-backed securities (ABS) as securities backed by installment loans, leases, receivables, home equity loans, and revolving credit. The ABS market has been in the upward trend for many years. The issuance grew from about $40 billion in 1990, to $107.9 billion in 1995, and to a total of $151.3 billion in 1996 and $185.1 billion in 1997. Growth in the ABS market can be attributed to a variety of factors, including strong investor demand, the entrance of new issuers, and the use of new assets. Demand for ABS has been soaring as a result of the attractive yields, high credit quality, and liquidity offered in this market. New structures have also contributed to the market's growth. Many cities are seeking investment bankers' advice on issuing ABS backed by tax liens in order to raise funds and remove delinquent property taxes off their books. In addition, Wall Street has devised collateralized bond obligations (CBOs) to transform default-prone junk bonds into solid, investment-grade credits.

Credit Card Receivables

The credit card sector has been the largest in the ABS market. The introduction of master-trust structures allows issuers to move on the market windows without the need for time-consuming trust creation and document drafting. The advantages to investors are significant. The structure reduces the risk of a shortfall on a given payment date, because of the broad diversification of asset pool and amortization of principal payments. However, the dominance of the credit card ABS has begun to slip as the ABS market has grown and become more diverse. The issuance totaled $37.5 billion in 1997 and $47.8 billion in 1996.

For credit card receivable ABSs, there is generally a *lockout period* or *revolving period* of 18 months to 10 years. During this period the principal payments made by the credit card borrowers are retained by the trustee and reinvested in additional receivables. After the lockout period, the principal is paid to investors based on one of the following:

- *Pass-through structure:* The principal cash flows are paid to investors on a pro rata basis.
- *Controlled amortization structure:* A scheduled principal amount is established, investors are paid the lesser of the scheduled principal amount or the pro rata amount.
- *Bullet-payment structure:* Investors receive the entire amount in one distribution.

Auto Loans and Receivables

The auto loan sector issued a total of $33.1 billion in 1997, a 10% increase from $30.3 billion in 1996, which was a 21% jump from 1995's level of $25.1 billion. The growing trend by consumers to lease new and pre-owned automobiles will help maintain strong growth. Additionally, a reduction in the luxury tax in 1997 will provide an added boost to this sector.

Prepayments in auto-loan backed securities are measured in terms of an absolute prepayment rate, which computes prepayment relative to the original number of loans in the pool. Causes of prepayment include sales or trade-ins, loss or destruction of cars, payoff of loan to save interest cost, and refinancing at a lower rate. Refinancing is not a major factor, and there is rich historical information on other causes of prepayments. Therefore, cash flows to investors in this sector tend to be more certain than in the MBS.

Home Equity/Revolving Credit

Issuance surged 76% in 1997 to $65 billion, versus $36.9 billion a year earlier, which more than doubled the 1995 level of $14.5 billion. The entrance of new issuers and an increase in the frequency of issuance by old issuers contributed to the growth.

Other Asset Types

Student-loan–backed ABSs account for a small share of the ABS market. Issuance climbed to $12.5 billion in 1997 from $8 billion in 1996 on the increased participation of Sallie Mae. In addition, volume may rise by possible entrance of not-for-profit student-loan finance companies in 1997, since legislation was passed permitting not-for-profit corporations to become taxable entities. As taxable entities, the student-loan companies will no longer be able to issue student pledge bonds, and thus will have to tap the ABS market in order to raise funds.

Other asset types include equipment leases, tax liens, home improvement loans, consumer loans, manufactured housing loans, and junk bonds. Securities backed by junk bonds are called CBOs (collateralized bond obligations). They are created the same way that investment bankers turned home mortgages into CMOs.

Catastrophe risk securitization was introduced in 1992. This is another method of transferring insurance risk, in addition to spreading the risk over a large number of policyholders and purchasing reinsurance. The development of securitizing property catastrophe risk is largely due to increases in the frequency and size of catastrophic events such as earthquakes, hurricanes, and other natural disasters. Total insured losses amounted to $75 billion between 1989 and 1995, compared with just $51 billion covering 1950 to 1988. The risk securitization products include insurance options and futures, contingent surplus notes, catastrophe bonds, and insurance swaps instruments.

FINANCIAL ASSET SECURITIZATION INVESTMENT TRUST

The Small Business Job Protection Act of 1996 established the Financial Asset Securitization Investment Trust (FASIT), effective September 1, 1997. FASIT is patterned after the Real Estate Mortgage Investment Conduit (REMIC) provision in the tax code. FASIT is a new type of statutory entity that will facilitate the securitization of debt obligations. Specifically, a FASIT is not subject to tax and is not treated as a trust or a partnership. Instead, all of the FASIT's assets and liabilities are treated as the assets and liabilities of the holder of the ownership interest. Plus, compliance with the FASIT qualification tests is all that is required for an entity's securities to be taxed as FASIT interests. The only disadvantages are that gains, but not losses, must be recognized upon contribution of assets to a FASIT, and that income on a FASIT high-yield or ownership interest is subject to tax in all events. Overall, because of their flexibility and certainty of tax treatment, FASITs will likely become one of the dominant vehicles in structured finance transactions in the years to come.[5]

FASIT Qualifications

To qualify as a FASIT, the entity must meet requirements relating to the composition of its assets, the nature of the interests in the entity, and the entity of certain interest holders. The first requirement is that the entity must elect to be treated as a FASIT. Once an election to be a FASIT is made, the election is applied from the date specified and all subsequent years until the entity ceases to be a FASIT. An entity loses its FASIT status on the date it ceases to qualify as a FASIT, and it may not be a FASIT for any subsequent year. However, an entity that inadvertently loses its FASIT status, in some cases, may apply to retain its status with the IRS's consent.

The second requirement is that, as of the date 90 days after the election and all times thereafter, substantially all of the entity's assets must be *permitted assets*. Permitted assets include:

- Cash and cash equivalents
- Certain permitted debt instruments and foreclosure property
- Certain hedging and credit enhancement contracts
- Regular interests in a REMIC or another FASIT

A permitted debt instrument is indebtedness for federal income-tax purposes and bears either fixed or qualified floating rate. Obligations, except for cash equivalent, issued by FASIT owners or certain related persons do not qualify as permitted debt instruments.

Third, all interests in a FASIT must be either ownership interest or regular interest. The ownership interest is generally the interest held by the entity creating the FASIT. The FASIT must have one ownership interest only and the interest must be held directly by a single eligible entity, generally a domestic C corporation. Exception is granted if each holder is a member of the same affiliated group. Regular interests are instruments treated as debt for federal income-tax purposes. The term *regular interest* includes a high-yield interest. A high-yield interest is any interest that fails to meet one of the regular interest qualifications.

Taxation Issues

A FASIT itself is generally not subject to tax. However, the FASIT is subject to a penalty exercise tax equal to 100% of net income derived from *prohibited transactions*. Prohibited transactions cover items such as income derived from a nonpermitted asset, any nonpermitted disposition of an asset, any loan originated by the FASIT, and any compensation for services other than fees for a waiver, amendment, or consent under permitted assets not acquired through foreclosure. The penalty tax is the principal mechanism to assure that the FASIT is a passive securitization vehicle and not an active financial services business.

Taxation of interests in the FASIT depends on the type of interests, ownership interest or regular interests. For FASIT owners, all of the FASIT assets and liabilities are treated as assets and liabilities of the holder of the ownership interest. The FASIT owner includes all FASIT's income, gain, deduction, or loss in computing its taxable income using the accrual method of accounting. A FASIT owner cannot offset income or gain from the ownership interest with other losses, if any. In the case of an owner's transfer of assets to a FASIT, gain but not loss generally is recognized immediately by the FASIT owner upon the transfer of assets, as if the assets were sold to the FASIT at the fair market value.

The taxation of holders of the regular interests is as follows. A holder of the regular interest or a high-yield interest is taxed in the same manner as a holder of any other debt instrument. However, the regular interest holder is required to account for interest income on an accrual basis, regardless of the method of accounting otherwise used by the holder. Furthermore, a holder of the high-yield interest is not permitted to offset any income derived from the high-yield interest with unrelated losses.

SUMMARY

Asset securitization converts illiquid individual loans and other debt instruments into liquid marketable securities. Investment bankers' creativity has been the driving force behind the powerful revolution in a new era of structured finance. This chapter describes the securitization process and the market for each asset type. Understanding the essence of the process will lead to more innovative products. Also, the newly enacted FASIT is an important vehicle available for use in the securitization process.

SELECT BIBLIOGRAPHY

Border, S., and A. Sarker. "Securitizing property catastrophe risk." *Current Issues in Economics and Finance* 2 (August 1996), Federal Reserve Bank of New York.

Britt, P. "Asset securitization." *America's Community Banker*, April 1996, v5n4, pp. 10-14.

Deloitte and Touche. "The 1996 tax changes." August 1996.

Fabozzi, F. J. *Bond Markets, Analysis and Strategies*. Upper Saddle River, NJ: Prentice Hall, 1996.

Fabozzi, F. J. *Handbook of Mortgage-Backed Securities*. Chicago: Probus Publishing, 1995.

Grant Thornton LLP. "Tax provisions in August 1996 laws: provisions affecting financial services business," 1997.

Hunton and Williams. "Asset securitization," 1997.

Johnson, D., and E. Eldridge. "Asset securitization as a corporate finance tool." *The Financier: ACTM* 2 (August 1995): pp. 7-13.

Johnson, H. J. *The Banker's Guide to Investment Banking*. Chicago, IL: Irwin Professional Publishing, 1996.

Kendall, L. T., and M. J. Fishman, eds. *A Primer on Securitization*. Cambridge, MA: MIT Press, 1996.

Kuhn, R. L. *Investment Banking*. New York: Harper & Row, 1990.

Lockwood, L. J. "Wealth effects of asset securitization." *Journal of Banking and Finance* 20 (January 1996): pp. 151-164.

Milbank, Tweed, Hadley & McCloy. "Capital markets updates: 1997-the year of the FASIT?" 1997.

Nirenberg, D. Z., C. J. Burke, and S. L. Kopp. "FASITs—the Small Business Act's new securitization vehicle," *Journal of Taxation* 85 (November 1996): pp. 1-11.

PSA Research Report. *U.S. Bond Markets at Record Levels in 1997*. New York: PSA, 1998.

Sundaresan, S. *Fixed Income Markets and Their Derivatives*. Cincinnati, OH: South-Western College Publishing, 1997.

7

Foreign Listing on Wall Street

With rapid advances in information technology and greater cooperation among financial regulators, the international capital markets are now more closely linked. Listing of foreign companies on Wall Street, in the form of depositary receipts,[1] is an important element in this process of market integration. Foreign companies seek listing on Wall Street to raise capital, gain liquidity, and stress shareholder information. On the demand side, U.S. investors are looking to take advantage of new capital growth opportunities and to add an additional element of diversification in international securities. Within the next few years, U.S. investors are expected to double the non–U.S. component of their equity portfolio from 5% to around 10%. Investment banking firms need to seize the opportunity to facilitate the global capital raising and capital allocating process. This chapter describes the structure and types of *American Depositary Receipts* (ADRs), including Rule 144As. The process of bringing ADRs to the marketplace and the legal requirements are described.

MARKET OVERVIEW

J.P. Morgan created the first ADR in 1927 to allow Americans to invest in the British retailer Selfridge. ADRs have since evolved in sophistication and in importance. ADRs are now among the commonly used vehicles to invest internationally and have become fully integrated into the U.S. capital markets. They are an efficient, transparent, cost-effective and liquid method for U.S. investors to make specific foreign investments. ADRs provide U.S. investors an additional venue to acquire and trade non-U.S. securities in U.S. dollars without concern for the differing settlement process, securities custody, and currency exchange. Through ADRs, Americans can also achieve the benefits of systematic risk reduction not obtainable in the U.S. domestic markets. For a foreign company, some structures of ADRs allow the company to raise U.S. capital, while others provide a mechanism that improves such company's visibility in the United States.

The process of creating a new ADR is as follows. Upon demand, a U.S. depositary bank contacts a broker in the issuing company's home market and acquires shares in that company. These shares are then deposited with the depositary bank's local custodian. Upon confirmation that the custodian has received the shares, the U.S. depositary then issues the requisite number of ADRs to the investor.

The ADR market is growing from both the supply side and the demand side. It is the preferred method of entering the U.S. markets. Foreign issuers are increasingly attracted to the U.S. markets for several reasons. The U.S. markets are efficient and the largest in the world. The United States presents fewer barriers to entry by foreign issuers than do other nations, and the hurdles are perceived to be worth the effort to overcome. On the demand side, U.S. investors have been looking for yield and diversity. And at times, certain ADRs offer greater liquidity in the United States than the underlying stocks in foreign local markets. Moreover, some pension funds and investment managers may have preference or may be legally required to invest in ADRs when they invest in non-U.S. securities. According to a survey[2] by Greenwich Associates, U.S. pension funds, foundations, and endowments at the end of 1993 owned $170 billion in foreign equities and planned to increase their foreign holdings to $300 billion by 1996. Many institutional investors favor investing in securities listed for trading in the United States. Certain listing requirements provide acceptable standards of corporate governance. There are also minimum capitalization requirements, which appeal to institutional investors who cannot invest their sizable sums in thinly capitalized or traded stocks. Also, accounting and disclosure standards associated with listing and trading in the U.S. markets give investors confidence. The top three ADR investors include Fidelity Management & Research, Brandes Investment Partners, and Capital Research & Management. Table 7.1 lists the top 10 ADR investors.

Over the years, the SEC has taken steps to simplify and lower cost of registration and reporting process for foreign companies. First, in April 1990, the SEC adopted Rule 144A and Regulation S. Rule 144A allows resale of restricted securities among qualified institutional buyers (QIBs). Regulation S permits resale of 144As internationally without registration. Second, in June 1991, the SEC proposed new rules to expedite cross-border right offerings and tender offerings. Furthermore, in October 1992, the SEC expanded its definition of QIBs to include trust funds and master trusts, and to allow inclusion of government securities in the $100 million threshold for QIB qualification. Additionally, the SEC adopted several measures in 1994 to forward deregulation:

TABLE 7.1   Top 10 ADR Investors

Institutional Investor	ADR Investments ($ million)[1]
Fidelity Management & Research	$11,573
Brandes Investment Partners	5,753
Capital Research & Management	5,607
Franklin Advisors	4,588
Invesco Capital Management	3,921
Putnam Investment Management	3,562
Capital Guardian Trust Company	3,479
J.P. Morgan Investment Management	3,301
Wellington Management Company	3,221
Merrill Lynch Asset Management	2,665

[1] Figures are as of December 31, 1996.
Source: Adapted from J.P. Morgan, 1997.

- Rule 135(c) affords some liability protection for issuer announcements of offerings. The safe harbor assists issuers in balancing the need to keep investors informed and the prohibition under Regulation S of no U.S. direct selling efforts.
- SEC's amendment of Form 20-F to permit foreign issuer's inclusion in the form,[3] without reconciliation, of a cash flow statement prepared in accordance with International Accounting Standards (IAS) No. 7 "Cash Flow Statements."
- Amendment of Form 20-F that enables first-time registrants to reconcile the required financial statements and selected financial data for only the most recent two fiscal years and any required interim period.

The total ADR programs listed in NYSE, AMEX, and Nasdaq have risen significantly. There were about 800 programs in 1990. By 1996, the total ADR programs[4] reached over 1,300. The trading dollar volume increased from less than $100 billion in 1990 to $350 billion in 1996. The trading dollar volumes of depositary receipts account for more than 4% of total exchange volumes in the United States in 1990 to 1992, 5% to 6% range in 1993 to 1995, and more than 7% in 1996. And the trend is still up.

ADR STRUCTURES AND BENEFITS

ADRs are registered certificates issued by U.S. depositaries in the names of particular foreign entities. An ADR guarantees that the issuing depositary will retain a specific number of the named entity's securities in trust for the buyer of the ADR. As such, the ADR represents ownership of such foreign issuer's security held on deposit in the home country of the issuer by a custodian engaged by the depositary. ADR is a certificate that usually represents a multiple or a fraction of a share of the foreign company deposited in the program, so that the ADR trades in a price range that is common in the U.S. market. ADRs are created when a broker purchases the foreign company's shares on its home market and delivers those shares to the depositary's local custodian bank, which then instructs the depositary bank to issue *Depositary Receipts*. The depositary receipts can be traded either on an exchange or in the over-the-counter market.

Citibank, J.P. Morgan, and Bank of New York are the three major depositary banks. Depositary banks typically act as more than just a depositary. The depositary is also a vital link between the issuer and investors. A typical depositary services package includes:

- Original issue of depositary receipts and provisions of transfer agency services
- Custodian services for the underlying securities
- Collection and payment of the underlying interest or dividends, including conversion of foreign currency
- Distribution of issuer's financial statements, notices and shareholder meeting materials
- Cancellation and exchange of ADRs for underlying debt or equity and vice versa
- Answering investor's inquiries and other investor relations services
- Program information to the issuer
- Tax reporting
- General program administration

Deposit Agreements

A sponsored ADR program is created pursuant to a *deposit agreement* between the foreign issuer, the depositary, and the holders of the ADR. Deposit agreements vary in length. A typical deposit agreement covers the following items:

- Deposit, transfer, and withdrawal
- Dividends, other distributions and rights
- Record dates
- Voting of deposited securities
- Reports and other communications
- Amendment and termination of the deposit agreement
- Charges of depositary
- Liability of owners for taxes
- Governing law

ADR Advantages

The ADR structure provides several distinct benefits, such as trading simplification, faster dividend payment, risk and cost reduction, investor barrier elimination, and investor communication facilitation. The increased efficiency in the ADR market further benefits brokers and market makers.

ADRs greatly simplify the trading of foreign equities for the issuers, brokers, market makers, and investors. Without ADRs, a single trade of a foreign security involves multiple parties, currency concern, and settlement delays. ADRs standardize the varying securities practices. Securities in ADR forms are easily transferable and the automated book-entry systems for clearing procedures are well established. ADR holders also have the benefit of a depositary collecting dividends, converting the currency, and issuing prompt payment in U.S. dollars or additional ADRs in the case of a stock dividend.

Because ADRs simplify securities processing, settlement risk is reduced. Without ADRs, U.S. investors must find a non-U.S. or U.S. broker to execute trade abroad. Investors buying ADRs save even more because they do not have to pay for safekeeping fees to a custodian abroad. ADRs are registered in the United States, therefore, records exist here to protect ownership rights. At the same time, ADRs save investors insurance fees necessary to protect securities abroad. In cases where tax treaty exists, the depositary can arrange tax withholding at a favorable rate which will prevent an extended claim period by qualified investors.

Institutions whose charters preclude holding foreign securities and currencies can invest through ADRs. Similarly, institutions that only invest in the U.S. because they have no custodian facilities or arrangements abroad can invest in ADRs. An ADR program helps investors avoid the regulations of countries that prohibit physical delivery of shares overseas as well. Another significant advantage ADR holders have over holders of foreign shares is that the price information is more readily available. It is important to note that ADR holders enjoy all the voting rights, as well as the equivalent cash value of non-U.S. subscription right and warrant offerings.

Securities dealers and brokers find ADRs attractive as well. The T+3 settlement cycle minimizes losses from fails. The depositaries can also prerelease shares to help traders overcome problems from differing settlement periods in different nations. In a

TABLE 7.2 Top Issuers with Most Widely Held ADRs

Issuer
1. Royal Dutch Petroleum Company
2. SmithKline Beecham Plc
3. Unilever N.V.
4. British Petroleum Company Plc
5. Ericsson LM Telephone Company
6. Nokia Corporation
7. Telefonos de Mexico, S.A.
8. Telecomunicacoes Brasileriras S.A.-Telebras
9. Reuters Holdings
10. YPF Sociedad Anonima

Source: Adapted from J.P. Morgan, 1997.

prerelease, the depositary with the knowledge that the trade of underlying shares has been executed, issues an ADR before the underlying shares are physically deposited in an overseas custodian.

For foreign companies, ADRs provide the most effective means of entering the important U.S. market. An ADR program provides a simple means of diversifying a company's shareholder base. It may increase the liquidity on the underlying shares of the issuer and its visibility and name recognition in the United States. An ADR program can also be used to help finance acquisitions or building a stronger U.S. presence. Features such as dividend reinvestment plans help ensure a continual stream of investment into an issuer's program. And ADR ratios are often adjusted to ensure that an ADR trades in a comparable range with those of its peers in the U.S. market. In addition, ADRs provide an easy way for U.S. employees of non–U.S. companies to invest in their companies' employee stock purchase programs. These benefits have motivated foreign companies to launch ADRs in the United States. During 1992 to 1996, the amount of capital raised by ADR public offerings per year were $5.3 billion, $9.5 billion, $11.4 billion, $7.9 billion, and $13.8 billion, respectively. Table 7.2 lists top-10 issuers with the most widely held ADRs.

PRINCIPAL TYPES OF ADR PROGRAMS

There are two categories of ADR programs: unsponsored and sponsored. The later includes Level I ADR, Level II ADR, Level III ADR, and Rule 144A ADR. Unsponsored ADRs are not supported by the foreign companies. Sponsored facilities are exclusive to one depositary and cannot exist simultaneously with unsponsored ADRs because sponsored and unsponsored ADRs for the same foreign security might trade at different prices, creating confusion. The prices might be different in part, because in a sponsored program the issuer reimburses the depositary for its expenses, whereas in an unsponsored facility the ADR holders bear such expenses.

Unsponsored Programs

An unsponsored ADR program is not initiated by the foreign issuer but by a bank in response to investor demand. The issuer has little, if any, control over the activity of the unsponsored program because there is typically no deposit agreement between the issuer and the depositary bank.

Registration of the underlying shares is not required, only the ADRs must be registered with the SEC. The depositary and the issuer together submit an application under Rule 12g3-2(b) to the SEC seeking exemption from the full reporting requirements. If granted, the issuer will be notified that it has been included in the list of foreign issuers eligible to claim exemption and assigned a file number.

Upon receipt of SEC approval, the depositary files Form F-6, which is a limited-disclosure registration statement. The foreign issuer is not a signatory to the document and generally has no obligation or liability in connection with the registration of the ADRs. SEC normally grants approval of Form F-6 registration statement within a short period of time. Once approved, the unsponsored ADR program can only be traded in the over-the-counter market and listed in the Pink Sheets or the Bulletin Board. The SEC requires that material public information in the issuer's home country be supplied to the SEC and made available to U.S. investors. The depositary will mail the issuer's annual reports and certain public information to U.S. investors upon request. The SEC does not require this material to be translated into English or adjusted for differences in U.S. GAAP practices.

Unsponsored programs provide two advantages to the issuers. They provide an inexpensive and simple way of expanding the U.S. investor base. The SEC compliance and reporting requirements are minimal. Other depositary banks can duplicate an unsponsored program by filing a Form F-6 with the SEC without the consent of the issuer. An unsponsored program can be converted to a sponsored facility. The issuer has to "buy out" the unsponsored ADRs, by contacting the depositary bank of the unsponsored program, having it exchange its ADRs for the new sponsored ADRs and paying such depositary the cash out fee.

Level I Program

This is the easiest and least expensive way for a foreign company to gauge interest in its securities and to begin building a U.S. presence. The company does not have to comply with U.S. GAAP or full disclosure. The company is required to obtain a Rule 12g3-2(b) exemption by providing its financial statements in English and the other information already required by the regulatory authorities of its home country. The issuer also has to file a Form F-6 and sign a deposit agreement. The issuer has greater control over a Level I facility because a deposit agreement is executed between the issuer and one exclusive depositary bank. The agreement defines the responsibilities of the depositary, including responding to investor inquiries, maintaining stockholder records, and mailing annual reports and other materials to shareholders.

The Level I sponsored ADRs can only be traded OTC, with bid and ask prices published daily in National Daily Quotation Bureau pink sheets. Prices may also be posted on the OTC Bulletin Board. Due to the SEC's recent permanent approval of the Bulletin Board, however, effective April 1, 1998, all non–U.S. equity securities (including ADRs) must be registered with the SEC pursuant to Section 12 of the Securities Exchange Act of 1934 to remain eligible for quotation in the Bulletin Board. Those who wish to continue relying on 12g3-2(b) exemption will trade exclusively on the pink sheets. As a result, investor interest might be limited. On the other hand, it has several advantages:

- Low set-up costs
- Exempt from full compliance with SEC's disclosure requirements

- Issuer has greater control than would be the case with an unsponsored program
- The depositary bank passes on dividends, financial statements, and material public corporate information to U.S. investors
- Can support a Rule 144A ADR facility, and is easy and relatively inexpensive to upgrade the program to Level II or Level III

Level II Programs

Companies wishing to list their shares on a U.S. exchange use sponsored Level II program. Level II ADRs must comply with SEC's full registration and reporting requirements. The issuers must file with SEC a Form F-6 for registering the ADRs and a Form 20-F to meet the reporting requirements. In addition, the issuer must submit its annual reports, which must be prepared in accordance with U.S. GAAP. The compliance allows the issuer to list its ADRs on NYSE, AMEX, or Nasdaq; each has its own reporting and disclosure requirements.

Full registration and listing increase liquidity and marketability, and hence enhance the issuer's name recognition in the United States. The issuer is also able to monitor the ownership of its U.S. shares. Because the foreign issuer must comply with the rigorous SEC requirements, it is well positioned to upgrade and make a public offering in the U.S. market. The foreign company may be qualified to use a short-form registration statement if it has been filing timely periodic reports to the SEC for a specified time period.

On the other hand, the program is more expensive and time-consuming to set up and maintain than for a Level I ADR. It must comply with SEC full registration and reporting requirements. Financial statements must be prepared in accordance with U.S. GAAP or a detailed summary of the differences in financial reporting between the home country and the United States must be submitted. Additional costs include legal and listing expenses. Another key disadvantage is that SEC regulations do not permit a public offering of ADRs under Level II program; that is, a foreign company cannot use Level II to raise capital in the United States.

Level III Programs

Companies wanting to raise capital use sponsored Level III facility. ADRs under Level III are similar to Level II ADRs. In both programs, the issuer initiates the program, signs a deposit agreement with one depositary bank, lists on one of the U.S. exchanges, and files Form F-6 and Form 20-F with the SEC. The major difference is that a Level III ADR allows the issuer to make a public offering. For this, the issuer is required to file a Form F-1 (similar to Form S-1 for U.S. companies). The reporting is more onerous than for Level I or II programs. The costs can be substantial, which include costs for listing, attorneys, accountants, investor relations, and roadshows.

In summary, among the three programs discussed, a Level I facility allows a foreign company to enjoy the benefits of a publicly traded security without changing its current reporting process. Companies wanting to list shares on a U.S. exchange use sponsored Level II programs, and companies wishing to raise capital use Level III. Each higher level of ADR program reflects additional SEC registration and increases the visibility and attractiveness of the ADR to institutional and retail investors.

Rule 144A ADRs

As an alternative to Level III sponsored programs, foreign companies can access the U.S. capital markets through 144A ADRs to accredited investors, thereby avoiding SEC registration and reporting. The SEC adopted Rule 144A in April 1990, in part to stimulate capital raising in the United States by foreign companies. Some of the previous restrictions governing resale of restricted securities were lifted under Rule 144A, if the resale is made to QIBs. A QIB is defined as an institution that owns and invests on a discretionary basis at least $100 million in securities of an unaffiliated entity. In the case of registered broker–dealers, the requirement is $10 million.

Through Rule 144A ADRs, foreign companies have access to the U.S. private placement market and may raise capital without conforming to the full burden of SEC registration and disclosure. The costs of issuing 144As are considerably less than the costs of initiating a Level III ADR. In addition, the NASD established a closed electronic trading system for 144A, Private Offerings, Resales and Trading through Automated Linkages (PORTAL). This system is designed to provide a market for privately traded securities. The system is available to both investors and market makers. Essentially, it allows institutions to claim 144As as liquid securities for regulatory purposes.

In summary, the key advantages to issuers are as follows. Rule 144A ADRs do not have to conform to full reporting and registration requirements. Though QIBs may demand certain disclosure, they are exempted if exemption under Rule 12g3-2(b) has been granted, as in the case where 144A coexists with Level I. 144As can be launched on their own or as part of a global offering. There are two disadvantages, however. First, 144As cannot be created for classes of shares already listed on a U.S. exchange. 144As can only be traded among QIBs, the market certainly is not as liquid as the public equity market.

Another pathway for lifting restrictions on restricted securities is under Regulation S, which can be used in conjunction with Rule 144A. Underwriters place 144A ADRs with U.S. QIBs and Regulation S depositary receipts with non–U.S. investors. Forty days after the conclusion of the offering, the depositary and the company may file a Form F-6 to set up an unrestricted, side-by-side Level I ADR program. Once filing is effective, Level I ADRs may trade among public investors in U.S. over-the-counter. Because Regulation S ADRs have now lost their restrictions, all the Regulation S ADRs automatically become Level I. Table 7.3 provides a summary of the different filings required by the SEC.

TABLE 7.3   ADR Filing Requirements and Trading

Type of ADRs	SEC Filing	Exchange Listing	Raising Capital
Unsponsored	Form F-6	OTC	No
	12g3-2(b)		
Sponsored:			
Level I	Form F-6	OTC	No
	12g3-2(b)		
Level II	Form F-6	NYSE, AMEX,	No
	Form 20-F	Nasdaq	
Level III	Form F-6	NYSE, AMEX,	Yes
	Form 20-F	Nasdaq	
	Form F-1		
Rule 144A	N/A	Private placement market	Yes

Global Depositary Receipts (GDRs)

With a GDR, the underlying shares are held with a local custodian and the depositary issues GDRs to foreign markets. GDRs are commonly used when the issuer is raising capital in its local market as well as in the U.S. and international markets, whether through public offerings or private placements. GDRs also allow issuers to overcome selling restrictions to foreign investors imposed in the home country.

A U.S. component of a GDR can be structured either as a Level III ADR or as a private placement under Rule 144A. With the global integration of the major securities markets, it is common to have fungible securities listed and cleared in more than one market. For example, the links between Euroclear and Cedel in Europe and DTC in the United States allow for efficient settlement of securities between these two markets.

REGISTRATION OF ADRS FOR EXISTING SHARES

The motivations for registration of ADRs for previously issued shares are either that a foreign issuer seeks visibility in the United States through sponsorship of an ADR program or that a depositary creates an unsponsored program as a result of perceived demand. The issuer is not engaged in a public offering of its shares. It is the issuance of ADRs that constitutes a public offering requiring registration. In this situation, Form-6 is used to register the ADRs under the Securities Act of 1933. The simplified registration procedures are available only where the issuer of the deposited shares has obtained exemption under Rule 12g3–2(a) or (b). The general eligibility requirements are:

- The ADR holder is entitled to withdraw the deposited securities at any time, subject only to the temporary delay caused by closing transfer books.
- Fees, taxes, and similar charges must be paid.
- As of the filing date, the issuer is reporting pursuant to requirements of Section 13(a) or 15(d) of the Securities Exchange Act of 1934, or the deposited shares are exempt by Rule 12g3-2(b) unless the issuer concurrently files a registration statement on another form for the deposited securities.

Under Rule 12g3-2(a), a foreign issuer is exempt from the 1934 Act reporting burden if it does not have a class of equity securities held by at least 300 persons resident in the United States. The exemption continues until the next fiscal year-end that the issuer has a class of equity securities held by 300 or more persons resident in the United States.[5] The exemption under Rule 12g3-2(a) is unlikely to be available if the ADR facility is successful. The issuer then must satisfy the reporting requirements of Section 12(g) or qualify for an exemption provided under Rule 12g3-2(b). Under Rule 12g3-2(b), a foreign issuer is granted exemption if it meets the following requirements:

- It does not have its ADRs or underlying securities listed on a U.S. exchange or quoted on Nasdaq.
- It submits to the SEC certain information that was made available to its shareholders or to foreign governmental entities.
- It provides the SEC the same information during each subsequent fiscal year.

The extent to which the foreign issuer is involved in the registration depends on whether the program is sponsored or unsponsored. Although the terms of deposit are different between these two programs, the sponsorship in and of itself does not result in different reporting or registration requirements under U.S. securities laws.

REGISTRATION OF ADRS FOR NEW SHARES

When ADRs representing newly issued shares or shares are distributed by a *statutory underwriter*,[6] the ADRs as well as the deposited shares must be registered under the Securities Act of 1933. As just discussed, Form F-6 is available only for the registration of ADRs.[7] The underlying securities must be registered on Forms F-1, F-2, or F-3, which are similar to Forms S-1, S-2, or S-3 used by domestic issuers.[8] Each "F" series form requires disclosure of the basic information regarding the issuer that is prescribed by Form 20-F under the 1934 Act. The forms differ primarily with respect to the amount of information that a foreign issuer has to include. Certain disclosure can be made through Form 20-F or other Exchange Act filings. Unless the foreign issuer has shares registered, or is otherwise reporting under the Exchange Act, Form F-1 must be used.

Form F-1 is the long form registration statement and does not allow information to be incorporated by reference to previously filed SEC reports. Form F-1 is available to all foreign issuers who have never filed reports with the SEC or are not qualified or choose not to use Form F-2 or F-3. Form F-1 is typically used for initial public offerings into the U.S. markets. To be eligible to use the short forms or the more streamlined Form F-2 or F-3 to register securities, the foreign issuer must already have been filing periodic reports with the SEC. Eligibility is also tied to the size of the issuer.

The most streamlined is Form F-3. The SEC adopted new rules in 1994 that lower the eligibility thresholds. The new requirements are a minimum global public float of $75 million and a reporting history of 12 months that includes at least one annual report on Form 20-F. There in no public float requirement for using this form to register investment-grade nonconvertible securities, qualified secondary distributions, rights offers, dividend or interest reinvestment plans, conversion of outstanding securities, or exercise of outstanding transferable warrants. Additionally, the SEC now allows foreign issuers registering securities on Form F-3 to use unallocated "shelf registration." Thus, qualified foreign issuers have the financing flexibility to register debt or equity securities on a single registration statement without having to specify the amount of each class of securities to be offered in the future.

Form F-2 may be used to register securities to be offered in transactions other than an exchange of securities with another issuer (which requires filing of Form F-4). The eligibility requirements are similar to those of Form F-3, except that the foreign issuer must have been filing Exchange Act reports for 36 months, and that all periodic reports referred to in the form must be delivered with the prospectuses. The 36-month reporting requirement is exempt if the foreign issuer has a global public float of $75 million, is a reporting company, and has filed at least one annual report with the SEC. The exemption is also available if the foreign issuer intends to offer only investment-grade or nonconvertible debt securities.

For eligible Canadian issuers, the multijurisdictional disclosure system (MJDS) applies. MJDS allows eligible Canadian companies to register securities under the Securities Act and to report under the Exchange Act by filing with the SEC documents prepared in accordance with Canadian requirements. Special registration forms, to which a Canadian prospectus is attached for filing as a single registration statement with the SEC, are available to specified Canadian issuers. Reconciliation of Canadian financial statements to the U.S. GAAP is required. However, Canadian registrants using MJDS forms may not invoke the unallocated shelf procedures available to other foreign issuers eligible to use Form F-3.

REGULATION S SAFE HARBOR

Regulation S was adopted in 1990 concurrently with Rule 144A. The intent of Regulation S is to define the registration requirements of the Securities Act of 1933 with regard to offerings made outside the United States to foreign residents. Regulation S differentiates between securities sold outside the United States, and not subject to the registration requirements, and those that are subject to the Securities Act registration requirements. There are two types of Regulation S safe harbors. One is the *issuer safe harbor*, which addresses offers and sales by issuers, their affiliates, and securities professionals involved in the initial offerings of securities. The second is the *resale safe harbor*, which addresses resales by securities professionals such as brokers. Two general conditions must be satisfied to take advantage of the issuer and resale safe harbors. The first condition is that any offer or sale must be made in an offshore transaction. The second general condition is that no direct selling efforts may be made in the United States.

For issuer safe harbor, there are three categories of securities offerings. Category 1 is the least restrictive; it encompasses securities for which there is minimum prospect of flowback (to the U.S.) because there is not much interest among U.S. investors. If the issuer is certain that U.S. market interest is unlikely to exist, the offering will qualify for safe harbor as long as the two general conditions just outlined are met.

Category 2 covers offerings of securities of both foreign and U.S. reporting issuers, offerings of debt securities, asset-backed securities, and specified preferred stock of nonreporting foreign issuers with a substantial U.S. market interest. In addition to the requirements of an offshore transaction and no U.S. direct selling efforts, Category 2 securities may not be offered or sold to or for the benefit or account of a U.S. person (resident) for a period of 40 days. Issuers and distributors further must ensure that any nondistributor to whom they sell securities is a non-U.S. person and is not purchasing for account or benefit of a U.S. person.

The most restrictive of the issuer safe harbor is Category 3. Category 3 includes any offers or sales of securities not covered in the first two categories. Distributions of equity securities by nonreporting issuers in which there is a substantial U.S. market interest is a typical type of Category 3 offerings. Additionally, there is a one-year foreign holding period requirement for equity securities.

For secondary trading under the resale safe harbor, Regulation S permits sales in an offshore transaction without any directed sales effort into the U.S. market. Such secondary transactions need only comply with the two general conditions. Securities acquired in Category 2 or Category 3 offerings may also be resold in the U.S. prior to the expiration of the holding period if the purchaser is unaffiliated with the issuer or any participant in the foreign distribution. The resale of these securities in the United States, however, would have to be registered with the SEC or qualify for an exemption.

Regulation S and Rule 144A are closely related. SEC has maintained the position that issuers may undertake private placements in the United States (Rule 144A) at the same time that they are making an offshore Regulation S offering without violating that regulation's prohibition against U.S. direct selling efforts. Substantial care must nevertheless be taken to avoid spillover of such securities into the U.S. public markets.

In recent years, the SEC has identified abusive practices in offshore Regulation S securities transactions. In an effort to address these abuses, a new SEC proposal would require Regulation S sales to be reported by the issuer on Form 10-Q. The SEC has also proposed to amend Rule 903 of Regulation S. The amendments will lengthen the restricted period to two years. This represents an increase from the current 40-day holding period applicable to reporting issuers and the one-year holding period applicable to nonreporting issuers. The SEC has also proposed to add a new Rule 905 that would classify as "restricted securities" covered equity securities placed offshore under the issuer safe harbor.

EVALUATING ADRS

Pricing usually originates in the ADR issuer's home market, with adjustment for exchange rates and transaction costs. Although various valuation models can be employed, analysis ought to include consideration for differing accounting principles, effects of currency swings, liquidity, and character of the home market.

Many foreign companies supply U.S. GAAP-adjusted information in their financial data. Though the information supplied is helpful in understanding the level of impact that differing accounting principles has on reported earnings, these adjustments should not be regarded as the company would have reported if it were a U.S. concern. Several reasons exist why these GAAP adjustments do not aid in achieving comparability with U.S. numbers. First, these numbers often are company estimates, not absolute figures. Adjustment also may carry differing tax implications that are not applicable in the U.S. In addition, managers of foreign companies plan and evaluate finances and performance within their own accounting principles, tax system, social, cultural, and political environment. They are not necessarily motivated to produce good earnings under U.S. GAAP.

ADRs are traded in dollars, hence, the translated earnings provide a point of reference. On the other hand, the level and trend of exchange rates often cloud the picture. For example, the same amounts of revenues taken in or expenses paid out in local currency could be translated into volatile dollar amounts simply due to volatility in the currency markets. Additionally, the dividend payout ratio is affected by timing. Earnings will likely be translated at some average, while dividends are paid on a specific date and translated on that date. Furthermore, in the area of emerging market ADRs, politics ranks higher than other factors when considering a stock. In emerging markets, political stability, regulation, and management are more important than GAAP accounting or disclosure.

Another important factor is liquidity, both as an ADR and as the underlying stock in its home market. The ADR market has been growing at a rapid pace, which certainly enhances liquidity. But some ADRs are not as successful. For example, Dixons Group of the United Kingdom dropped its NYSE ADR program and Svenska Cellosa of Sweden packed in its Nasdaq listing.[9] Liquidity of the underlying security is also important. In some countries (e.g., Germany and Japan), cross-holdings decrease liquidity. In such situations, the companies can be less responsive to minority shareholders and their interests. Additionally, ADR and the underlying security should be traded at "an equivalent price." At times split market pricing occurs due either to market inefficiencies or new information. This is primarily where ADR depositaries make their money, when arbs need to convert an ADR to shares or shares into ADRs.

TRADING ADRS

ADR trading involves several factors that are not common in trading domestic equities. These factors include local price, exchange rate, local commissions, local taxes, and ADR conversion fees.

An ADR is not a U.S. domestic stock in the sense that the foreign company's local political, economic and market valuations will significantly affect the local price. A trader must be keenly aware of local price and market movements, and not just to watch the U.S. market. As is clear, ADRs represent foreign stocks, and apart from being affected by the local price, they are also affected by currency fluctuations. Local commissions are another cost factor in calculating ADR price, unless the trader or dealer can deal net or without commission in the local market.

In some markets, such as the United Kingdom and Japan, local taxes are a factor when calculating an ADR price. In the United Kingdom there is a 0.5% transfer tax in case of purchases and also a 1.0% ADR tax. There are no taxes on sales. In Japan, a 0.3% tax is charged on sales and in Hong Kong there is a 0.2% transfer tax on purchases. Many other ADR-issuing countries—such as China, Taiwan, Korea, and Australia—all have local or registration taxes. Depositary banks charge the ADR conversion fees, for issuance when buying and for cancellation when selling sponsored ADRs. The charges range from 3 cents to 5 cents. If the ADR is unsponsored, then there are no issuance fees at all, only cancellation fees.

As an example, ABC stock is offered at £10.00/share in London. The cost factors when a U.S. trader is offering are listed in Table 7.4. The U.S. trader's offer price should be $34.628. If only the local price of £10.00 had been used in the calculation without

TABLE 7.4   ADR Offer and Bid Price Calculations

Offer price	
Local offer price	£10.00
0.5% transfer tax	0.05
1.0% ADR tax	0.10
0.2% local commission	0.02
TOTAL	£10.17
In U.S.$ (U.S.$/£ exchange rate 1.700)	$17.289
ADR price (ADR ratio 2:1 + ADR creation fee 5 cents)	$34.628
Bid price	
Local bid price	£9.95
–0.2% local commission	0.02
SUBTOTAL	£9.93
In U.S.$ (U.S.$/£ exchange rate 1.700)	$16.881
Bid price (ADR ratio 2:1—ADR creation fee 5 cents)	$33.712

including the transfer, local tax, and commission, then the equivalent U.S. price would have been $34.00. The costs have added $0.628 to the price. On the other hand, the bid price is $33.712. Therefore, on a mathematical basis the bid and offer are $33.712 and $34.628. In practice, however, traders would quote a narrower spread because of competition and other factors such as their own position in the stock. In the United Kingdom, if market makers can buy back the stock that they have sold to create ADRs within the UK account period, then it is possible for them to get credited with the 1% ADR tax and the 0.5% transfer tax. The possibility to mitigate these costs can be carried forward for as long as two account periods, or 28 days. The cost savings certainly can lead to a narrower spread.

SUMMARY

ADRs are an efficient vehicle for foreign issuers to access the U.S. capital markets and for U.S. investors to acquire interests in foreign companies. As the globalization of the securities markets continues, investors want to diversify their portfolio by investing in foreign stocks. At the same time foreign companies want to raise capital and gain liquidity in the U.S. capital markets. Investment banking houses are well positioned to bridge these two needs. Investment bankers must be knowledgeable about the process of listing foreign companies on Wall Street. Compliance with SEC regulation is basic to a successful underwriting and listing. Trading ADRs involves several factors that are not common in trading domestic securities, including local taxes, commission, currency fluctuations, and characteristics of the home market.

SELECT BIBLIOGRAPHY

The Bank of New York. *The Complete Depositary Receipt Directory*. New York: 1997.
Bankers Trust. *Depositary Receipt Handbook*. New York, 1997.
Brancato, C. K. *Getting Listed On Wall Street*. Burr Ridge, IL: Irwin, 1996.
Coyle, R. J., ed. *The McGraw-Hill Handbook of American Depositary Receipts*. New York: McGraw-Hill, 1995.
Darby, R. "ADRs shine again." *Investment Dealers Digest* (August 12, 1996): pp. 12–17.
Hubbard, D. J., and R. K. Larson. "American depositary receipts: Investment alternatives or quicksand?" *CPA Journal* (July 1995): pp. 70–73.
Muscarella, C. J. "Stock split: Signaling or liquidity? The case of ADR solo-splits," *Journal of Financial Economics* (September 1996): pp. 3–26.
Ogden, J. "Should all those foreign companies be listing on the NYSE?" *Global Finance* (July 1996): pp. 54–58.
Webb, S. E. "An examination of international equity markets using American Depositary Receipts." *Journal of Business Finance & Accounting* 22 (April 1995): pp. 415–430.

8

Euromarkets and European Markets

Euromarkets are global, trading around the clock in all major financial centers throughout the world. The euromarkets are attractive to both borrowers and investors because of a high degree of flexibility and anonymity. Major activities in eurobonds, floating rate notes, eurocommercial paper, and euro medium term notes are covered in the first four sections of this chapter. The subsequent sections focus on the three largest European markets. The discussion provides a roadmap on how to participate in the major exchanges in London, Paris, and Frankfurt. The European Monetary Union of 1999 effectively brings about a merger of the capital markets of the member states. The implications for the equity markets, bond markets, and settlement challenges are examined as well.

OVERVIEW OF EUROMARKETS

After World War II the U.S. dollar replaced sterling as the main trading currency. Communist countries held large reserves of U.S. dollars, mostly at U.S. banks, to support their international transactions. Later, because of the cold war and concern over possible U.S. seizure of their U.S. deposits, they transferred deposits to banks in Europe.[1] These were the first eurodollars. The lifting of foreign exchange restrictions in Western Europe, which permitted multinational corporations to shift to the currency of lower interest, also helped create an environment for the development of euromarkets. In the United States, Interest Equalization Tax (1963) and banking regulations such as reserve requirements, deposit insurance, and legal lending limit forced the dollar-denominated business out to the newly developing eurodollar market. The first eurodollar bond was issued in 1963.

The explosive growth of euromarkets began in the late 1970s. The change in U.S. monetary policy, coupled with spiraling inflation, caused interest rates to skyrocket. Investors began to take money out of the U.S. banks, limited by interest-rate ceilings, and deposit in foreign banks. Other new sources of funds—oil surpluses of OPEC countries and new wealth from emerging countries—poured into the euromarkets. Blue-chip multinationals were increasingly tapping into the euromarkets for floating rate loans.

The introduction of International Banking Facilities (IBFs) in the United States in 1981 created a euromarket in the United States. Furthermore, the growth is also, in part, attributable to the success of currency swaps. A significant proportion of funds raised through the sale of Euro issues is swapped into other currencies. And the improvement in clearing operations provided the necessary infrastructure for the explosive growth. Without the electronic clearing systems such as Euroclear and Cedel, it is impossible for the market to grow. Physical delivery of the bearer certificates is inefficient and risky. In order to receive the annual interests and the final capital redemption, coupons must be cut from the certificates and sent to the issuer's agent.

The euromarkets have become a global financial market, trading around the clock in all major financial centers throughout the world. Trading in Euro issues spread from London to other European centers and later to financial centers throughout the world. Major euromarket centers include London, New York, Paris, Brussels, Frankfurt, Luxembourg, Tokyo, Hong Kong, and Singapore. The five major currencies in Euro issues are the U.S. dollar, Japanese yen, German deutschemark, British pound sterling, and French franc. The impressive growth is expected to continue in the largely unregulated euromarkets, in which borrowers could raise funds in almost any currency and swap to the desired currency and the desired form of interest liabilities.

EUROBONDS

Eurobonds are denominated in a currency different from the currency of the country in which they are issued. Corporate or sovereign borrowers, on an internationally accepted market, issue eurobonds. In addition to those paying fixed-rate coupons (*Euro straights*) with a stated redemption date, there are alternative types of eurobonds, such as floating-rate coupons, convertible bonds, and zero coupon bonds. Fixed-rate eurobonds typically pay interest only once a year on a basis of 360/360. That is, it is assumed that each year has only 360 days and each month has 30 days. The interest payments are without the deduction of any withholding tax. Eurobonds are generally not registered with any particular regulatory agency. However, they might be listed in London or Luxembourg or other exchanges. Listing is mainly to circumvent restrictions imposed on some institutional investors that are prohibited from purchasing nonlisted securities. Most eurobond trading is in the OTC market. Table 8.1 lists the major features of eurobonds.

A key driving force behind the eurobond market is that, by selling outside of the country of origin, the issuer can often escape local regulation and securities laws. For companies in the United States, eurobond issues are not subject to SEC registration and disclosure requirements. In addition, the eurobond market is largely a name market. Only the most creditworthy borrowers can issue securities. Another advantage is that they are bearer bonds; the ownership of the bonds is not recorded. As such, eurobonds are effectively tax-free. The bonds are cleared through Euroclear and Cedel.

Because fixed-rate straight bonds pay interest annually, instead of semiannually, investors should expect a higher yield. The calculation of an equivalent yield on a eurobond that would be necessary to equal the yield of a U.S. semiannual coupon bond is

$$y = r(1 + r/4),$$

TABLE 8.1 Major Features of Eurobonds

Issuer	Top-quality borrowers
Currency	Any widely used international currency
Average issuing size	U.S. $50 million to $500 million
Type	Bearer
Regulation	Not subject to regulation of any sovereign governments
Tax	No withholding tax
Interest payments	Annual for fixed rates, semiannual or quarterly for FRNs
Listing	London or Luxembourg
Security covenants	Unsecured
Investors	Institutional and individual
Structure	Bullets are common
Issuing procedures	Placed through an international syndicate
Trading	OTC, spreads vary among currencies
Settlement	Book-entry via one of euromarket clearing systems, Euroclear and Cedel

where y is the annual equivalent yield and r is the yield for semiannual coupon bonds. As an example, to be equivalent to a U.S. bond with 8% yield, a eurobond would have to yield 8.16%.

Conversely, an adjustment is required to make the U.S. bond yield comparable to the eurobond yield. Given the eurobond yields, its equivalent yield on a semiannual coupon bond is calculated as follows:

$$r = 2\left[(1+y)^{1/2} - 1\right].$$

For example, suppose a eurobond yields 10%. Then the U.S. bond equivalent yield is 9.76%.

The volume of issuance has increased to $735 billion in 1997 from $276 billion in 1992. From 1993 to 1995, eurobonds supply remained relatively flat in the $368 to $394 billion ranges. The five major currencies (U.S. dollar, deutschemark, sterling, French franc, and yen) represent 80% or more of the total issuance from 1992 to 1997. Among the top five currencies, the U.S. dollar is the most widely used. During the period 1992–1995, the U.S.-pay averaged at close to 40% of the total supply each year. The average surged to 45% and 49% in the following two years. Table 8.2 lists the detailed annual volume (1992–1997) by currency.

Innovations in the Eurobond Markets

A significant volume of Eurobonds in the past has been issued with attached warrants. A popular type is *debt warrant*, which allows holders to purchase additional debt at a fixed price. These warrants are basically interest-rate call options, and are attractive in a perceived trend of downward rate movements. A typical debt warrant issue allows holders to purchase additional bonds with the same maturity bearing a lower coupon rate (than the host bonds). There are also bonds issued with attached currency warrants or commodity (gold and oil) warrants. A *currency warrant* permits the holder to exchange one currency for another at a predetermined rate, and hence, it protects the

TABLE 8.2   Euro Issues by Currency ($ billion)

Currency	1992	1993	1994	1995	1996	1997
U.S. dollar	103.2	147.7	149.4	144.4	268.7	361.7
German deutsche mark	33.8	54.7	31.6	72.7	100.1	130.2
British pound sterling	23.3	42.7	30.4	21.6	51.8	68.6
French franc	24.3	39.9	27.4	12.7	46.1	49.8
Japanese yen	33.7	44.4	67.3	64.5	41.2	28.4
Subtotal	218.3	329.4	306.1	315.9	507.9	638.7
(% of total)	(79%)	(83%)	(83%)	(85%)	(86%)	(87%)
U.S. dollar as % of total	37%	37%	40%	39%	45%	49%
Total of All Euro Issues	276.1	394.6	368.4	371.3	589.8	735.1

Source: Adapted from OECD. *Financial Market Trends.* June 1997 and February 1998.

bondholder against a depreciation of the currency in which the cash flows are denominated. Similarly, a *commodity warrant* allows the warrant holder to purchase the commodity from the issuer at the specified price.

Another type is convertible eurobonds. U.S. and Japanese companies have issued the majority of these bonds. They generally pay a fixed rate but may, at the option of the holder under certain conditions, be converted to shares of common stock. Or they may be converted from one currency of denomination to another.

Dual-currency bonds pay interest in one currency and the bonds are redeemed in another currency. They resemble a portfolio of annuity (periodic coupons) and a zero coupon bond (face amount at maturity) in two different currencies. The exchange rate may be specified at the time the bond is issued or is the prevailing market rate at the time a cash flow is made. The zero-coupon eurobond (called *streaker bond*) was introduced in the early 1980s. The advantage of a streaker bond is that the yield is guaranteed if held to maturity, since there is no reinvestment risk. Another innovation is the global bond, which is a hybrid between a eurobond and a foreign bond. The World Bank pioneered the global in September 1989. The 10-year notes ($1.5 billion issue) were placed in the U.S. and other markets simultaneously. Pricing was based on market yield in the U.S., but the distribution is broader.

The Primary Markets

In the eurobond market, there are no requirements for filing an issue with any regulatory agencies, except for listing requirements of London and Luxembourg. In earlier years, issues were frequently "mandated" to a lead manager who would form a syndicate to distribute the issue. Today, most issues are bought deals. The underwriter offering the best all-in cost in the desired currency buys the issue from the borrower. The lead manager should be keeping constant dialogue with trading and sales staff to be on top of where the comparable issues are trading in the secondary market and to have a feel of investor demand.

Recently, most of the major eurobond issues are under fixed price re-offer. When bonds are in syndication, they can only be offered at the fixed price set by the lead manager. This prevents syndicate members from selling their allotments at a lower price. Thus, the price is fixed during the offering period, until the lead manager disbands the syndicate formed for the issue. Under the fixed-price approach, total fees are generally smaller and there are fewer houses in the syndicate. The period during which the deal is in syndication is very short, as short as one hour is not impossible. Pricing is typically in relation to comparable government securities.

When an underwriter is asked to bid on a new issue, the choices are bid to miss, bid to win, or refuse to bid. If the underwriter is not comfortable with the market, it might bid to miss or decline to bid. In a bid to win situation, the strategy is to win by the narrowest margin possible. In order to win, an underwriter has to come up with a rate to the issuer below competitors. There are several ways to search for attractive terms. First, often an underwriter will scour investors in different time zones who might purchase the bonds at a yield that offers a low cost of funds to the company. Second, the underwriter may find a way to create a synthetic dollar bond using swaps to obtain a lower cost of funding. Finally, the underwriter could decide to bid for the bond at an aggressive rate, because it predicts a bull market environment or simply needs to drum up volume to climb up on the league tables. The Street does attach enormous importance to league tables.

Once syndication has begun and terms are known, the issue generally will appear in the *gray market*. This is an informal electronic quotation service provided by *Reuters* and *Bloomberg* and other networks to the market. All market participants stay tuned to the gray market pages to keep abreast of market development. If the issue is tightly priced and other syndicate members are unable to locate buyers for the issue, they might go to bond brokers to arrange a sale of the bonds in the gray market. The lead manager is likely to purchase much of the bonds if it decides to stabilize the market. Such risk from stabilization purchases can be hedged by shorting governments or other similar bonds. If the cost of financing the bond inventory is less than the coupon yield (a positive carry), some dealers are willing to carry the unsold bonds for some time or until the market improves. Sometimes they have to take a loss.

The gross spread or commissions in the 1980s averaged at $1^3/_8$% for a 3-year, $1^5/_8$% for a 5-year, $1^7/_8$% for a 7-year, and 2% for a 10-year. The current market is quite different. Total commissions for AAA-rated borrowers are generally $1/_8$% for a 2-year deal, $3/_{16}$% for a 3-year, $1/_4$% for a 5-year bond, 30 basis points for a 7-year, and 32.5 basis points for a 10-year maturity. It is worth noting that many deals are awarded based on all-in cost, including commissions.

FLOATING RATE NOTES

Floating rate notes (FRNs) are simply eurobonds with a variable rate coupon. As the coupon reset ensures that the FRNs pay returns in line with the market interest rate, the market value is typically close to the issue price before coupon reset and is at par at reset. The most significant variations that may occur are due to the unanticipated changes in the creditworthiness of the issuer or the guarantor. Interest rate cycles have a lesser effect. In times of falling interest rates, investors tend to turn to fixed coupon bonds to secure their yields, whereas issuers prefer FRNs as they do not want to be locked into high financing costs. The reverse situation applies in times of rising interest rates. However, the impact is not significant as institutional investors are able to participate in the swap market and banks can balance FRNs against short-term deposits or loans.

Coupon Reset

The rate on a FRN is generally quoted as a margin over or under a specific benchmark rate. The coupon is reset semiannually or quarterly, commonly based on LIBOR plus a margin reflective of issuer's credit. Less commonly used benchmarks are LIBID (London InterBank bid), which is the rate London banks offer to borrow from each other, and LIMEAN, which is the midpoint between LIBOR and LIBID. The majority of issues carry a margin over LIBOR, while a few of very high-quality issues may carry a margin below.

Hybrid FRNs

Perpetual (undated) FRNs have no fixed maturity date, and can be treated as tier-1 capital for compliance with international banking regulation. U.K., Canadian, and U.S. banks issued large volumes of perpetual FRNs in 1985 and 1986. But soon investors became concerned about the financial soundness of the banking sector, and they sold large amounts back to market makers. Since then there is no significant investor interest.

Another innovative structure is the *collared floater*, which is a floating rate debt with a cap and a floor on its interest rate. The coupon may float within the range. In order to attract investors, the minimum coupon often is set higher than the prevailing rates at that time. If market interest rates soar above the maximum rate, the market value will fall. Conversely, the market value will appreciate when interest rates plummet.

Some issues give the purchasers the right to convert the floating coupon into a fixed rate at some future date. If the FRNs carry an automatic conversion feature under certain circumstances, they are called *drop-lock bonds*.

Trading and Settlement

Floating rate notes are traded at a clean price, to which any accrued interest since last coupon date until settlement date must be added. The accrued interest is calculated actual/360. There is one exception, though; the EuroSterling bonds use the actual/365 unless trading a new issue, in which settlement is on a specific date. Settlement in the secondary market is typically T+7, usually via Euroclear or Cedel.

The yield of a euro FRN is quoted in terms of its spread (discount margin) in relation to a chosen benchmark such as LIBOR. Pricing an FRN involves discounting all future "unknown" cash flows back to their present value. Since the future coupons are resent periodically and unknown before the reset, the calculation requires a certain explicit forecast of the future path of the interest rate. Specifically, to apply the bond equation to an FRN, the trader must forecast the value of the reference benchmark on each of the remaining reset dates. Assume that all coupons after the next one occur at equal intervals during a 365.25-day year.[2] The clean price of an FRN is calculated as

$$P = d_{sn} \left[\sum_{n=1}^{N-1} d^n C_n + R d^{N-1} \right] - AI \, ,$$

where

d_{sn} = the discount factor from settlement to next coupon date,
d = discount factor for future cash flows,
C_n = coupon at n,
R = redemption value,
N = total number of future coupons,
AI = accrued interest.

EUROCOMMERCIAL PAPER AND EURO-MTN

Eurocommercial paper (Euro-CP) and euro medium-term notes (Euro-MTN) represent a significant sector in the eurocapital markets. Euro-CP is a short-term bearer, unsecured zero coupon security with maturity in the range of 7 to 365 days. Euro-MTN issues offer tranches tailored to investor requirements. Euro-MTNs started in 1985 and have become the predominant way of issuing international debt in recent years.

Euro-CPs

Major development of the Euro-CP market occurred after the early 1980s. Initially, only private corporations with the highest credit ratings issued Euro-CP. The high-grade Euro-CPs offered a higher rate than Euro CDs. The Euro CDs often returned investors only LIBID less $1/4$% while Euro-CPs offered 10 to 15 basis points more. If investors were prepared to accept a lower grade paper, they could look for an even higher yield. Unrated paper required up to 10 basis points higher than lower rated. After several defaults in 1989 to 1990, ratings became increasingly important. The increase in overall activity is strong. The volume each year over the period 1992 to 1997 is $28.9 billion, $38.4 billion, $30.8 billion, $55.9 billion $81.3 billion, and $48.5 billion, respectively.

The market has been successful in providing cheaper funds to borrowers and filling a need by international investors for a spectrum of bearer money market paper that was free of withholding taxes. The spectrum gradually expanded to include lesser-quality names.

The expansion of the Euro-CP market threatened the wholesale bank's business of providing short-term credit to major industrial and government borrowers. Hence, banks introduced *note issuance facilities* (NIFs), in which the corporate customer had the choice of drawing down a loan at an agreed formula based on LIBOR or selling Euro-CP through banks. In NIFs, borrowers retain all benefits of an Euro-CP program and secure a committed bank facility. As an example, a borrower enters into an agreement with a bank for $300 million revolving credit facility for 7 years. The lead bank syndicates the credit facility with other banks. Funds can be drawn and repaid any time without penalty. The borrower also obtains a rating for its Euro-CP. The issuer could issue the Euro-CP to the syndicate at the rate the dealer group offers for distribution to investors. If the CP market is not attractive, the banks are ready to make the loan. Thus, for a modest fee, the borrower can have the lower rates of the Euro-CP market and the guaranteed assurance that funds will be available. Most NIFs have tender panels, in which a group of banks and dealers bid for the Euro-CP at an auction when the paper is issued or renewed.

Another approach is through the *revolving underwriting facilities* (RUFs). An RUF is similar to a NIF, except for NIF's use of a designated placement agent(s) to distribute the paper. Members of the tender panel and the placement agents can bid whatever rate they want, so their role is largely best efforts. But the borrower can replace them if their participation is not satisfactory. The aim is to obtain competitive money market rates by way of aggressive bidding. A well-known issuer may be able to obtain bids at LIMEAN or lower, thus saving 20 or 30 basis points over bank loans. If the fees for the facility are no more than the cost savings, the issuer comes out ahead.

Euro-MTN

The continuous evolution was to the Euro-MTN market. There was no Euro-MTN market before 1985. By 1996, the Euro-MTN has passed over $500 billion in outstandings. Annual supply has steadily increased from $99.0 billion to $113.6 billion to $222.1 billion to $346.1 billion and to $375 billion from 1992 to 1996. An emerging area in the Euro-MTN market is programs set up to repackage securities, mostly by special-purpose vehicles arranged by investment banks. A partial list of major borrowers includes the World Bank, Kingdom of Sweden, GE, Fannie Mae, Ford, Toyota, and Citicorp. Top arrangers are Merrill Lynch, Morgan Stanley Dean Witter, Lehman Brothers, Goldman Sachs, Citicorp, Salomon Smith Barney, J.P. Morgan, Credit Suisse, and Deutsche Bank.

The success of the market is attributable to three basic reasons: cost, speed, and flexibility. The costs of setting up an MTN program and issuing debt off it are falling over time. In 1996, the upfront costs of a Euro-MTN were at about $131,500, compared with a total cost of $100,000 for a stand-alone eurobond. Issuers thus benefit from continuous offerings. The programs save on documentation as well. The convergence of different instruments under one single form of documentation is a major trend in the MTN market, thanks to the ever-decreasing costs of documentation and increasing liberalization. Pricing supplements for vanilla MTN deals are typically two pages only. In addition, the modern MTN market gives issuers tremendous flexibility and variety of issues that may be done with the same documentation. The programs could be structured as pre-placed, nonsyndicated tranches tailored to specific requirements of institutional investors, as well as public, syndicated issuance.

The MTN provides more options, such as subordinated and perpetual debt and an increasing range of currencies. In 1991, MTN tranches were issued in eight currencies. By 1997, the market had seen more than 30 currencies.

Recently, the Euro-MTN market has become the predominant way of issuing international debt. The short maturities are cutting into the traditional commercial paper domain. In terms of documentation, there may be no difference between a eurobond and a Euro-MTN. Increased transparency and dealer rivalry have greatly improved the competitiveness of secondary trading. Investors are as comfortable with syndicated Euro-MTNs as they are with stand-alone eurobonds.

The market received a big boost by the introduction of the issuing and paying agencies (IPAs) that include Bankers Trust, J.P. Morgan, Citibank, and Chase Manhattan. The technological innovation enables the IPAs to send right information to different players in each MTN transaction: issuers, investors, dealers, swap counterparties, the stock exchange, clearing house, and central bank. In addition, a new system, Capital Net, developed by Euromoney Publications and Computasoft, provides capabilities for issuers to post rates to dealers, receive reverse inquiries and discuss terms on-line.

EUROPEAN MARKETS

The major exchanges in the 15 EU Member States are Amsterdam, Athens, Brussels, Copenhagen, Dublin, Frankfurt, Helsinki, Lisbon, London, Luxembourg, Madrid, Milan, Paris, Stockholm, and Vienna. These exchanges are mostly segmented. In 1997, though, a European network of stock exchanges (EURO.NM) aimed at young companies with high growth potential was launched. The EURO.NM currently includes Le Nouveau Marché in France, Euro.NM Belgium, Amsterdam's Nieuwe Market, and Germany's Neuer Market.

Before the mid-1980s, these markets were mostly operated under call auction markets and commissions were fixed. The European markets have undergone substantial reforms since the mid-1980s. The following discussion provides a brief review of the recent development in London, Paris, and Frankfurt. The section discusses the recent formation of EURO.NM as well. A detailed description of each of the three largest exchanges in Europe follows in the next three sections.

Development

The London Stock Exchange (LSE) was the first to launch the *Big Bang* reforms in October 1986. Major changes include lifting the separation of jobbers and brokers, extending dealership to banks and other financial institutions, deregulating commissions, and introducing SEAQ.[3] These changes were extended to the London market for non-UK stocks through SEAQ International (SEAQ-I). In addition, the stamp duty on UK equity trades was cut in half and no such duty was levied on non-UK equity trades. In September 1995, several former LSE executives launched a proprietary trading system, *Tradepoint*, that allows institutional investors and broker–dealers to trade directly and anonymously.

In response to London's Big Bang, Paris Stock Exchange (SBF-Paris Bourse) implemented several reforms. First, Paris replaced the old system of open outcry call auctions with a continuous electronic auction called *Contation Assistée en Continu* (CAC). The CAC system was extended to six regional exchanges in 1991. For liquid stocks, the call auction is used at open and close only. The second major step was taken in 1988 to substitute the old publicly appointed brokers (*agents de change*) with new corporate broker–dealer intermediaries (*sociétés de bourse*). The change is aimed at enhancing market liquidity by attracting better-capitalized intermediaries. Furthermore, fixed commissions became a term of the past in July 1989. The stamp duty caps at FFr 4,000 beginning in July 1993 and nonresidents were exempt from such duty beginning January 1994. Later in September 1994, Paris instituted new block-trading rules, which permit trading of French equities off the central trading system.

Germany lacks an equity culture. The market capitalization is far behind the United Kingdom, and trading activities cluster at several big name stocks such as Deutsche Bank, Daimler-Benz, and Siemens. The equity market development has been hindered by the role of large universal banks in providing corporate funding and by the cross-holding structure. Frankfurt is the largest exchange. Exchange-floor trading is similar to that in the United States. Every stock is assigned to one specialist (*Kursmakler*), who runs the limit book and receives a commission. An electronic trading system, *Integrirtes Börsenhandels-und Informationssystem* (IBIS), was adopted in 1991. In May 1995, *Deutsche Börse* announced its plan to develop an improved trading system for both stocks and bonds, supplemented with three daily call auctions. The new system, Xetra, was introduced in several releases beginning in June 1997.

The settlement cycles are T+5, T+3, and T+2 in the United Kingdom, France, and Germany. This poses significant problems for cross-border trading. A trader selling in Paris and buying in Frankfurt would have to borrow funds for one day to cover for the one-day difference in settlement.

EURO.NM

The establishment of stock markets specifically for innovative high-growth companies is spreading over Europe. NMAX in Amsterdam, EURO.NM Belgium in Brussels, Neuer Market in Frankfurt, and Le Noveau Marché in Paris have joined forces to create EURO.NM to set up and promote a European-wide network of markets for fast-growing companies. The four core members were all established recently:

- Le Nouveau Marché was established on February 14, 1996. Trading began a week later on March 20.
- The Nieuwe Market in Amsterdam was established on February 20, 1997. The first listing company came on board in April 1997.
- Frankfurt's Neuer Market began operation on March 10, 1997.
- EURO.NM Belgium had its first listing in April 1997.

EURO.NM members have signed a *Markets Harmonization Agreement* that establishes rules and standards of the network. The common rules for listing, membership, and market are specified. Listing applications are submitted to the listing exchange. The exchange approves the application based on the prospectus, as well as a minimum commitment of the listing advisor/market makers of one year. Once listed, companies are required to publish quarterly reports. Management must retain 80% of their shares for a minimum of six months. Participants and trading must be in compliance with the European Investment Services Directives (ISD).

Call Auctions

Periodic call auctions have been used in securities trading in Europe and Japan. In a call market, orders are collected for execution at predetermined points in time. A clearing price is determined to maximize the trading volume. All buy orders at or higher than this level and all sell orders at or lower than this price get executed at the clearing price. A market order is in essence an order to trade at whatever the clearing price is. A limit order is generally not executed at the specified price, but it only specifies conditions under which the order will execute at the call. This is in contrast to a continuous trading system, in which a limit order, if executed, is generally executed at the specified price.

The call auction process can be illustrated with an example. Assume that before the next call time, there are seven limit buy orders and seven limit sell orders, as listed in Table 8.3. These orders are held until call. A clearing price is determined at the next call to maximize the number of shares traded; at $25, in this example. Limit orders to buy 100 shares each at $25, $26, and $27 and limit orders to sell at $23, $24, and $25 are all filled at $25. There are 300 shares changing hands.

TABLE 8.3 Buy and Sell Orders at a Call

Price	Limit Buy Order	Limit Sell Order
29		100 shares
28		100 shares
27	100 shares	100 shares
26	100 shares	100 shares
25	100 shares	100 shares
24	100 shares	100 shares
23	100 shares	100 shares
22	100 shares	
21	100 shares	

LONDON STOCK EXCHANGE

The LSE is one of the world's top three stock exchanges. London is regarded as the most international of the world's great financial centers. More international companies choose to list in London than in any other exchange. Plus, a third of the world's institutional equity holdings are managed in Europe, and London provides access to the largest pool of institutional equity capital in the world.

At yearend 1996, there were 2,171 UK companies with market capitalization of £1.011 trillion and 533 international companies with a capitalization of £2.258 trillion listed on the LSE. As is clear, the average capitalization for international firms (£4.7 billion) is much higher than UK companies (£157 million). There were 299 member firms. UK securities are quoted on SEAQ or SEATS. Trading hours are from 8:30 A.M. to 4:30 P.M. The standard settlement is T+5. A new settlement system CREST was introduced in July 1996, which is capable of providing a three-day settlement.

IPO and LSE Listing

In the United Kingdom, there are various methods of flotation, including *public offers, placings*, and *introductions*. A public offer is typically underwritten by the company's sponsor. The shares offered may be new shares issued for cash or existing shares held by current shareholders. Shares normally are offered at a fixed price,[4] determined immediately before the offer period. The second method is through a placing, in which the company's sponsor and brokers sell the shares to their own clients. Placings are geared for smaller companies, and are the most frequently used method of making an initial public offering. Finally, in an introduction, shares are "introduced" to the market. There is no money raised. The LSE permits this approach only if the company's shares are already widely held.

The key members of the flotation include the company's management and board of directors, the sponsor, the corporate broker, the accountant, the solicitors, and other advisors. The success of the flotation critically depends on the company's ability to assemble and appoint high caliber professional advisors.

The sponsor's role is vital both at the time of the flotation and during the period leading up to it. The sponsor may be a merchant bank, stockbroker, or a professional advisor. The sponsor's key responsibilities include:

- Assessing the suitability for a public offering
- Advising the company and ensuring that its board of directors is of a structure and caliber suitable for a listed company
- Advising on the method of flotation
- Planning the flotation process and coordinating the activities of other professional advisors
- Helping prepare the company for the offering and drafting the prospectus
- Pricing and underwriting the issue

The corporate broker advises on market conditions and the potential demand. The corporate broker represents the company to private and institutional investors. In addition, a main responsibility of the broker is to act as the principal point of contact between the company, its advisors, and the LSE. The broker is frequently asked to give advice on compliance with Listing Rules (known as the Yellow Book). When required, the broker will organize subunderwriting and placing agreements with institutions.

The reporting accountant's main function is to prepare a "long form" report. The long form report is a detailed financial and business analysis of the company, its financial status, financing, and forecasts. Solicitors are primarily concerned with ensuring that all legal requirements are complied with, both in readiness for flotation and in information disclosure in prospectus. Specific responsibilities also cover:

- Amendments to articles of incorporation and director's service contracts
- Agreements between the company, shareholders, and the sponsor; including the underwriting agreement
- Employee stock options programs

Other members of the flotation team may include public relations advisors, registrars, financial printers, and receiving bankers (to handle share applications).

Assembling the flotation team is part of the process. The complete process of preparing the company for a public flotation may take up to two years, though it may take just six months from the preparation of the accountant's report to the commencement of dealings on the LSE. An illustrative timetable for the process provided by the LSE is included in Table 8.4. The *impact day* is the day when details of the new issue are published and when the underwriting or placing agreements become effective.

The total costs of an offering depend on a variety of factors. The average is roughly at 4% to 8% of the total sale proceeds, while the percentage may rise for small offers. The expenses for obtaining a listing are determined by the size of the company, the marketing involved and the method of admission. According to the LSE, for a market capitalization of between £20 million and £100 million the fee would be between £6,500 and £22,500, and for a market capitalization of between £100 million and £500 million it would be between £22,500 and £62,500.

An international company can apply for a listing on the LSE, irrespective of whether it already has one on its domestic exchange. International companies not already listed may apply for a primary listing, and companies listed on another exchange may apply for a secondary listing. The general requirements for listing are:

- Represented by an approved sponsor
- A three-year trading record, except for scientific research based companies and those undertaking major capital projects

TABLE 8.4   The Flotation Process

12–24 weeks before admission	Appoint advisors; prepare detailed instructions to advisors, detailed timetable, and documents list.
6–12 weeks before admission	Produce short form report in draft, draft prospectus and derogation letter; submit other documents in first draft, initial review of pricing issues to the LSE, review PR presentations.
1–6 weeks before admission	Draft meetings on prospectus; review cash flow and profit forecast; verify legal documents; hold PR meetings; formally submit and agree all documents and derogation with LSE; appoint registrars.
Admission week	Complete all documents; get LSE approval; hold completion and pricing meeting; register prospectus; make investment presentations; apply for listing; sign underwriting agreement.
Impact day	Advise availability of prospectus and announce flotation; press/analysts briefing; complete sub-underwriting.
1 week after impact day	Get listing granted; close application lists; receive applications and cash.
2 weeks after impact day	Announce basis of allotment; when listing becomes effective, begin dealing in new shares.

Source: Adapted from London Stock Exchange, 1997.

- A market capitalization of at least £700,000
- At least 25% of its shares in public hands
- A prospectus that complies with LSE's listing rules

The international equities are traded on SEAQ-I. There are currently about 50 registered international market makers in more than 1,000 securities from 36 countries. Share prices are typically quoted in the home currency and transactions are settled through the home market or one of the global clearing systems.

In August 1994, the LSE adopted rules to list depositary receipts (DRs). According to the LSE, the DRs are often issued by companies where their exchanges are lesser known or not as accessible to foreign investors. Companies from nations such as Argentina, Brazil, Hungary, India, Poland, South Africa, South Korea, and Taiwan have their DRs listed on the LSE. The LSE does not operate a system for settlement of DRs. This is organized by the company's advisors and the depository.

The LSE also lists gilts, eurobonds, warrants, and options. There are 25 firms registered as gilt-edged market makers. Around one-third of eurobonds are listed on the LSE. London's eurobonds listing rules are based on EU listing directives that apply in all member states. London offers a number of benefits as a listing center for eurobonds. The listing charges are competitive, in the range of £1,000 to £4,000, payable initially. There is no annual charge. In addition, more than 75% of eurobonds are executed by dealers based in London. The general listing requirements are:[5]

- The issuer must present a three-year record of business.
- The issuer must prepare a listing document complying with the listing rules.
- The securities must be freely transferable.
- The market capitalization must be at least £200,000.
- The application for listing must relate to all securities of that class, issued or proposed to be issued.

- Convertible securities may be admitted only if the securities into which they are convertible are or will become listed in London or another market.

New Development

The Stock Exchange Electronic Trading Service (SETS) came live on October 20, 1997. SETS is an electronic order book that provides fully automated trading capabilities. For FTSE 100 stocks, SETS will replace SEAQ. The SETS trading will be extended to the next 250 companies in the near future. Shares that fall out of the FTSE 100 will continue to be traded on the order book. Investors will be able to place orders on to the order book through a member firm. These orders will be displaced on screen via a central electronic system and will be executed with matching orders.

Investors will be able to deal via brokers directly on to the order book for large trades or through a *Retail Service Provider* for smaller trades. For super large trades, a special regime will provide the flexibility of negotiating around the order book but transacting on the exchange.

Another significant step is LSE's announcement of a lower pricing structure on September 9, 1997. The new prices took effect on October 20, 1997. For trading outside of SETS, the maximum charge is reduced from £10 to £2.35 while the minimum stamp duty remains at 2.5 basis points. For trading on the new order book, charges are cut to 0.6 basis points from the previous 15 basis points, with a cap of £10 per trade.

Alternative Investment Market (AIM)

AIM was launched in June 1995. AIM is LSE's section for young and fast-growing companies. As of September 16, 1997, AIM had 260 listed companies, including 18 from overseas. According to the data published by the LSE, 80% of AIM companies have a market capitalization of less than £30 million. Many companies raised amounts in the range of £1 million to £10 million.

AIM places no restrictions on the listing company regarding the size of the company, the length of operating record, or the percentage of shares in public hands. AIM does require companies to provide an admission document, similar to a prospectus. A listing company must appoint an LSE-approved nominated advisor and a nominated broker. The nominated advisor helps the company comply with AIM rules, particularly timely disclosure of information to investors. The nominated broker must be a member of the exchange. In the absence of a market maker, the advisor provides a means for investors to trade.

SBF–PARIS BOURSE

The Paris Stock Exchange (SBF–Paris Bourse) is a fully computerized stock market. The trading system *Supercac* came on line in April 1995. It is an automated system linked to member firms and other intermediaries collecting client orders, and to France's computerized DVP settlement system *Relit*. Paris Bourse acts as a clearinghouse for trades between member firms.

There are the Official List (Premier Marché) and the Second Market (Second Marché). In the main market, there are two types of listing: monthly settlement market and cash. At yearend 1997 the monthly settlement market listed 174 French companies and 78 foreign firms, while the cash section listed 202 French corporations and 100 foreign firms. The second market listed 307 stocks, of which 1 was foreign. There were 1,842 French bonds and 1,345 foreign bonds under cash at the Official List.

The application to listing on the Primier Marché or the Second Marché must be submitted to SBF-Paris Bourse by the issuer, in collaboration with its sponsor. For equities, all listed shares must have the same rights. Listing on the Primier Marché requires that the company submit three years of financial statements, and that the public must hold at least 25% of shares no later than the first day of trading. The requirements for listing on the Second Marché are two years of audited financial statements and 10% public holdings. For admission to listing debt securities, the SBF-Paris Bourse requires two years of audited financial statements. In addition, SBF-Paris Bourse may require a rating for the issue and the issuance of guarantee for principal and interest. SBF-Paris Bourse also verifies that the issue ensures a liquid market.

Admission to listing is announced in an official *Avis*, describing the procedures for placing and initial trading of the admitted securities. The placing of securities immediately preceding their initial trading can be done through a complete or partial underwriting. The lead manager shall provide the SBF–Paris Bourse with a statement detailing the results of the placing. The SBF–Paris Bourse may allow a placing in part through a fixed price offer.

The initial trading is effected through one of the three procedures: *direct trading, minimum-price tender,* and *fixed-price offer.* The direct trading procedure is carried out under the standard conditions of trading. The direct trading may allow a stated number of securities offered through a bought deal on behalf of the selling shareholders or of the underwriters. In a minimum-price tender, the SBF-Paris Bourse collects all buy orders sent in by members. The initial fixing price is the limit set on the last order filled. There is only one price on the first day of trading. Under a fixed-price tender procedure, only orders placed at the offer price are accepted. If the conditions of the offer are met, the price quoted is the offer price.

Trading is conducted on the NSC-Supercac trading system. The system has been successful in Paris, and has been acquired by exchanges in Brussels, Toronto, Sao Paolo, Warsaw, Chicago, and other locations. Also, Paris Bourse and MATIF SA will adopt the *Clearing 21* clearing system, which was jointly developed by CME and NYMEX. The systems were expected to be up and running in all three markets by the second half of 1998. Using the Clearing 21 system will enable Paris Bourse, MATIF (France's futures market) and MONEP (options trading) to reduce margin calls and reduce costs for member firms. The combination of NSC-Supercac and Clearing 21 will become an unchallenged standard and open new horizons for harmonization of trading systems in the global marketplace.

SBF–Paris Bourse is a clearinghouse. It clears and guarantees final settlement of trades on the exchange. Delivery and payment between clearing members are made in respect of the net cash and securities position of each member at the end of each business day. Instructions for delivery and payment of these net positions are submitted to the delivery and payment bodies selected by SBF–Paris Bourse. Alternatively, delivery and payment between clearing members and order collectors are based on the procedures defined by SICOVAM if the security is admitted to it.[6] In the case of securities not admitted to SICOVAM, delivery and payment shall conform to procedures defined by SBF-Paris Bourse.

Le Nouveau Marché

There is another exchange for young and smaller companies, Le Nouveau Marché. The listing requirements are less stringent than the Paris Bourse Official List or the Second Market. There are no requirements to offer 25% equity (as there is on the Official List or 10% on the Second Market), or to provide audited financial statements. The Official List requires three years of such statements and the Second Market requires two years. The listing requirements at Le Nouveau Marché are:

- Equity must be FFr 8 million.
- 100,000 shares must be offered.
- Float must be FFr 10 million.
- For companies that have been in business for less than two years, listing must be for raising additional capital.
- Founders, managers and individuals who acquired ownership in the preceding 12 months must agree to retain 80% of their ownership for 3 years (100% for first 2 years and then 80% in the third year for companies that have been in business for less than 2 years).

FRANKFURTER WERTPAPIERBÖRSE

The Frankfurt Stock Exchange[7] (Frankfurter Wertpapierbörse, FWB) is the largest in Germany, and ranks the fourth in the world. Trading is carried out through IBIS for stock and warrants, and through IBIS-R for fixed-income securities. Deutsche Börse AG operates the FWB. Table 8.5 lists the major events in the history of FWB.

The FWB is governed by the Exchange Council. The Council is composed of a maximum of 24 members, including banks, specialists (*Kursmakler*), independent brokers (*Freimakler*), insurance companies, issuers, and investors. A company applying for listing must undergo a formal listing process supervised by the Securities Admission Board. As in most other exchanges, the main objective is to ensure timely and full disclosure.

Trading

Trading hours are from 8:30 A.M. to 5:00 P.M. There are orientation phases before the open (8:15 A.M.–8:30 A.M.) and after the closing (5:00 P.M.–5:30 P.M.). During the orientation phase before the open, traders can begin entering quotes that will become binding when the market opens. At 5:00 P.M., after the market closes, a similar orientation phase follows until 5:30 P.M. All quotes in the system after 5:30 P.M. are deleted. There are no market makers in IBIS. The system does not match orders automatically. Traders must enter proper instructions in order to match quotes; once matched, a confirmation immediately appears on screen.

IBIS-R is the system for bond trading in the third largest bond market, next to the United States and Japan. IBIS-R is an electronic trading system and offers interfaces with the clearing and settlement systems of Deutsche Kassenverein AG (DKV). Also, the primary market is integrated into IBIS-R, which shortens the time between listing and trading. The two largest segments of the fixed-income market, mortgage bonds and bonds issued by public entities, are traded on IBIS-R.

TABLE 8.5 History of Frankfurt Stock Exchange

Year	Event
1585	The exchange is founded.
1820	The first share is traded in Frankfurt.
1896	The Stock Exchange Act is passed.
1945	The exchange is reopened.
1953	A Foreign Exchange Market is introduced.
1958	The first foreign company is listed.
1969	Computerized settlement is introduced.
1969	The first foreign bank is admitted as a member.
1984	Daily volume exceeded DM 1 billion.
1988	The DAX is launched.
1990	pcKiss information system is launched.
1990	Frankfurter Wertpapierbörse AG is founded to operate FWB.
1991	IBIS is introduced.
1991	REX (bond index) is launched.
1991	BOEGA (settlement system) begins operation.
1992	BOSS (securities order routing system) is introduced.
1993	The newly established Deutsche Börse begins operating FWB.
1995	Federal Securities Supervisory Office is founded.
1995	IBIS-R is launched.
1996	The MDAX (midcap index) is launched.
1996	Deutsche Börse opens access point to IBIS in London.
1996	Transition of bond trading from IBIS to IBIS-R.
1998	Xetra electronic trading system begins operation.

Source: Adapted from Frankfurter Wertpapierbörse, 1998.

A new electronic trading system, Xetra, is in operation and replacing IBIS in 1998. Xetra is aimed at enhancing the quality of trading in equities, fixed-income securities, and warrants. Market participants have participated in the development of the new system. Xetra will expand the decentralized low-cost access to the German markets. Xetra is being introduced in several releases:

- Release 1: Introduction of Xetra Front End, June 1997
- Release 2: Introduction of Xetra Back End, November 1997
- Release 3: Complete Xetra Functionality, October 1998
- Release 4: Fully implemented market model, to be announced

Settlement

IBIS trade settlements are automatically forwarded to the Exchange's system (BOEGA). IBIS transactions are settled under the regular T+2. Parties to the transaction receive a trade confirmation called a *contract note,* on the trade day. On the next business day, the seller releases the securities on-line for delivery. On the value date, stocks are credited to the purchaser's account at the securities depositary and the purchaser receives a statement to that effect. At the same time, payment is made through the LZB (the regional Bundesbank office). The corresponding offsetting entries are then made for the seller.

FIGURE 8.1   FWB Settlement Process

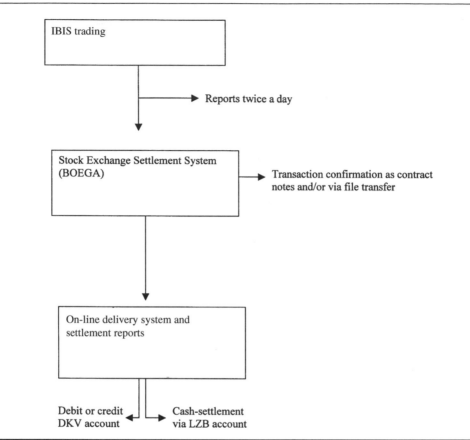

Market participants can take over settlement for their transactions through their membership at DKV. Or they can use the services of a settlement bank. Official brokers, as well as independent brokers who do not have accounts at DKV, rely on this service.

IBIS transactions are divided into two periods. All transactions made up to and including 3:59 P.M. are forwarded to BOEGA on the same day. All transaction made between 4:00 P.M. and 5:00 P.M. are submitted "for next-day settlement." Reports are generated twice a day, the first for transactions before 4:00 P.M. and the second for those between 4:00 P.M. and 5:00 P.M. If a transaction is settled through a settlement bank, the bank will receive a so-called "settlement bank record" that details the transactions through the bank. The settlement process can be depicted in Figure 8.1.

The Neuer Market

Deutsche Börse launched a new trading segment at the Frankfurt Stock Exchange, the Neuer Market, on March 10, 1997. Companies that seek listing on the Neuer Market must satisfy the following requirements:

- Minimum issue volume of DM 10 million
- Issue of common stock only
- Minimum 15% float
- At least one Betreuer (market maker) for the stock
- Prospectus based on international standards
- Lock-up of 6 months for original shareholders
- Acceptance of German takeover code
- At least 50% of the flotation for a capital increase

Once listed, companies must publish quarterly and annual reports in English and German. Listed companies must disclose management ownership and their corporate action timetable.

The Deutsche Börse integrates the Neuer Market into its existing system but as an independent trading segment of the FWB. In 1998, trading on the Neuer Market was to be transferred to the new Xetra system.

EUROPEAN MONETARY UNION

Based on the 1991 Maastricht Treaty, the European Monetary Union (EMU) will go into effect in January 1999, when the euro becomes a currency of the euroland. There will be a three-year transition period during which the euro will be used alongside national currencies. Full integration is scheduled for 2002. Table 8.6 lists the timetable of the EMU.

Only EU countries with sound monetary and fiscal policies will be admitted to the monetary union. The Maastricht Treaty requires a low inflation rate, stable exchange rates, comparably low interest rates, and a sustainable level of government debt for participation in EMU. Specifically, the requirements are:

- A low inflation rate: inflation rate within 1.5% of the 3 best performing EU countries
- Exchange rate stability: kept within the normal fluctuation margins of Europe's exchange rate mechanism for at least two years
- Low interest rates: within 2% of the 3 lowest interest rates
- Sustainable government debt: a budget deficit of no higher than 3% of GDP, and a ratio of public debt to GDP of no more than 60%

Selection of participating countries and directors of the new central bank were made in 1998. At the May 1998 special summit, the European leaders also determined at which exchange rates their currencies would be locked in when the euro is launched (Table 8.7). The 11 first-round members are Germany, France, Spain, Italy, Austria, Luxembourg, Netherlands, Belgium, Portugal, Ireland and Finland. Other EU countries such as England, Denmark, Greece, and Sweden plan to remain out in the first round. There is still uncertainty as to when and which of these four will or will not join. J.P. Morgan's EMU Calculator derives the financial market's expectation of a country participating in EMU based on analysis of spreads in the interest-rate swap market. For example, the EMU Calculator suggested a probability of 52% for the United Kingdom's joining in 1999 based on spreads on May 4, 1998. On the same date, the Calculator predicted a probability of 78% for its joining in 2002.

TABLE 8.6   EMU Timetable

July 1, 1990	Jan 1, 1994	Dec 15/16, 1995	Early 1998	Jan 1, 1999	Jan 1, 2002
Start of stage one	Start of stage two	Resolution of Madrid meeting	Resolution of the European Council	Start of stage three	Conversion of currency
Stage One	*Stage Two*	*Stage Two*	*Stage Two*	*Stage Three*	*Stage Three*
Full liberalization of capital movements	Establishment of European Monetary Institute	Euro will be the new single currency	Confirmation of 1999 as starting date	Irrevocable fixing of conversion rates between member states	The euro becomes legal tender
Coordination of economic, fiscal, and monetary policies	Autonomy of national central banks	Preparation of legal framework by end of 1996	Group of participating countries	ECB assumes monetary policy responsibility	Exchange of note and coin
			Establishment of European Central Bank	Start of currency changeover	Conversion of all monetary values not yet denominated in euro

Source: Adapted from Deutsche Bank. *European Monetary Union: What It's All About*, 1997, p 2.

The EMU effectively brings about a merger of the capital markets of the countries that join the union. The European Monetary Institute (EMI) published the blueprint of the European Central Bank (ECB) in January 1997. The ECB will control and oversee a common European monetary policy. The ECB will deal only in euros during the transition period. The Federation of European Stock Exchanges (FESE) announced its inten-

TABLE 8.7   Exchange Rates against the Euro

Country	Currency	Dollar Rate[1]	Euro Rate
Austria	Schilling	$0.08	13.91
Belgium	Franc	0.0271	40.78
Finland	Mark	0.1842	6.01
France	Franc	0.1666	6.63
Germany	Mark	0.558	1.98
Ireland	Punt	1.405	0.80
Italy	Lira	0.000566	1958.00
Luxembourg	Franc	0.0271	40.78
Netherlands	Guilder	0.496	2.23
Portugal	Escudo	0.00545	202.70
Spain	Peseta	0.00658	168.20

[1] Dollar rate is as of May 1, 1998, and euro rate is announced May 2, 1998.
Source: Wall Street Journal, May 4, 1998, A17.

tion to move all trading and settlement in euro at the outset. In the bond market, all new tradeable governments will be issued in euro. France, Belgium, Finland, Spain, Austria, Italy, and the Netherlands have decided to re-denominate their outstanding debts. Germany is expected to come to a formal decision soon. The following discussion focuses on the implications of EMU for bonds, equities, and settlement issues.

The Equity Markets

The single euro removes the option of products or services re-pricing through currency. This implies that productivity will now determine corporate profits and economic growth. Valuations will be enhanced through higher growth rates and lower capital costs, resulting from the elimination of currency risk and the reduction of inflation risk. Companies in Europe will save on foreign currency exchange and hedging costs as much as $65 billion a year.

The stock markets will benefit from the movement toward private pension and other privatization programs, as member states have to meet the Maastricht convergence criteria on budget deficits. The maturing equity markets in Germany, France, and other EMU member states will lead to more funds flowing into the stock markets. The market capitalization of German, French, and Italian stock markets is currently less than half the GDP, much lower than in the United States and United Kingdom. Furthermore, pension funds in EMU countries allocate a small proportion of their assets in equities. For example, German pension funds held only 12% of their assets in equities in 1995, compared with the United Kingdom's 82%. Funds allocated to the equity market will increase exponentially if EMU countries match the United Kingdom in pension funds asset allocation. A single euro helps movement toward this direction because funds can match liabilities to any European financial asset without currency risk.

The Bond Markets

The bond markets benefit from fiscal discipline, low interest rates, and reduced currency risk. The single currency will lead to lower operating costs and better liquidity, which will provide a major boost for corporate borrowers and investors. However, one currency does not mean one yield curve for all governments. Clearly, different sovereign borrowers will have different credit ratings and pay different interest rates in line with credit quality. Another aspect is the ratings on local currency and foreign currency debts. Among the first-round participating states, Belgium, Finland, and Ireland have local currency ratings higher than their foreign ratings (Table 8.8). Their local ratings are expected to be downgraded before EMU.

The bond markets after EMU will expand. The euro zone government bond market is about $1.9 trillion and is apt to diversify. The strapped central governments are expected to push spending onto municipalities, which will provide a boost to municipal finance. According to a report by Goldman Sachs, the corporate fixed-income market will quadruple from the current $160 billion to $640 billion after EMU. The effect of sovereign risk on the credit risk of other issuers within a participating nation will be reduced. By 2002, a new and integrated euro-denominated "domestic" market will emerge. As Euro has become reality, high-yield eurojunk market will be in the spotlight because yields on European government debt have been dropping as European economies align themselves under the EMU, leaving investors looking for alternatives. The eurobond sector is likely to attract new issuers to tap into this new market.

TABLE 8.8   Local and Foreign Currency Ratings of Participating States

Country	Foreign Currency	Local Currency
Austria	Aaa/AAA	NR/AAA
France	Aaa/AAA	Aaa/AAA
Germany	Aaa/AAA	Aaa/AAA
Luxembourg	Aaa/AAA	NR/AAA
Netherlands	Aaa/AAA	NR/AAA
Belgium	Aa1/AA+	Aa1/AAA
Ireland	Aa1/AA	Aaa/AAA
Finland	Aa1/AA	Aaa/AAA

Source: Adapted from *Euromoney* (August 1997): p 45.

Furthermore, a euro-denominated Yankee market—a euro-denominated debt issued by nonmember issuers to European institutional buyers—is expected to emerge.

A potential negative effect comes from the need for diversification after EMU. A portfolio of government bonds denominated in the same euro and under the influence of the same monetary policy does not offer investors diversified risk. This may lead to greater investments in equities outside the EU to obtain diversification.

Settlement and Custody

During the transition period, local currencies will coexist with the euro until the entire payment and settlement systems become euro-denominated. The transition period posts a number of technical challenges to custodians. Global custodians need to add capacities to provide services in euro-denominated securities. Reporting and accounting will need to be in local currency and/or euro terms between 1999 and 2002. On top of that, the settlement cycle, the day-count convention, and price quotations have to be changed. Preparation is complicated by the uncertainty of participating countries, especially the United Kingdom, given the size of the UK market and the importance of UK institutional investors.

SUMMARY

This chapter covers the euromarkets and the largest three European markets. Euromarkets are international, trading around the clock in all major financial centers in the world. The European markets are expected to be consolidated after the EMU. Investment bankers should be ready for the upcoming changes. Euromarkets represent a significant segment in the capital markets. The size and significance will continue to rise. Investment bankers will continue to structure and design new products that better fit the needs of borrowers and investors in the "unregulated" markets.

SELECT BIBLIOGRAPHY

Canals, J. *Universal Banking*. Oxford: Oxford University Press, 1997.
Euromoney. Various issues.

Deutsche Bank. *European Monetary Union: What It's All About*. Germany, 1997.

Ho, T. S. Y., ed. *Fixed Income Solutions: New Techniques for Managing Market Risks*. Chicago, IL: Irwin Professional Publishing, 1996.

J.P. Morgan. *What Is EMU?* New York, 1997.

OECD. *Financial Market Trends*. Washington, D. C., Various issues.

Steil, B., ed. *International Financial Market Regulation*. New York: Wiley, 1994.

Steil, B., ed. *The European Equity Markets*. London: Royal Institute of International Affairs, 1996.

Stigum, M., and F. L. Robinson. *Money Market and Bond Calculations*. Chicago, IL: Irwin Professional Publishing, 1997.

Temperton, P., ed. *The Euro*. New York: Wiley, 1998.

Thompson, V. *Mastering the Euromarkets*. Chicago, IL: Irwin Professional Publishing, 1996.

Tran, H. Q., L. Anderson, and E. Drayss. "Eurocapital markets." In *The Handbook of Fixed Income Securities*. F. J. Fabozzi, ed. Burr Ridge, IL: Business One Irwin, 1991.

Walter, I., and R. C. Smith. *Investment Banking in Europe*. Oxford: Basil Blackwell, 1990.

Walter, I., and R. C. Smith. *Global Banking*. Oxford: Oxford University Press, 1997.

9

Japanese Securities Markets

Japanese *Big Bang* will reshape its securities markets and financial system. Deregulation is based on the principles of fair market, free entry, and global competition. The 1997 reform plans, as part of the Japanese Big Bang, focus on instruments, markets, and intermediaries. The aim is to upgrade the Japanese market so it rivals New York and London by the year 2001. The Japanese securities business is a potentially lucrative market, especially in the areas of capital markets and fund management. Individual savings amount to ¥1,200 trillion, a tremendous market for pension planning and asset management. The Big Bang will include greater freedom for savers to invest outside of Japan, and will thereby earn a true market return on their savings. This chapter provides a brief overview of the market and the major reform plans introduced in 1997. This chapter also covers the microstructures of the equity and fixed income markets.

INTRODUCTION

From the 1960s until 1997, the *Big Four* (Nomura, Daiwa, Nikko, and Yamaichi) dominated the Japanese securities market. On November 22, 1997, Yamaichi Securities[1] announced that it would shut down its business. Foreign firms were first allowed to enter the Japanese market in 1972. Foreign firms now are becoming serious competitors to the remaining *Big Three*, as they possess advantages in providing sophisticated services to institutional investors.

The Japanese securities industry experienced unprecedented prosperity in the 1980s. In the 1990s, the markets are confronted with scandals, increased competition, and regulatory changes. The legal violations of compensating customers for trading losses and company payoffs to alleged racketeers cost Nomura Securities and Yamaichi Securities their top management. Japanese securities companies are facing an increasingly competitive market environment, both home and abroad, due to globalization of the financial markets and rapid advances in information technology. The increased competition, an extended (since 1990) decline in real estate and stock prices, and a weakening convoy system[2] also resulted in the failure of Sanyo Securities in November 1997, Hokkaido Takushoku Bank in November 1997, and Nissan Mutual Life in April 1997.

Recently, the Securities and Exchange Council (SEC) established the General Committee to conduct comprehensive reviews of the securities market. The committee has published its plan for reform, outlined in Section 7 of this chapter. The objectives of the reform are to upgrade the Japanese market to a level that rivals New York and London by the year 2001 and to obtain higher returns from its ¥1,200 trillion household savings to finance the care of the aging population. According to a recent study by Sanwa Bank, the process will cost as many as 320,000 jobs in Japan's financial services industry, which accounts for 16% of its work force. But such changes are seen as necessary if Japan is to regain its competitiveness in financial services.

DEVELOPMENT OF THE SECURITIES MARKET

The development can be divided into five phases. The first phase was the growth in the 1950s, followed by the stock market crisis of 1965 and the restructuring of the industry in the second phase. The securities market entered into a new stage of development in the 1970s. The fourth phase is the dramatic expansion in the 1980s. Finally, the changing environment in the 1990s presents new challenges to the securities industry.

The Securities and Exchange Law (SEL) was enacted in 1948.[3] But the balanced budget principle restricted the central government from issuing bonds. Moreover, the government placed strict controls on the flotation of corporate bonds in order to protect the banking industry (companies had to rely on bank loans for funding). In the late 1950s, the securities market grew rapidly, which was paced by the accumulation of personal wealth from the recovery of the economy. During this period, the Big Four aggressively expanded their sales networks. They also had permission to operate investment trusts. The Big Four hence established themselves as the dominant players in this period. They represented 33.2% of stock transaction volume in 1953, and their share rose to 64.9% in 1960.

The securities market experienced a sharp downturn in the early 1960s. There were minimal activities in both stock and bond markets. As a result, several securities companies ran into financial difficulties. The Bank of Japan had to provide financial support for several failing securities companies. The SEL was revised in 1965. The revision introduced a new licensing system requiring separate licenses for brokerage, dealing, underwriting and distribution. The minimum equity capital required for obtaining all four licenses was ¥1 billion. Firms with ¥3 billion equity capital can become lead underwriters (*Sogo-Shoken*).

The securities market gradually recovered after the crisis. The Japanese government began to issue a large volume of long-term bonds in 1975 to meet the shortfall in revenues because of the oil crisis. The issuance of stock and corporate bonds also increased. As a result, the demand for underwriting services increased. During this period, the movement of economic activities toward Tokyo and the improvement in telecommunications technology led to the concentration of securities business in Tokyo.

The securities industry experienced unprecedented growth and profits in the 1980s. The transaction volume surged from ¥3.528 trillion in 1980 to ¥40.824 trillion by 1987 and then after the crash declined to ¥23.302 trillion in 1990. The commissions and fees rose from ¥8.741 billion to a peak of ¥45.085 billion in 1989. The financial liberalization, high valuation of yen, and low interest rates fueled this extraordinary growth. The Ministry of Finance (MOF) first permitted banks to sell long-term public bonds in 1983, to deal in public bonds the next year, and later to trade in futures and options. The securities companies were also permitted to expand into transactions in CDs, yen-denominated BAs, and CPs issued overseas.

In the 1990s, the markets have been confronted with scandals, increased competition, and regulatory changes. Major scandals involving the Big Four broke out in the summer of 1991. The legal violations of compensating customers for trading losses and company payoffs to alleged racketeers cost Yamaichi Securities and Nomura Securities their top management. As a result of the scandals, compensation by a brokerage firm to its customers for trading losses is now explicitly prohibited.

Additional amendments to the SEL were passed in 1992. First, MOF established a market surveillance committee to monitor and enforce mandatory disclosure and anti-fraud rules. The second major amendment was to broaden the definition of security to include:

- Debt security issued by government, municipalities, and corporations
- Stock issued by corporations
- Beneficial certificates under a securities investment trust or loan trust
- Securities issued by foreign government or companies that have characteristics resembling the domestic issues
- Any other security designated by cabinet order

Then the rules on private placement were relaxed. An exemption from disclosure requirements is available when securities are issued to certain qualified institutional investors.

Japanese securities companies are facing an increasingly competitive market environment at home and abroad, due to globalization of the financial markets and advances in information technology. To be competitive in the global markets, the Japanese government has decided to carry out the Big Bang shakeup of Tokyo's capital markets. Japanese competitiveness and being the Land of the Rising Sun depend on the success of the upcoming reforms.

THE BOND MARKETS

The Japanese bond market is the second largest in the world. The Japanese bond market consists of Japanese government bonds (JGB), government agency bonds, local government bonds, corporate bonds, and foreign bonds. The largest sector is the JGB market.

Japanese Government Bonds

There are four types of Japanese government securities: short-term Treasury bills, medium-term notes, long-term bonds, and super long-term bonds. The Japanese government began issuing short-term bills in February 1986. Medium-term notes include 2-year, 4-year, and 6-year coupon notes and zero-coupon 5-year notes, usually issued monthly. Long-term bonds are the 10-year noncallable coupon bonds and are usually issued monthly. Super long-term bonds have a maturity of 20 years and are noncallable.

The super long-term bonds are issued three times a year. The 10-year bonds have occupied the central part of government securities. As of the end of the first quarter in 1998, the outstanding marketable JGBs totaled ¥258 trillion, long-term bonds (including 20-year bonds) accounted for 83% at ¥215 trillion. For the long-term bonds, there is a quarterly maturity cycle. As a result, the maturity typically occurs on the twentieth day of the last month of the quarter and the first coupon payment is made six months after the final month of that quarter.

Yields in Japan have been much lower than in the United States in recent years. Table 9.1 lists the yield for each maturity segment, from 1-year to 20-year government securities, on January 2, 1998. On the same date the U.S. 1-year bills yielded 5.442%, 5-year notes yielded 5.614%, and 10-year notes yielded 5.649%, considerably higher than the yields seen in Table 9.1 on Japanese government debt.

The MOF approves the issue and sets the coupon rate before the auction, but the Bank of Japan implements the issuance of JGBs.[4] The coupon rate is set at such a level so that the security is most likely auctioned below par. Issue sizes range from ¥400 billion to ¥3.2 trillion. Japanese government securities have been traditionally offered through a syndicated underwriting system, in which the syndicate members commit to purchase the unsold portion of the offering at the average of the successful bid prices. Almost all the securities companies and financial institutions belong to the underwriting syndicate. The competitive bidding method was introduced in 1989, and this method is like the first price auction in the United States, where each accepted bidder pays its own bid price. Except for 40% of the 10-year bonds, JGBs are now issued through the auction method. The syndicate at the average auction price underwrites the remaining 40% of the 10-year bonds. Both long-term and super long-term bonds are numbered serially and are referred to by the number rather than the maturity and coupon, as in the United States.

The JGB auction process is as follows. The MOF announces the terms of the issue at 8:30 A.M. on the day of the auction, after consultation with the syndicate. Financial institutions submit bids in price, to two decimal places, between 11:30 A.M. and 1:30 P.M. The result is announced at 4:30 P.M. As this is a first-price auction, each accepted bid is filled at the price bid until the announced amount is sold.

TABLE 9.1   Yield Curve for Japan

	Coupon	Date	Yield (%)
1-year	4.80	12/21/98	0.523
2-year	5.10	12/20/99	0.632
3-year	7.20	12/20/00	0.785
4-year	6.00	12/20/01	1.017
5-year	4.80	12/20/02	1.219
6-year	3.60	12/22/03	1.425
7-year	4.50	12/20/04	1.501
8-year	2.90	12/20/05	1.703
9-year	2.90	12/20/06	1.789
10-year	2.00	12/20/07	1.940
15-year	5.70	03/20/13	2.036
20-year	2.70	03/20/18	2.565

Source: Adapted from Bloomberg Online, January 2, 1998.

Government Agency and Local Government Bonds

Government agency bonds are backed by general mortgages or government guarantee. Those guaranteed by the Japanese government require prior approval by the Diet (legislature). The privatization in Japan has resulted in a decline in the volume of government guaranteed bonds. Local government bonds typically have a maturity of two years or longer. These bonds are issued either via a public offering or a private placement.

Corporate Bonds

Bank debentures are bonds issued by long-term credit banks and other financial institutions under special laws. Bank debentures are the second largest fixed-income sector. Industrial Bank of Japan, Long-Term Credit Bank of Japan, Nippon Credit Bank, and Bank of Tokyo-Mitsubishi are among the major banks permitted to issue bank debentures.

A formal bond rating system was introduced in 1977. Major Japanese rating agencies are Nippon Investors Service, Japan Bond Rating Institute, Japan Credit Rating Agency, and Mikuni & Co. Mikuni is the only independent credit rating agency. In addition, Moody's and Standard and Poor's provide rating services in Japan as well. Since a credit rating downgrade helped sink Yamaichi Securities, Japan's financial industry has paid a lot more attention to credit ratings. As an example, according to a *Wall Street Journal* report (November 26, 1997), a major Japanese nonfinancial firm considering acquiring a financial institution called off the deal after it considered S&P's response on how the purchase might affect its rating. This was unheard of in Japan before.

A shelf registration rule was introduced in 1987 that permits issuers to come to the market faster. Equity-linked securities such as convertible bonds and bonds with warrants have been popular. Japanese companies in 1995 issued a total of ¥6.950 trillion of bonds. The issuance reached ¥10 trillion in 1996. The market has seen an increase in structured deals such as dual-currency bonds, reverse dual-currency bonds and callable notes. International issuance has also increased. The growth is a sign of breaking free from banks that have supplied the bulk of their financing needs until recently. The decline in the proportion of bank loans to total external financing is due to low interest rates, deregulation, and the changing relationship between banks and corporate borrowers.

During the 1990s, Japanese interest rates have fallen to extremely low levels. The official discount rate reached a historical low of 0.5% in September 1995 and is not expected to rise any time soon (see Table 9.2). The low-interest-rate environment has motivated both retail and institutional investors to shift money from bank deposits into the bond market. Most of the bond issues have been fixed-rate bonds in the maturities of three to five years. With investors hungry for higher coupons, several top-rated companies (including Tepco, Chubu Electric, and NTT) have been able to extend maturity to 10 to 20 years.

The Japanese government has taken steps to gradually implement deregulatory policies. Deregulation will contribute to the expansion of the fixed-income market. Deregulatory measures introduced in 1996 include the following:

- Permit noninvestment grade companies to issue domestic bonds.
- Lift regulation on collateral and size of issuance.
- Allow asset-backed deals.

TABLE 9.2   The Official Discount Rates

	Official Discount Rate (%)
January 1976	6.50
March 1977	6.00
April 1977	5.00
September 1977	4.25
March 1978	3.50
April 1979	4.25
July 1979	5.25
November 1979	6.25
February 1980	7.25
March 1980	9.00
August 1980	8.25
November 1980	7.25
March 1981	6.25
December 1981	5.50
October 1983	5.00
January 1986	4.50
March 1986	4.00
April 1986	3.50
November 1986	3.00
February 1987	2.50
May 1989	3.25
October 1989	3.75
December 1989	4.25
March 1990	5.25
August 1990	6.00
July 1991	5.50
November 1991	5.00
December 1991	4.50
April 1992	3.75
July 1992	3.25
February 1993	2.50
September 1993	1.75
April 1995	1.00
September 1995	0.50

Source: Bank of Japan, 1998. The table lists the new rate and the month when the rate change occurred.

- Modernize settlement system to a rolling T+7 (later to T+3) process from the inefficient settlement only on dates ending in a five or a zero.
- Create a repurchase agreement market.

The 1997 reforms of the securities markets will certainly provide additional impetus to further expand the scope and size of the Japanese capital market.

The close ties between banks and borrowers in the past deterred the development of the capital market in Japan. After the banking crisis in the past few years, banks are now lending less and demanding tighter covenants. Also, big banks such as the Industrial Bank of Japan, Long-Term Credit Bank, and Norinchkin are now permitted to underwrite bonds. To shore up their securities business, they encourage corporate clients to refinance their loans in the bond market, instead of rolling over bank loans. Consequently bank lending to corporate clients fell to ¥11 trillion in July 1996, from ¥32 trillion in yearend 1994.

Finally, another healthy development is that there has been an increased use of spread-based pricing. In the past, most bonds in Japan were priced on a coupon basis. An AAA bond might be priced at almost the same level as an A-rated issue. The new spread-based pricing will result in more bond supply and a more efficient allocation of funds. The continued growth means more demand for underwriting services.

Foreign Bonds

Foreign bonds are issued in Japan by foreign institutions or by Japanese institutions in foreign markets. Table 9.3 lists samples of government-guaranteed foreign bonds issued overseas by Japanese institutions. *Samurai* bonds are yen-denominated bonds issued in the Japanese market under domestic regulations. Major samurai issuers include supranational institutions, sovereign governments, governmental institutions from various countries, and corporate issuers. The first samurai issuers were the Asian Development Bank (1970), the World Bank (1971), Australia (1972), and Sears Roebuck (1979). *Shibosai* bonds are privately placed foreign bonds in the Japanese capital markets. *Shogun* bonds are publicly offered bonds denominated in foreign currencies. *Daimyo* bonds are foreign-currency denominated, listed on the Luxembourg exchange, and settled through Euroclear or Cedel.

The samurai bond market has grown rapidly in recent years. For example, the supply totaled ¥3.9 trillion in 1996, a big surge from 1995's ¥1.9 trillion and 1944's ¥1.1 trillion. Hedging strategy and a low-interest-rate environment have contributed to the growth. Non–Japanese borrowers may use samurai bonds to hedge against foreign exchange risk. Foreign institutions may also tap into the samurai market and simultaneously swap the issue into another currency to take advantage of the lower costs of funding in Japan. The cost advantage outweighs the higher issuing expenses, averaging 0.78% as compared to 0.28% in the Euroyen market.

Before January 1996, bonds issued in Japan required a minimum credit rating of Baa3/BBB-. Packer and Reynolds (1997) observe that the elimination of minimum credit rating requirement increased bond issues ¥507 billion[5] in 1996, that accounts for 23% of the growth from 1995 to 1996. Japanese rating agencies used to assign several-notches-higher ratings, both samurai and domestic bonds, than U.S. agencies. But the ratings differentials do not lead to underestimation of credit risk, because Japanese investors consider the rank ordering of default risk in formulating required yields. The new-issue pricing practice of samurai reflects a strong correlation with U.S. and Japanese agency rankings of credit risk.

Yield Quotes

Yields in the Japanese bond market are quoted on a simple yield-to-maturity basis. This convention reflects a general discomfort with compound interest calculations. The simple yield is calculated as follows:

$$ y = \frac{c \times F + \dfrac{F - P}{M}}{P} $$

TABLE 9.3 Japanese Government-Guaranteed Foreign Bonds

	Amount (in millions)	Currency	Maturity	Issue Date
Japan Finance Corporation for Small Business Deutsche Mark Bonds	450	D-Mark	5 years	08/07/97
The Metropolis of Tokyo French Francs Bonds	1,700	French Francs	10 years	07/25/97
The City of Yokohama Swiss Francs Bonds	120	Swiss Francs	10 years	07/16/97
Japan Finance Corporation for Municipal Enterprises Eurodollar Bonds	400	Dollar	10 years	07/03/97
Hokkaido-Tohoku Development Finance Public Corporation Swiss Francs Bonds	150	Swiss Francs	5 years	06/24/97
The Export–Import Bank of Japan French Francs Bonds	2,000	French Francs	11 years	06/05/97
Japan Finance Corporation for Municipal Enterprises French Francs Bonds	1,000	French Francs	10 years	05/09/97
Japan Development Bank Eurodollar Bonds	500	Dollar	5 years	05/02/97
Japan Finance Corporation for Municipal Enterprises Dutch Guilders Bonds	300	Guilders	10 years	02/13/97
The Export–Import Bank of Japan Europound Bonds	400	Pound	10 years	02/05/97
Japan Development Bank Euroyen Bonds	50,000	Yen	10 years	12/20/96
Japan Highway Public Corporation Eurodollar Bonds	300	Dollar	10 years	11/27/96
Trans-Tokyo Bay Highway Corporation Bonds	200	Dollar	10 years	11/21/96
Japan Finance Corporation for Municipal Enterprises Swiss Francs Bonds	250	Swiss Francs	10 years	10/30/96
The City of Yokohama Eurodollar Bonds	200	Dollar	10 years	10/18/96
Metropolis of Tokyo Eurodollar Bonds	250	Dollar	10 years	10/16/96
Hokkaido-Tohoku Development Finance Public Corporation Deutsche Mark Bonds	150	D-Mark	7 years	10/15/96
Kansai International Airport Company, Ltd. Eurodollar Bonds	200	Dollar	10 years	10/02/96
Japan Finance Corporation for Small Business Deutsche Mark	350	D-Mark	3 years	09/30/96
Export–Import Bank of Japan Eurodollar Bonds	750	Dollar	5 years	08/02/96
Japan Finance Corporation for Municipal Enterprises Eurosterling Bonds	150	Pound	10 years	07/18/96

In the expression, y is the simple yield, c the annual coupon rate, F the par amount, P the clean price, and M the years to maturity.

As is clear from this expression, the simple yield reduces to coupon rate if the bond is traded at par. If an investor purchases the bond at a premium, the simple yield earned will be less than the coupon rate because *drag to par* will lead to capital loss as the bond approaches maturity. Conversely, if an investor purchases the bond at a discount, his simple yield will exceed the coupon rate as the drag to par produces capital gains.

THE SECONDARY JGB MARKETS

The JGB market is the most important bond market in Japan. The outstanding volume in 1998:Q1 was about ¥250 trillion. During the past two decades the rapid growth was attributable to steps taken by the government to gradually open up the market. For example, banks were permitted to sell government bonds in 1977 and to deal in government bonds in 1984 (*bank dealing*). In 1985, the bond futures market began trading. Option on JGB futures was introduced in 1990. In government bond trading, the Big Three and Industrial Bank of Japan claim the top positions.

The Growth in the Interdealer Market

The interdealer market consists of direct trading, trading through bondbrokers, and trading on the stock exchanges. The formation of the Japan Bond Trading Corporation (broker's broker) in 1973 and the authorization of bank dealing in government bonds in 1984 contributed to the rapid growth in the interdealer market, which, in turn, led to rapid growth in the JGB market and the overall fixed-income market.

The Benchmark Issues

A unique feature in the JGB market is that the 10-year benchmark issue dominates trading activities in the secondary market. A benchmark issue is the most actively traded and has the greatest liquidity, similar to the on-the-run issue in the U.S. government securities market. Unlike the on-the-run issues in the United States, however, the benchmark issue in JGB is not necessarily the most recent government bond issue. The Big Three typically play a big part in designating the benchmark issue. A benchmark issue generally has several characteristics:

- A coupon close to the prevailing rate
- A large outstanding amount (¥2.0 trillion or more)
- A wide distribution
- A current maturity close to 10 years

The benchmark issue generally retains its status for 5 to 10 months before a new benchmark is selected. When the current benchmark begins to lose support, the Big Three begin to speculate on which issue will be the next benchmark. Since there is a large liquidity premium for the benchmark, from 10 to 100 basis points, the transition can be costly. The succession process usually takes several weeks.

The benchmark bond accounts for the majority of trading volume. This has led to a bid/offer yield spread of 0.5 basis point. For issues deliverable into the JGB 10-year bond futures contract (7- to 11-year maturities), the spread ranges 1 to 2 basis points. The spreads for other issues can be as large as 2 to 3 basis points.

Reverse Coupon Effect

The reverse coupon effect is another unique characteristic in the Japanese debt market. High coupon bonds are traded not at a higher yield, but instead at a lower yield, than equivalent-duration bonds with lower coupons. This is in contrast to other fixed income markets, because high coupon bonds have a higher reinvestment risk and are taxed at a higher income tax rate. However, Japanese life insurance companies are legally obligated to make their payouts from interest and dividend income. In order to compete with other types of financial institutions, life insurance companies are hence motivated to invest in high-coupon JGBs.

Clearing and Settlement

Japan adopted a T+7 settlement system in 1996 (settlement in 7 business days), as part of the government bond market reforms. The settlement cycle was further reduced to T+3 in April 1997. Even though this is still behind the T+1 or same-day settlement abroad, this is a vast improvement over the replaced settlement system. Under the old system introduced in 1987, settlement took place only on dates ending in five or zero (or last day of the month). The introduction of that system did bring bond speculation under control, but the inefficiency is clearly evidenced by conflicts it has with the Western calendar, Japanese holidays, and the securities association's own rules that require three to six trading days for paperwork. That could delay delivery 15 days or more.

THE PRIMARY EQUITY MARKET

The SEL governs the issuance and trading of securities in Japan. For the purpose of issuing a security, a *Securities Registration Statement* must be filed with the MOF. After the issuance, companies are required to disclose specified matters, prepared in accordance with Ministerial Disclosure Ordinance, in Annual Securities Reports and other reports. Listing requirements are established by exchanges themselves. The securities business has concentrated in the Tokyo Stock Exchange (TSE), as a result of concentration of economic activities in Tokyo and improvement in information technology.

TSE Listing Requirements for Domestic Stocks

Companies applying for initial listing must meet the requirements on the number of shares to be listed, number of shareholders, history of incorporation, shareholder's equity, and dividend (see Table 9.4). The TSE conducts a rigorous examination of an applicant. If satisfied, the TSE accepts the listing application with the approval of the MOF. If the applicant's main business is in an emerging or a new industry, the alternative listing requirements apply (Table 9.4).

The TSE requires listed companies to provide an immediate notice to the TSE of any material information. The TSE also requires listed companies to file various documents on matters relating to shareholder rights.

The listed domestic stocks are assigned to either First Section or Second Section, and foreign stocks are assigned to the Foreign Section. Newly listed stocks are generally assigned to the Second Section. The requirements for First Section are much more stringent. At the end of each year the TSE examines the listed companies to determine whether they meet reassignment criteria, from First Section to Second Section or vice versa.

TSE Listing Requirements for Foreign Companies

A foreign company in principle must apply for listing of all its outstanding fully paid-up stocks with voting rights. A listed foreign company must also apply for listing of all new issued stocks in the same class as the listed stocks at the time of issuance. The TSE's policy is to require that all common stocks have the same voting rights and have no restrictions on the exercise of such rights.

TABLE 9.4   TSE Listing Requirements

Application	All Requirements Must Be Met
Shares to be listed	4 million or more if issuer is based in or around Tokyo; 20 million or more, elsewhere
Minimum number of shareholders holding 1,000 shares or more (excluding "special few")	800 if shares listed are less than 10 million; 1,200 for listed shares between 10 and 20 million; 2,000 plus 100 per each 10 million in excess of 20 million (up to 3,000)
History of incorporation	3 years of continuous operation
Shareholder equity	¥1 billion (and ¥100 per share)
Net profits before taxes	(1) Total for last 3 years: first, second year: ¥100 million; latest year: ¥400 million
	(2) Amount per share: 15
Dividends	Paid in cash within the latest year, and able to maintain ¥5 or more in cash after listing
Alternative Listing Criteria	
Number of shares	2 million
Number of shareholders with 1,000 shares or more	300
Number of shares publicly offered at the time of listing	0.5 million
Shareholder equity	¥200 million
Net profits before taxes	Amount per share for latest year ¥10 or more, if the applicant who had a deficit must make a profit at the end of latest fiscal year at ¥10 per share (except for new business)

Source: Adapted from Tokyo Stock Exchange, 1997.

A foreign company seeking listing at the TSE is subject to two types of examinations: formal examination and substantial examination. A formal examination focuses on eligibility criteria and a substantial examination looks at fairness of pricing, liquidity, and merit. For foreign companies, there are two kinds of eligibility criteria. One is for ordinary companies and the other for privatized companies. Privatized companies are subject to less stringent requirements. The following is a brief list of the areas of eligibility for an ordinary company seeking listing at TSE:

- Number of listed shares and average closing price in the preceding year
- Liquidity of stocks and number of shareholders in Japan
- Share distribution
- History of incorporation
- Shareholder equity
- Pretax profits
- Appointment of shareholder service agent and dividend payment bank

Once a foreign company has passed the formal examination, the TSE will conduct a substantial examination, looking into matters like fair price formation, good liquidity, investor protection, and public interest. For this purpose, the TSE examines continuity of applicant's management and profitability, full and timely disclosure, and other items the TSE deems important for public interest and investor protection. In summary, the illustrative listing timetable is summarized as follows:

Day 1 **Primary examination**
Documents to be submitted: preapplication report, articles of incorporation, annual and semiannual reports (5 years), press releases (latest year)

Day 15 **Listing application**
Documents to be submitted: Securities report for Listing Application (Part I), resolution of board of directors authorizing the listing application, and Application for Original Listing of Securities

Day 85 **TSE's preliminary application to MOF and MOF's preliminary approval**

Day 100 **TSE's formal application and listing approval from MOF**
Public offering: filing of Securities Registration Statement with MOF, effective date of the registration statement (15 days later), public offering or sale of securities

Day 130 **Listing date**

The TSE charges an initial fee[6] of ¥1 million for examination and ¥2.5 million for listing fee. After listing, the annual listing fee is calculated based on the number of listed shares. The annual fee is payable to the TSE in two installments on or before the last day of the fourth and tenth months of the company's financial year.

As of August 3, 1998, there were 55 listed foreign companies on the TSE. These are mostly well-known companies from Hong Kong (1), Malaysia (1), Australia (4), United States (21), Canada (1), U.K. (8), Netherlands (1), Switzerland (3), Sweden (2), Spain (3), Germany (9), and France (1). Dow Chemical and Citicorp were the first two companies listed in the foreign section, on December 18, 1973.

Top Underwriters

A company seeking listing at the TSE is advised to select a member firm who is knowledgeable about listing procedures and policy. There are 102 Japanese firms and 22 foreign securities companies who are members of the TSE. Foreign-member firms include BZW, Credit Lyonnais, Credit Suisse First Boston, Deutsche Morgan Grenfell, Dresdner Kleiwort Benson, Goldman Sachs, HSBC James Capel, Indosuez Capital, ING Baring, Jardine Fleming, Lehman Brothers, Merrill Lynch, Morgan Stanley Dean Witter, NatWest, Paribas, Salomon Smith Barney, SBC Warburg Dillon Read, Schroder, Societe Generale, and UBS. Top equity underwriters include the Big Three, Merrill Lynch, Goldman Sachs, and J.P. Morgan.

SECONDARY EQUITY MARKETS

There are several exchanges in Japan, including TSE, Osaka Stock Exchange, Nagoya Stock Exchange, and Hiroshima Stock Exchange. The TSE has risen to be the largest

---

TABLE 9.5   Major Instrument Introduction at Tokyo Stock Exchange

06/01/1951: Margin trading introduced
04/02/1956: Bond trading started
10/01/1966: JGBs listed for the first time after World War II
07/01/1969: Tokyo Stock Price Index (TOPIX) introduced
05/11/1970: Trading in convertible bonds began
07/19/1971: Book entry clearing system for stocks introduced
04/02/1973: Yen-denominated foreign bonds started listing
12/18/1973: Foreign stock section opened
04/01/1977: Ad valorem brokerage commission system introduced
01/23/1982: Computer-assisted Order Routing System introduced
05/13/1985: Trading in 10-year JGB futures started
09/03/1988: Trading in TOPIX futures started
10/20/1989: Trading in TOPIX options started
12/01/1989: Trading in U.S. T-Bond futures started
05/11/1990: Trading in options on JGB futures started
11/26/1990: Floor Order Routing and Execution System introduced
10/09/1991: Central Depository & Clearing System began operation
04/01/1994: Partial deregulation of commission schedule
07/18/1997: Equity options introduced
04/01/1998: Partial (over 50 million yen) deregulation of brokerage commission was effected

---

Source: Adapted from Tokyo Stock Exchange, 1998.

exchange in Japan, accounting for 85% or more of trading volumes. Its development provides a catalyst to the progress of the Japanese securities market. Table 9.5 lists the time of major instrument introduction at the TSE.

The OTC market in Japan is relatively insignificant and provides a trading place for stocks of companies that do not meet exchange listing requirements. In October 1991, the Japanese Association of Securities Dealers Automated Quotations (JASDAQ) was set up to integrate computerized trading of OTC securities.

At exchanges, there are regular members and *saitori* members. Regular members are securities firms trading securities in the market of the exchange. Saitori members function as intermediator of transactions between regular members. They are not permitted to trade on their own accounts or deal with nonmembers. Securities companies submit all orders to the saitori member for order matching. Even in the OTC market, Japan OTC Securities plays a role of saitori member. In brokerage business, securities companies still operate under a regulated commission schedule. The 1997 reforms will gradually deregulate brokerage commissions beginning in April 1998.

Trading on the TSE

Members are generally not permitted to trade listed securities off the market of the exchange. This ensures that a large amount of orders trades on the exchange, resulting in fair price formation and high liquidity. Trading hours are 9:00 A.M.–11:00 A.M. for the morning session and 12:30 P.M.–3:00 P.M. for the afternoon trading session. Stocks may be traded on the floor of the exchange or the Computer-assisted Order Routing and

Execution System (CORES). Regular transactions are on a T+3 basis. Special-agreement and cash transactions can be arranged, but the special-agreement transactions must be settled within 15 days. When-issued transactions require a 30% margin. There are 1,805 companies listed on the TSE; among them, 1,585 are eligible for margin transactions, of which 1,046 issues are also eligible for loan transactions.[7] The TSE sets minimum price fluctuations for each stock. The exchange also maintains daily price limits for individual stocks based on their previous day's closing prices, as outlined in Table 9.6.

Price Formation

The Japanese stock exchanges can be characterized as auction markets, using both the *itayose* method and *zaraba* method of auction. The itayose method is a call auction used to establish prices at open, at the end of a trading session, or after an interruption. Under the itayose method, all orders are collected to set the opening price for each stock. After the opening, the zaraba method, a continuous auction, takes over during the trading session.

Settlement

For settlement of domestic shares, the TSE opens a settlement account at JASDEC (Japan Securities Depository Center) to use its Central Depository and Book Entry Transfer System. The TSE's wholly owned subsidiary JSCC (Japan Securities Clearing Corporation) handles the practical aspects of securities settlement for its members.

Here is how settlement works. Transactions on the TSE are generally settled on a T+3 basis. On trade date, the trade report is transmitted to members upon execution of orders. Member firms compare the reports received with their internal records. At the

TABLE 9.6   Daily Price Limits at Tokyo Stock Exchange

Previous day's closing price, less than	Price limits
100	30
200	50
500	80
1,000	100
1,500	200
2,000	300
3,000	400
5,000	500
10,000	1,000
30,000	2,000
For stocks with par value of 50,000 or more	
500,000	80,000
1,000,000	100,000
1,500,000	200,000
2,000,000	300,000
3,000,000	400,000

Source: Adapted from Tokyo Stock Exchange, 1997.

same time, trade data are compiled at Tosho Computer System Corporation (a subsidiary of TSE). On T+1, member firms report any errors or discrepancy to the TSE for correction. On the morning of T+2, post-trade data are compiled in accounting format for net settlement between counterparties. By 8:00 P.M. the TSE provides JASDEC with transfer instructions effective on T+3. The settlement is carried out by book-entries from net-selling member's account to the net-buying member's account. The book-entry transfers for settlement are completed at 9:00 A.M. on T+3. If the net-selling firm does not have sufficient stock in account, it must make up the deficiency by 3:00 P.M. The settlement of funds on a net basis is done on T+3 by checks for next-day funds. The paying members pay their checks to the TSE, and in turn, the TSE issues its checks payable to receiving members.

SECURITIES FINANCING AND MARGIN TRADING

Margin transactions in Japan traditionally did not account for a significant portion of trading volume. There was no viable call market for brokers to refinance (margin purchase), nor did brokers have stocks to lend (short sale). Hence, three securities finance companies were established to loan funds and stocks to securities companies. Japan Securities Finance by far is the largest, set up to service exchanges in Tokyo, Fukuoka, Niigata, and Sapporo. Osaka Securities Finance covers exchanges in Osaka, Kyoto, and Hiroshima. Chubu Securities Finance was set up to finance transactions at Nagoya Stock Exchange. Major business areas of securities finance companies have evolved to include:

- Loans to securities companies for margin transactions
- Loans collateralized by bonds
- General loans to securities companies for working capital and loans to individuals and corporations for securities financing
- Custody business, which includes settlement and clearing

Article 49 of the SEL stipulates that margin trading is the purchase or sale of securities or other securities transactions on credit extended to a customer by a securities company. Margin transactions can be made only on eligible issues. Currently, issues eligible for margin transactions at TSE are 1,585 (out of 1,805 listed). Among these eligible issues, 1,046 issues are eligible for loan transactions and 539 issues are eligible only for margin transactions.

In order to trade on margin, a customer must open a margin account. The customer must also specify the period of settlement—either 3 months or 6 months. Once decided, it cannot be changed. Hence, a margin position is settled when the investor closes out the position or at the end of the specified period (3 or 6 months) by the broker. The SEL requires an initial margin of 30% of the transaction value or of ¥300,000, whichever is greater. Investors are required to maintain a 20% maintenance margin. Securities can be used as margin in lieu of cash.

A stock exchange member firm each day nets its balance of margin purchases and sales for each issue and applies for a loan at the securities finance company. The securities finance company, within the credit limit, transfers funds or equity directly to the clearing section of the stock exchange and, in return, receives securities or payments from the exchange. The stock exchange then notifies its member of outstanding balance based on the closing stock prices. When a broker closes out a position financed through the securities finance company, the finance company transfers money or equity to the exchange. The exchange, in turn, transfers it to the member firm.

1997 REGULATORY REFORMS IN SECURITIES MARKETS

As part of the Japanese Big Bang, the SEC released its *Comprehensive Reform of the Securities Market* on June 13, 1997. The reforms are called for because of globalization and deregulation in major financial markets, advancements in information technology, and the need to better manage the ¥1,200 trillion savings. The urgency of regulatory reforms is due to Japan's huge lag in reforming and competitive status, behind the United States and Europe. For example, trading commissions are 40% cheaper in London; hence, many institutional investors have bypassed Tokyo for London. Commissions have been gradually deregulated, beginning in April 1998. Also, the SEC has opened the door to innovative financial products that were common in the West but banned in Japan. For example, equity options on 33 big companies were cleared for trading for the first time in July 1997.[8]

Pension funds and asset management are lucrative areas. The deregulation of the financial system will allow banks to sell the investment trust funds through their extensive branch networks. The reforms will permit savers to invest outside of Japan to earn market returns on their savings. This is imperative, because Japan's population needs better returns on savings to prepare for a growing percentage of retirees. U.S. institutions have been aggressively lobbying Japanese banks to include U.S. funds in the lineup to be sold at branch counters beginning in 1998. Many asset managers are setting up joint ventures with Japanese banks and insurers in a bid to penetrate the world's second largest pension market, currently at $1 trillion. Table 9.7 lists selected transpacific linkups between foreign investment houses and Japanese financial giants.

TABLE 9.7   Selected Transpacific Joint Ventures in Money Management

Foreign Firm	Japanese Partner	Founded
Rosenberg International Equity Management (U.S.)	Nomura Securities	1987
Foreign & Colonial Management (UK)	LTCB Investment Management[1]	1988
Miller Anderson & Sherrerd (U.S.)	LTCB Investment Management	1989
Barclays Global Investors (U.S.)	Nikko Securities	1992
Lord, Abbet & Co. (U.S.)	Fuji Investment Management	1993
Dresner RCM Global Investors (U.S.)	Fuji Investment Management	1993
Gartmore Investment Management (UK)	Nippon Credit Bank	1996
New York Life/Crédit Commercial de France (U.S./France)	Taiyo Life	1997
AIG Global Investment (U.S.)	Mitsubishi Trust and Banking	1997
Brison Partners, Swiss Bank Corp. (U.S.)	LTCB Investment Management	1997

[1] LTCB Investment Management is the money management arm of Long-Term Credit Bank of Japan.
Source: Adapted from *Institutional Investor* (September 1997): 69.

Objectives of the Reforms

The goal of the reforms is to upgrade Japan as an international financial market that rivals New York and London by the year 2001. The Japanese government believes that a modern financial system is the foundation of a sound economy. The structural reforms will enable the Japanese economy to retain its vigor in an aging society and to continue its contribution to the international community. In order to meet these objectives, the reforms are to be structured and implemented based on three principles: Free, Fair, and Global.

Under a free market principle, the reforms aim at promoting freer entry into banking, securities, and insurance sectors. The activities and products in which banks and securities companies can engage will expand. The stock exchange commission rates will be gradually deregulated. Also, the government will take steps to provide a better environment for asset management business.

Under the fairness principle, the reforms are to establish a transparent and credible market. Regulations will require full and timely disclosure of material information. Rules will be strictly enforced, and violators will be punished.

Globalization is key to the success of the reforms. Japan needs to establish a legal system that lays the ground rules for new financial services and products, as well as an accounting system comparable to the international standards. The revision of Foreign Exchange Law in May 1997 was a front runner in the overall reform efforts. With the foreign exchange deregulation, the Japanese capital markets can be truly integrated into the global market and the Japanese companies may offer better services and compete effectively in the global marketplace.

Reform Plans

The reforms target products, markets, and financial intermediaries. Financial engineering and product innovation are essential to meeting preferences and requirements of investors and borrowers. All products require an efficient and trusted market for transactions. Moreover, encouraging competition among intermediaries will lead to better services to market participants. The reform plans are summarized in Table 9.8. In summary, the Big Bang is aimed at lifting restrictions on overseas bank accounts, lowering barriers separating bank and securities operations, deregulating trading commissions, and promoting entry of foreign money managers. With this, Japan has entered the early stages of structural revolution toward a more Western-style financial system.

Wall Street firms must develop strategies to deal with the challenges and opportunities posed by the upcoming changes, including gradual deregulation of commissions and the dismantling of barriers to the types of business they are allowed to do. According to the reform timetable, brokerage on trades of more than ¥50 million for listed equities will be deregulated in April 1998 and retail brokerage rates will become negotiable from March 2000. For OTC stocks, commissions have been transformed from the previous "informal administrative guidance" to a more competitive schedule. Matsui, a small Tokyo broker, took the lead and cut its rates to half of those charged under previous consensus scales. Paribus followed by making a further 20% reduction. Many believe that there is a scope for discount brokerage in Japan. Fidelity has already obtained a license for this purpose. Other houses are expected to follow.

Money management is another attractive area. There is a huge amount of savings in Japan. In addition, past poor returns might force Japan to switch to defined-contribu-

---

TABLE 9.8   Reform Plans

A. Products

Diversify the types of bonds

Diversify derivatives products

Develop investment trust products

- Introduction of Cash Management Account
- OTC sales of investment trusts by banks
- Private placement of investment trusts
- Investment Company type funds

Review and broaden the definition of securities

B. Markets

Improve transaction system in stock exchanges

Improve the OTC market system

Deregulate the solicitation by securities companies for
  unlisted and unregistered stocks

Improve the stock lending market

Improve the clearing and settlement for securities

Strengthen inspection, surveillance, and enforcement

Disclose material information in a full and timely manner

C. Financial Intermediaries

Deregulate brokerage commissions

Deregulate activities by intermediaries

Employ holding company structure

Improve asset management services

Enhance the monitoring system

Deregulate entry into securities businesses

Protect investors

---

tion pension schemes rather than the current underfunded defined benefit. This will lead to a sharp increase in the demand for fund management.

SUMMARY

The 1997 securities market reforms are called for because of globalization and deregulation of the financial markets, advancements in information technology, and the need to better manage the ¥1,200 trillion savings. This chapter provides an overview of the securities markets and identifies promising areas of investment banking business in Japan, particularly underwriting services, securities brokerage, and asset management.

SELECT BIBLIOGRAPHY

Essex, M., R. Pitchford. *The Reuter's Guide to World Bond Markets*. New York: Wiley, 1997.

Fabozzi, F. J., ed. *The Japanese Bond Markets*. Chicago, IL: Probus Publishing, 1990.

Packer, F., and E. Reynolds. "The samurai bond market." *Current Issues in Economics and Finance*. Federal Reserve Bank of New York, June 1997.

Patrick, H. T., and Y. C. Park, eds. *The Financial Development of Japan, Korea, and Taiwan*. Oxford: Oxford University Press, 1994.

Securities and Exchange Council (Japan). *Comprehensive Reform of the Securities Markets*. June 1997.

Shirakawa, M., K. Okina, and S. Shiratsuka. "Financial market globalization: Present and future." Bank of Japan, December 1997.

Suzuki, Y., ed. *The Japanese Financial System*. Oxford: Claredon Press, 1987.

Takagi, S., ed. *Japanese Capital Markets: New Developments in Regulations and Institutions*. Cambridge, MA: Blackwell, 1993.

Walter, I., and T. Hiraki, eds. *Restructuring Japan's Financial Markets*. Homewood, IL: Business One Irwin, 1993.

10

Emerging Markets

Emerging markets are an integral part of the global capital markets. They present unique opportunities to bankers. To capitalize on the profit potential in investment banking operations in emerging markets, bankers should be aware of the specific environment in each sector of the market. This chapter describes the complex process involved in doing business in emerging markets. First, several risk factors are unique to emerging markets. This includes liquidity risk, political instability, insufficient legal infrastructure, and risk of contagion effects. Issuance and trading of Brady bonds have dominated emerging market activities for many years. However, there is no longer a pipeline of Brady restructuring to feed the market. Most Bradys will eventually be paid off, exchanged, or bought back in the secondary market. This chapter also covers equity trading and privatization programs in emerging markets, clearing and settlement of emerging market instruments, and emerging market derivatives, which are essential in winning business and hedging risks in emerging markets.

OVERVIEW

The term *emerging market* describes the securities markets of a developing country and the use that country makes of international capital markets. Emerging markets are increasingly an integral part of today's global capital markets. The implementation of economic reforms throughout emerging markets has created great expectations and optimism. Even though these emerging countries are still far behind the United States, Western Europe, and Japan, many developing countries are taking steps to build more efficient capital markets. These steps should target three areas:

1. *Legal infrastructure for investor protection:* The fundamentals behind investor protection are full, accurate, and timely company financial reports and disclosure; fair securities issuance and trading practices; and the sanctity of contract law. All are essential if emerging markets are to achieve their key objectives.
2. *Establishment of modern banking and securities laws:* A good start for any country is a contract law, a company law, a banking law, and a justice system that enforces the law effectively.
3. *Corporate ownership and governance:* Expanding enterprise ownership is perceived as a means of increasing social stability in emerging markets. In recent

years, this has been central to privatization programs. Policies that increased the supply of equities can create their own demand from savers that were never recognized before. The local demand, plus international capital inflows, is fundamental to successful privatization programs. This is especially essential in markets where governments limit foreign ownership of equities.

Regions of Emerging Markets

Emerging markets can be divided into the following regions:[1]

- *Latin America and Caribbean:* Argentina, Bermuda, Bolivia, Brazil, Chile, Colombia, Costa Rica, Cuba, Dominican Republic, Ecuador, Guatemala, Honduras, Jamaica, Mexico, Nicaragua, Panama, Peru, Trinidad and Tobago, Uruguay, and Venezuela
- *Central and Eastern Europe and CIS Countries:* Albania, Bulgaria, Croatia, Czech Republic, Estonia, Hungary, Latvia, Lithuania, Poland, Romania, Russia, Slovakia, Slovenia, Ukraine, and Yugoslavia
- *Africa:* Algeria, Angola, Cameroon, Congo, Gabon, Ghana, Ivory Coast, Kenya, Libya, Madagascar, Mauritius, Morocco, Mozambique, Namibia, Nigeria, Senegal, South Africa, Sudan, Tanzania, Togo, Tunisia, Zaire[2] (Democratic Congo), Zambia, and Zimbabwe
- *Asia:* Bangladesh, China, Hong Kong, India, Indonesia, Kazakhstan, Malaysia, North Korea, Pakistan, Philippines, Singapore, South Korea, Sri Lanka, Taiwan, Thailand, and Vietnam
- *Middle East:* Bahrain, Egypt, Iran, Iraq, Israel, Jordan, Lebanon, Oman, Syria, and Turkey

RISK FACTORS

Investment banking business in emerging markets involves much higher risks than those associated with developed capital markets. Bankers preparing to commit capital to an emerging market should be aware of the following six primary risks:

- Volatility risk and risk of contagion effects
- Liquidity risk
- Clearance and settlement risk
- Political risk
- Currency risk
- Limited disclosure and insufficient legal infrastructure

Volatility Risk and Risk of Contagion Effects

High volatility is expected in emerging markets. Emerging markets are immature, sometimes vulnerable to scandal, and often lack the legal and justice infrastructure to enforce the law. Accounting, disclosure, trading, and settlement practices may, at times, seem overly arbitrary and naive. Against this backdrop, many emerging markets have had to cope with unprecedented inflows and outflows of capital in recent years. The sudden movement of highly speculative, short-term capital has the potential of taking with it much of a market's price support. This was seen in the 1994–95 Mexico peso crisis and in the 1997–1998 financial crisis in Asia that included Malaysia, Thailand, Hong Kong, Indonesia, Japan, and South Korea. Such sudden flight of capital, triggered by events in one emerging market, can spread instantly to other markets, even when those markets have quite different conditions (contagion effects). When Mexico's currency collapsed in 1994–1995, the panic quickly spread to other Latin markets (the so-called *tequila effect*). More recently, the impact of the financial crisis in Asia spilled over to all markets in the world. In just a few days at the end of October 1997, some Brady bonds shed up to 15% of their value as volume zoomed. Traders stared at their screens as bid–ask spreads widened from 15 to 200 basis points.

The International Finance Corporation publishes, in its annual *Emerging Markets Facts Book*, a summary of stock price volatility for the emerging markets. It is quite common to observe a standard deviation of monthly stock returns of 30% or higher. Research has found that the price movement of stocks within the market tend to be highly correlated with one another, and the higher the volatility, the higher the correlation. This implies that being in the right market at the right time is more important than the stock selection ability.

Liquidity Risk

Emerging markets are generally small and often illiquid. A country's entire market capitalization may be less than that of a single large U.S. company. Many companies in some markets are closely held family businesses. Shares of only several hundred companies trade in several markets, and total daily trading volume may reach only a few million shares. According to a *New York Times* report (November 11, 1995), the average value of trading in NYSE per minute was $30,707,692 in 1994. The time it would take to trade that same value in Malaysia was 2 hours and 8 minutes, in Chile it was 2 days, 3 hours, and 7 minutes, and in Hungary it was 41 days, 12 hours, and 18 minutes. Thin trading activity often leads to higher market impact costs. Buyers of large blocks of shares may have to pay up to complete a transaction. Sellers may receive a mark-down price. In addition, in some countries (e.g., Russia and parts of Latin America), it is sometimes difficult to sell shares in a falling market because stock markets are underdeveloped and riddled with corrupt practices.

Some countries restrict foreign investments. In Taiwan and Korea, for example, foreigners are not permitted to own more than a certain percentage of a company's equity. In some emerging markets, foreign investors must wait a certain period of time to withdraw capital from the market.

Clearance and Settlement Risk

Among the emerging market risks, inadequate settlement procedures rank high on the list. This risk may not have been apparent to stock exchange officials or regulators until made so by the increasing transaction volume. The settlement fail rates (trades failing to settle on settlement date) in emerging markets are much higher than in the more developed markets. To the extent such problems occur, the purchaser could miss attractive opportunities in the event it were unable to consummate securities purchases. Also, a seller in a fail situation could experience losses due to a decline in the security price after the time the trade was entered if the counterparty is not held accountable.

Even in Brady bonds, the settlement system lags far behind. The system struggled with 4,500 trades a day for about a week in late October 1997. The rate of mismatches soared. Euroclear wound up stretching its deadline for receipt of settlement instructions by two hours to allow customers to sort out transactions.

Political Risk

Many emerging markets are undergoing major changes in structures of government, and economic and financial markets. The very fact of an emerging market may entail variability of returns associated with political risk. Certainly, some are subject to such political risks as coups, assassinations, or paralyzing power struggles. Governments moving toward democracy might be grappling with long-standing political and social problems, and at times might suddenly retreat toward socialism. Progress could also be stalled by economic reversals that have often gripped emerging economies.

Equally important is that the government may change the way capital gains, dividends, or interests due to foreign investors are taxed. They may also restrict repatriation of earnings, or change the conditions under which funds may be repatriated. Restrictions may take the form of new foreign exchange regulations or limitations on the convertibility of the local currency.

Several advisory services and financial publications rank political risks. Most vendors charge high fees. Also, *Institutional Investor–International* periodically publishes the results of surveys of sovereign political risk. *Euromoney* regularly publishes political risk ratings as well.

Currency Risk

Fluctuations in the foreign exchange markets have a dramatic effect on profits earned abroad. High profits from underwriting, trading, M&As, or privatization programs could be turned into losses from falling local currencies. Currency devaluation and stock market downturns can produce steep losses to bankers. One of the primary causes of currency risk in emerging markets has been runaway inflation. Other factors to consider include large external indebtedness, volatility in their balance of payments position, and inexperienced central banking authorities. Also to blame is large hedge funds' speculative trading.

Disclosure and Property Right Risk

Many emerging markets lack the legal structure for investor protection. Investor protection in many emerging markets is not perceived as important as broadening and deepening the securities markets. Nevertheless, investor protection is the key to confidence in the capital markets. More and more countries have moved toward better investor protection, toward full, accurate, and timely financial reporting and disclosure. In addition, many are taking steps to ensure fair securities issuance and trading practices, and sanctity of contract law. Updating laws relating to securities markets is another step. The market environment in emerging markets will not be improved unless the emerging countries set forth a contract law, a company law, a banking law, and a justice system that enforces the law effectively.

Overall, progress has been made. Capital market participants still need to recognize that disclosure is often limited and fundamental data are imprecise in emerging markets.

BRADY BONDS

Major emerging market debt instruments include loans, Brady[3] bonds, non-Brady sovereign and corporate bonds, local market instruments in local currency and in U.S. dollars, and options and warrants. Brady bonds are created under the 1990 *Brady Plan*. Each Brady restructuring resulted in the issuance of collateralized securities. By 1997, all major Brady restructurings had been announced or completed.

In recent years, there have been many conversions and redemptions of Bradys and the amount is declining. Much of the Brady debt will eventually be exchanged or bought back. Still, trading volume of Bradys accounted for more than half of the total volume in emerging market debt instruments each year from 1992 to 1996.[4] Top houses in Brady bonds include J.P. Morgan, Citicorp, Salomon Smith Barney, Bear Sterns, Morgan Stanley Dean Witter, Chase, Merrill Lynch, ING Barings, ABN Amro Hoare Govett, and Credit Suisse First Boston.[5] Major interdealer brokers in Bradys include Euro Brokers, Garban Securities, and RMJ Securities. The business of interdealer brokering proliferated because it allowed big dealers to trade huge positions without revealing themselves. Between 1993 and 1997, the interdealer brokering soared from 10% to 90% of Brady trading.

Description of Brady Bonds

Brady bonds are securities that have resulted from the exchange of commercial bank loans into new bonds. They come in many types and options, but there are several consistent characteristics. The similarity stems from the fact that creditor banks were provided with three options for the restructure of the commercial debt. The first set of options allowed banks to exchange loans for a series of new sovereign bonds. Banks could either exchange original face value of the loans for new 30-year par bonds that paid below-market fixed interest rates, or they could exchange the discounted amount (usually 30–50% discount) of the loans for new 30-year bonds that paid a floating interest of LIBOR + 13/16%. Hence, a new class of securities called Brady bonds were created. The third option allowed creditor banks to carry the full principal amount of the loans on their books while providing new lending of at least 25% of old loans over several years.

The debtor country's foreign reserves were to be used for purchase of the collateral enhancement. Since the first Brady bond was issued for Mexico in 1990, no country has ever defaulted on payment and the Brady bond market has become the largest and most liquid of the emerging markets. Overall, there is around $190 billion of eligible loan debt from countries in Asia, Africa, Eastern Europe, and Latin America. By 1997, more than $150 billion of Brady bonds had been issued.

For many Bradys, their principal and semiannual interest payments are collateralized by 30-year zero-coupon U.S. Treasury bonds and by high-quality assets. If a Brady bond defaults, and its principal is collateralized, holders can only collect the principal when the bond matures. Some Bradys have embedded warrants whose value is often tied to the world price of raw products native to the debtor country. The majority of outstanding Brady bonds are U.S.-dollar denominated. Although some bonds have been issued in other currencies, including deutsche marks, those nondollar issues tend to be relatively illiquid.

The market is largely a longer dated market. More than 72% of outstanding Brady bonds have maturities longer than 10 years, and more than half have maturities of longer than 20 years. Outstanding issues are evenly divided between fixed- and float-ing-rate instruments.

Investment banking houses and commercial banks make active markets in Brady bonds. The investor base has widened to include mutual funds, hedge funds, and insurance companies and pension funds. Portfolio managers are looking to these instruments as the core of the emerging markets or yield enhancement and portfolio diversification.

Issuers

Since Mexico issued the first Bradys in 1990, many countries have followed. By 1997, a total of more than $150 billion of Brady bonds had been issued by Mexico, Argentina, Brazil, Bulgaria, Costa Rica, the Dominican Republic, Ecuador, Jordan, Nigeria, Panama, Peru, the Philippines, Poland, Uruguay, and Venezuela. The Ivory Coast and Vietnam are expected to issue Brady Bonds in the near future.

The first Mexico issue ($48 billion) offered banks two options for exchange of their loans into tradable securities. The Mexico *par bonds* were issued in March 1990 with $29^3/_4$-year maturities and fixed $6^1/_4$% coupons. They are dollar denominated, and zero-coupon U.S. government securities back the principals. Initially, two series of *Par bond* were issued: Series A and Series B. Alternatively, the *discount bonds* gave a 35% discount in face value of debt, but offered a floating rate of LIBOR + 13/16%.

The principals on both types of bonds were fully collateralized by zero-coupon U.S. Treasury bonds, and there was a rolling interest guarantee covering 18 month's worth of interest payments. Structures of Bradys have become more complex over time; but the basic principles were based on the first Mexican deal. One major bond feature added to later issues was the buy-back option that allows a country to repurchase part of its debt at an agreed discount, enabling it to participate in a debt-reduction program. In 1995, Argentina repurchased some of its par and discount bonds in the secondary markets. In April 1996, Mexico completed a $1.75 billion swap deal to repurchase mainly par bonds in exchange for a 30-year uncollateralized global bond, which represents pure sovereign risk. The Central Bank of Brazil had legislation approved to buy back or restructure all $57 billion of its Brady bonds. Mexico, Ecuador, and Brazil have already bought back more than $8 billion of Bradys since 1996. Venezuela announced in September 1997 its plan to swap $1.5 billion of Bradys for new global bonds. In many of these buyback deals, investors from Europe, Asia, and the United States exchanged the Bradys for unsecured, higher-yielding 30-year global bonds.

Types of Bradys

There are four basic types of Brady bonds: *Par or discount bonds, debt conversion or new money bonds, front-loaded interest-reduction bonds* (FLIRBs), and *interest arrears capitalization*.

Par bonds are loans exchanged for fixed-rate bonds, issued with below-market interest rates at par. *Discount bonds* are loans exchanged for floating-rate debt, issued at a discount. Both are backed by U.S. Treasury zero-coupon bond principal collateral. These bonds have long-term maturities and are the most liquid. These have bullet amortization and represent the most common Brady bonds outstanding.

Debt conversion bonds are short-term floating-rate bonds without collateral. Creditors exchanged loans for bonds at par and provided additional funds to the Brady issuing nation at a floating rate of interest. This proved positive in the emerging markets, as these countries had the ability to service their debt obligations but were unwilling to pay before the conversion.

Front-loaded interest-reduction bonds (FLIRB) are loans exchanged for medium-term step-up bonds at below-market interest rates for the initial 5 to 7 years, then at a floating rate until maturity. These bonds provide partial interest collateral in the form of cash, with collateral rolled over for subsequent periods upon timely interest payments. These bonds are less liquid than the par/discount, but they contain a much shorter average life, as amortization payments begin typically after 5 to 7 years.

Interest Arrears Capitalization Bonds were created when commercial banks rescheduled interest in arrears of Brazilian, Argentine, and Ecuadorian debt. The interests were used to create new short-term floating-rate bonds. These bonds have been issued prior to the rescheduling of principal into the Brady format.

The Chicago Mercantile Exchange has listed futures and options contracts on four individual Brady bond issues: Mexican par bonds (Series A and B), Argentine floating-rate bonds (FRBs), and Brazilian C and eligible-interest bonds. Bankers and traders use these contracts for purposes such as hedging, asset allocation, yield enhancement, and spread trading.

Valuation

Brady bonds have three distinct features: principal collateral, interest collateral, and the sovereign portion. When evaluating a Brady, it is necessary to strip out the enhancements attached in order to understand and analyze the risk and relative valuation ascribed by the market to each respective sovereign issuer. Removing the value of U.S. Treasury strips and the portion of interest guarantee will produce the yield of the unenhanced income stream. This is based on the credit quality of the issuing nation. Table 10.1 lists Standard & Poor's long-term credit ratings[6] of emerging countries.

Further analysis of collateralized Brady bonds includes assessing the present value of the collateral as a percentage of the Brady market price. The value of the U.S. Treasury component acts as a floor, in that the bond would not trade below the value of the collateral. The respective countries—both in the open market and also through special Treasury issue—purchased such collateral. Par/discount bonds and FLIRBs also include a partial guarantee of interest. The Brady-issuing government deposits money with the New York Federal Reserve in amounts covering 12 to 18 months of interest payments. Additionally, some bonds have detachable warrants or recovery rights predicated upon economic/industry performance. The highest profile is Mexico's Value Recover Rights based on numerous variables including oil price, GDP, and oil production levels.

TRADING

Trading in emerging markets instruments or in local markets involves special risks such as volatility risk, liquidity risk, clearance and settlement risk, political risk, currency risk, and limited disclosure and insufficient legal infrastructure. These risks should not deter investment-banking operations in these markets. Emerging markets have become an integral part of the global capital markets, and these risks can be managed through diversification and the use of derivatives.

TABLE 10.1 Standard & Poor's Long-Term Credit Ratings of Emerging Countries

Issuer	Local Currency	Foreign Currency
Taiwan	NR	AA+
Bermuda	NR	AA
Korea	NR	AA–
Malaysia	AA+	A+
Slovenia	AA	A
Thailand	AA	A
Hong Kong	A+	A
Czech Republic	NR	A
Chile	AA	A–
Israel	AA–	A–
Indonesia	A+	BBB
Latvia	A–	BBB
China	NR	BBB
Colombia	A+	BBB–
Slovak Republic	A	BBB–
Croatia	A–	BBB–
Egypt	A–	BBB–
Hungary	A–	BBB–
Poland	A–	BBB–
Oman	NR	BBB–
Philippines	A–	BB+
India	BBB+	BB+
South Africa	BBB+	BB+
Trinidad and Tobago	BBB+	BB+
Uruguay	BBB	BB+
Panama	BB+	BB+
Mexico	BBB+	BB
Argentina	BBB–	BB
Jordan	BBB–	BB–
Romania	BBB–	BB–
Brazil	BB+	BB–
Lebanon	BB	BB–
Russia	NR	BB–
Dominican Republic	NR	B+
Pakistan	NR	B+
Turkey	NR	B
Venezuela	NR	B

Source: The ratings are obtained from *Sovereign Credit Ratings: A Primer*, Standard & Poor's, 1997. NR stands for *not rated*.

Trading of Emerging Debt

According to the EMTA survey of bank participants, turnover in emerging debt instruments rose to U.S.$5.296 trillion in 1996, which nearly doubled the turnover in 1995 and was more than sevenfold the 1992 volume of $733 billion. Sharp trading increases were reported for all major instruments. All regions participated in the growth of debt trading. Although Latin America debt accounted for more than 80% of total trading,

TABLE 10.2   Trading Volume of Emerging Market Debt Instruments (in U.S.$ millions)

	1996	1995	1994	1993	1992
Latin America	4,265,869	2,284,193	2,259,349	1,621,562	666,444
Argentina	1,292,462	609,678	590,488	544,236	156,315
Brazil	1,441,454	877,412	597,118	259,144	209,030
Mexico	946,396	510,135	601,397	465,421	189,503
Venezuela	397,122	194,080	400,040	287,782	93,596
Eastern Europe and Russia	612,673	314,145	172,274	104,495	26,116
Russia	380,499	144,977	71,417	24,697	678
Asia	165,775	26,204	23,506	16,403	7,169
Africa	222,413	108,813	109,965	78,751	20,489
Middle East	21,198	5,343	2,630	2,859	0

Source: Adapted from Eng and Lees (1997), which contains comprehensive, detailed EMTA Survey results. This table lists only data for each region and several countries with significant trading volumes.

Middle East and Asia trading demonstrated impressive percentage gains. Table 10.2 lists annual trading volume by region from 1992 to 1996.

Trading in debt of Brazil, Argentina, Mexico, and Venezuela was 77% of all reported emerging market trading activity in 1996. Brazil topped the trading volume with $1.441 trillion, 27% of all reported activity. Trading in Argentine assets came in second at $1.292 trillion. This more than doubled the trading volume in 1995. Trading in Mexico instruments rose significantly to $946 billion. This followed from Mexico's swap of $1.75 billion of outstanding Brady bonds for new uncollateralized 30-year bonds, and better-than-expected economic developments. Venezuelan debt trading was reported at $397 billion in 1996.

Russian asset trading approached the level of Venezuelan debt trading, reaching U.S.$380 billion in 1996. Volumes in other Eastern European debts also showed impressive gains. Trading of African instruments was up dramatically, from $20.489 billion in 1992 to $222.413 billion in 1996. Trading in Asian instruments rose 375%, of which much was attributable to local instrument trading. The EMTA Survey notes that Asian trading may be underreported. Many Asian countries have been rated investment grade and are not categorized as emerging markets by some participants. Finally, trading in the Middle East region still remains far behind other regions.

Since 1993, Bradys have accounted for more than half of the emerging market turnover. Reported shares of local market instruments rose to $1.188 trillion, mostly in local currency. The trading volume of options and warrants has risen steadily during the time period 1992–1996 and is expected to continue upward. Annual trading volume by instruments is listed in Table 10.3.

According to a more recent EMTA survey, Brady bonds represented 41.4% of total trading volume in the first quarter of 1997. The volume of Bradys is expected to decline, as many countries have taken steps to repurchase or swap new uncollateralized issues for their outstanding Brady debt.

Equity Trading in Emerging Markets

The emerging stock markets should not be viewed as a static universe, but as a constantly evolving group of markets. Each market is unique, characterized by its capitalization, trading hours, settlement process, transaction costs, ownership structure, and

TABLE 10.3   Trading Volume of Emerging Market Debt Instruments (in U.S.$ millions)

Instrument	1996	1995	1994	1993	1992
Loans	248,564	175,108	244,435	273,563	229,312
Bradys	2,685,985	1,580,099	1,684,003	1,021,290	247,698
Non-Bradys Eurobonds	658,145	233,255	164,863	176,628	22,661
Local Market Instrument	1,187,899	571,141	518,928	N/A	N/A
-Local currency	850,760	461,163	370,735	207,204	N/A
Options & Warrants	471,044	179,212	142,378	57,407	15,340
Others	45,293	N/A	11,574	N/A	119,947

Source: Adapted from Eng and Lees (1997).

regulation. Growth in market capitalization of emerging equity markets has been impressive. Some emerging equity markets are rival in size to industrial country equity markets. Although many emerging markets have removed restrictions on foreign equity ownership, entry barriers still exist. U.S. investment banking participation of the local equity market is generally quite limited. Most of the equity activities are in ADRs in London and New York.

Trading in local markets is gaining importance, even though not all markets are able to give large investors ready access, due to size of market, lack of liquidity, concentrated trading, and limitation on foreign ownership. It is worth noting that J.P. Morgan publishes *Emerging Local Markets Index* monthly, which tracks total returns for local-currency-denominated money-market instruments in the emerging markets. In addition, *IFC's Emerging Stock Markets DataBase* tracks most emerging stock markets.

Execution costs are very dramatic in emerging markets. According to an Elkin/McSherry report published in *Institutional Investor* (November 1997), the total trading cost at NYSE in 1996 was 34.1 basis points and an average trade on an international exchange cost 49.8 basis points. The total execution costs include commission, fee, and market impact.[7] In emerging markets, the 13 exchanges with complete data averaged 92.3 basis points in trading costs (see Table 10.4). Hong Kong was the lowest cost

TABLE 10.4   Execution Costs in Emerging Markets in 1996 (Basis Points)

Country	Average Commission	Average Fees	Market Impact	Total
Brazil	35.7	6.0	21.4	63.1
Hong Kong	41.6	12.2	5.4	59.2
Indonesia	74.8	12.5	21.2	108.5
Malaysia	65.9	9.8	11.6	87.3
Mexico	33.2	1.7	34.4	69.3
Philippines	84.0	23.1	7.8	114.9
Portugal	37.5	6.5	18.7	62.7
Singapore	57.4	3.4	11.1	71.9
South Africa	33.3	3.8	52.5	89.6
South Korea	46.6	23.2	159.1	228.9
Taiwan	31.2	23.8	17.9	72.9
Thailand	76.8	2.3	14.7	93.8
Turkey	38.5	10.2	28.5	77.2
Average	50.5	10.7	29.6	92.3

Source: Adapted from "How the cost of executing trades varies in 42 countries (table)," *Institutional Investor* (November 1997): 73.

place to trade, at 59.2 basis points. The costs of executing equity trades were modest (60 to 75 basis points) in Brazil, Mexico, Portugal, Singapore, and Taiwan. South Korea was the most expensive place to trade equities, at 228 basis points, due to an unusually high market impact. The average market impact was 29.6 basis points. As listed in Table 10.4, the commissions and fees averaged at 50.5 basis points and 10.7 basis points, respectively.

PRIVATIZATION IN EMERGING MARKETS

In emerging markets, a strong consensus has emerged that the achievement of more dynamic economic growth requires a greater role for the private sector, because production resources will be used more effectively. A key element of the transformation to the private sector is the privatization of state-owned enterprises (SOEs). Between 1988 and 1995 (the latest year with complete data at the time of the writing), developing governments took in more than $132 billion from sale of the SOEs. This represents the transfers of control of more than 3,800 entities from public to private hands. The number of developing countries undertaking privatization has grown from 14 in 1988 to more than 60 in 1995. Table 10.5 shows selected privatization revenues from 1988 to 1995. These privatization programs represent only a small portion of net private capital flows to emerging markets. According to data released by the Institute of International Finance, total net private capital flows to the leading emerging markets reached $232

TABLE 10.5 Privatization Revenues from Selected Countries (1988–1995, U.S.$ millions)

Country[1]	Revenues	Number of Privatization
Argentina	18,355	131
Brazil	9,998	54
Chile	1,297	24
China	7,033	89
Czech Republic	2,297	39
Czechoslovakia	1,909	40
Hungary	7,957	207
India	5,205	62
Indonesia	4,014	15
Korea	3,274	8
Malaysia	9,158	38
Mexico	27,331	211
Pakistan	1,576	92
Peru	4,458	90
Philippines	3,417	82
Poland	2,994	224
Russia	1,234	36
Slovak Republic	1,482	148
Thailand	1,040	10
Turkey	3,081	145
Venezuela	2,510	29

[1] The table lists only those countries with at least $1 billion in privatization revenues.
Source: The figures are obtained from Bouton and Sumlinski (1997).

billion in 1997, $304 billion in 1996, $218 billion in 1995, and $155 billion in 1994. The 1998 projections are at $220 billion.

Governments in emerging countries are under pressure to speed up privatization. The IMF is pressing governments to rid themselves of state dinosaurs. There are also signs that the strong investment inflows from the United States are drying up. In Western Europe, the need to reduce public debt to levels[8] that will qualify countries to join the EMU single currency has brought a new urgency to previously stalled programs. It is expected that the privatization will remain focused on more marketable sectors such as telecoms, utilities, energy companies, banks, and industrials. The trend of speeding up privatization provides bankers around the world with tremendous opportunities.

Although offerings will continue to rely on international investors, the strength of domestic demand is the overriding factor in the success of privatization. This is especially true because government regulation limits foreign ownership in many emerging markets. Incentives such as long-term employee ownership encourage participation in big offerings will certainly help.

The flood of issues adds an element of risk. Because the markets are dominated by large institutions, an increased interest is expected. This is because privatization will bring a change in the composition of that country's stock market indices. Examples include Deutsche Telekom entering the DAX, and ENI entering the MIB30. The large size of the offerings means they must constitute a big part of the market indices, and investors wishing to maintain their country and sector weightings will increase their positions on these stocks.

Underwriters are facing the squeeze between demands for good investments of increasing sophistication with a wide range of menus to choose from, and those of experienced vendors keen to extract the highest possible valuations from the market at the least expense. The squeeze has caused the privatization fees to fall from 4% in 1994 to 2.5% and 3% on certain high-profile European secondary sales. Bankers need to be aware that efforts to compensate for the low fees with high issue volumes may tempt banks to overstep the limits of a saturated market that has the potential for disaster.

CLEARING, SETTLEMENT, AND CUSTODIAL SERVICES

Settlements in emerging markets are often more complex than in the more established markets. The key to minimizing problems and maintaining a good settlement record in these markets is the use of a knowledgeable and efficient global custodian. This section discusses the custodian issues involved in the international trading of equities and debt.

Custodian Issues of Equities

In emerging markets, many traders and fund managers care more about settling on time than they do about sophisticated services. The global custodian plays an integral part in the settlement/clearing process by providing a subcustodian network, custody and registration, foreign exchange service, reporting, cash management, income collection, tax reclamation, and daily settlement duties related to trading.

It is important when doing business in emerging markets to have a global custodian (such as Chase Manhattan, Citibank, Bankers Trust, and State Street Bank) that can quickly establish agent bank relationships in new markets. Custodians with better networks receive online reporting from their agent banks and maintain daily communications, thus enabling them to quickly resolve any problems that may arise. The global custodian is responsible for custody of the investment bank's assets. Some are held locally by its subcustodian agents. The registration process varies from market to market and the subcustodians are familiar with the practices of their respective markets.

If foreign exchange service will be needed, it is crucial to know that the chosen custodian can perform the service in all the needed markets. Some custodians may not perform foreign exchange services for certain highly volatile currencies. Custodian agents differ tremendously in the area of corporate actions such as proxies, rights issues, and splits. Custodians with a good corporate action department provide more than just the basic information by also noting special information, such as whether rights are tradable. Another essential piece of information needed on corporate action is whether new share entitlements will rank *pari passu* with the old shares. *Pari passu* refers to new shares issued that rank equally with the old shares. New shares that do not rank *pari passu* with old shares may differ in many ways; they may not have voting rights, they may not be entitled to dividends, or they may be valued at a different level.

The custodians rely on their subcustodian banks for collection of income in local markets. Most custodians perform well in providing this service; however, difficulties may arise if proper registration of shares has not been accomplished. Very few institutions want to keep local currency on hand, because there is always a risk of devaluation. This is especially a big concern after the peso devaluation and the recent shakeouts in the Asian financial systems. They may place standing instructions with the custodian to bring back all local currency to U.S. dollars on a regular basis. The custodian is responsible for placing the uninvested funds into income-generating short-term investments.

Another important function of a custodian bank is to provide a good tax reclamation procedure, which includes timely filing of recoverable taxes and tracking of all outstanding claims. This is important due to the administrative red tape in some local governments. Global custodians differ in the area of routine settlements as well. It is essential to have a custodian who specializes in all of the markets in which the investment bank has holdings.

The common settlement practices are DVP (delivery versus payment). However, in certain emerging markets with short settlement periods, the settlement cannot be DVP in local currency unless a local currency account is maintained. In Mexico and Turkey, settlements are often made in U.S. dollars instead of local currency, although delivery is made and shares are held in the local market. Instructions to the custodian may state that the custodian is to "receive shares free" (not delivery versus payment) and wire U.S. dollars after receipt of shares. For sales, shares may be released to local brokers either "free of payment" on settlement date or after payment is made in U.S. dollars from the local broker's U.S.-agent bank. Argentina is an emerging market in which the trader may decide to settle DVP in local currency or "free" in U.S. dollars.

Bradys and Other Debt Instruments

Beginning in 1991, Daiwa Securities America began building a solid business of clearing Brady bonds. By late 1994, Daiwa had a near monopoly. There was a fear that a failing interdealer broker could hinder Daiwa operation, which, in turn, could spread the problem throughout the market.

To keep up with the increased pace of trading activity, the EMTA (*Emerging Markets Traders Association*) developed Match-EM that permits nearly simultaneous confirmation and matching of bond and loan trades, as well as the real time dissemination of accurate market price and volume data. Furthermore, the EMTA and the *International Securities Clearing Corporation* (ISCC) signed a memorandum of understanding in August 1996 to jointly develop the *Emerging Market Clearing Corporation* (EMCC) as a net settlement guarantee system among global dealers, interdealer brokers, and correspondent clearing firms for Brady bonds and other emerging-market debt instruments. It is owned initially by EMTA (38%), NSCC (38%), and the *International Securities Market Association* (ISMA) (24%). All major emerging market dealers and interdealer brokers participate in EMCC. Big dealers have to keep up to $200 million in accounts and interdealer brokers have agreed to maintain $10 million in net excess capital and meet special margin requirements. The SEC approved the EMCC as a U.S. clearing agency in February 1998. The EMCC has been up and running since April 1998.

Here is how the system works. Emerging market debt trades will be entered by EMCC participants, matched by Match-EM and Trax,[9] and transmitted to EMCC for acceptance and multilateral netting. After the trades are entered, they are evaluated for eligibility. Accepted transactions are guaranteed by the EMCC and reported to members on an *Accepted Trade Report*. EMCC also transmits settlement instructions to Cedel or Euroclear to complete the process. In addition, EMCC will calculate appropriate margin requirements daily, based on existing positions as well as new net trades, mark positions to market, issue margin calls when needed, and manage the resulting collateral. According to an EMTA report, anticipated benefits from the EMCC include:

- Guarantees on trade date the ultimate settlement of accepted transactions
- Calculates exposures and collects collateral to secure those exposures
- Strengthens the post-trade settlement chain by linking trade clearance to settlement
- Provides fail compensation for undelivered items
- Insulates the clearing process from overdependence on commercial clearers
- Reduces cost and increases efficiency through standardization and centralization

It is estimated that the EMCC would reduce Daiwa's exposure to the interdealer brokers to $8 million from $50 million per day. In addition, the EMCC would benefit the market by lowering the daily market risk from $100 million to $25 million.

EMERGING MARKET DERIVATIVES

The growth of emerging market derivatives is driven by continued allocation to emerging market asset classes, increased sophistication of emerging market investors, recognition of downside risk, innovation in new instruments, and the emerging country's attempt to lower costs. Bankers looking to gain access to or compete in emerging markets need to understand the impact of derivatives on emerging market finance. Several derivatives—such as currency swaps, equity swaps, derivative enhanced securitization, and credit-default swaps—have been used to increase the availability of and reduce the cost of capital for borrowers in emerging markets and to maximize the funding advantages of securitizable assets. Emerging market options, futures, forwards, and credit spread contracts can be used to facilitate investment in countries with capital restrictions.

Currency Swaps

Historically, investors in markets with low interest rates, excess liquidity, and narrow credit spread have provided capital flows into emerging markets. In 1992 and 1993 capital flows were primarily in U.S. dollars. More recently, capital flows have been in yen, deutsche marks, and Swiss francs. Issuers have used currency swaps to lower costs by more than 1% a year and to open up an entirely new funding source.

A currency swap works as follows. In a straight currency swap, a borrower issues a foreign currency debt (such as yen) and immediately exchanges that debt for its chosen currency (such as dollar). The counterparty of the exchange is typically a swap dealer. The borrower periodically pays the dealer dollar coupon interest (could be either floating or fixed), and the dealer pays the interest to the creditor in yen. When the loan comes due, the borrower reverses the transaction with the swap dealer, swapping dollar to get back yen needed to pay off the yen debt. The borrower has received dollars at the beginning of the loan and experiences a dollar outflow when the loan is paid off. The currency swap has facilitated the borrower's ability to borrow dollars from foreign markets, possibly at a lower cost, with currency risk hedged. The process is described in Figure 10.1.

The combination of cheap debt in certain markets and a currency swap allows emerging market borrowers to reduce funding costs without taking incremental currency exposure. The combination can generate significant savings. For example, in November 1995, Argentina issued a 3.3-year yen-denominated debt and swapped to U.S. dollars. This generated a synthetic U.S. dollar funding at LIBOR +4.1%. At the time, comparable dollar debt cost LIBOR +5.3%. The yen-debt-plus-currency-swap combination saved 1.2% per year.

Equity Swaps

In an equity swap, an investor receives capital gains plus dividends in a target market and, in turn, pays to the swap dealer LIBOR and any decrease in the market index, a total return swap. This is one of the most efficient ways of gaining exposure to emerging markets. The structure saves investors on commission, stamp duty, clearing fees, and spreads. This is especially useful for investors who, for legal or regulatory reasons, cannot invest directly in a particular country but would like to have exposure to that market. Many players opt for price return swap, instead of total return swaps, because of the administrative headaches of dividend accounting. There have been wild swings in equity swap pricing in Taiwan, Korea, and especially Thailand.

Derivative Enhanced Securitization

Emerging market borrowers can use derivatives to maximize the amount of low-cost funding with securitizable assets. A recent example of this is YPF's structured export notes. In November 1995, Argentina's largest company, YPF, issued $400 million of 7.5% structured export notes due 2002. The notes were issued at a yield of 2.0% over comparable-maturity U.S. Treasury notes. This is lower than the 4.0% spread YPF might have to pay on unsecured debt. The right to receive certain payments from Empresa

FIGURE 10.1   Foreign Debt Plus Currency Swap

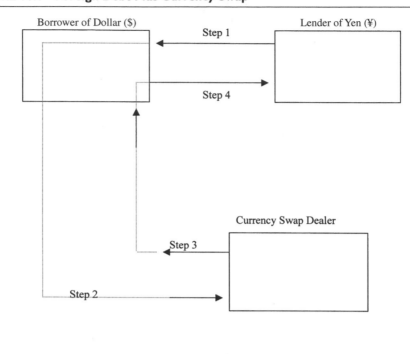

Step 1: Receive a loan in yen.
Step 2: The yen are swapped for dollars for the borrower's use during the life of the loan.
Step 3: Dollars are swapped back for yen to pay off the loan.
Step 4: Pay off the loan in yen (plus interest).

Nacional del Petroleo (ENAP) in Chile and the right to receive payments under a long-term oil price hedge agreement secured the transaction. Moody's, Standard & Poor's, and Duff and Phelps rate the notes Baa1, BBB and BBB, respectively. A similar private placement of $400 million was issued in June 1995.

The idea was simple but highly effective: YPF had long-term agreements to deliver oil to, and receive payments from, ENAP in Chile. The rating agencies had indicated that a note backed by the ENAP receivables would result in investment-grade ratings. The disadvantage of this approach was that YPF would need to commit a large number of barrels of oil to secure the issue against lower oil prices. The solution was to use put options on the oil price from an investment-grade bank rather than to over-collateralize the transaction.[10] The incremental cost of purchasing the put options was outweighed by the benefit of securing investment-grade ratings. The puts maximized YPF's access to this low-cost source of funds.

Credit Default Swaps

A credit default swap[11] is a synthetic instrument, in which one counterparty pays a premium in return for a contingent payment triggered by the default of one or more third-party reference credits. In project finance, an equity sponsor to a large project might want to hedge the portion of sovereign risk not guaranteed by an export-credit-agency-backed facility. It could enter into a credit default swap with a notional principal equal to the amount not covered by the sovereign guarantee. For example, a German bank with a Mexican loan might have 95% of the principal covered by the guarantee. It cannot sell part of the loan, but it can hedge the 5% stub with a credit default swap.

Emerging Market Options, Futures, and Forwards

Emerging market equity derivatives, such as futures and options on an equity index, are attractive because of wide bid–ask spreads, custodial fees, broker commissions, and liquidity problems in the cash markets. Many markets have been successful in launching options and futures contracts on equity indexes.

Also, the nondeliverable forwards (NDFs) have been widely used to facilitate investment in countries with capital restrictions or to hedge market exposure. An NDF contract is an agreement in which the returns of a specified notional investment in an indexed asset are settled for cash in the reference currency, often U.S. dollars. Transactions are entirely offshore, and counterparties settle the contract on maturity on a net basis. There is no transfer of any local currency.

Credit Spread Contracts

A credit spread is generally expressed as the yield spread of an emerging market instrument over the yield of a "risk-free" bond. The credit spread is a measure of the market's perception of the default risk of the emerging market issuer. Many structures allow investors to bet on a specific credit spread or a basket of credit spreads. For example, when the sovereign Brazil 2027 global bond was offered at a spread of 525 basis points over the U.S. Treasury long bond, an institutional client of Lehman Brothers "locked in" a spread of 575 over the settlement in one year. The net settlement on the end date is determined by the credit spread of Brazil 2027 bond at that time. In this trade, the notional size is $10,000 per basis points of spread tightening or widening. The investor will receive $10,000 at the end date for each basis point by which the Brazil credit spread is below 575, but will pay $10,000 for every basis point the spread is greater than 575.

Another related instrument is the credit-linked note. The note typically contains provisions linking its value to the default risk of an emerging market credit. For example, an investor looking to invest in Peru would be forced to buy a long-term Brady bond because the country has not yet issued shorter-term debt. Instead, a dealer can create a shorter-term note with payment linked to the risk of Peru default. Using credit-linked notes, money managers can tailor the specific exposures in terms of currency, maturity, and default.

Other structures, such as step-up callable notes and digital options, have also been traded. Step-up note buyers pick up additional yields by implicitly selling to the issuer an option to call back the note on specified dates. The basic risks are the credit risk of the issuer and the reference credit. A digital option pays either a large lump sum or nothing, depending on the credit spread of a bond.

SUMMARY

In the process of international capital markets integration, emerging markets have become more important for international investors and for investment banking business as well. Bankers need to be knowledgeable about the unique characteristics of each emerging market, the needs of issuers, and the objectives of investors. The requirement of satisfying demands from all sides presents a unique challenge and opportunity to bankers. Regulatory reforms in emerging markets are expected to be a significant factor in the banking business.

SELECT BIBLIOGRAPHY

Bouton, L. and M. A. Sumlinski. "Trends in private investment in developing countries." *IFC Discussion Paper* 31 (February 1997).

Brown, K. "Talking Stock in Third World," *New York Times*, November 11, 1995, pp. 37–38.

Chrystal, J. "Using derivatives to lower borrowing costs." *Latin Finance: Latin Derivatives Supplement* (Jan/Feb 1996).

Eng, M., and F. A. Lees. "Sharp increase in trading volume of emerging debt in 1996." *Journal of Emerging Markets* 2 (Spring 1997): pp. 79–88.

Euromoney. The 1998 Guide to Emerging Market Derivatives. 1998.

Featherstone, J. "Looking after Latin paper." *Euromoney* (May 1997): pp. 133–138.

Kaplan, P. "Stocks, bonds, and currencies: Investment opportunities in Latin America." *Emerging Market Quarterly*, forthcoming.

Hargis, K. "The globalization of trading and issuance of equities from emerging markets." *Journal of Emerging Markets* 2 (Spring 1997): pp. 79–88.

Molano, W. T. "From bad debts to healthy securities: the theory and financial techniques of the Brady plan." *Economic and Financial Research*, SBC Warburg, 1996.

The J.P. Morgan Emerging Markets Bond Index. J.P. Morgan Securities, Inc. Emerging Markets Research, 1997.

The J.P. Morgan Emerging Local Markets Index. J.P. Morgan Securities, Inc. Emerging Markets Research, 1997.

Park, K. H., and A. W. Van Agtmael, eds. *The World's Emerging Stock Markets*. Chicago, IL: Probus Publishing Company, 1993.

Standard and Poor's. *Sovereign Credit Ratings: A Primer*. New York: Standard and Poor's, 1997.

Stanley, M. T. *The IRWIN Guide to Investing in Emerging Markets*. Chicago, IL: Irwin Professional Publishing, 1995.

Willougby, J. "Trade Secrets," *Institutional Investor*, November 1997, pp. 69–75.

II

Trading and
Trading Techniques

Successful traders take home millions of dollars in bonuses. Many investment banks put up huge amounts of capital for proprietary trading. The most notable is, of course, Salomon Brothers (now Salomon Smith Barney). Other outstanding players include many of the best-known investment banking houses and hedge funds. Trading for market making is part of a dealer's business. Day trading involves taking advantage of short-term volatility. Scientific approach-based trading and arbitrage play high-stake games. Headlines like George Soros made $2 billion betting against Bank of England and John Meriwether took a $12 billion position in Italian tax-driven arbitrage trade are fascinating. This chapter discusses the fundamentals for successful trading, arbitrage strategies, and technical trading techniques.

INTRODUCTION

This is a great story for trading.[1] One cold winter morning a young man walks five miles through the snow to the jademaster's place to learn about jade. The young man comes in and they sit by the fire, sipping hot green tea. The jademaster presses a green stone deeply into the young man's hand and begins to talk about tree frogs. After a few minutes, the young man interrupts. "Excuse me, I am here to learn about jade, not tree frogs." The jademaster takes the stone and tells the young man to go home and return in a week. The following week the young man returns. The jademaster presses another stone into the young man's hand and continues the story about tree frogs. Again, the young man interrupts. Again, the jademaster sends him home. The young man interrupts less and less. The young man also learns how to brew the hot green tea, clean up the kitchen, and sweep the floors. Spring comes. One day the young man observes, "The stone I hold is not genuine Jade."

In trading, you may look at hundreds of systems, study with dozens of gurus (genuine or fake), or spend money and time on various books on trading. Probably for most people, they teach you that you cannot use them. And that is a great lesson, which you will never learn until you have learned it. Put it differently, you cannot buy success. You have to make it yourself. It comes from within. You need to have the feel for it and have to work hard for it. The scientific approach, especially convergence trading, requires a comprehension of advanced financial theories and advanced computer capabilities. Day trading, on the other hand, requires the trader's feel of the market. Successful day traders often say that there is no system to it. It is nothing more than this: "I think the market is going up, so I buy. It's gone up enough, so I am going to sell. I do not know where the intuition comes from, and there are times when it goes away." That is the art of day trading.

Successful traders buy low and sell high, or short high and cover low, making gains that are greater than their losses when they are wrong. This seems simple, but it is not. To succeed, traders must understand that they are competing with the sharpest minds. In addition, trading is a negative sum game. Brokers, exchanges, and advisory services constantly drain money away from the market. A trader has to be right more than half of the time just to break even. Making money requires a higher winning percentage.

Risk Management and Discipline

The first step to successful trading is to ensure survival by making risk management a top priority. Most losers wash out trying to trade their way out of a hole. Many of them have difficulties taking a loss and keep hanging on to losers. It is essential to understand that a 10% loss requires a gain of more than 11% just to get even, and a 50% loss will require a gain of 100% to get back in the game.[2] Typically, a trader would place a stop right after getting into a position. The level of stop is chosen in such a way that any loss from a single position will be limited to a small percentage of the account.

Taking a profit is sometimes emotionally hard as well. When the market moves in the anticipated direction, a trader needs to decide whether to stay put, take profits, or add to position. A successful trader sets a certain objective for each position. Once the objective is accomplished, the trader might take profits or might prefer to let it run. In such a case, the stop needs to be adjusted in the same direction. The worst mistake is when a trader cashes out too quickly and then decides to hang on the next time to a position that is going sour. Another mistake is for a trader who missed a profit to grab a quick profit the next time and miss a major move.

Trading Approaches

There are many markets, many instruments, and many techniques. Each market has its own unique characteristics and its own trading hours. Certain instruments continuously trade in different time zones. Fundamentals in the market where they are traded and the events in other markets affect certain instruments. Most major currencies and U.S. government securities are traded in all major markets and the economic fundamentals in the United States and the financial market conditions in other countries affect their prices. Euromarkets are global, trading around the clock in all major financial centers throughout the world.

The number of trading techniques is limited only by the trader's imagination. There are three basic approaches. The first is fundamental analysis that bases a security price on corporate and economic fundamentals. The fundamental approach for a security involves the analysis of the economy, industry, and company. This applies to equities and fixed-income securities. In commodities, fundamentalists study factors that affect market demand and supply, such as weather and politics. Currencies are affected by economic fundamentals such as production and inflation, and political factors as well. In futures, expectations of interest rate and cash market conditions are important. Volatility and expected direction of price movements are key in determining options valuation.

The second approach is the market efficiency hypothesis, in which securities prices are based on all available information so as to offer an expected rate of return consistent with their level of risk. There are three different degrees of informational efficiency. The least restrictive form is the *weak form efficiency*, which states that any information contained in the past is already included in the current price and that its future price cannot be predicted by analyzing past prices. This is because many market participants have access to past price information, and hence, any free lunches would have been consumed. The second form of informational efficiency, *semi-strong form efficiency*, states that security prices fully reflect all relevant publicly available information. Information available to the public includes past prices, volumes, economic reports, brokerage recommendations, advisory newsletters, and other news articles. Finally, the *strong form* of informational efficiency takes the information set a step further and includes all public and private information. This version implies that even insiders who have access to nonpublic material information cannot make abnormal profits. Most studies support the notion of semi-strong form market efficiency, but do not support the strong form version of efficient market hypothesis. In other words, insiders can trade profitably on their knowledge of nonpublic material information. This advantage is unfair, and hence, insider trading is illegal.

Finally, technical analysis attempts to use information on past price and volume to predict future price movement. It also attempts to time the markets. Technical analysis is based on four key assumptions:

- Demand and supply determine market price.
- Securities prices tend to move in trends that persist for long periods.
- Reversals of trends are caused by shifts in demand and supply, which can be detected in charts.
- Chart patterns tend to repeat themselves.

Technicians have developed numerous techniques, which attempt to predict changes in demand (bulls) and supply (bears). Later in this chapter we will briefly cover the definition and use of several popular techniques.

MARKET MAKING AND DAY TRADING

Market making is an integral part of a dealer's business. Dealers stand ready to buy at bid and sell at offer. The bid–ask spread is largely determined by the dealer's perception of risks such as price uncertainty and carry in making the market. During volatile periods market makers widen the spread to protect themselves. A trader who is making a market but feels that the market is going the wrong way will hedge with other highly correlated securities.

In day trading, traders make money by buying securities or currencies and then selling them again in a short period of time, hoping to gain an eighth or a quarter of a point on the sale. Day trading is not investing, however. Day trading is a tough profession that is not for the "faint of heart." It is a risk-versus-reward scenario that may allow the astute and disciplined trader who studies the art and science of day trading to make consistent profits greater than what he or she would make at most other professions.

ARBITRAGE TRADING

Arbitrage trading is situated on the proprietary trading desks of Wall Street. There are various types of arbitrage. The classical riskless arbitrage opportunities are practically nonexistent in many active markets, which are the results of constant pursuit by arbitrageurs who have low-cost capital, state-of-the-art technology, and an intimate understanding of intra-day market-making activities. In developing sectors or markets, however, riskless arbitrage opportunities do occasionally present themselves. This section reviews several major types of arbitrage plays on Wall Street.

Index Arbitrage

Theoretically, a stock index futures price will differ from the cash price by an amount equal to the cost of carry. Because of transaction costs and other factors, there are boundaries around the theoretical futures price within which there are no arbitrage opportunities. An index arbitrage positions trades in the cash and futures markets when the differences between the theoretical futures price and actual futures price are sufficiently large to generate arbitrage profits. A trader can generate arbitrage profits by selling the futures index if it is expensive and buying the underlying stocks, or by buying the futures contract when it is cheap and selling short the underlying stocks. Index arbitrage plays an important role in linking futures prices and cash prices. Program trading is used to execute the buy and sell orders.

Convertible Arbitrage

A convertible arbitrage involves purchasing convertible bonds or preferred stocks and then hedging that investment by selling short the underlying equity. The resulting position generates income from the accrued interest or preferred dividends and interest earned on the short-sale proceeds. The short sale is to protect the investment from adverse stock market movements so that the overall position, if correctly hedged, will be nondirectional. The objective is to correctly position trades that produce certain current income and preserve principal, regardless of stock market conditions.

As an example, suppose a convertible debenture maturing in one year trading at $1,050 is convertible into 100 shares of nondividend-paying common and the common is trading at $10 a share. There is a $50 premium over the conversion value of $1,000. Assume that a bond of similar characteristics without the conversion feature is traded at $920. The $920 is the investment value.

Assume the common stock has an even chance of going to $7.5 or $12.50 over the next year. The conversion value is hence $750 or $1,250 one year later. The convertible arbitrageur could take advantage of this expected relationship by being long one bond at $1,050 and short 60 shares of common at $10. At a price of $7.50 the short position would be in the money for $150 while the bond would be traded at an $130 loss, for a gross profit of $20 per bond. If the price goes up to $12.50, the bond will be converted and result in a gain of $200 while the short position would lose $150. The net profit is $50. This example illustrates the basics of convertible bond arbitrage. In practice, the convertible bet is more complex, and strategies are constantly changing.

M&A Risk Arbitrage

Risk arbitrage is an integral part of proprietary trading. Arbitrageurs take a position in firms in a merger or a takeover. They are interested in the deal, not in becoming shareholders. In order to commit funds, they must have reasonable belief that the deal will go through. The standard strategy is to go long on the target and short on the acquiring firm. The position is not at the mercy of the market, but is at risk with respect to the consummation of the transaction.

A transaction can involve a cash exchange, an exchange of securities, or a combination of both. First, consider the case of a cash offer. This example was discussed in Chapter 3. Suppose an acquirer is offering to buy the target's stock at a price of $50 per share at a time when it is traded at $40 per share, a 25% premium. The target's stock can be expected to rise to about $50. There is a chance that the acquirer might withdraw or change the offer. It is likely that the target's stock may rise to, say, $46 rather then $50. An arbitrageur purchases the target at $46 will realize a profit of $4 per share if the acquisition takes place at $50. The arb will lose $6 per share if the deal does not go through and the target's share declines back to $40.

When the transaction involves an exchange of securities, the arb would long the securities of the target, expecting them to rise in price, and short the securities of the acquiring company, expecting them to decline. There are two risks involved: Either the acquisition would not be consummated or the length of time it would take is longer than anticipated. As an example, assume that the stock of an acquirer is trading at $50 per share. The company offers to exchange one share of its stock for one share of the target, which is traded at $40. The transaction is expected to be complete in three months. Suppose that the arb offers the target stock $46 per share. The target's shareholders can immediately take a $6 profit from the proposed deal by selling now to the arb. Or these shareholders can wait three months and receive one share of the acquirer's stock. This gives an extra $4 per share profit, but only if the acquisition is completed and only if the shares of the acquirer are still traded at $50 per share.

Suppose the target's shareholder decides to sell to the arb and take a profit of $6 per share. The arb will have a profit of $4 per share if the deal is closed as proposed. The same outcome remains even if the shares of the acquirer are traded at a level lower than $50. For example, the acquirer's shares are traded at $48, instead of $50. The arb has a $2 profit from the short position (acquirer) and another $2 profit from the long position (target). The primary risk is that the deal will not go through and the prices of both companies will go back to their levels before the announcement.

The level of complexity in risk arbitrage varies, depending on the structure of the transaction. To reduce risk, the arbs must perform comprehensive research to examine the likelihood of the proposed transaction and the structure of the deal.

Structural Arbitrage

Structural arbitrage is also called primary market arbitrage. It capitalizes on a financial innovation that meets certain investor needs and makes the overall marketplace more complete. The objective is to identify opportunities through the recombination and restructuring of securities. For example, financial innovations such as index-linked bonds, CMOs, Treasury strips, and swaps all enhance the market's completeness. Historically, structural arbitrage has generated handsome profits for pioneering investment banks. Many forms of structural arbitrage have been implemented across the capital markets, but this activity is most prevalent in the global fixed-income markets.

A good example of structural arbitrage via financial engineering is securities stripping. In the early 1980s, several investment banks realized that they could sell the stripped components of a coupon Treasury security at a total price that is significantly higher than the price of the bond. The first STRIPS (Separate Trading of Registered Interest and Principal of Securities) made their debut in 1983. They were created from Treasury bonds by separating the periodical coupons and their principal. Each piece is treated as a separate security. The resulting instruments are the first zero-coupon bonds. The zero-coupon bonds' lack of reinvestment risk appeals widely to both domestic and foreign pensions and insurance companies that try to match assets and liabilities.

Another example of structural arbitrage was the stripping of the FNMA passthroughs. In late January 1987, the FNMA Trust 1 was traded at 102.19% of par (total value at $750 million). Bankers stripped the security and created IO strip and PO strip in February. The IO strip issued at 58.16% and the PO strip issued at 48.00%, for a total of 106.16%. This process created 3.97% structural arbitrage profits.

Convergence Trading

Salomon Brothers was a powerhouse in bond trading, especially in convergence trading. The firm devotes half of its capital to proprietary trading. John Meriwether pioneered fixed-income arbitrage at Salomon Brothers, building its arbitrage desk into one of the biggest money-spinning machines on Wall Street in the 1980s. After leaving Salomon Brothers, he started his own hedge fund, Long Term Capital Management (LTCM), in Greenwich, Connecticut, in 1994. This group has been prized as the best finance faculty in the world. They are very focused and very analytical. They generally believe that the markets are efficient but markets can get out of line for a period of time. Taking advantage of its considerable computer power and analytics, LTCM scours the universe of financial assets and find mispricings or out-of-line values of bonds or derivatives relative to one another. Traders then construct trades to capture the spread in what they anticipate will be an eventual convergence back to their projected fair value. They calculate the probability and timing of the convergence, formulate the duration weighting, and monitor and manage risk. The temporary out-of-line relationships and eventual convergence can appear between different bonds of the same maturity, a cash bond and its futures contract, different maturities on the yield curve, Treasury and mortgage-backed securities, or between bonds in different countries. The opportunities may also appear in emerging market equity and equity indexes.

Here are several examples of John Meriwether's successful convergence trading.[3] The first example involves positioning trades on Treasuries and mortgage-backed securities. The second is about an Italian tax-driven arbitrage, and the third involves a convergence bet in Italian, Spanish, and German bonds.

First, the yields for different types of bonds have a historical relationship to each other. In turbulent times, those relationships get out of line as some bonds become undervalued relative to others. Meriwether's traders (then at Salomon Brothers) use computers and economic models to find and exploit these anomalies. Here is one example:

1. *The opportunity:* In late 1988, Larry Hilibrand and Greg Hawkins noticed that because of worries about the mortgage market, mortgage-backed prices had declined relative to treasuries, widening the spread to 1.5% from the historical norm of 1.0%.
2. *The bet:* They believed that mortgage-backeds would regain their historical value versus treasuries by increasing in price, reducing the spread back to 1.0%.
3. *The strategy:* They purchased mortgage-backeds and sold short treasuries to hedge. Salomon would earn more interest on the higher-yielding mortgage securities than it would have to pay out in interest on the shorted treasuries. And when the spread narrowed as expected, the value of the mortgage-backeds would rise more or fall less than that of the Treasuries.
4. *The risks:* There are two risks. First, if the market for mortgage securities tanked, the spread would widen disastrously. They believed that this would be highly unlikely. Second, if interest rates went down a lot, mortgage holders would prepay their mortgages, decreasing the value of the mortgage securities that they purchased.
5. *The play:* They purchased $5 billion worth of mortgage-backeds yielding 10.5% and sold short $5 billion worth of treasuries at 9.0%. To hedge against prepayments, they also purchased interest-rate options costing 0.5% of the value of the mortgage-backeds, or $25 million.
6. *The payoffs:* Every year for three years, the mortgage-backeds earned $75 million more in interest than Salomon had to pay on the treasuries. But the prepayment hedge cost $25 million. Over the three-year period, the positive carry amounted to $150 million. When the spread narrowed to 1.0%, Salomon covered its short position and sold its mortgage securities. Each $1,000 bond had risen $25 more than treasuries, for a $125 million gain. Total profit for the trading strategy: $275 million

The second example involves an unusual spread between Italian government bonds and the rate for lira interest-rate swaps, due partly to Italian political risk but primarily to a 12.5% withholding tax imposed on investors from countries lacking a reciprocal tax treaty with Italy. The tax withheld could be reclaimed only by filing an application to the Finance Ministry. The process was so cumbersome, the market traded as though the 12.5% could not be reclaimed. This drove government bond yields above lira swap rates, making an arbitrage possible. LTCM reportedly bought Italian government bonds and financed the purchase in the lira repurchase market, resulting in LTCM's receiving of a fixed rate from the bonds and paying floating rates in the financing. LTCM then entered into a lira interest-rate swap to receive a floating rate and pay a fixed rate. LTCM is believed to have made $600 million to $700 million in this arbitrage. LTCM made money on two levels. First, the interest cost of the below-market repo was less than the income stream from the floating leg of the lira swap.[4] Second, the convergence between government yields and the swap rates led to mark-to-market gains.

Another example was related to the convergence in bond yields in anticipation of the 1999 single European currency (1999 EMU). Traders made a bundle betting on the once-weak bonds of Italy and Spain. Fears of political and currency gliches kept government bonds in those countries virtually in the junk category, and hence there were wide spreads over the Bunds. Italian 10-year bonds had a yield of 12.09% in July 1995 and in July 1997 its yield was 6.52%. Spanish 10-year bonds that yielded 11.25% the same time in

1995 were traded at 6.23% two years later. During the same time span, the yield on the German 10-year bonds declined from 6.79% to 5.57%. Hence, the Italian–German spread declined from 5.30% to 0.95% and the Spanish–German spread dropped from 4.46% to 0.66%. According to a report in *Institutional Investor* (1996), LTCM made a lot of money in this type of convergence bet.

Those are examples of profitable trades at LTCM. Unfortunately, the very same type of highly leveraged trades, placing huge bets on the spreads between interest rates on various types of bonds with insufficient capital backing them, failed the firm in 1998.

Yield Curve Arbitrage

A yield curve arbitrage involves trading bonds of different maturities on the yield curve. A trader would long the "cheap" part of the curve and short the "rich". A successful arbitrageur will be able to unwind the positions at a profit because the abnormal yield spread will have returned to the expected norm in one of several ways:

- The security shorted will have fallen in price and risen in yield.
- The security purchased will have risen in price or fallen in yield.
- A combination of these two will have occurred.

In such a yield curve play, the trader is not exposed to parallel shifts in yield curve. If the yield curve shifts up, the resulting loss on the long position will be offset by the profits on the short position. If the yield curve shifts downward, the reverse will occur. Thus, the trader is not predicting the direction of interest rates, but is concerned about the yield spreads between two maturity segments along the yield curve. But this strategy can produce major losses if the shape of the yield curve twists in the opposite direction of the prediction. Wall Street firms actively play this type of arbitrage game. They all have access to database containing all sorts of information on historical spreads and have programmed a computer to identify anomalies in prevailing spreads. Wall Street firms use this type of information to set up arbitrages themselves and to advise clients. Here is an example of an arbitrage along the yield curve.[5]

In late October 1981, the yield curve in the 3- to 4-year area was relatively flat. A dealer expected the Fed would ease the Federal Funds rate causing the yield curve to steepen. On October 21, for next-day settlement, he bought the current 3-year note, 13 1/8s of 8/15/85, at a yield of 10.95%. Simultaneously, he shorted the current 4-year note, 12 1/4s of 9/30/86, at a yield of 11.00%. The current 3-year note was traded at a dollar price of 105:03+, and the yield value of 1/32 was 0.126. The current 4-year note was traded at a dollar price of 103:28+, and the yield value of 1/32 was 0.096. The smaller yield value of 1/32 on the 4-year note meant that, for a given movement up or down in interest rates, the 4-year note would move 131% in price as much as the 3-year note would. To minimize the market risk, the dealer set the arbitrage in a ratio based on the yield values of 1/32 on the two notes. This would insulate the arbitrage against general shift in the yield curve up or down but not against a relative movement between yields on the two securities.

The dealer bought $1.31 million of the current 3-year note and financed at a repo rate of 7.5%. Simultaneously, he sold short $1 million of the current 4-year note and reversed in the security at a reverse repo rate of 7.15% to make good delivery. Thirty-one days later when the dealer's expectation had come true, the yield curve steepened. The dealer sold the 3-year note at 106:02+ (a yield of 10.49%) and covered the short position in the 4-year note at a dollar price of 105:01 (a yield of 10.65%). The net profit was \$2,611 per million of securities arbitraged. In practice, such arbitrage bets are commonly done for \$100 million or more.

Covered Interest Arbitrage

Covered interest arbitrage involves trading of an instrument denominated in dollars and another in a foreign currency on a hedged basis.[6] In markets that are actively traded, the arbitrage profits are quickly traded away. In markets that are less arbitraged, taking a long position in a foreign instrument on a hedged basis and shorting a similar dollar-denominated instrument can generate arbitrage profits. There are several alternatives for hedging the currency risk, including forward contracts, currency futures, currency option contracts, and currency swaps. Traders frequently hedge by doing a swap. At the time a trader buys the foreign currency in the spot market for the purchase of the foreign security, the trader will simultaneously sell that currency forward (swap). This eliminates exposure to the foreign exchange risk.

The arbitrage-free condition is

$$y_f - y_\$ = \left(\frac{S}{F} - 1 \right) \left(\frac{360}{T} + y_\$ \right) ,$$

where y_f = money market rate of the foreign instrument, $y_\$$ = rate on a dollar denominated instrument similar to the foreign instrument, S = spot rate quoted in dollars per unit of foreign currency, F = forward rate, T = number of days. The rate differential (left-hand side of the equality) should equal the rate of return on the swap used to hedge the currency risk (right-hand side of the equality). If a foreign currency is expected to appreciate, the forward rate will exceed the spot rate and hence, the hedge will produce a gain. For the hedged instrument to yield the same rate as a similar dollar-denominated instrument, y_f must be less than $y_\$$. If, alternatively, the foreign currency is weak, the spot rate will exceed the forward rate. The yield on the foreign instrument must be higher than that on a similar dollar-denominated instrument; otherwise arbitrage opportunities exist.

Put differently, if the rate differential is greater than the return on the swap, then the trader will take a long position on the foreign instrument and a short position on the dollar-denominated security to profit from the anomalies. This will result in a higher demand for the spot foreign currency and an increase in the supply of the forward. If the positions taken are significant, then the yield on the foreign security will decrease and the yield on the dollar-denominated security will rise. The market adjustments in the securities and the currency markets will restore the equality of rate differential and the swap returns. Similarly, if the rate differential is less than the rate of return on the swap, the opposite processes will restore the equality.

TECHNICAL ANALYSIS

Technical analysis is based on the assumptions that prices tend to move in trends that persist for certain periods and that these trends can be detected by charts. This approach is a dramatic departure from the *fundamental analysis* or *efficient market hypothesis*. Many academicians equate technical analysis with mystics. Technicians often criticize fundamentalists and the market efficiency theorists as "divorced from the reality of the markets."

Charting is at the heart of technical analysis. Chartists often use *support* or *resistance* to describe whether it is a trading or a trending market. Prices generally move within the support–resistance range (trading range). Traders buy at support and sell at resistance. A breakout above a resistance point signals an upward trending market, while a breakout below a support indicates that the market is trending downward. Volume is an essential supporting factor. A new high on heavy volume is considered bullish, while a new high on light trading volume may indicate a temporary move that is not likely to sustain.

There is no magic for identifying trends and trading ranges. Technicians generally combine several methods. When they confirm one another, the signal is considered valid. When they contradict one another, it is better to pass up a trade. This section provides a brief description of several indicators frequently used by technicians.

Moving Average

Moving average (MA) is one of the oldest technical indicators. This method is very popular among technical practitioners. This is easy to formulate and is less open to interpretation than other methods. A moving average is the arithmetic average price of a security or an index over the past predetermined number of days:

$$\text{MA} = \frac{\sum_{t-(N-1)}^{t} P_T}{N}.$$

In the above expression, P is the security price or index value, N the chosen time span, and t is the most recent trading date, and T is the time variable.

As each day passes, the earliest day is dropped and the most recent one is included. Connecting each day's moving average produces an MA line. The most important message of a simple moving average is the direction of its slope. When it falls, it shows bearish sentiment. When it rises, it signals a bull market. When the market is bullish, prices rise above an MA. When the bears dominate, prices fall below an MA. Hence, a buy signal is given when the security price crosses above the MA line and the moving average is directed upward. A sell signal is given when the security price crosses below the MA line and the moving average is trending downward. There are no valid signals when the moving average changes direction but the price does not cross over the *MA*. When price fluctuates in a broad sideways pattern, the moving average at times gives false signals. Hence, technicians always use other indicators to confirm the direction of price.

Alternatively, a more complicated scheme involves the use of several moving averages. For example, a technician might plot 4-week, 13-week, and 50-week MAs on the same graph. A buy signal is generated when the shorter-term 4-week and 13-week averages cross over the 50-week MA from below. A sell signal is given when the shorter two averages fall through the 50-week MA. The two shorter moving averages are used to filter false signals.

A weighted moving average favors the most recent observations. A frequently used method is described as follows. For simplicity, assume the time span chosen is 7 days. Multiply the first price by 1, the second price by 2, ..., and the seventh price by 7. Then divide the sum of these multiplications by the sum of the weights. The divisor is $1 + 2 + ... + 7 = 28$. With a weighted MA, a buy or sell signal is given when the weighted MA changes direction.

Exponential Moving Average

An exponential moving average (EMA) is another form of weighted MA. Technicians believe that EMA is a better trend-following tool because it assigns a greater weight to the latest data and responds faster to changes than a simple MA. The mathematical expression of EMA is

$$EMA = P_{t+1}H + EMA_t(1 - H),$$

where $H = 2/(N + 1), P$ = security price, t = time point, N = the chosen time span. The very first EMA is proxied by a simple MA. Then the line connecting all EMA points obtained from repeating the calculating process gives the EMA line. The trading rule is, trade from the long side when EMA rises, and trade that security from the short side when the EMA falls. When the EMA moves repeatedly from side to side or remains flat, it is a trendless market.

Moving Average Convergence–Divergence (MACD)

Moving average convergence–divergence (MACD) consists of two statistics: a difference in short-term and long-term EMAs, and the smoothing of this difference. The smoothing is used to generate signals of buys and sells. Hence, MACD consists of three EMAs. The first is the shorter EMA (for example, a 12-day EMA[7]). The second is a longer EMA (for example, a 26-day EMA). Then the difference is calculated by subtracting the longer EMA from the shorter EMA. This is the so-called fast MACD line. The final step is to calculate a 9-day EMA of the fast line, which results in the slow signal line. A buy signal is given when the fast MACD line crosses above the slow signal line. A sell signal is given when the fast line crosses below the slow line.

Many MACD systems also use histograms. Some technicians believe it offers more insight into the balance of power between bulls and bears. It shows not only whether the market is bullish or bearish, but also whether it is growing stronger or weaker. The MACD-Histogram plots as a histogram the difference between the MACD fast line and the slow signal line. The histogram is positive when the fast line is above the slow line, and it is negative when the opposite is true. Hence, when the MACD-Histogram stops falling and ticks up, it gives a buy signal. When the MACD-Histogram stops rising and ticks down, it gives a signal to trade on the short side.

Filter Trading Rule

The idea behind a filter rule is to get in on a trend as the trend is starting and to get out as it begins to reverse. A filter trading technique specifies when a security will be bought or sold. Typically, it specifies that when a security price moves up by x% above a previous low, then buy and hold until price falls by y% below a previous high, at which time the trader should trade on the short side. A trader using this rule would believe a positive breakout (the security price would continue to rise) if the security rises x% from some base. In contrast, a y% decline from some peak would be considered a breakout on the downside. The trader would expect a downward trend and would sell any holding and might even sell short.

The specification of x% and y% will determine the frequency of trading. A small percentage specification will result in a large number of transactions. A large percentage specification might miss certain market movements. Studies have found that filter rules might be effective when the filter is small, in the range of 1% to 5%.

Directional Movement Indicator

The directional movement indicator (DMI) is used to determine if a security is trending or is not trending. The directional movement is the portion of today's trading range that is outside of the previous day's trading range. The process of calculating the DMI is briefly described as follows.

If today's range extends above yesterday's, the directional movement is positive (+DM). In contrast, if today's range extends below yesterday's range, the directional movement is negative (–DM). If today's range is inside yesterday's trading range or extends above and below it by an equal amount, there is no directional movement. If today's trading range extends both above and below yesterday's, the directional movement is either positive or negative, depending on which outside range is larger.

The next step is to identify the true range (TR) of the market. The TR is the largest of (1) today's trading range, (2) the distance from today's high to yesterday's low, or (3) the distance from today's low to yesterday's close. Then the directional indicator (DI) is defined as

$$+DI = +DM/TR \text{ and } -DI = -DM/TR.$$

Once the DIs are calculated, they are moving averaged to get smoothed directional lines. The relationship between positive and negative lines identifies the trend. When the smoothed +DI line is on top of the smoothed –DI line, the trend is up. When the smoothed –DI line is on top of the smoothed +DI line, the trend is down. The crossovers of +DI and –DI lines give buy and sell signals.

Many technicians also calculate the average directional indicator (ADI). ADI measures the spread between the smoothed +DI and smoothed –DI lines. It is calculated in two steps. The daily directional indicator (DDI) is calculated as

$$DDI = \frac{\text{smoothed } (+DI) - \text{smoothed } (-DI)}{\text{smoothed } (+DI) + \text{smoothed } (-DI)} \times 100.$$

Then use EMA on DDI to obtain the ADI. In an upward-trending market, the DDI rises and the spread between +DI and –DI lines increases. When the trend reverses, the DDI declines.

Relative Strength Index

Relative strength index (RSI) analysis is an index based on the momentum concept. It measures the strength of a security or an index by monitoring changes in its closing prices. It is based on the assumption that higher closes indicate strong markets and lower closes indicate weaker markets. The RSI is defined by the following formula:

$$RSI = \frac{AU}{AU + AD} \times 100.$$

AU is the average *net up* closing changes for a selected number of days. Traders first choose a time span (e.g., 10 days), then find all days when the security closed higher than the day before and add up the amounts of increases. The AU is equal to the sum divided by 10. AD is the average *net down* closing changes for the same number of days. Traders need to find all days when the security closed lower than the day before and add up the amounts of declines. AD is equal to the sum divided by 10. RSI is obtained by inputting the values of AU and AD into the formula. As is clear from the formula, RSI fluctuates between 0 and 100. If the ratio is 50, the ups and downs are equally divided. As the ratio goes above 50, more closes are ups than downs, indicating an upward trend. Technicians would state that when the RSI passes 70, the market has reached its top. Conversely, if the RSI falls below 30, the market is near its bottom and a reversal is in sight. Many analysts have widened the band to 20 and 80.

Stochastic Oscillator

Stochastic oscillator (SO) compares a security closing price relative to its trading range over a certain period of time. There have been observations that in an upward-trending market, prices tend to close near their highs, and in a downward trending market, they close near their lows. Further, as an upward trend matures, price tends to close further away from its highs; and as a downward trend matures, price tends to close away from its lows.

The SO is plotted as two lines: one fast line called %*K* and a slow line called %*D*. First, %*K* of fast stochastic is defined as

$$\%K = \frac{P_t - P_L}{P_H - P_L} \times 100.$$

where P_t is today's closing price, P_L is the lowest price traded during the selected number of days, and P_H is the highest point during the selected time span. Then %*D* is obtained by smoothing the %*K* over a three-day period. The %*D* is smoothed once again to *obtain* %*D* of slow stochastic. The *slow stochastic* does a better job in filtering out market noise. The stochastic is plotted on a chart with value ranging from 0 to 100. References lines are drawn at 20 and 80 to mark overbought and oversold. Readings above 80 are strong and indicate that price is closing near its high. This means the market is overbought and is ready to turn down. Readings below 20 indicate that price is closing near its low. This implies that the market is oversold and is ready to turn up.

Breadth of Market

This technique measures the strength of advances over declines. The advance/decline (A/D) line shows each day the difference between the number of advancing issues and the declining issues, ignoring the unchanged. For example, if 1,234 stocks were traded higher for the day and 891 stocks declined, the A/D is +343. A cumulative A/D line is created by adding each day's A/D to the previous day's total. The cumulative A/D is then compared with the Dow Jones Industrial Average (DJIA). An uprising cumulative A/D line supported by a higher DJIA signals a strengthening market. Conversely, a declining line coupled with a lower DJIA signals market weakness. Additionally, if a new high in the Dow index is accompanied by a new high in the A/D line, then the rally has broad support. When the DJIA reaches a new high but the cumulative A/D line only ups to a lower peak than the previous run, it shows that fewer stocks are participating and the bull run may come to an end. Similar analysis applies on a down market.

A variation of the technique is *breadth advance/decline* (BAD). Data on NYSE-listed stocks are generally used to construct the BAD. The BAD index is the simple moving average of the ratio of advances over the sum of advances and declines. Technicians believe that when the reading reaches 0.66, significant bull gains can be expected. When the ratio is 0.367 or lower, it is a bearish signal.

For an individual security, there is a technique called *on balance volume* (OBV) that creates a volume line along with a price chart at the bottom. If the stock closed higher, that day's volume is added. If the day closed lower, the volume is subtracted from the starting number. So volume is added on up days and subtracted on down days. The OBV often rises or falls before prices; hence, technicians believe that the OBV is a leading indicator of market trend.

Arm's Short-Term Trading Index

Arm's short-term trading index (ASTTI) measures the relative strength of the volume associated with advancing stocks and declining stocks. ASTTI is the ratio of advances to declines divided by the ratio of the volume of advances to the volume of declining issues:

$$\text{ASTTI} = \frac{A/D}{V_A/V_D}.$$

In the above expression, A is the number of advancing issues, D the number of declining issues, V_A the total volume of advances, and V_D the total trading volume of declines. At a level of 1, the market is in balance. Readings of above 1 indicate that more volume is moving into declining stocks. Readings of below 1 indicate that more volume is moving into advancing stocks. Some technicians have found the indicator useful when it reaches 1.3 on the upside or 0.4 on the downside.

Momentum and Rate of Change

Momentum and rate of change (RoC) show when the trend speeds up or slows down. Momentum subtracts a past price from today's price, while RoC divides today's price by a past price. They can be expressed as

$$\text{Momentum} = P_t - P_{t-N},$$

$$\text{RoC} = \frac{P_t}{P_{t-N}},$$

where P_t is today's closing price and P_{t-N} is the close N days ago. For example, a 10-day momentum equals today's closing price minus the closing price 10 trading days ago. A 10-day RoC divides today's price by the closing price 10 days ago. The time window is kept short to detect short-term market changes. A long time window is for trend following.

When momentum or RoC rises to a new high, it signals that the prices are likely to rally higher. Conversely, when momentum or RoC falls to a new low, lower prices are expected. When prices rise but momentum or RoC declines, the market is near its top and it is time to take profits or consider shorting. Reverse this approach during down trends.

William %R

William %R is a momentum indicator. It compares the closing price to the recent high–low range. It is the ratio of the difference between the highest high during the selected days and today's close over the difference between the highest high and the lowest low. Specifically,

$$\text{William } \% \, R = \frac{P_H - P_0}{P_H - P_L} \times 100,$$

where P_H is the highest high during the selected number of days, P_L is the lowest low, and P_0 is today's closing price. William %R fluctuates between 0 and 100. It is near 0 when prices reach the top of the trading range. It is approaching 100 when prices close at the bottom of the recent range. Oversold readings tend to occur in the 80 or higher range and overbought readings tend to occur in the 20 or lower range. When William %R reaches 80, go long and place a protective stop below the recent price low. When the reading drops to 20 or lower, go short and place a protective stop above the recent price high.

Barron's Confidence Index

Barron's confidence index (BCI) is the ratio of Barron's average yield on 10 top-grade corporate bonds ($y_{\text{top-}10}$) to the average yield on Dow Jones 40 bonds (y_{DJ}). Specifically, the formula is

$$\text{BCI} = \frac{y_{\text{top-}10}}{y_{\text{DJ}}}.$$

The BCI measures the relative yield ratio between top-quality bonds and a large cross-section of bonds. The BCI is always less than 1. Technicians feel that the BCI gives a bullish signal when the index rises above 95% and gives a bearish signal when the index falls below 85%. The reasoning is that during periods of prosperity, investors are willing to invest more in lower-quality bonds for added yield. This causes a decrease in the average yield for the large cross-section of bonds (relative to the average yield of the top-quality bonds), leading to an increase in the BCI value. Conversely, during periods when investors are pessimistic about economic outlook, the BCI falls.

Head and Shoulder Tops

A technician studies the price pattern to decide when a trend is likely to continue or reverse. Head and shoulder (HS) tops indicate the market has reached its top. The head is a price peak surrounded by two lower tops (called shoulders). Volume is often higher on the left shoulder than on the head. An uptrend continues as long as each rally keeps reaching a new high. Rising volume serves as a confirmation. Volume falls when the market is near its top. The decline from the head to the right shoulder is the beginning of a downtrend. Trading strategies on the existing long position include sell, tighten stop level, or sell some and hold the rest. Another strategy is to short the security and place a protective stop.

In an inverse HS, the head is at the lowest point, surrounded by two shoulders. An inverse HS develops when a downtrend is near an end and a reverse is likely. In a downtrend, each new low falls lower than the previous low and each rally fails to reach a higher level. High volume confirms all declines. The decline to head usually comes with low volume. The rally out of the head breaks out of the downtrend and signals a likely bull market. During the right shoulder, there is usually a low volume. An increasing volume associated with each new high confirms that an uptrend has developed.

Mutual Fund Cash Ratio

Mutual funds hold cash for several reasons. One obvious reason is for possible shareholder redemption. Second, the money from new purchases of funds may not have been invested. Third, a fund manager might build up its cash position if the manager has a bearish outlook. Some technicians interpret the mutual fund cash ratio (cash/assets) as a contrarian indicator. They consider mutual funds to be a proxy for the institutional investor group, and mutual funds are generally wrong at market timing. Therefore, a bullish sign is given when the cash ratio rises and a bearish signal is given when the cash ratio declines.

Additionally, a high cash ratio can be considered a bullish sign because of potential buying power, because the funds have to be and will be invested. Alternatively, a low cash ratio would mean that institutions have bought heavily and are left with little potential buying power.

Short Sales by Specialists

Short sales by exchange specialists are closely watched statistics. This is because specialist operations consistently generate high returns. Those who want to follow smart money watch the specialists. Specialists regularly engage in short selling as part of their market making function, but they will be more aggressive in executing shorts when they feel strongly about the market direction.

The specialist short sale ratio is the ratio of short sales by specialists to the total short interest. Technicians view a decline of this ratio below 30% as a bullish sign, because it means that specialists are attempting to minimize their participation in short selling. In contrast, a reading of 50% or higher is a bearish sign.

Short Interest Ratio

Short interest is the total number of shares that have been shorted and not covered. Technicians compute a short interest ratio (SIR) as the outstanding short interest divided by the average daily trading volume on the exchange. As an example, suppose the short interest totaled 750 million shares and the average daily trading volume is 500 million shares; then the SIR is 1.50. This means the short interest equals about 1.5 day's trading volume. The SIR can also be computed based on an individual stock.

Technicians interpret the SIR as a contrarian indicator, contrary to short-seller's belief. Traders selling short expect stock prices to decline, so an increase in SIR could be a bearish sign. On the contrary, technicians consider a high SRI bullish because it indicates potential demand for the security by those who have sold short and have not covered the sales. Recent experience suggests that technicians using this technique would be bullish if the SIR approaches 3.0 and bearish if it declines toward 2.0.

Options Ratio

The put/call ratio is used as a contrarian indicator. Technicians reason that a higher put/call ratio indicates a more pervasive bearish attitude, which to them is a bullish indicator. The ratio is typically less than 1 because investors tend to be relatively more bullish than bearish and avoid selling shorts or buying puts. A buy signal is given when the ratio is approaching 0.70. In contrast, a put/call ratio of 0.40 or lower is considered a bearish sign. A put/call reading of between 0.40 and 0.70 is neutral.

Odd-Lot Theory

The odd-lot technique focuses on the trading activities of small investors. Most small investors do not engage in short selling except when they feel especially bearish. Technical analysts interpret heavy short selling by individuals as a signal that the market is close to trough because small investors only get pessimistic after a long decline in prices, just when the market is about to turn around. A buy signal is given when the ratio of odd-lot short sales as a percentage of total odd-lot sales is rising above 3%. A sell signal is given when the ratio declines to 1% or lower.

Another interpretation of the odd-lot behavior is based on a similar belief that small investors are unsophisticated and frequently make mistakes in market reversals. Small investors often do all right but frequently miss on key market turns. Specifically, the odd-lot investors are generally in the money as the market is going up. However, as the market continues upward, small investors get greedy and buy strongly just before the market reverses direction. Similarly, small investors are also assumed to be strong sellers right before the market bottoms out.

Investment Advisory Opinions

Technicians practicing this approach reason that most investment advisory services tend to be trend followers. Technicians develop a trading rule from the ratio of the number of advisory services that are bearish as a percentage of the number of services expressing an opinion. A bearish sentiment index of 60% indicates a pervasive bearish attitude by advisory services; contrarians would consider this a bullish sign. Conversely, a decline of the bearish sentiment index to below 20% indicates a sell signal.

SUMMARY

This chapter describes the fundamentals for successful trading, including talent, discipline, risk management, and hard work. The chapter outlines different approaches to trading and presents several real examples of successful arbitrages. The last section reviews major technical techniques and indicators. In the next chapter, we describe the market for repurchase transactions and how Wall Street uses repos in dealer financing, customer funding, and matched-book trading.

SELECT BIBLIOGRAPHY

Achelis, S. B. *Technical Analysis From A to Z*. Chicago: Probus Publishing, 1995.

Bernstein, J. *The Complete Day Trader: Trading Systems, Strategies, Timing Indicators, and Analytical Methods*. New York: McGraw Hill, 1995.

Elder, A. *Trading for a Living*. New York: Wiley, 1993.

Eng, W. F. *The Day Trader's Manual: Theory, Art, and Science of Profitable Short-Term Trading*. New York: Wiley, 1993.

Equity Analytics. *Technical Analysis*. New York: Equity Analytics, 1997.

Friedfertig, M., and G. West. *The Electronic Day Trader*. New York: McGraw-Hill, 1998.

Liaw, K. T. "Book review—The day trader's manual: Theory, art, and science of profitable short-term trading." *Journal of Finance* 50 (June 1995): pp. 758–761.

Lynch, P. *Beating the Street*. New York: Simon & Schuster, 1994.

Muehring, K. "John Meriwether by the numbers." *Institutional Investor*, November 1996, pp. 69–81.

Murphy, J. J. *Intermarket Technical Analysis*. New York: Wiley, 1995.

Schwager, J. D. *The New Market Wizards*. New York: Harper Business, 1992.

Stigum, M., and F. L. Robinson. *Money Market and Bond Calculations*. Burr Ridge, IL: Irwin Professional Publishing, 1997.

12

Repurchase Transactions

Repurchase agreements (repos) are extensively used in dealer financing, customer funding, and matched book trading. The repo desk has become the hub around which revolve the trading, hedging, and arbitrage strategies. At many firms the repo desk has become a key profit center. In addition, understanding the market is essential to assessing value in the securities markets. For example, the status of a bond in the repo market can be used to understand the relative values between bonds and also to assess the valuation of futures contracts. This chapter first describes the structure, development, trading mechanics, and market practices. Subsequent sections cover the upper and lower bounds of special repo rates, and the brokering and matched book transactions. It is important for bankers to understand the clearing process, fail consequences, the PSA-recommended trading guidelines, and GSCC netting services as well. Finally, the chapter also examines key issues related to the emerging equity repos.

THE BASICS

The repo market is the biggest money market, with the estimated market at $17.5 trillion and turnover at perhaps $500 billion a day.[1] This is much larger than the Fed funds and is the biggest short-term money market in the world. In July 1996, the Fed adopted changes to Regulation T by loosening its provisions on valuing certain securities pledged as collateral from the previous 50% to discretionary "good faith." The relaxation of Regulation T will further benefit the development of the fixed-income repo market and will, together with the National Securities Markets Improvement Act of 1996, help give birth to the equity repo market.

Purpose of Repurchase Transactions

In a typical repo transaction, a dealer puts up liquid securities as collateral against a cash loan while agreeing to repurchase the securities at a future date. The *start-leg*, or leg one, is usually settled the same day. The *close-leg*, or leg two, repurchase is a forward transaction. A repo is, in format, a securities transaction, but is, in essence, a collateralized loan to finance the purchase of the underlying security. The repo markets are therefore often called financing markets.

Securities market participants enter into repo transactions because they have cash and want a short-term investment or because they have securities and need funding. For example, a securities dealer purchases and plans to hold overnight $100 million of 6 1/2 May-05 Treasury notes. The dealer can finance the position with its own funds or by borrowing from a bank. Typically, however, the dealer uses the repo market to obtain financing. Suppose a customer, a municipality, a mutual fund, or an insurance company, has excess funds of $100 million to invest. The overnight repo rate is 5.00%. In leg one, the dealer delivers these notes to the customer for cash. In leg two of the repo trade, the dealer buys back the same notes at $100 million plus one-day interest of $15,556. The result is that the customer has invested $100 million and the dealer has financed the position overnight at an interest of 5.00%. For the transaction, the securities dealer does a repo with the customer and the customer is said to do a reverse with the dealer. Market participants in some circumstances refer to a repo or a reverse as selling or buying collateral. Also, the expressions of "to repo securities" and "to do repo" mean someone is financing a position using securities as collateral and a party is going to invest in a repo, respectively.

The Treasury and agency securities, mortgage pass-throughs, money market instruments, investment grade debt, and convertible bonds may be used for repo collateral. It is common in a repurchase transaction for the collateral seller to have the right to take back that security and simultaneously substitute other collateral of equal value and quality for it, known as the *right of substitution*. Also, the market practice is that the coupon interests coming due on the collateralized securities are passed through from the buyer back to the seller of collateral.

Repo rates in part depend on the collateral used. The higher the credit quality and the easier the security is to clear, the lower the repo rate. Treasury repos trade at lower levels than federal agency repos, which, in turn, trade at lower levels than mortgage-backeds. The second factor is the term of the repo, which is usually for maturities between one day and one year. Most of the repo transactions have maturities of three months or less. One-day transactions are called *overnight repos;* longer maturities are called *term repos*. An *open repo* is an overnight repo that rolls over automatically until terminated by either party.

Government securities are the most frequently used collateral. Numerous issues—in particular, on-the-run or current issues—are frequently on special. The specialness of the given issue is the difference between the general collateral rate and the specific repo rate for that issue. The special rate may be quoted either as an absolute rate or as a spread below the general collateral rate. For example, if the general collateral rate is 5.25%, a special issue trading at 4.50% may be quoted as being 75 basis points special.

Both parties to a repo transaction are exposed to credit risk, due to changes in the market value of the collateral. The cash lender usually receives a margin, or *haircut,* in which the mark-to-market value of the securities put up as the collateral is more than the loan as an added cushion against a fall in securities value during the term on the repo. In addition, it is helpful to review the counterparty's financial status, its legal and corporate authority to enter into repurchase transactions, and specifics of the transaction.

In general, collateral buyers' control of collateral is not crucial. There are two situations, however, in which the control of collateral is crucial to the buyer: *reverse to cover shorts* and *reverse to maturity.* In the case of covering a short, the collateral buyer needs a specific security to cover a previously established short. On a reverse to maturity, the dealer reverses in security and sells it to lock in a profit on the trade. To unwind the position on a reverse to maturity, the market practice is usually doing a pair-off and exchanging a difference check. For example, suppose a customer owns $50 million of May 31, 1999 notes, repos out the note for cash at a rate of 5.00%, and reinvests the proceeds by reversing in mortgage-backed collateral until May 31, 1999 at a rate of 5.10%. The customer picks up 10 basis points in incremental yield. The dealer reverses in the note and sells it outright to lock in a certain spread.

Fixed-Income Repo Products

A *flex repo* is a term repurchase agreement lasting for several years that provides for principal drawdowns prior to its final maturity. The flexibility is popular for structured municipal financing that requires a fixed reinvestment rate even though there is substantial cash-flow uncertainty. As an example, suppose a state housing authority issues a certain amount of bonds to subsidize mortgages to stimulate home ownership. However, the proceeds need to be invested until the mortgages are originated. Since the actual origination schedule can only be estimated, fixed-term investments are impractical. A flex repo allows for drawdowns of principal as needed. In return for the flexibility, the housing authority accepts a lower rate on this repo transaction than on an equivalent one.

An *indexed repo* is a term repo with interest rate reset periodically based on a certain benchmark such as the Fed funds rate, LIBOR, or the bill discount. The investor can draw or add to the principal as needed. Indexed repos are an attractive reinvestment vehicle for corporations with floating-rate liabilities wanting to match their book of assets and liabilities.

The Fed does several types of repurchase transactions. A *system repo* is the Fed's purchase of collateral for its own account. When the Fed buys collateral on behalf of customers, it is called a *customer repo*. A *matched sale* is when the Fed sells securities for its own account and commits to a subsequent repurchase at a price that reflects the financing rate.

Commodity repos are a recent innovation by Merrill Lynch (1991). For example, Merrill Lynch agrees to pay 90% of the inventory value for a term of 30 days or up to 6 months. In return, the company agrees to repurchase back the commodities at a specified price that reflects the mutually agreed-on interest rate for the term. The commodity repo formula could be more attractive than factoring or a bank loan.

HISTORY OF DELIVERABLE AND TRIPARTY REPOS

One of the first all-private repo trades was between General Motors (GM) and Discount Corporation in the early 1950s. At that time, the portfolio manager at GM had cash to invest for several days. There were no maturing bills that fit the schedule. The manager could not do a collateralized loan. The Discount Corporation proposed a repo trade, in which Discount Corporation was to sell bills to GM at a discount rate slightly below the market rate, and simultaneously contract to repurchase the same bills at the same rate on the date when GM needed cash. The Discount Corporation obtained a fixed rate financing for the term and GM invested an amount and a term of their choosing with no market risk.

The reverse repo by a dealer was developed through brokering or running a matched book. For example, corporations like GM asked Discount Corporation to do a term repo when the dealer was not bullish, and hence, was not willing to purchase securities outright and repo out to GM for funding. The need to service GM motivated the dealer to look for a counterparty who needed funds but was not willing to sell securities at a loss. Therefore, Discount Corporation did a reverse with that client and repoed out the securities it reversed in to GM. Discount Corporation earned a spread in those two matched transactions. This marked the start of the matched book activities.

Many repo participants were not empowered to make collateralized loans, but they could buy and sell securities to stay fully invested. Many investors (such as municipalities and financial institutions) cannot take a capital loss because of legal or self-imposed restrictions, but they can take an interest loss. Suppose a municipality thinks that it has cash available for six months, but that it might need it sooner. The municipality cannot invest in 6-month bills because of the potential capital loss that results from an unfavorable market movement should it need the money before the bills mature. The municipality can invest either in open overnight repo or in a 6-month repo. Should it have invested in a term reverse repo and need money sooner than anticipated, the municipality can repo out the securities it has reversed in. If yield has risen, the municipality may incur a loss of interest; the rate on the reverse (interest income) is lower than that on the repo (interest expenses). There is, however, no capital loss.

Defaults in Repo Market

Back in the beginning of repo development, participants priced collateral at market value. The cash lender usually received a haircut. The practice was inconvenient, because it led to odd amounts of money. An investor with $10 million to invest would prefer getting all $10 million invested rather than investing $9,988,255.25 and getting an adequate protection against credit risk. This gradually led to the practice of *flat pricing*, *par flat*, or *round price flat*. In par flat pricing, the collateral was priced at par regardless of market value, or the collateral was priced at some round price, *round price flat*, such as at 99 flat. The practice of flat pricing was an opportunity for abuses by dealers who were short on capital and integrity. In a bullish environment, they would buy bills at discount, repo them out for par, and use the excess cash to do more speculative trading. Alternatively, if they were bearish or at least not bullish, they would be tempted to reverse in high-coupon securities nearing the coupon date and sell them at market value. The extra funds generated were used to cover trading losses or to finance more speculation. This type of abuse led to the bankruptcy of Financial Corporation in 1975. Another failure story involves Drysdale Government Securities in May 1982. Drysdale reversed in high-coupon securities nearing the 1982 May coupon date at flat prices and sold the borrowed securities for full accrual prices, generating significantly more cash than it had paid out. Drysdale lost money in its shorts and was unable to pass onto collateral lenders the coupon interest when the May coupon date arrived. The bankruptcy cost its agent, Chase Manhattan Bank, about $160 million. The New York Fed ordered the primary dealers, beginning in October 1982, to adopt full accrual pricing in repo and reverse transactions.

Unlike Financial Corporation or Drysdale Government Securities, the downfall of Lombard-Wall in August 1982 was not due to abuse but instead to its inability to manage risk. Central to the bankruptcy of Lombard-Wall was the huge volume of flex repos it had with housing and other authorities. The flex repo was often done as part of a package in which the dealer agreed to underwrite the bond issue if the borrower would accept a flex repo. A safe way for the dealer to provide a fixed rate in the flex repo is to buy securities with matched maturities. Lombard-Wall mismatched maturities based on incorrect interest-rate predictions. When Lombard-Wall failed, the NYS Dormitory Authority was reported to have a $55 million unsecured claim against Lombard-Wall.

Other examples include the failures of Lion Capital, RTD Securities, ESM Government Securities, and Bevill Bressler and Schulman, resulting in significant losses to their repo counterparts in the early 1980s. To minimize operational costs (clearing), dealers in these cases did hold-in-custody repos[2] in which dealers held the repo collateral instead of delivering to customers. Lenders of money in the "trust me" repos realized significant losses because the collateral was pledged two or three times.

The losses arising from these bankruptcies led to the amendment of the Bankruptcy Act in 1984 that exempted repo collateral from the automatic stay provisions of the bankruptcy code. Coverage of the amendment is limited to repo of one year or less for collateral of government, agency, and certain money market securities. Also, the Government Securities Act of 1986 requires greater disclosure in the repo market and an executed repurchase agreement as a prerequisite for hold-in-custody transactions.

Triparty Development

The expenses associated with deliverable repos and the loss experience from letter repos prompted bond dealers to devise the *triparty agreement*. A custodial bank stands between the repo counterparties. The custodial bank maintains accounts for both parties and hence, the actual delivery of collateral and cash can be reduced to just credit and debit transfers within the same bank that simplifies the transaction. Triparty is a convenient, secure, and recognized option. In a triparty setup, all of the burden of obtaining pricing and marking to market becomes the contractual obligations of the custodian. Typically, broker–dealers pay the fees. The wire charges and fail risk are eliminated as well. The triparty repos are estimated to finance about 75% to 80% of large U.S. primary dealers' bond inventory. It is worth noting that the Bank of New York and Chase Manhattan handle most of the triparty custody market. These two banks are large government securities clearing banks, serving about 30 dealers and 500 to 600 cash providers.

Another factor contributing to the popularity of the triparty formula is the Federal Reserve Board regulations on daylight overdraft that took effect on April 14, 1994. The Fed started charging daylight overdrafts—the amounts overdrawn on the Fed wire—on an intraday basis. For the big clearing banks, bond dealers are largely responsible for the overdrafts every morning when they return borrowed cash from the conventional deliverable repo transactions. The overdraft charges give dealers strong incentives to abandon the deliverable format. The triparty agreements, of which most are open, eliminate the need for cash transfers and hence the daylight overdrafts.

In addition, the repo market has moved online. For example, Credit Suisse First Boston's RepoTrade has been successful. About 350 counterparties trade through RepoTrade. As the repo margin has narrowed to about 8 or 10 basis points (2 to 5 in a tight market), it is necessary to employ a more efficient processing mechanism. Credit Suisse First Boston also operates the International RepoTrade, which allows counterparties to trade online in a dozen currencies. Morgan Stanley introduced an online trading system in June 1996. These online trading systems provide greater transparency in which investors with access to online systems can see live bids/offers. The increased transparency in the U.S. repo market is also due to the introduction of the repo index by GovPX in November 1995. GovPX updates repo rates for overnight on-the-run treasuries and general collateral several times a day.

Europe

Development in Europe has been slow. The triparty repo has been available in Europe since 1993, direct corporate access to Cedel and Euroclear's systems since 1994, and standard legal documentation (the PSA/Isma global master repurchase agreement) since 1992. European corporate interest in repos remains lukewarm. This is due to several factors. Most companies need board approval, so repo brokers and dealers have to persuade the treasurer, who, in turn, has to explain it to the board of directors. This is a slow process. Some treasurers who traded repos have stopped because the yields are not good enough. Another reason is that Europe securities are in many different currencies and there is a great variety of issuers and structures. Hence, the repo market is neither as liquid nor as transparent, which again hinders development. Another problem for the repo market in Europe is the strength of the banking relationship and the decreased pressure that treasurers are under to produce short-term investment performance.

Despite these unfavorable factors, many in the repo market remain bullish. For one, the United Kingdom opened the gilt repo market in early 1996, and many companies have become more interested. The willingness of U.S. subsidiaries to use repo transactions in the European market is a good reason for European treasurers to eventually come to the market. Plus, European-based money market funds are beginning to invest in the nondollar repo market.

In France, the repo market took off in 1994, subsequent to the approval by the French Treasury of 15 primary dealers in Treasury bond repos, known as SPVTs. These dealers quote prices on screen in fixed amounts: Ffr 500 million for one week, Ffr 200 million for one month, and Ffr 100 million for three months. In December 1995, the repo transactions cleared through the two French clearing systems (Sicovam and Saturne) totaled Ffr 3,860 billion. The 1995 yearend outstanding amount was Ffr 1,300 billion. Furthermore, the increasing use of margin calls and the plan to extend online trading could make France a model for the development of other European repo markets.

In Germany, the domestic market is quite limited, and most repo trades (70% to 90%) are booked in London because the Bundesbank requires reserves on domestic transactions. This is changing and the German repo market is expected to be on a path of rapid growth. The first catalyst for change is the Bundesbank's decision to exempt repos from its minimum reserve requirements (took effect in January 1997). The market is now free to take advantage of broader changes in the capital markets. The second catalyst for change is the implementation of EU's Capital Adequacy Directive, which came into effect in Germany in January 1998. It will encourage a shift from unsecured to collateralized financing such as repos. As the capital markets become more international, German banks will find themselves dealing with institutions with which they do not have long-term relationships and large credit lines. This increases the value of collateralized lending. In addition, repo trades save capital. Another factor that sets the market for growth is the introduction of a standard contract in German law.

The triparty arrangements are gaining acceptance in Europe. The transaction between Swiss Bank Corporation and the European Bank for Construction and

Development in 1992 was one of the first triparty agreements in Europe. Bank of New York established RepoEdge in 1992 to provide Europe's cash-rich nonfinancial institutions, which do not have accounts with either Cedel or Euroclear, to access the system. The RepoEdge has been used actively by several dealers.

Euroclear, Cedel Bank, and Bank of New York are the three largest triparty repo custodians in Europe. The average daily triparty repo volume more than doubled from 1995 to 1996. The fees are generally between 1 and 4 basis points depending on volume.

Japan

The onshore bond repo market started in Japan in 1996. This is striking because Japan has the second largest government bond market in the world. The Japanese public debt is ¥249 trillion. The development of a real repo market was part of the 1996 government bond market reforms. The reforms include (1) modernizing the settlement system to a rolling T+7 process from the inefficient settlement only on dates ending in a five or a zero, (2) introducing a five-year JGB futures market, (3) creating a repurchase agreement market, and (4) introducing the strips technique in borrowing. The change in the settlement process took effect on October 1, 1996. A further change to T+3 took effect in April 1997. The change means that traders need to settle every day. This need will stimulate the securities lending market, and hence help the development of the repo market.

In addition to the offshore repo transactions, there are two repo-like markets. One is called *gensaki*. The *gensaki* market follows similar principles to other repo markets; however, the taxation on interest has prevented it from taking off. The total *gensaki* turnover was estimated at ¥66 trillion in 1994, a relatively small amount compared to the U.S. market. In addition to the sales tax levy, the borrower cannot specify the bond of choice but has to take whatever is available. Another repo-like market is called *taishoku*. It has developed primarily to avoid the transaction tax and the inefficient settlement system. The disadvantage is that it has existed in a state of legal limbo. Fund lenders accept unsecured transactions to avoid tax and a lengthy settlement process.

One aspect of the new onshore repo market is that the 15% taxation of interest payments to foreigners will remain. This will ensures the dual existence of the onshore and offshore repo markets. Another aspect is that the new onshore repo market is more of securities lending than a repo because the cash lender sets an interest rate and the bond lender sets a fee for the use of the bond.

Emerging Markets Repo

Emerging markets repo has, until recently, focused on international issues such as eurobonds and Brady bonds. Brady bonds are international and the most liquid because they are Euroclear eligible and as convenient and cheap to settle as OECD government bonds. Domestic emerging market debt is different, which may be denominated in dollar or local currency. The settlement and custody are also in local market. Liquidity risk and currency volatility are a big challenge. Domestic emerging market debt is the latest form of repo collateral.

Depending on the counterparties and countries involved, Brady bond repo might pay an investor LIBOR flat to LIBOR plus 8–10 basic points if the counterparty is an

A-rated U.S. investment bank, 15–20 basic points more for a weaker house. For domestic emerging market debt, the investor can expect an additional 10–20 basic points.

MECHANICS OF REPOS AND MARKET PRACTICES

Suppose an investor purchases $100 million of a 6 1/2 February-05 Treasury notes from dealer X at an offer of 100 28/32. Suppose that the last coupon was paid 60 days ago and the next coupon date is 123 days away. This customer is obligated to pay the dealer the clean price plus the accrued interest the next day against delivery. The total payment next day is

$$\$100,000,000 \times \left(100\,\frac{28}{32} + 3.25 \times \frac{61}{183}\right) = \$101,958,333.33$$

(A same-day settlement exists, but it is much less liquid.) Payments are made from the customer's clearing bank account to the dealer's clearing account. The notes are in a book-entry form, and hence, the transfer would be made through the Fedwire service. The Fedwire service handles amounts of at most $50 million, so this trade would be done in three transfers. The transfer involves a fee paid to the clearing bank.

Suppose the investor finances the purchase the next day with an overnight repo, same day settlement, with dealer Y.[3] Assume the next morning the dealer quotes the customer a repo rate of 5.20% and a bid price of 101 2/32 for these notes. The dealer requires a 1% haircut. The amount of dealer financing is

$$\$100,000,000 \times \frac{1}{1.01} \times \left(101\,\frac{2}{32} + 3.25 \times \frac{61}{183}\right) = \$101,134,488.45.$$

The customer's clearing bank will thus have the following list of transactions to perform:

1. Pay dealer X $101,958,333.33 in cash.
2. Accept $100 million of the 6 1/2 February-05 notes from dealer X.
3. Transfer $100 million of these notes to dealer Y.
4. Receive $101,134,488.45 in cash (loan) from dealer Y.

The overnight repo could be rolled over or be terminated by either party. Suppose it is terminated the next day. The customer is to pay dealer Y

$$\$101,134,488.45 \times \left(1 + \frac{0.052}{360}\right) = \$101,149,096.76$$

via clearing house to dealer Y in return for the same $100 million notes. The one-day interest is $14,608.31.

In practice, however, it is not unusual for them to roll over the open repo for another day. In this case the base price for repo purposes would often remain at the same original price, 101 2/32. If the repo is rolled at a rate of 5.1%, the amount payable the next day will be

$$\$101{,}134{,}488.45 \times \left(1 + \frac{0.052}{360} + \frac{0.051}{360}\right) = \$101{,}163{,}424.15.$$

Note that the interest is not compounding. This open arrangement eliminates the need to repeatedly transfer the collateral for cash on a daily basis; each transfer incurs clearing fees.

The customer could do a term repo if it needs a term financing instead of overnight. The calculation is similar to the earlier example (e.g., the customer did a 2-day term repo instead of rolling open repo over). For the 2-day financing at a rate of 5.2%, the customer would have to repay the following amount in return for getting back the collateral:

$$\$101{,}134{,}488.45 \times \left(1 + \frac{0.052}{360} \times 2\right) = \$101{,}163{,}705.08.$$

This assumes a haircut of 1%. The margin is an added cushion against a fall in securities value. Typical margin ranges from 1% to 3%. Higher percentages are required for illiquid collateral or weak credit counterparty. For customers with established good business relationships or for collateral with short maturities, the margin is often waved. The current market practice is that a dealer financing a hedge fund client's position generally will demand a daily margining on the firm's net market exposure across all products requiring margin. Dealers argue that new technology and netting across products makes traditional haircuts irrelevant.

Another way to limit the credit exposure is to mark the securities collateral to market regularly on a term repo. The trade can be adjusted either through a margin call or a repricing. For example, if the market price declines, the adjustment takes one of the two options:

1. *Margin call:* The customer sends the dealer additional collateral to restore the margin.
2. *Repricing:* The loan is reduced, restoring the original margin. The customer wires the difference to the dealer's account.

Interest is paid on the principal amount outstanding. If the additional collateral is delivered, the principal of the trade remains at the initial amount and interest is paid on that amount. If the transaction is repriced, interest will be paid on the initial amount until repricing and on the new reduced amount thereafter.

Substitution and Coupon Pass-Through

During the term of the repo transaction, the seller of the collateral may need the specific security for delivery to another party. The seller may then request a substitution. For example, the customer may need the specific notes for other purposes. If the right of substitution is granted in the repo agreement, the customer can then request to deliver other securities of equal market value and similar characteristics to dealer Y. The principal amount of the trade remains the same.

Even though the lender of money owns the collateral during the term of the repo trade, the collateral seller is entitled to any principal or interest received. The buyer is responsible for wiring to the seller any such funds while holding the collateral.

Trading Practices

Nearly all repo trading is done on a same day settlement basis. This necessitates close contact between the repo desk and the clearance area. In addition, repo trading tends to be compressed to an 8:00 A.M. to 10:00 A.M. window to allow for the trade to be processed and cleared same day.

Repo rates are quoted on an actual/360 basis, as shown in the previous calculations. A round lot in the repo market is $25 million (special) or $50 million (others). Because of the short-term nature of the market, operational costs affect rates on smaller pieces of collateral.

On Special

At any given time, most governments are generic and traded at the same rates, often at a level close to the Fed Funds rate. These issues are referred to as the general collateral; lenders of cash are indifferent as to which issue they receive as collateral. At the same time, there are issues (called special) traded at lower repo rates. The specials usually include the on-the-run issues and some more actively traded off-the-run securities. In this case, the lender of money wants to receive a specific issue as collateral.

Securities go on special for a number of reasons. They may be in short supply because they are snapped up by institutions that are not active in the repo market or because they were distributed through dealers with a large retail client base. Trading and hedging strategies play a big part, too. A security can also go on special when one or more big players in repos are holding back a large chunk of an issue from the market. The number of such squeezes has declined sharply since the Salomon scandal.

Most of the variation in Treasury repo rates is based on the demand for and supply of particular collateral. This is particularly evident for the current issues that are often on special. The on-the-run treasuries have the greatest liquidity of issues with similar maturities. They are frequently used for hedging or speculative trading. It is also common for traders and money managers who prefer as much liquidity as possible to maintain positions in the most recently issued security by regularly rolling into the on-the-run issues.[4] The process of trading rolls leads dealers to short the when-issued securities and buy the recently off-the-run issues. This tends to relieve repo market pressure in the newly off-the-run security and begin building pressure in the new on-the-run issue.

The spread between the special repo rate and general collateral rate, or specialness, reflects the relative scarcity of the security involved. The collateral buyer (cash lender) demands the specific security to cover short and, hence, is willing to accept a lower rate in return for that specific collateral. The spread between the specials and general collateral repo rates can be highly volatile, tightening or widening over the course of weeks or days, or sometimes within an hour. The average specialness for 2-year, 3-year, 5-year, non-reopened 10-year, reopened 10-year are 27 basic points, 41 basic points, 58 basic points, 143 basic points, and 62 basic points, respectively. The associated costs per month to short sellers are amounted to 2 basic points, 3 basic points, 5 basic points, 12 basic points, and 5 basic points.[5] The on-the-run 10-year notes have consistently gone on special. The main reason is that mortgage-backed and corporate bond trading desks routinely short the 10-year notes to hedge their inventories against interest rate, duration, and convexity risks. Proprietary trading desks deploying global bond arbitrages often require shorts in the 10-year notes to capture yield spread.

The status of a bond in the repo market is important in assessing the relative values of bonds and in understanding the valuation of futures contracts. The status is one of the reasons[6] why a bond may trade at a different level from implied by a smooth yield curve. If a trader is considering shorting a particular bond that looks rich compared with the yield curve, the trader needs to know the bond's status in the repo market. This is because the cost of borrowing that issue may be large enough to erode or even eliminate the potential profits. In the futures market, a cash-and-carry trade is when a trader buys a bond that is deliverable into a futures contract and shorts the correctly weighted number of contracts. This is similar to a repo trade. At the beginning, the trader pays a cash amount and receives a bond. At the expiry of the contract, the trader receives cash and delivers bond. The implied repo rate can be calculated accordingly. The bond with the lowest implied repo rate is the cheapest to deliver. The *net basis,* the difference between actual and implied repo rate, is the value the market has assigned to the delivery option.

The lower bound on repo rates is practically at zero. However, under certain circumstances, the repo rates could be negative in which the collateral buyer does not charge interest on money lent and is willing to pay a fee for using the collateral. First, a trader might accept a negative repo rate to reverse in the specific collateral to prevent a fail. If a trader needs only an additional relatively small quantity of an issue to completely cover a large short position, the trader might offer a collateral usage fee (negative repo rate). Furthermore, there was an instance in which a specific repo rate of −21% was offered for a specific Treasury note needed to fill a delivery requirement on a futures contract. Failure to deliver would have had severe adverse consequences.[7] Finally, a cheapest-to-deliver Treasury issue, by a wide margin, against a futures contract could also have a significant negative repo rate.

FAIL AND CONSEQUENCES

On the settlement date, if the security seller does not make timely delivery of the securities sold, the trade becomes a fail. When a fail occurs, the buyer does not have to make payment until proper delivery is made. This is equivalent to an interest-free loan for as long as the fail persists. Furthermore, the buyer is entitled to the accrued interest, starting on the initial agreed-on settlement date.

In the repo market, a fail occurs when the collateral buyer does not make timely return of the collateral to complete leg two of the repo transaction. Failure to deliver collateral under a standard repurchase agreement is not viewed as default, but is instead covered under terms of the agreement by requiring the collateral buyer (money lender) to renew the trade at a repo rate of zero.[8] This effectively limits the extent to which a repo rate can become negative. The reason is that a negative repo rate will induce the short to fail and accept a more favorable zero repo rate.

BROKERING AND MATCHED BOOK

In the early stages of the repo market, dealers and banks often executed repo transactions to finance their portfolios. They could do these transactions directly and efficiently with their customers. Also, executing repos was viewed as part of customer services. As the market developed, dealers are using repo not just as a financing tool, but also as a trading strategy. The average daily amount of outstanding repos and reverses

TABLE 12.1   Average Daily Amount Outstanding for Repos and Reverses ($ billions)[1]

Year	Reverses	Repos	Total
1981	46.7	65.4	112.1
1982	75.1	95.2	170.3
1983	81.7	102.4	184.1
1984	112.4	132.6	245.0
1985	147.9	172.9	320.8
1986	207.7	244.5	452.2
1987	275.0	292.0	567.0
1988	313.6	309.7	623.3
1989	383.2	398.2	781.4
1990	377.1	413.5	790.5
1991	417.0	496.6	913.6
1992	511.1	628.2	1,139.3
1993	594.1	765.6	1,359.7
1994	651.2	825.9	1,477.1
1995	618.8	821.5	1,440.3
1996	718.1	973.7	1,691.8
1997	883.0	1,159.0	2,042.0

[1] Figures cover activities by U.S. government securities dealers.
Source: Adapted from The Bond Market Association, 1998.

by government securities dealers is about $2 trillion (Table 12.1). Dealers can only do the huge volume by relying on brokers.

Brokering

Major repo brokers include EXCO RMJ Secs. Corp., Patriot Secs.,[9] Darban LLC, Tullett & Tokyo Secs. Inc., CF Kross,[10] GFI Group Inc., Prebon Secs. USA Inc., Euro Brokers Maxcor Inc. Brokers used to quote rates by giving runs over the phone. Then they switched to posting rates on CRTs. Table 12.2 is an example of the CRT screen.

Most repo brokers act on a give-up-name basis. They reveal who the counterparty is after crossing a trade. Brokers charge a fee from both sides of about five basis points for an overnight repo, and of about two basis points for term repos. For example, suppose a broker arranges a repo transaction of $100 million. The fee on an overnight repo amounts to

$$(0.0005 + 0.0005) \times (\$100 \text{ million}) \times \frac{1}{360} = \$277.78.$$

The fee on, say, a 10-day term repo on the same amount is charged from both counterparties for 10 days. The total amount of the fee earned by the broker is

$$(0.0002 + 0.0002) \times (\$100 \text{ million}) \times \frac{10}{360} = \$1,111.11.$$

Repo brokers earn the fee by providing timely market information to participants, including the availability of and demand for the collateral. Participants can obtain more

TABLE 12.2   Repo CRT Screen

O/N <10/<10		2 YR 9–30	
O 2Y 100 3/8	5.20 (25) – 5.125 (25)	GSCC 2Y 9–30	
2 YR 99$^1/_2$		OLD 3Y 1WK	
O 3Y 101$^5/_8$		OLD 3Y 11–15	
GSCC O3YR[1]		3 YR 11–15	5.30 (50) – 5.20 (50)
3 YR 98$^7/_8$[2]		1–01 11–15	
GSCC 3YR	5.18 (25) – 5.10 (25)	OLD 5Y 9–17	
O 5Y 100$^1/_8$	5.15 (25) – 5.00 (25)[3]	5 YR 9–30	4.80 (25) – 4.65 (25)
5 YR 99–	4.625 (old) – 4.30 (25)	2–06 11–15	
GSCC 5YR		OLD10Y 11–15	
2–06 91$^3/_4$	4.50 (OLD) – 4.25 (25)	10 YR 9–16	
DELTA 2–06[4]		10 YR 9–30	5.00 (25) –
O10Y 101$^3/_4$		10 YR 10–15	4.90 (50) – 4.80 (25)
10YR 101$^1/_2$		10 10–15S9–16	
GSCC 10YR		10 YR 11–15	
8–25 96$^1/_2$		10 YR 2–14	
O BD 86$^1/_4$	5.05 (25) – 4.95 (25)	8–25 9–16	
BOND 96–[5]	– 5.00 (25)	8–25 11–15	
GSCC BOND		OLD BD 9–16	
11$^1/_4$ 2–15		OLD BD 11–15	
9–30		OB11–15S9–16	
12–31		BOND 10–1	
5$^3/_4$ 8–03		BOND 11–15	4.50 (25) – 4.25 (25)
12–31		BD11–15S10–1	

[1]**GSCC 03YR** GSCC stands for the Government Securities Clearance Corporation. The clearing facility will be used for this instrument. 03YR denotes the instrument as old 3-year Treasury. There are no bids or offers at this moment.

[2]**3YR 98 7/8** GSCC or DELTA is not mentioned; therefore, this trade would clear on a "Name Give-Up" basis. 3YR denotes the instrument as the current, or on the run, 3-year Treasury, priced at 98 7/8.

[3]**5Y 100 1/8 5.15 (25)–5.00 (25)** This instrument is a current 5-year Treasury traded at 100 1/8. 5.15 is the bid represented as a yield. (25) represents the size of the amount that could be traded; in this case, 25 million notional. 5.00 is the offer represented as a yield.

[4]**DELTA 2–06** DELTA is mentioned; therefore, this trade would clear through DELTA. 2–06 denotes the instrument as a "Term Repo." At this moment there are no bids or offers for this security.

[5]**BOND 96–5.00 (25)** BOND denotes this is the current 30-year Treasury, priced at 96.00. At this moment there is no bid, however, there is an offer of 5.00. (25) represents the size of the amount that could be traded.

Source: This is the Market Page Display for Page 31 as of Thu Sep 05 08:00:04 1996, Liberty Brokerage Inc.

accurate and timely information from repo brokers than they would obtain by calling dealers. The increased market transparency is provided not only to dealers, but also to their customers.

Among the major brokers, some are "principal brokers," which often act as a principal when it brokers repos and reverses. It reverses in collateral against money, and repos out these securities for cash. This is, in essence, a matched book. This could be more profitable than pure brokering, especially when it finds a firm wanting to repo out stock collateral and another wanting to borrow as a special.[11] By acting as a principal, however, the firm is exposed to delivery risk when it takes in securities late in the day and cannot make timely delivery. If this occurs, the firm has to provide overnight financing for these securities. The cost to a delivery fail are significant, especially over the weekend. Second, the firm needs to set up facilities to clear the trades. Furthermore, it also requires capital to support these positions.

The GSCC (Government Securities Clearing Corporation) provides netting services for brokered repos executed on an anonymous or blind basis, in lieu of name give-up. Brokers and dealers would execute the settlement of intra-day settling of start legs directly with each other. Brokers and dealers would send transaction details to GSCC for comparison, netting, and guaranteed settlement of close legs. The following brokers are eligible for netting participation: EXCO RMJ, Liberty, Garban, Tradition, Tullett & Tokyo, CF Kross, GFI, Prebon, and Euro Brokers. In addition, 55 repo dealers are eligible for the GSCC blind-brokered repo netting services. These dealers are listed in Table 12.3.

The value of repo transactions cleared by the GSCC has been soaring from $68 trillion in 1994 to $148 trillion by 1997. The red-hot repo market of recent years is attributable to the confluence of FASB Fin 41 and GSCC's netting services. The 1994 FASB Fin 41 allows repo dealers to net gross exposures to the same counterparty with the same end date. Then, in 1995, the GSCC began to provide clearing and netting services

TABLE 12.3   Dealers Eligible for GSCC Repo Netting Services

Number	Dealer	Number	Dealer
9510	BancAmerica Robertson Stephens	9549	Prudential Securities Incorporated
9511	Bankers Trust Company	9550	Sanwa Securities (USA) Co., L.P.
9512	Bear, Stearns & Co., Inc.	9552	Salomon Brothers, Inc.
9513	HSBC Securities, Inc.	9554	Smith Barney Inc./Dealer
9515	Chase Securities, Inc.	9555	Warburg Dillon Read LLC
9516	Citibank, N.A.	9558	Schroder & Co. Inc.
9519	Refco Securities, Inc.	9561	BZW Securities, Inc.
9520	NationsBanc Montgomery Securities	9562	BT Alex. Brown Incorporated
9521	Daiwa Securities America Inc.	9563	Citicorp Securities, Inc.
9522	Dean Witter Reynolds Inc.	9564	Scotia Capital Markets (USA)
9524	Zions First National Bank	9565	CIBC Oppenheimer Corp.
9525	Donaldson, Lufkin, & Jenrette	9566	Deutsche Morgan Grenfell Inc.
9526	Spear, Leeds & Kellogg	9567	First Chicago Capital Markets Inc
9527	Eastbridge Capital Inc.	9569	Dresdner Kleinwort Benson
9528	Credit Suisse First Boston Corporation	9580	Daiwa Securities America, Inc./OddLot
9530	The First National Bank Of Chicago	9581	CIBC Oppenheimer Corp./WG
9531	Goldman, Sachs, & Co.	9584	ABN Amro Incorporated
9532	Greenwich Capital Markets, Inc.	9586	TD Securities (USA) Inc.
9533	Nesbitt Burns Securities Inc.	9589	Commerzbank Capital Markets Corp.
9536	Fuji Securities Inc.	9592	Credit Lyonnais, NY
9538	Lehman Brothers Inc.	9595	Societe Generale, NY
9539	Aubry G. Lanston & Co., Inc.	9597	BancBoston Securities Inc.
9541	Merrill Lynch Government Securities	9633	Scotia Capital Markets (USA) Inc./CCS
9542	J.P. Morgan Securities Inc.	9637	Paribas Corporation
9543	Morgan Stanley & Co., Incorporated	9644	Sumitomo Bank Securities, Inc.
9545	The Nikko Securities Co. Int'l, Inc.	9653	Rosenthal-Collins Group
9546	Nomura Securities International, Inc.	9661	Marine Midland
9548	Paine Webber Incorporated		

Source: Government Securities Clearing Corporation, September 1998.

for repos to member dealers. Before 1995, if a bond dealer, say, HSBC Securities repoed $200 million with Goldman Sachs and reversed $150 million with Morgan Stanley Dean Witter, it had $350 million of gross position on its balance sheet. Now the GSCC serves as the counterparty, HSBC would have to shoulder only $50 million net exposure. And this $50 million exposure could be easily netted out by reversing in $50 million with the same end date with a GSCC member dealer.

Dealers' Repo Desk and Matched Book

Securities dealers use repos both to finance their inventory and to execute matched book activities. In a matched book, the dealer would reverse in securities and simultaneously repo out the collateral at a lower rate. The dealer makes a profit on the bid–asked spread, which is in the vicinity of 8 to 10 basis points, and 2 to 5 basis points in a tight market. In a perfectly matched book, the dealer would not have any interest rate risk.

In practice, dealers tend to regard a wide range of transactions as part of the matched book. The range of repo desk activities includes financing dealer's positions, covering shorts, acting as intermediary, and providing funding to customers.

A dealer's repo desk is usually first responsible for obtaining financing as much as possible dealer's inventory and trading positions. For dealers, repo is the cheapest financing alternative. The overnight rate is usually at a spread below the Fed funds rate, whereas the dealer loan rate from clearing banks is a spread above the Fed funds rate. Financing at the clearing bank is only the last resort. With a matched book, there are other profitable opportunities. For one, a trader might reverse in securities in anticipation of future shorts. The trader could repo out these securities until the trader needs them to deliver. Another example is that a matched book trader who anticipates an issue to go on special in the future will reverse in now while it is still a general collateral.

The second responsibility of a repo desk is to reverse in securities traders sold short to make good delivery. In a reverse to cover short, the objective is to have the specific security. This is in contrast to most repos, in which the lender of money demands collateral to limit its credit risk exposure.

Third, when the repo desk runs a matched book, it provides a financial intermediation function. It buys in collateral at a rate and sells out at a lower rate. The dealer is earning a spread in the process. Furthermore, repurchase transactions are an important source of funding to customers and are therefore facilitating sales of securities.

Of course, the dealer might mismatch the repo and reverse maturities, creating a tail, to profit from the anticipated rate movements. For example, suppose a dealer anticipates that interest rates will fall in the next three months. To take advantage, the dealer does a 91-day reverse of $100 million collateral at 5.7% and does a 7-day repo of the same securities initially at 5.6%. If rates decline as anticipated, the dealer profits from the weekly rolling over of the repos at lower rates. If the 7-day repo rates stay at 5.6% and the dealer rolls over weekly the trade with the same counterparty, the trader is making a gain of 10 basis points, or $25,277.78 in dollar terms.

However, if the trader does the repo with a different counterparty every week or a certain event causing the closing and reopening of repo every week, the trader will not make the 10 basis points profits. The interest income from reverse is

$$\$100,000,000 \times (5.7\%) \times \frac{91}{360} = \$1,440,833.33.$$

The weekly interest is paid out every 7 days at

$$\$100,000,000 \times (5.6\%) \times \frac{7}{360} = \$108,888.89.$$

The total value of these weekly interest payments at repo maturity, 91 days later, is $1,424,738.56. The net interest income is only $16,094.77.

In the example, the dealer is said to long collateral. If the maturity of the reverse is shorter than that of the repo, the dealer is short collateral. Both parties to a repo transaction are exposed to credit risk because the market value of collateral changes constantly. The risk exposure can be limited by requiring a haircut, regular repricing of collateral, and thoroughly reviewing the counterparty's financial status. Furthermore, the position in reverse might eat up capital during a bear market. As an example, suppose the dealer did a $10 million, six-month reverse on the long bond and the market dropped three points because of an unexpected strong employment number as it did in early 1996. The dealer would be out $300,000 of capital. Collateral repricing reduces risk. In the repo and reverse market, repricing can be done any time during the life of the agreement; there is no set time period on repricing.

CLEARING OF REPOS AND REVERSES

The discussion here focuses on two important aspects. One is on the dealer's accounting and operations systems. The second is on the process at the clearing banks.

Dealers' Operations and Accounting Systems

At least seven pieces of information are required to get a bond trade into the dealer's system. These are the trade date, value date, the bond, nominal amount, counterparty, buy or sale, and the clean price. To book a plain-vanilla repo trade requires all these plus the term, deal type, dirty price, repo rate, and cash principal. For settlement, a bond trade settles once with possible complications of a fail, both of which are relevant to a repo trade. Various adjustments such as margin calls and collateral substitution might take place during the repo term period. Each of these adjustments must be represented as a combination of cancelled and rebooked trades. The accounting of repos is more complex. A repo trade is accounted for as a collateralized loan, with the securities remaining on the balance sheet and coupon continuing to accrue. Therefore, a repricing affects the main account but a substitution of collateral does not.

A repo trade can look like a number of different things. In a matched book, the trader is taking on interest-rate risk. In a financing book, the same repo is used to manage cash and inventory to reduce the cost of funding for the firm. The very same trade is viewed differently according to its purpose. But the purpose ceases to matter in settlement, when it becomes a cash purchase and a forward sale. Turning to accounting, the purpose matters again. Is it a matched book profit and loss, or is it cost of carry?

Clearing of Repos and Reverses

The clearing of repos and reverses is on the underlying collateral. The securities could be in book-entry or physical form. Repurchase transactions are more complex than the outright sales or purchases. A bond trade settles once, the only complication is a fail or partial fail. A repo has two legs, each leg looks like a bond trade. In addition, there is a right of substitution.

A repo involves a cash sale and a forward purchase. The sell side of the transaction is typically settled the same day and the buy side is for forward settlement. In a basic deliverable repo trade, the operations department makes up and sends out instructions to its clearing bank to clear the trade and confirmation to its counterparty. The dealer's clearing bank sends out the collateral against payment. The cash lender's clearing bank wires the cash to and accepts delivery of the collateral from the dealer's clearing bank. The opposite process occurs in close leg.

In a letter repo, the dealers will safekeep the collateral for the customer. This is often done by transferring the collateral from the dealer's clearing account to some other account maintained by the dealer. Dealers offer to safekeep securities for customers for several reasons. First, safekeeping is provided at no cost to the customer as a service. The second reason is to prevent a subsequent fail by the customer. Another reason is to save clearing fees. Finally, in a dealer safekeeping arrangement, the dealer benefits if another counterparty fails to deliver the collateral that the dealer has promised to safekeep for the customer.

In a triparty repo, a custodial bank stands between the repo counterparties. The custodial bank maintains accounts for both parties and hence, the actual delivery of collateral and cash can be reduced to just credit and debit transfers. The wire charges and fail risk are eliminated.

PSA REPO TRADING GUIDELINES

This section briefly explains PSA-recommended repo trading practices guidelines.[12] The confidentiality guideline indicates that it is the responsibility of dealers and brokers to maintain the confidentiality of the names of parties to a trade. The identity is disclosed only after the bid is hit or the offer lifted. A broker may disclose to a dealer that it does not have a line of credit with the other side before a trade is completed.

Repo trading has come online. Parties to all trades have a maximum of 20 seconds to clear the picture. All bids and offers are good until cancelled or the end of the business day. Trading in odd lots means (1) a lot less than $50 million for mortgage securities, overnight and term general collateral and (2) a lot less than $25 million for specials. If all or nothing is not specified, dealers bidding or offering an amount greater than $50 million should accept transactions in $50 million increments.

All overnight and open trades are assumed cash trades until the end of reversal time[13] at 3:30 P.M. on Fedwire. All other trades done before 12:00 noon are assumed to be cash trades. Trades done after 12:00 noon are regular trades. The pricing on all current-issue specials should be done within five minutes, except for trades with longer than regular settlement such as when-issued trades that should be priced the night before settlement. Margin calls on all dealer-to-dealer repos are to be met the same day with transfers of collateral or cash. A party wishing to "mark to market" its counterparties should do so by 10:00 A.M. The counterparty can refuse to be marked when there is no net credit exposure.

In CMO repo transactions, IOs, POs, inverse floaters, residuals, Z-tranches, superfloaters, re-remics, and accumulation bonds are not acceptable collateral. Only Fedwire securities are acceptable in agency CMO repos.

The collateral buyer need not pass through any due payments from the security if the issuer fails to make such payments. Finally, parties to trades with the right of substitution executed through brokers should notify counterparties of the substitution by 10:00 A.M. and provide a description of the substituted collateral by 11:00 A.M. (EST).

EQUITY REPOS

The National Securities Markets Improvement Act (NSMIA) of 1996 and the relaxation of Regulation T removed significant legal barriers to the development of a U.S. equity repo market. NSMIA eliminated previous restrictions, which stated that only banks and broker–dealers could lend to broker–dealers against listed securities. NSMIA also paved the way for the removal of Federal Reserve Board minimum margin requirements for qualifying broker–dealer financing transactions. An ad hoc committee on equity repo was set up to examine potential issues in the emerging equity repo market. The committee members include representatives from securities companies, the PSA, and the NYSE. Based on suggestions and recommendations by the ad hoc committee, the PSA and the Securities Industry Association (SIA) have jointly released Annex VIII and Guidance Notes.

The fundamentals of equity repos are the same as the fixed-income repos. There are several differences, though. First, settlement is the standard T+3 through the Depository Trust Company. Because the transaction is terminable upon demand, either party can terminate the transaction by delivering a notice specifying a termination date, which could be same day or the following business day. However, the seller is required to give a termination date no earlier than the standard settlement date. The expansion of the notice period is intended to address situations in which the buyer does not possess the *purchased securities* (collateral), so it requires more than one business day to obtain the securities for delivery back to the seller on the termination date.

The PSA/SIA Annex III requires the seller to pay any transfer taxes, stamp taxes, and similar cost with respect to the transfer of securities. The parties involved may agree to any alternative arrangement. The market value of securities traded primarily in the United States shall be determined by the last reported sale prices, whereas securities cleared and settled outside of the United States are valued in accordance with market practice in the principal market for such securities.

In an equity repo, the seller is entitled to all dividends and distributions during the term of the repo. Cash distribution is passed along from buyer to seller, whereas non-cash distributions such as stock dividends or stock splits are added to the purchased securities. This is intended to protect the ability of collateral buyer to use the purchased securities to satisfy an outstanding delivery obligation. The issue on whether to transfer the voting rights to the buyer has been subject to heated debate. Under the PSA/SIA Annex VIII, the seller transfers all rights to vote the purchased securities to the buyer. Also, the seller may wish to require the buyer to provide notice of corporate events, such as proposed conversion, subdivision, consolidation, takeover, preemption, option, or other right. With such events, the seller may request a substitution of other securities for the affected purchased securities (right of substitution) or to terminate the transaction (demand transaction).

SUMMARY

This chapter describes in detail many important aspects of the repo market. It is the largest money market in the United States and is gaining rapidly in size in the global markets. It is a significant market itself and is essential to other areas of business as well. In addition, understanding the repo market is key to assessing value in the underlying securities, and is therefore becoming more and more important to all participants. The equity repo market is expected to present a tremendous opportunity and to post a big challenge to the traditional stock loan business.

SELECTED BIBLIOGRAPHY

Duffie, D. "Special repo rates," *Journal of Finance* 51 (June 1996): 493–526.

International Securities Lending. Euromoney Publications PLC (London, UK). Various issues.

Jordan, B. D., and S. D. Joedan. "Special repo rates: an empirical analysis." *Journal of Finance* 52 (December 1997): pp. 2051–2072.

Keane, F. "Expected repo specialness costs and the Treasury auction cycle." Federal Reserve Bank of New York, Research Paper #9504, 1995.

Keane, F. "Repo rate patterns for new Treasury notes." *Current Issues In Economics and Finance*, Federal Reserve Bank of New York (September 1996): pp. 1–5.

Liaw, T. "Pricing Treasury coupon rolls." *Corporate Finance Review* (March/April 1997): 12–15.

Reichard, R. "Commodity repos—a new way to cut inventory costs." *Purchasing* (July 13, 1995): pp. 133–137.

Repo Trading Practices Guidelines. Public Securities Association, New York (August 1996).

Rogg, O. H. "Repurchase agreements." In F. Fabozzi, ed. *Handbook of Fixed Income Securities*. Burr Ridge, IL: Irwin, 1991.

Sollinger, A. "The triparty is just beginning." *Institutional Investor* (January 1994): pp. 133–135.

Stigum, M. *The Repo and Reverse Markets*. Burr Ridge, IL: Irwin, 1989.

Stigum, M., and F. L. Robinson. *Money Market & Bond Calculations*. Burr Ridge, IL: Irwin, 1996.

The Worldwide Directory of Securities Lending and Repo 1997/1998. Euromoney Publications PLC (London), 1997.

Financial Engineering

Financial engineering is the investment banker's creativity successfully put into practice. The competition among investment banking professionals to meet the needs of borrowers and investors—such as hedging, funding, arbitrage, yield enhancement, and tax purposes—drives the explosive growth in the structured and derivatives markets. The development of the junk bond and asset-backed markets provides borrowers additional funding sources at lower costs. Structured notes add another dimension in the funding and investment spectrum. Transactions in repurchase agreements provide borrowers lower funding costs and give lenders legal title to the collateral. Through swap contracting, borrowers and investors obtain a high degree of flexibility in asset–liability management at better terms. Credit derivatives are the new trend with widespread applications. This chapter first provides an illustration of the financial engineering process, from why to how and to the end results. Subsequent sections cover the most widely used products and the new trend in the derivatives markets.

OVERVIEW

Financial engineering is the successful implementation of the investment banker's creativity in security design. The rapid pace of financial innovation is driven by the competition among investment bankers in response to increased price volatility, tax and regulatory changes, demand for new funding sources, arbitrage, and yield enhancement. The application of mathematical and statistical modeling, together with advances in computer technology, provides the necessary infrastructure for financial engineering. The notional principal of swaps and related derivatives outstanding worldwide grew from $3.45 trillion in 1990, to $25 trillion by 1996, and to more than $29 trillion in 1997. Table 13.1 lists volume summary of derivative market data from 1990 to 1997.

Since 1991, many banks and investment banks have created AAA-rated derivatives subsidiaries. These subsidiaries and vehicles with guaranteed pool of collateral offer them as more acceptable counterparties for derivative transactions in order to gain access to the world's most select clients. The 1998 *Institutional Investor* poll ranked J.P. Morgan, Citicorp, Chase Manhattan, Deutsche Morgan Grenfell, and Union Bank of Switzerland the top dealers in interest-rate derivatives. In foreign exchange derivatives,

TABLE 13.1   Summary of Derivative Market Data[1]

Year	Derivative Activity ($ billion)	Total Outstanding ($ billion)	Interest Rate Swaps Outstanding ($ billion)
1990	$1,769	$3,450	$2,312
1991	2,333	4,449	3,065
1992	3,717	5,345	3,851
1993	5,517	8,474	6,177
1994	8,133	11,303	8,816
1995	11,169	17,712	12,811
1996	17,775	25,453	19,171
1997	22,181	29,035	22,291

[1]Derivative market data include interest rate swaps, currency swaps, and interest rate options.
Source: ISDA Market Survey, August 1998.

the top ranks include Citicorp, Deutsche Morgan Grenfell, Chase Manhattan, SBC Warburg Dillon Read, and J.P. Morgan. The top-ranked dealers in equity derivatives are Goldman Sachs, Morgan Stanley Dean Witter, BT Alex. Brown, Merrill Lynch, and SBC Warburg Dillon Read. At the same time, Goldman Sachs, J.P. Morgan, Citicorp, BT Alex. Brown, and Chase Manhattan are regarded as the best in providing tailored derivative solutions. In overall ranking of derivative dealers, Citicorp, Goldman Sachs and J.P. Morgan claim the top positions. Table 13.2 lists the top 20 derivatives dealers.

TABLE 13.2   Top Derivatives Dealers

Rank	Firm
1	Citicorp
2	Goldman Sachs
3	J.P. Morgan
4	Chase Manhattan
5	Deutsche Morgan Grenfell
6	Morgan Stanley Dean Witter
7	SBC Warburg Dillon Read
8	Union Bank of Switzerland
9	Merrill Lynch
10	BT Alex. Brown
11	HSBC Capital Markets
12	Credit Suisse First Boston
13	BankAmerica Robertson Stephens
14	Societe Generale
15	BZW
16	NatWest Markets
17	Dresdner Kleinwort Benson
18	Banque Paribas
19	Salomon Smith Barney
20	Lehman Brothers

Source: Institutional Investor (February 1998): 53–60.

Risk Management

Futures, options,[1] swaps, credit derivatives, commodity price indexed securities, and pass-throughs all involve some form of risk reallocation. These securities transfer risks away from issuers or investors to others better able or more willing to bear them. For example, credit derivatives can help banks, financial companies, and investors manage the credit risk of their investment by insuring against adverse movements in the credit quality of the issuer. Also, companies can use currency swaps to manage foreign exchange risk and use interest rate swaps to hedge against interest rate volatility. Many companies have used put options or collar to better manage stock repurchase programs.[2] Investors also find inverse floaters useful for immunization purposes.

New Funding Sources

High-yield bonds provide smaller and less-known companies access to the corporate debt market. Without the high yield market, those companies would have been shut out of this funding source. Asset securitization packages illiquid individual loans and other debt instruments into securities, with credit enhancements, to further their sale in the marketplace. As such, it has created a new source of funding for the ultimate borrowers. A debt issue structured with currency swaps broadens the investor base from national to global, and frequently at a lower rate of interest. Plus, a borrower could design a structured note with interest payment rise and fall with certain indices or spreads, attracting a new group of lenders that otherwise are prohibited from investing in the indices or spread derivatives directly. Furthermore, fixed-income repurchase agreements (repos) broaden the funding sources to include those that will not or cannot make a collaterialized loan. The new emerging equity repo markets will allow broker–dealers to finance from firms other than commercial banks.

Lower Funding Costs

Mortgage-backeds and asset-backed securities transform individual loans into marketable securities. Liquidity is much enhanced because mortgages and receivables can be sold in the liquid secondary markets, despite the fact that the underlying assets individually are highly illiquid. The pricing transparency resulting from active secondary market trading provides an objective valuation standard. The securitization process also broadens the market from local to national and to global. Naturally the enhanced liquidity, pricing transparency, and a higher demand lead to a lower yield and thus a reduction in funding costs. Repos also lower funding costs, to a level generally at or lower than the fed funds rate.

Reduction in Transactions Costs

Securities backed by a pool of assets benefit investors with a degree of diversification that could otherwise be obtainable but might be significantly more expensive to accomplish on their own. For issuers, securities such as extendable notes and renewable notes reduce flotation expenses and transactions costs by giving either the issuer or investors the option to extend maturity without additional issuance expenses for registration and underwriting. Similarly, an interest rate swap agreement provides corporate borrowers flexibility in changing the nature of its interest rate obligation. To accomplish the same objective, the costs could be significantly higher if the company has to retire the outstanding bonds and float another security.

Tax and Regulatory Issues

The pattern often goes like this: An investment banker has a tax-advantaged product and convinces companies to issue it. Then Washington takes actions to stop it. For example, prior to the passage of the Tax Equity and Fiscal Responsibility Act of 1982, zero-coupon bonds produced tax savings for corporate issuers because the tax code allowed an issuer of zero-coupon bonds to amortize interest expenses on a straight-line basis. Adjustable-rate, convertible notes were typically issued at par and convertible into common stock, but redeemable at just half the issue price so they were certain to be converted. A 1983 IRS ruling treated them as equity from the start. As another example, the deferred-interest debentures were issued in recapitalization, and buyers were allowed to defer recognition of implied interest until the bonds were redeemed. Congress ruled out that trick in 1984.

More recently, Congress is considering eliminating interest deductions on debt that is either more than 40 years in maturity or payable as stock. The government, in search of more tax revenues, has targeted a host of corporate-financing vehicles. Included are 50- and 100-year bonds, discounted convertible debt, step-down preferred, and hedge fund investor tax avoidance strategy.

Advances in Computer Technology and Quantitative Finance

Technological breakthroughs and applications of quantitative methods in finance help a great deal of financial engineering. High-speed processors and sophisticated software programs allow for sophisticated modeling that track the complex mathematical relationships in the financial world. Pricing and arbitrage in derivatives require such advanced computer technology. During the past two decades, the market has witnessed a flood of "quant" people joining the securities industry. This is true in trading, especially in convergence trading that exploits the out-of-line relationships among various securities under differing market conditions. This is even more so in financial engineering. Technical advances and development of financial theory are basic to the design of a new security, its pricing, and trading.

The following sections present the major financial innovations. The sequence of the coverage is junk bonds, asset-backed securities, structured products, swaps, credit derivatives, equity-linked securities, step-down preferred, and a tax-avoidance strategy that converts short-term gains to long-term gains.

JUNK BONDS

The high-yield market has been on a roll in recent years. Investors are rushing into the high-yield mutual funds at a breakneck speed. Institutional investors, searching for incremental yields, have poured in large sums of money. Even blue-chip-grade investors are competing with traditional high-yield investors for junk bonds by investing in *Collateralized Bond Obligations* (CBOs), which are securitized pools of junk bonds and leveraged loans. Investors pumped $55 billion into these portfolios in 1997. Wall Street, aggressively seeking to snare a piece of the burgeoning junk bond market, are offering to do back-stopped and bought deals to win an underwriting mandate. Many companies, taking advantage of Rule 144A as a shortcut through the registration and disclosure maze if the deal is sold to QIBs, are tripping to bring new bonds to market. In addition, refinancing is likely to be a big driver of new issues in the low-interest-rate environment.

Market Overview

Junk bonds are bonds with below-investment-grade ratings, Ba or lower by Moody's or BB or lower by Standard & Poor's. Unrated corporate bonds are usually included in the junk bond category as well. Quality difference among high-yield issues is huge. B3 bonds are found three times more likely to default than B1 bonds.

The market has evolved from a collection of fallen angels into an established capital market for raising funds. The issuance totaled $123.8 billion in 1997. This level surpassed the full-year 1996 total of $71.3 billion and the 1993's record level of $72.5 billion. Several factors have contributed to the growth, including bank-loan substitution, technological improvements, investor preferences, and advancements in hedging techniques.

After the late 1970s, the surge in M&As and LBOs created new opportunities and new ways to raise capital. Investment banking firms, notably Drexel Burnham Lambert, devised new ways of allowing firms of less than investment grade access to the capital markets. No longer were high-yield bonds only those of *fallen angels.* Once the new ways of financing were available, some little known and riskier borrowers began tapping into high-yield debt as a substitute for bank loans. The growth of the high-yield sector has been accompanied by a reduction in the corporate debt share of bank loans. There are high-yield municipals as well. Unlike the taxable market, a majority of high-yield municipals are not rated. Most are sold by not-for-profit organizations, such as hospitals, nursing homes, and airports and power authorities.

Information technology has cost banks part of their comparative advantage in information gathering and monitoring. Technological improvements have greatly reduced the cost of obtaining and processing information about the financial status of the borrowers. Shifts in investor preferences toward marketable securities away from illiquid debt contracts are another contributing factor. Junk bonds have some form of liquidity and provide investors a higher return. In exchange for these returns, high-yield investors can expect to bear higher levels of risk. Even allowing for default risk, junk-bond investors still earn a wide spread over comparable treasuries. Moreover, many researchers have observed that the higher yields often come with lower volatility than treasuries and corporate issues.

Developments in hedging techniques enable investors to effectively manage the risk. As such, investors might have become more willing to take on risk. Innovative securitization techniques such as collateralized bond obligations attracted more money. The ERISA of 1974 brought pension funds into the market. This has allowed pension funds to compete more broadly for investment opportunities.

The Junk Bond Revolution

The first reported high-yield bonds were issued in 1901 when financier J.P. Morgan merged eight steel companies (to become U.S. Steel) for a total cost of $1.4 billion and took on $570 million in high-yield debt to finance the transaction. From 1909, when bond rating began, until World War II, junk bonds accounted for about 17% of all publicly issued straight debt. The largest increase in junk bonds occurred during the Great Depression, when the number of fallen angels exploded. Junk bonds were not as widely used in subsequent years.

In 1977, however, demand for junk bonds reignited. Much of the growth was attributable to Michael Milken, who successfully demonstrated that the rewards of high-yield bonds far outran the risks. The first step he took was to convince investors to buy such securities. At the same time, because of out-of-control inflation, newer and less established companies were paying higher and higher interests. In addition, the equity market experienced high volatility. Milken seized the opportunity to push for high-yield debt by explaining that it was far less volatile in terms of price movements than government bonds and stocks, and that investors had a higher rate of return (than governments) and were more senior in the capital structure (than stocks). Junk bonds could be an excellent investment, outperforming investment grades over time.

Drexel Burnham began developing new-issue high-yield debt in 1977. Drexel Burnham also created distribution channels for these high-yield bonds. Junk bonds were now issued and marketed successfully, and not just as fallen angels. Annual issuance of junk bonds exploded from a mere $1.1 billion in 1977 to $45.6 billion in 1986. The junk bond market cooled off in the late 1980s in the wake of the market crash in October 1987 and the ongoing investigations by the SEC and U.S. Attorney's office of Drexel Burnham Lambert. Drexel Burnham Lambert eventually went bankrupt in 1990, and Milken was convicted of securities fraud and barred from securities business for life.

After issuance set a record of $72.5 billion in 1993, the market cooled off in 1994. Since then the high-yield bond market has been on a roll not seen since the 1980s. In 1996, total supply was $70.8 billion, with more underwriters getting into the act as upstart domestic and foreign banks battle the big houses for lucrative underwriting fees (as high as 3%). High-yield debt soared to $123.8 billion in 1997, surpassing the full-year 1993 level. In the first six months of 1998, more than $110 billion in high-yield debt was issued.

On the buy side, the junk bond market is primarily institutional, including pension funds, mutual funds and financial institutions. Risk-based capital standards have encouraged banks and insurance companies to invest in better-quality assets than in junk bonds. But more and more pension funds are turning to junk for enhanced yields. Many participants take the view that high-yield bonds have a place in a large portfolio. Junk bond mutual funds[3] have invested about $100 billion and cash inflows are running at $15 billion to $20 billion a year. The total inflows in 1997 were $18 billion. In addition, private equity funds are moving into the debt market for small- to mid-sized companies, because it offers an investment horizon typically shorter than for venture capital, and investment risks as a creditor are often lower than the risks facing long-term equity investors.

Risks and Returns

The high yields on low-quality bonds primarily reflect their greater risk of default, especially during a slowing downturn. The default rate[4] during the 1990–1991 recession soared to 9%, while few issuers defaulted (averaged at 1.58%) on their obligations to creditors during the 1980–1982 severe recession. The default rate varies considerably from year to year, ranging from a low of 0.156% in 1981 to 9.008% in 1991. The long-term average since the junk bond revolution began in 1977 is close to 3%. Researchers have identified three factors that significantly affect the pattern of default: credit ratings, state of economy, and the aging factor. *Credit ratings* can be viewed as a proxy of financial strength. The distribution of ratings in the high-yield market at the beginning of the year should provide a clear indication about the default rate in the upcoming year. The *state of the economy* affects the level of default. Profits decline in downturns, leaving companies less cash to service their debt. The *aging factor* is the length of time that bonds have been outstanding. Low-rated bonds are less likely to default in the first year after issuance and most likely to default three years after issuance.

Although media reports often focus on the par value default rate, this is not the most relevant measure for holders of the bonds. The main concern is the impact of default on a bond's price, because that determines the actual dollar loss on the bond. Even bonds in default typically retain some value; investors should look at the *default loss rate*. In 1991, for example, the default rate was more than 9%, while the default loss rate was much lower at 5.4%. Since 1993, the default loss rate has been less than 2%. The default rate dropped further, to less than 1%, in 1997. As long as the economy stays robust, the high-yield market should thrive as companies meet their debt service. This is good news, but—in striking contrast to investment grade bonds—most junk bonds are issued with call features. Moreover, many high-yield bonds issued by private companies contain *clawback* provisions. The clawback grants the company the right, if it goes public within a certain time (usually 3 to 5 years), to use the proceeds to call a certain percentage of the bonds. Another risk is related to the speed with which new issues are sold. With 80% of high-yield debt placed through 144A market, investors have a day or two, sometimes just hours, to make a decision whether to buy any of the offerings. That can lead to sloppy credit analysis.

The yield spread of high-yield bonds over treasuries varies from year to year, following the pattern of defaults. From 1982 to 1987, the yield spread on high-yield bonds averaged 411 basis points. In late 1990, with the U.S. economy in recession and junk bonds suffering through a severe bear market, that spread was more than 9%. Since 1990, the average spread has been on a downward trend, declining to about 275 basis points in mid-1997 and then remained at 3% in early 1998. By August 1998, default rates had risen with demand falling off. The yield spread has risen dramatically to more than 4%.

ASSET-BACKED MARKETS

Asset securitization substitutes efficient capital markets for less-efficient, higher-cost financial intermediaries in the funding of debt instruments. Financial engineers' creative design in response to new opportunities has been the driving force behind the powerful revolution. It provides businesses with access to new sources of capital at lower costs, even when the upfront analysis, structuring, and credit enhancement costs are factored in. Also, securitization provides a crucial source of funding for companies with limited access to other forms of credit because asset-backed securities (ABS) are rated on their own merit, independent of the issuing company's financial standing. The revolutionary process first began with mortgage pass-throughs. Issuance of agency mortgage securities increased from $269.2 billion in 1995 to $370.5 billion in 1996. Issuance of agency MBS recorded a slight decline to $368.0 billion in 1997. Other asset-backed securities totaled $185.1 billion in 1997 and $151.3 billion in 1996, up from the

$107.9 billion sold in 1995. The upward trend is expected to continue. Asset types used in securitization include mortgages, auto loans, credit card receivables, equipment leases, tax liens, and junk bonds. Chapter 6, "Asset Securitization", provides detailed coverage on the securitization process and major asset types.

STRUCTURED NOTES

Structured notes are debt securities. The interest and, at times, principal payments depend on formulas and terms specific to the security. These formulas can incorporate the direction of interest rates, the range of volatility, the shape of the yield curve, and the performance of equity market, commodity prices, and embedded options such as caps, floors, or call features. Customized complex features are difficult to evaluate, which reduces their liquidity.

Government agencies, banks, and corporations have participated in the structured markets as issuers. These institutions achieve low-cost, variable-rate financing. Institutional investors and money managers receive high-grade customized bonds designed to fit their preferences. For investment bankers, they earn underwriting fees while generating additional derivatives business.

Floaters

One of the earliest structured notes is a *floater*. The most basic type has its interest rate tied to LIBOR or T-bill rate. After a coupon reset, a floater trades at par and will make its next coupon payment on the following reset date. Between reset dates, the price of the floater fluctuates, depending on the market environment and credit quality of the issuer. Therefore, a floater is equivalent to a bond with one coupon remaining and with maturity equal to the time until next reset date. The Macaulay duration of a floater, regardless of maturity, is hence the time until its next coupon reset date.

A floater might have its interest rate tied to an index or a commodity price. For example, consider an oil refinery with a poor credit rating wanting to borrow money. It could issue a note with interest rate payment increases with oil price. If oil price rises, the refinery has more cash flow to pay for the higher interests. When oil prices decline, its interest burden is lower. There are also de-leveraged floaters. These notes generally give investors above-market initial yield and tie subsequent coupon adjustments to a formula on a fraction of the changes in an index (leverage factor). Furthermore, some types of structured notes pay a promised fixed-rate and additional payments based on the movement of a commodity price or stock index, in the latter case it is like a market indexed certificate of deposits.

Inverse Floaters

An *inverse floater* is a floating rate security whose interest rate moves inversely with market rates. The coupon on an inverse floater is the difference between the fixed rate on the underlying bond and the rate on the floater. The interests on the floater and inverse floater must total the fixed rate paid by the underlying bond from which they are created. The value of an inverse floater varies inversely with the market interest rates. As rates increase, the inverse floater loses value from a higher discount rate and lower cash flows. When rates decline, the inverse floater gains from a lower discount rate and from an increase in cash flows. A floor, typically at zero, is usually established for the inverse floater. As a result, a cap is imposed on the floater.

The duration of an inverse floater is longer than its maturity. This has often caught investors off guard. The duration of an inverse floater exceeds the duration of the underlying fixed-coupon bonds. The explanation is quite simple. The duration of the fixed-rate coupon bond is the weighted average of the duration of the floater and inverse floater. The duration of a floater is quite short, equal to the time until the next coupon reset date. Hence, the duration of the inverse floater exceeds the duration of the underlying fixed-rate bond.

Step-Ups

These securities pay an initial yield higher than a comparable government security and have coupons *step-up* at a prespecified date if the issue is not called. If the coupon has more than one adjustment period, it is called *multi-step-up*. The higher initial yield compensates the investor for implicitly having sold a call option to the issuer.

Index-Amortizing Notes (IANs)

IANs amortize the outstanding principal according to a schedule linked to the level of a designated index such as LIBOR or CMT (constant maturity treasury index). The final principal repayment date is fixed. The future cash flows, average life, and the yield to maturity are all subject to uncertainty. IANs are generally issued at par and have final maturities of 5 to 10 years.

Dual Index Notes

Dual index notes are also known as yield curve anticipation notes. The coupon rate is determined by the spread between two market indexes such as the prime rate, LIBOR, and CMT yields of different maturities. Yield curve anticipation notes are among the most risky of various structures. One of the investments by Orange County was on yield curve anticipation notes. The notes would pay higher (lower) interest rates when the yield curve steepens (flattens). Orange County financed the purchase with open repos. In 1994, the Fed raised the Fed funds rate seven times. The yield curve flattened and financing costs moved up, resulting in a negative carry and a capital loss. Investment strategies like this and borrow-short-lend-long at a time of rising interest rates brought about the financial debacles of Orange County and others.

Range Notes

Range notes are a recent innovation. These securities accrue interest periodically at a coupon tied to an index. Most range notes have two interest levels, a higher accrual rate during periods when the index remains within a designated range and a lower rate or no interest at all if the index moves outside of the range. These notes generally perform poorly in volatile interest rate environments. The direction of the interest rate is not important, but rather, the volatility matters. These notes are most risky when they are of a barrier nature, in which purchasers would lose all accrued interests once the index breaks out the range.

REPURCHASE AGREEMENTS

Repurchase agreements (repos) are extensively used in dealer financing, customer funding, and matched book trading. At many firms, the repo desk has become a key profit center. In addition, understanding the market is essential to assessing value in the securities markets. For example, the status of a bond in the repo market can be used to understand the relative values between bonds and also to assess the valuation of futures contracts. Chapter 12, "Repurchase Transactions", provides a detailed coverage of the repo and reverses markets. The following is a brief description of the fundamentals.

The repo market is the biggest money market. The estimated market is $17.5 trillion and turnover is perhaps $500 billion or more a day.[5] This is much larger than the Fed funds and is the biggest short-term money market in the world. In July 1996, the Fed adopted changes to Regulation T by loosening its provisions on valuing certain securities pledged as collateral from the previous 50% to discretionary "good faith." The relaxation of Regulation T will further benefit the development of the fixed-income repo market and will, together with the National Securities Markets Improvement Act of 1996, help give birth to the equity repo market.

In a typical repo transaction, a dealer puts up liquid securities as collateral against a cash loan while agreeing to repurchase the securities at a future date. The start-leg is usually settled the same day. The close-leg, repurchase, is a forward transaction. A repo is in format a securities transaction, but is in essence a collateralized loan to finance the purchase of the underlying security. The repo markets are therefore often called financing markets.

Securities market participants enter into repo transactions because they have cash and want a short-term investment or because they have securities and need funding. Repo rates, in part, depend on the collateral used. The higher the credit quality and the easier the security is to clear, the lower the repo rate. Treasury repos trade at lower levels than federal agency repos, which, in turn, trade at lower levels than mortgage-backeds. The second factor is the term of the repo, which is usually for maturities between one day and one year. Most of the repo transactions have maturities of three months or less. One-day transactions are called overnight repos, longer maturities are called term repos. An open repo is an overnight repo that rolls over automatically until terminated by either party.

Government securities are the most frequently used collateral. Numerous issues, in particular the on-the-run or current issues, are frequently on special. The specialness of the given issue is the difference between the general collateral rate and the specific repo rate for that issue. The special rate may be quoted either as an absolute rate or as a spread below the general collateral rate.

SWAPS

A swap is an agreement between two parties to exchange payments based on identical *notional principal*. Swaps are popular financial transactions that have come to be the most widely used derivatives. The efficacy and flexibility of swaps are best in managing financial risk or making an arbitrage play in a volatile interest rate, exchange rate, commodity price, or equity return environment. The notional principal of swaps and related derivatives grew from $866 billion in 1987 to more than $25 trillion by 1996, and to more than $29 trillion in 1997. The explosive growth has been mainly driven by interest rate swaps, which had an outstanding volume of $19 trillion in 1996 and $22 trillion in 1997.

Interest-Rate Swaps

An interest-rate swap is a contract between two parties in which each party agrees to make a series of interest payments to the other on scheduled dates in the future. In most interest-rate swaps, there are two legs. One counterparty pays a floating rate of interest such as LIBOR and the other pays a fixed rate or a different floating interest rate. The basic structure of an interest-rate swap is depicted in Figure 13.1. Company A borrows in the floating-rate market by issuing a 7-year floater at 6-month LIBOR +0.50%. Company B has issued a 7-year fixed-rate bond at 1.50% over 7-year Treasury. They then enter into an interest-rate swap transaction with an AAA swap dealer. Under the swap agreement, counterparty A receives 6-month LIBOR from the swap dealer and will pay a fixed-rate of 7-year Treasury plus 0.50%. The cost to Company A is then 1.0% over 7-year Treasury, and A has converted floating-rate obligation to fixed-rate. Counterparty B pays a rate of 6-month LIBOR and receives from the dealer the 7-year Treasury plus 0.30%. Company B has changed the interest payments to floating at a cost of LIBOR + 1.20%. The swap dealer profits 20 basis points from the transactions.

Swaps can also be arranged to manage the risk of a specific asset or liability exposure. An *asset swap* combines an existing asset such as a bond with an interest rate swap to create a different return profile. The investor might use the fixed coupon to swap for floating rate income or vice versa. If the asset is a MBS, *index amortizing swaps* can be used to mirror the asset's remaining principal amount. Some swaps have a *clean up call* whereby the swap can be called away if the remaining notional principal drops to about 5% of the original amount. A mortgage swap falls into this type. The notional principal amortizes over the life of the swap and the tenor of the swap is shorter than the final maturity of the mortgage pools.

FIGURE 13.1   Interest Rate Swaps

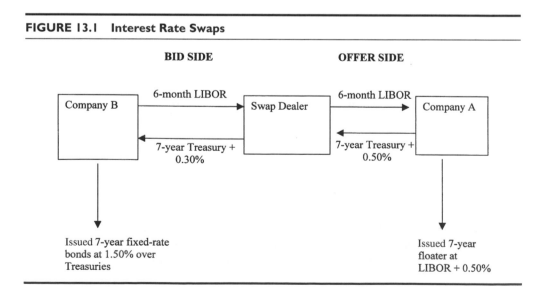

A derivative consisting of an option to enter into an interest-rate swap or to cancel an existing swap in the future is called *swaption*.

Currency Swaps

In a straight currency swap, a borrower issues a foreign currency debt (such as yen) and immediately exchanges yen for its chosen currency (such as dollar). The counterparty of the exchange is typically a swap dealer. The borrower periodically pays the dealer dollar coupon interest and the dealer pays the interest to the creditor in yen. When the loan comes due, the borrower reverses the transaction with the swap dealer, swapping dollars to get back yen needed to pay off yen debt. The borrower has received dollars at the beginning of the loan and experiences a dollar outflow when the loan is paid off. The currency swap has facilitated the borrower's ability to borrow dollars from foreign market, possibly at a lower cost, without currency risk.

Commodity Price Swaps

In a commodity swap agreement, each counterparty promises to make a series of payments to the other, and of which a commodity price or index determines at least one set of payments. Commodity swaps are becoming increasingly common in energy and agriculture areas. The user of a particular commodity who does not want to risk price uncertainty for the long term may agree to pay a financial institution a fixed price, in return for receiving payments based on the market price for the commodity involved. A producer, however, who wants a fixed income may agree to pay the market price to a financial institution, in return for receiving a fixed-payment stream. Both counterparties now have obtained their preferred structures.

The vast majority of commodity swaps involve oil. Airlines, for example, will often use commodity swaps in which they agree to make fixed payments for a number of years, and receive payments from the swap dealer on the same dates determined by an oil price index. For oil swaps, it is common to base the variable payment on the average value of the oil index over a defined period of time. As such, the airlines substantially lower the exposure to just the basis risk.

Although most commodities are priced in dollars, commodity swaps are also available in other currencies.

Equity Swaps

In an equity swap, an investor receives the return on some type of market index and in exchange pays to the swap dealer LIBOR (or a fixed rate or another market index).[6] This was developed primarily to deal with the problems in cross-country investing. For example, a portfolio manager in the United States wanting to diversify 30% of his portfolio into the Japanese market may agree to pay the S&P 500 return to the swap dealer based on a notional principal equal to 30% of his portfolio and in exchange the dealer will pay him the return on the Nikkei index.

An equity swap agreement is also one of the most efficient ways of gaining exposure to emerging markets. The structure saves investors on commission, stamp duty, clearing fees, and spreads. This is especially useful for investors who, for legal or regulatory reasons, cannot invest directly in a particular country but would like to have exposure to that market.

There are many ways to structure an equity swap. The notional principal can be fixed or variable. It can be structured so that the party either absorbs or hedges against the currency risk.

Real Estate Swaps

Morgan Stanley and Bankers Trust were the first to be in the real estate swaps market in 1993. In such a swap, the property owner agrees to pay the counterparty who wants to get into the real estate market a rate of return linked to the performance of the real estate market such as Russell-NCRREF Property Index. In exchange, the counterparty agrees to pay the property owner another type of return, such as a floating interest rate. Banks, pension funds, and insurance companies that are strapped with too much real estate might find this market attractive, because if they sell properties, not only would they incur heavy transactions costs in a time-consuming selling process, but could also suffer a loss. On top of that, they risk missing out if the market later takes off. The swaps provide investors, who have money to invest and think real estate promises big gains, exposures to the real estate market without the headaches of being a landlord.

CREDIT DERIVATIVES

Credit derivatives are becoming increasingly popular. Credit derivatives can help banks, financial companies, and investors manage the credit risk of their investment by insuring against adverse movements in the credit quality of the issuer. Specific applications include:

- Commercial banks to change the risk profile of loan books
- Investment banks to manage bond and derivatives portfolio
- Manufacturers to manage the exposure to a single customer
- Equity investors in project finance to deal with unacceptable sovereign risk
- Institutional investors to enhance yield or to speculate
- Employees to secure deferred remuneration

There are four broad types of credit derivatives: credit default swaps, credit-spread options, total return swaps, and credit-linked notes. The first deals were done in 1993 when Bankers Trust and Credit Suisse Financial Products in Japan sold notes whose redemption value depended on specified default events. The market got a slow start because of the disasters in financial derivatives. But by 1997, the market has approached some $200 billion and is rapidly expanding.

Credit Default Swaps

A *credit default swap* is a bilateral contract in which one counterparty pays a premium in return for a contingent payment triggered by the default of one or more third-party reference credits. The premium is typically expressed in basis points of the notional amount, while the contingent payment is determined by the decrease in the price of the security below par after the reference credit has defaulted. For example,[7] in June 1997, an international bank that already had a basket of 20 loans totaling more than

FIGURE 13.2 Credit Default Swap

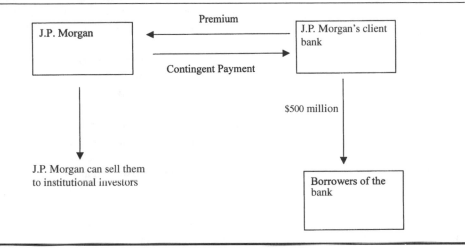

$500 million to mostly investment-grade companies but wanted to lend more money to the same companies. J.P. Morgan sold the bank the right to require Morgan to pay off any of the loans if a borrower goes bankrupt. J.P. Morgan can retain the default risks in its portfolio and collect the premium, or sell them to institutional investors such as insurance companies, hedge funds, or other banks. Meanwhile, J.P. Morgan's client retains the actual loans and the customer relationship. The transaction can be depicted in Figure 13.2

This transaction is actually a put option on a portfolio of loans or bonds. The client bank receives a payoff if a borrower goes bankrupt—that is, it has the right to sell the default loans to J.P. Morgan at par. In a similar manner, bond investors can use this type of credit options to hedge against a decline in the price of a bond. As an example, an institutional investor has a portfolio of 5-year Italian government bonds. The investor pays the counterparty a premium of, say, 20 basis points a year. The counterparty is obligated to make a payment if Italy defaults on its debt, in which case the contingent payment is par less the final price. Of course, the notional principal and maturity can be tailored to provide the exact amount and tenor of protection required.

Corporates and investors in projects stand to benefit, as well. Take an engineering company: All of its heavy drilling equipment in the next several years may be sold to just a few customers. If a customer goes bust, the equipment will be idled in inventory with no one else to sell to. To hedge against this risk, the engineering company can buy a credit swap on a notional principal that compensates for the loss of the sale. In project finance, an equity sponsor to a large project may want to hedge the portion of sovereign risk not guaranteed by an export credit-agency-backed facility. It could enter into a credit default swap with a notional principal equal to the amount not covered by the sovereign guarantee.

Credit Spread Options

Credit spread plays focus on the yield differential between credit-sensitive instruments and the reference security. *Credit spread options* can be used by bond issuers to hedge against a rise in the average credit risk premium. As an illustration, suppose a Baa company is planning to issue $50 million of 2-year bonds in three months. The interest rate the company anticipates paying is the current spread of 65 basis points over the 2-year Treasury notes. If the average risk premium for Baa companies increases before the bond's issuance, the interest payments will rise.

To hedge against the widening of the spread, the company could purchase a put option with a strike at the current level of spread. If the average risk premium rises above the strike rate in three months, the higher interest payments will be offset by gains from the option. Since the payments from the put option offset the increased borrowing costs, purchasing the put option provides a hedge against increases in the credit premium. Alternatively, suppose that the credit risk premium falls. The put option has no payoff, but the company saves financing costs at the lower spread. Thus, purchasing the put option allows the corporate user to insure against increases in the credit risk premium while maintaining the benefits of lower funding costs if the spread declines.

Credit spread contracts have also been successfully used in emerging markets. In emerging markets, a credit spread is generally expressed as the yield spread of an emerging market instrument over the yield of a "risk-free" bond. Many structures are available that allow investors to bet on a specific credit spread or a basket of credit spreads. For example, when the sovereign Brazil 2027 global bond was offered at a spread of 525 basis points over the U.S. Treasury long bond, an institutional investor of Lehman Brothers "locked in" a spread of 575 basis points over the settlement in one year. The net settlement on the end date is determined by the credit spread of the Brazil 2027 bond at that time. In this trade, the notional size is $10,000 per basis points of spread tightening or widening. The investor will receive $10,000 at the end date for each basis point by which the Brazil credit spread is below 575, but will pay $10,000 for every basis point the spread is greater than 575.

Total Return Swaps

In a *total return swap,* the market risk of the underlying asset is stripped out and transferred without actually transferring the asset. For example, a bank originates a loan and then collects and passes along the loan payments (total returns) to the swap dealer. In return, the dealer pays the bank a floating rate of interest, such as a spread over 3-month LIBOR. Periodically the swap is settled on the market value of the loan. Any positive change in value is paid by the bank to the swap dealer, the default risk holder. Conversely, the dealer pays any negative change to the bank. The effect of this swap for the bank is to trade the total return from its loan portfolio for a guaranteed return of a spread over a 3-month LIBOR. Because the swap dealer now guarantees the return, the bank has eliminated the credit risk on this loan.

Total return swaps offer two advantages. First, they allow banks to diversify loan credit risk while maintaining confidentiality of their client's financial records. Second, the administrative costs of the swap transaction are lower than for a loan sale.

Credit-Linked Notes

A *credit-linked note* is a structured note in which the bond has an embedded option that allows the issuer to reduce the note's payments if a key financial variable specified deteriorates. For example, an automobile-financing company may use debt to fund a portfolio of auto loans. To reduce the credit risk, the company's credit-linked note promises to pay lenders a higher coupon rate and the principal if the delinquency is below, say, 5%. However, if default exceeds 5%, investors accept a formula with potential loss of interest and principal. Some banks market a product known as *zero-one* structure. Instead of some coupon or principal loss, investors lose their entire principal if there is a higher default rate.

An auto financing company would issue a credit-linked note because it provides a convenient mechanism to reduce the company's credit exposure. If default rates are high, the earnings are reduced, but the company pays a lower interest. Investors would consider buying such a security because they earn a higher expected rate of return than a comparable bond.

OTHER FINANCIAL ENGINEERING PRODUCTS

This chapter so far has covered major financial engineering products, including high-yield bonds, ABSs, swaps, credit derivatives, and structured notes. This section briefly reviews several other important innovations and tax strategies.

Equity-Linked Securities

Standard and Poor's Indexed Notes (SPINs), market-indexed CDs, Stock Index Growth Notes (SIGNs), Preferred Equity Redemption Cumulative Stock (PERCS), and equity bonds are among the instruments whose payoffs are linked to the performance of the equity market.

Salomon Brothers Inc. issued $100 million of 4-year S&P 500 Indexed Notes (SPINs) on September 1, 1986. The SPIN carries a 2% annual coupon, payable every 6 months, and at maturity pays its holders the principal, accrued interest, and any positive growth in S&P 500 multiplied by a predetermined multiplier. The SPIN is a combination of 2% coupon plus a 4-year call option on S&P 500 index. To Salomon, there could be substantial interest savings, but it needs to hedge the exposure against gains in the stock market. Investors are offered a guaranteed low fixed return with the possibility of additional payoffs from favorable movement in the stock market.

Similar to SPINs, the market-indexed CDs (MICDs) pay interest tied to the performance of S&P 500 index. Chase Manhattan Bank first offered the MICDs in March 1987 in response to increasing competition for funds. MICDs pay investors interest contingent upon the growth in stock market index, but with a guaranteed minimum interest rate that limits their risk exposure. The call version of MICDs offers an interest rate that rises proportionally with the stock market. The put version pays higher interest rate when the stock market index declines. MICDs have the potential to expand significantly the investment opportunities available to investors, while offering financial institutions a means to compete with stock market for funds.

PERCS were engineered by Morgan Stanley and adapted by Goldman Sachs (YES, yield enhanced stock), Merrill (mandatory conversion premium dividend preferred stock), and Sallie (dividend enhanced convertible stock, debt exchangeable for common stock, and equity-linked securities). AVON was the first issuer of PERCS. Other issuers of PERCS include GM, Boise Cascade, Olin, Sears Roebuck, Kmart, RJR Nabisco, Tandy, Tenneco, and Texas Instruments. There are several unique features of PERCS. First, they have a very short final maturity, usually about 3 years. Second, they are redeemable at maturity at the issuer's option in either cash or common stock. Third, they are redeemable at the issuer's option any time subject to a schedule of declining redemption prices. PERCS provide investors with an enhanced dividend rate but limited potential for capital appreciation.

The Republic of Austria issued $100 million of 5.5-year SIGNs on January 28, 1991. There are no coupon payments prior to maturity. All payments are paid at maturity, with gains set equal to the growth in S&P 500. The value of SIGNs can therefore be expressed as the sum of several components. According to Finnerty's estimates,[8] the value of each component is as follows. The zero-coupon bond component of each SIGN was worth $6.48 per $10 par. The call option component was valued at $2.30. The value of tax arbitrage through the creation of SIGNs totaled $0.20, the tax benefit resulting from the investor's ability to defer income taxes. The savings in transaction costs amounted to $0.14 per SIGN. The value added through the creation of a new investment alternative was $0.88 per SIGN.

Equity bonds are secured by stocks. An equity bond allows investors to invest in the underlying company at a discount by giving up potential return above a predetermined cap price. At the time of the issuance the issuer will place in an escrow account either the underlying stock or a cash amount equal to the amount of the outstanding bonds. At maturity, if the share price is above the cap, the investor will be paid the bond face value. Conversely, investor receives the shares if the price is below the cap at maturity. Equity bonds offer a significantly lower risk level while maintaining an attractive yield. They are either listed or traded in unlisted form.

Other equity derivatives include synthetic convertibles and inverse synthetic convertibles. Many of these instruments are with embedded equity index puts or calls as a kicker. These products have been popular in the volatile Asian markets. They are sold as yield enhancement structures for investors willing to take some risk for higher returns.

Exchangeable Debt

Exchangeable debt gives the purchasers the option to exchange the debt for stock of a second company (*convert firm*). Exchangeable debt has been used since the 1970s. There are several reasons for companies to issue such a security. First, the issuing firm is able to capitalize on a security holding while delaying the recognition of capital gains. Second, the issuing firm collects the tax-preferred dividend income until conversion is exercised. Third, it is an efficient way of divesting a security holding, the negative effect on the convert firm price is less pronounced than a block sale.

Auction-Rate Preferred Stock

The predecessor is the adjustable-rate preferred stock whose dividend rate is adjusted quarterly to reflect changes in money market yields. The adjustable-rate preferred was popular, but later weakened because the dividend rate could not adjust quickly enough in response to changes in the interest-rate environment or the credit quality of issuer. This led to the development of the auction-rate preferred stock. The dividend yield is determined in a Dutch auction every 49 days. There are significant savings to issuers, since the auction-rate preferred typically carry a lower dividend yield than a comparable fixed-rate preferred.

Indexed Sinking-Fund Debentures

Indexed sinking-fund debentures (ISFDs) represent an effective new technique for financial institution asset–liability management. FNMA first issued $500 million of this security in 1988. Billions of supplies follow. ISFDs contain an interest-rate-contingent sinking fund. Sinking fund payments accelerate when market interest rates decline and decelerate when interest rates rise. Mortgage prepayments exhibit a similar pattern. The sinking fund schedule enables the FNMA to better manage the sensitivities of asset and liabilities. An ISFD can be characterized as consisting of a conventional bond and strips of calls and puts with time to expiry corresponding to the sinking fund dates. If interest rates decline, the calls are in the money and are exercised on the sinking fund dates. If interest rates rise, the puts come into money and are exercised.

Step-Down Preferred

The structure was invented by J.P. Morgan and adapted by Bear Sterns and Morgan Stanley Dean Witter. Federal Home Loan Mortgage, Walt Disney, Wal-Mart, Time Warner, and Union Carbide issued more than $10 billion of the step-down preferred. In a step-down preferred, a company in partnership with a pension fund creates a real estate investment trust. The company provides the real estate and receives common stocks; the pension fund supplies cash and receives preferred in exchange. The REIT then lends the company funds secured by its real estate holdings. The borrower (company) pays a high interest but no principal on the loan. The REIT, whose income is not taxable, passes all the funds received to the pension fund in the form of high preferred dividends. Those high dividends will "step down" sharply to almost nothing after 10 years when the investor has gotten back most of its money. The pension fund receives additional money by selling the REIT preferred stock back to the borrower. Finally, the REIT is merged into the borrower, returning the borrower its initial investment. The end result is that the borrower could deduct all payments. The government responded quickly, announcing that these transactions are taxable.

Hedge Fund Investor Tax Avoidance Strategy

Congress recently proposed legislation to end a tax-avoidance strategy that has been used mainly by hedge fund investors to reduce their tax liabilities. Hedge funds often have short-term gains from their bets on various types of assets. As a partnership, the funds pass such tax liability to investors. The tax-avoidance strategy involves Wall Street firms such as Merrill Lynch, Bankers Trust, and Lehman Brothers buying the hedge-fund stakes in place of investors. The banks then hold any gains for more than 18 months and then pass on the gains to investors. Investors left with long-term gains are now qualified for a lower tax rate.

SUMMARY

This chapter describes the key factors that have contributed to the success of financial engineering. This chapter covers many of the important innovations: junk bonds, structured notes, repos, swaps, credit derivatives, and other structures. Interest-rate swaps have been the most successful innovation, but the new trend seems to point to credit derivatives.

SELECT BIBLIOGRAPHY

Allen, F., ed. *Financial Management: Security Design Special Issue* 22 (Summer 1993).

Altman, E. I., ed. *The High-Yield Debt Market: Investment Performance and Economic Impact*. Homewood, IL: Dow Jones-Irwin, 1990.

Braddock, J. C. *Derivatives Demystified: Using Structured Financial Products*. New York: Wiley, 1997.

Chen, A. H., and J. W. Kensinger. "An analysis of market-index certificates of deposit." *Journal of Financial Services Research* 4 (1993): pp. 93–110.

Chen, K. C., and R. S. Sears. "Pricing the SPIN," *Financial Management* 19 (Summer 1990): pp. 36–47.

Das, S. "Credit risk derivatives." *Journal of Derivatives* (Spring 1995): pp. 7–23.

Finnerty, J. F. "Financial engineering in corporate finance." *Financial Management* (Winter 1988): pp. 14–33.

Finnerty, J. F. "Financial engineering in practice: an analysis of PERCS." mimeo, 1993.

Jeresky, L. "CBOs increase popularity of junk bonds," *Wall Street Journal*, July 7, 1997, C1.

Meder, M. S. "Structured notes: investment for your banks?" *Dialogue*, v2i1, Federal Reserve Bank of Cleveland, 1997.

Neal, R. S. "Credit derivatives: New financial instruments for controlling credit risk." *Economic Review*, Federal Reserve Bank of Kansas City (Second Quarter, 1996): pp. 15–27.

Phillips, A. L. "1995 derivatives practices and instruments survey," *Financial Management* 24, (Summer 1995): pp. 115–125.

Schwartz, R. J., and C. W. Smith, eds. *Derivatives Handbook: Risk Management and Control*. New York: Wiley, 1997.

Yago, G. *Junk Bonds*. Oxford: Oxford University Press, 1991.

14

Money Management

Money management is an important segment of the capital markets and is becoming an integral part of the investment banking business. Wall Street firms are buying into fund management because it is one of the most attractive segments of the financial services industry. It expands the menu of products and services investment banks offer to clients. Furthermore, the income stream is less volatile than trading, underwriting, or merger and acquisition activities. The affiliated funds also provide synergy to the bank's underwriting business. This chapter explains the rationale behind Wall Street's push into investment management and the issue of interdealing between underwriting and money management. In mutual funds, the chapter describes the structure and organization of a mutual fund, the regulatory environment, and the growing importance of the institutional players. In hedge funds, this chapter explains the structure of a hedge fund and the typical ranges of management fees and incentive fees. Where relevant, the discussion points out the regulatory changes contained in the National Securities Markets Improvement Act of 1996 and the Investment Advisers Supervision Coordination Act of 1997.

INVESTMENT BANKS ENTER MONEY MANAGEMENT BUSINESS

Banking, stockbroking, and fund management are converging. For investment banking houses, money management business is not a question of whether to enter, but rather to "buy" or to "build." In 1970, only 7 of top 15 underwriters had affiliations with units that ran money. By 1998, nearly all major investment banks had drifted into fund management.[1] Several factors have contributed to the growing importance of money management operations within investment banking business umbrella. First, it is to keep up with competition by providing a one-stop financial store. Running affiliated funds expands the range of products and services investment banks offer to clients. Second, it helps balance out banks' volatile income streams with a relatively stable source of income. Affiliated funds provide support for Wall Street parents' underwriting business as well. Investment bankers take in revenues to underwrite securities issues and fee income with the help of fund management operations. It is one of the most attractive segments of the financial services industry. The total industry net assets have grown from $135 billion in 1980 to $4.49 trillion by December 1997. By the end of the first half of 1998, the assets of the nation's mutual funds grew to more than $5 trillion.

The driving force behind such explosive growth includes the fast-growing defined contribution plans, retirement funding fears that create seemingly inexhaustible demand, new opportunities abroad, and new distribution channels such as mutual fund supermarkets and the Internet. According to a 1997 survey by the Investment Company Institute, about 80% of those surveyed (187) have created Web sites since 1995. They opened the sites mainly to enhance communication with current and prospective shareholders. Funds reported a median of 14,500 "hits" and 10,272 "visits" during the month of March 1997. Online marketing represents a huge opportunity. The number of U.S. households dialing into the Web is expected to increase from 20 million in 1997 to 26 million in 1998. For foreign funds, the creation of a Web site is an unsettled issue. The SEC in January 1998 has begun to prepare guidance on how creators of Web sites, especially for a foreign fund that has a Web site accessible to U.S. investors but that is not interested in attracting U.S. money, can avoid U.S. laws governing the offer or sale of securities.

Investment management business itself is undergoing radical reshaping. According to a widely read report from Goldman Sachs published in 1995, consolidation is the wave of the future. Within the next few years, the industry will emerge as a handful of dominant companies and some smaller niche players. To establish and secure a position in the marketplace quickly, Wall Street firms favor buying over the build-it-yourself approach.

Prices for money management firms have risen steadily overall as commercial banks and investment banks are eager to buy into investment management business. Most takeovers of fund managers are done at a price about 11 times cash flow. Top-notch fund companies command higher prices. In June 1997, Zurich Group paid Scudder, Stevens & Clark $2 billion, or 20 times cash flow. In November 1997, Merrill Lynch paid $5.3 billion, or 19 times cash flow, to acquire Mercury Asset Management (UK). Prior to this acquisition, Merrill Lynch also acquired Hotchkis & Wiley (a Los Angeles mutual fund giant) in 1996, and purchased Master Works, a division of Barclays Global Investors, to expand its 401(k) plan assets. In September 1997, J.P. Morgan spent $900 million to acquire a 45% stake in American Century to service the fastest-growing portion of the pension business, 401(k) plans. BankAmerica acquired Robertson Stephens in June 1997 for a price of $540 million. NationsBank acquired Montgomery Securities in June 1997 for $1.2 billion. Goldman Sachs, in a series of acquisitions, has also expanded its fund management business. Table 14.1 list major recent mergers and acquisitions of fund managers.

There are several important observations from Table 14.1. First, the money management industry itself has been through restructuring in recent years. Second, commercial banks have been buying into asset management business as well. Third, investment banking houses are also in play.

The high prices paid by private market buyers are one of the reasons money management firms do not come to the public market. According to Putnam, Lovell & Thornton, fewer than 20 publicly traded firms derive more than one half of the pretax profits from asset management. In addition, asset managers prefer to avoid the public scrutiny that comes with a listing. Table 14.2 lists the recent financial data from 14 publicly traded money managers.

TABLE 14.1   Major Recent Mergers and Acquisitions of Fund Managers

Date	Target	Type	Acquirer	Assets ($million)
02/98	Grosvenor Capital Mgmt	Institutional	Value Asset Mgmt	2,900
01/98	Essex Investment Mgmt	Institutional	Affiliated Managers	4,300
12/97	Brandywine Asset Mgmt	Institutional	Legg Mason	7,000
12/97	Founders Asset Management	Mutual fund	Mellon Bank	6,900
11/97	Mercury Asset Mgmt	Diversified	Merrill Lynch	180,000
11/97	Craig Hester Capital Mgmt	Private Client	Morgan Keegan	375
10/97	O'Connor Realty Advisors	Institutional	J.P. Morgan	4,100
10/97	Advanced Investment Tech	Institutional	State Street Corp.	160
10/97	Stolper & Co	Private Client	PNC Bank Corp.	N/A
10/97	ANB Investment Mgmt	Institutional	Northern Trust	28,000
09/97	Equitable Asset Mgmt/Trust	Private Client	Sun Trust Bank	1,500
09/97	Heartland Capital Mgmt	Institutional	Fifth Third Bancorp	900
09/97	Boston Financial	Institutional	Banc One Corp.	5,700
08/97	Common Sense Trust	Mutual Fund	Smith Barney	5,700
08/97	Colombia Management	Institutional	Fleet Financial Gp	22,000
08/97	J. Bush & Co	Private Client	Riggs Bank, NA	240
08/97	Westfield Capital Mgmt	Private Client	Boston Private Bancorp	1,300
07/97	American Century	Mutual Fund	J.P. Morgan (45%)	60,000
07/97	Washington Squares Advisors	Institutional	Piper Jaffray	2,700
07/97	Investors Management	Institutional	AMCORE Financial	1,700
06/97	Scudder, Stevens & Clark	Diversified	Zurich Group/Kemper	120,000
06/97	ASB Capital Management	Institutional	Chevy Chase Bank	4,000
05/97	Security Capital Corp.	Institutional	Security Capital Pacific	2,150
04/97	Fleet Financial Corp Trust	Institutional	State Street Boston	N/A
03/97	Montgomery Asset Mgmt	Diversified	Commerzbank	7,400
03/97	Commodities Corp.	Institutional	Goldman Sachs	2,000
02/97	Oppenheimer Capital	Institutional	Pimco Advisors	48,000
02/97	Pecksland Associates	Institutional	WR Lazard	106
01/97	Ganz Capital Management	Private Client	Mellon Bank	400
11/96	AIM Management	Mutual Fund	INVESCO plc	57,000
10/96	Liberty Investment Mgmt	Institutional	Goldman Sachs	54,000
10/96	Aldrich, Eastman & Waltch	Institutional	New England Invstmt	5,000
10/96	JP Investment Mgmt	Mutual Fund	Oppenheimer funds	172
09/96	Keystone Investments	Mutual Fund	First Union Corp.	11,600
09/96	Jurika & Voyles	Institutional	New England Invstmt	5,200
09/96	Lehman Br. Money Market	Mutual Funds	Federated Investors	5,000
07/96	Clay Finlay	Institutional	UAM	6,000
07/96	Chancellor Capital Mgmt	Institutional	LGT Group	33,000
07/96	Flagship Resources	Mutual Fund	John Nuveen	4,400
07/96	Mentor Investment Group	Mutual Fund	Everen Capital Corp.	5,200
06/96	Van Kampen/American Cap	Mutual Fund	Morgan Stanley	57,123
06/96	Heine Securities	Mutual Fund	Franklin Resources	17,000
06/96	Hotchkis & Wiley	Institutional	Merrill Lynch	10,600
05/96	Institutional Capital	Institutional	John Nuveen	4,300
04/96	National Mutual Fund	Mutual Fund	Alliance Capital Mgmt	1,200
04/96	Chase Manhattan Prvt Client	Private Client	Swiss Bank	1,000
04/96	Vaughan, Nelson, Scarborough & McConn	Institutional	New England Invstmt	1,614

(continues)

TABLE 14.1   (continued)

Date	Target	Type	Acquirer	Assets ($million)
04/96	OSV Partners	Institutional	United Asset Mgmt	1,000
03/96	The Clifton Group	Institutional	Voyageur Asset Mgmt	2,800
01/96	Gateway Investment Advisers	Institutional	Alex. Brown (24%)	700
01/96	Aetna-Real Estate Mgmt Unit	Institutional	T/A Associates	3,475
01/96	First Quadrant	Institutional	Affiliated Managers	10,252
11/95	RCM Capital Mgmt	Institutional	Dresdner Bank AG	25,500
11/95	Affiliated Managers	Institutional	NationsBank & ITT (50%)	5,000
10/95	Cursitor Eaton Asset Mgmt	Institutional	Alliance Capital Mgmt	8,813
10/95	MacFarlane Partners LP	Diversified	GE Capital Realty	1,800
10/95	Bear Sterns Unit Inv. Trust	Mutual Fund	Reich & Tang	3,800
10/95	The Rochester Funds	Mutual Fund	Oppenheimer Mgmt	2,900
08/95	Renaissance Inv. Mgmt	Institutional	Affiliated Mgrs (70%)	1,462
08/95	New England Inv. Mgmt	Institutional	General Re	7,500
08/95	Quest for Value Funds	Mutual Fund	Oppenheimer Mgmt	1,617
07/95	Martingale Asset Mgmt	Institutional	Commerzbank (60%)	400
07/95	Graystone Partners	Private Client	New England Inv Mgt	NA
06/95	Miller, Anderson & Sherrerd	Institutional	Morgan Stanley	32,500
06/95	Harris Associates	Diversified	New England Inv	6,000
06/95	Lehman Latin Am Growth	Mutual Fund	American Express	2,000
06/95	Wells Fargo Nikko Investment Advisors	Institutional	Barclays plc	171,900
05/95	Dreman Value Mgmt	Institutional	Kemper Corp.	1,600
04/95	Zirkin-Cutler Investments	Private Client	First Maryland Banco	1,200
04/95	Kemper	Mutual Fund	Zurich Insurance	65,366
03/95	RCB International	Institutional	Northern Trust	4,400
03/95	ABT Funds	Mutual Fund	First Union	468
03/95	Certus Financial Corp.	Institutional	Mellon Bank	5,000
03/95	Skyline Investment Mgmt	Institutional	Affiliated Managers	500
02/95	Sheffield Mgmt	Mutual Fund	Signet Banking Corp.	1,008
02/95	Benham Int'l Group	Mutual Fund	Twentieth Century	10,800
02/95	Pilgrim Baxter & Associates	Diversified	United Asset Mgmt	4,120

Source: Adapted from Putnam, Lovell & Thornton, Inc., 1998; and *Wall Street Journal*, various issues.

TYPES OF MONEY MANAGEMENT OPERATIONS

There are many types of investment management, including mutual funds, unit investment trusts, hedge funds, private client services businesses, leveraged buyout funds, and private equity funds. Private equity funds are funds that invest primarily in private equity such as venture capital (see Chapter 2 for a detailed coverage on venture capital investing). Leveraged buyout funds invest in corporate buyouts. The best-known leverage buyout specialist is Kohlberg Kravis Roberts. Unit investment trust is a registered investment company that buys and holds a relatively fixed portfolio of securities or assets. Units in the trust are sold to investors who receive a share of principal and interest or dividends. Unit investment trusts typically have a stated date for termination. Private client services business manages money for wealthy clients. Almost all invest-

TABLE 14.2 Financial Data on Publicly Traded Investment Services Companies

Name	Stock Price on 1/7/98	52-Week Range	Earnings per Share	Market Capitalization ($ million)	Beta
New England Investment	$29 $^9/_{16}$	$21 $^7/_8$ – $31	$2.05	1,310	0.86
Affiliated Managers	27 $^1/_4$	23 $^7/_8$ – 30 $^3/_{16}$	N/A	452	N/A
Alliance Capital	40 $^1/_4$	24 – 42	1.25	3,341	0.97
T. Rowe Price	61 $^5/_8$	36 $^1/_2$ – 73 $^3/_4$	2.07	3,573	1.34
PIMCO Advisors	30 $^1/_2$	19 $^3/_{16}$ – 34 $^9/_{16}$	2.47	789	0.81
Allied Capital	6 $^3/_8$	4 – 6 $^7/_8$	0.24	62	N/A
Franklin Resources	87 $^3/_4$	44 $^5/_{16}$ – 103 $^{13}/_{16}$	3.43	10,964	1.87
Equitable Co.	46 $^{15}/_{16}$	15 $^1/_8$ – 53	1.62	10,216	1.55
Phoenix Duff & Phelps	7 $^7/_8$	6 $^1/_2$ – 9 $^3/_8$	0.43	345	1.18
John Nuveem	34 $^3/_{16}$	26 $^1/_4$ – 37 $^3/_4$	2.14	1,087	0.60
United Asset Management	24 $^1/_{16}$	23 $^1/_2$ – 30 $^1/_4$	1.44	1,671	1.03
Pioneer Group	27 $^3/_8$	22 $^3/_4$ – 33 $^7/_8$	1.05	690	0.03
Eaton Vance	38 $^3/_8$	20 $^7/_8$ – 38 $^3/_8$	2.08	700	0.87
U.S. Trust	61 $^7/_8$	27 $^1/_2$ – 65 $^3/_4$	2.27	1,184	0.27
AVERAGE				2,599	0.95

Source: Adapted from Yahoo Finance, January 8, 1998; *Wall Street Journal*, various issues.

ment and commercial banks run private client services businesses. For example, Goldman Sachs has some 365 brokers who specialize in money management for wealthy clients managing more than $125 billion of investor's money.

A *mutual fund* is an investment management company that pools money together from investors who have similar investment objectives, such as obtaining current income, maximizing long-term capital growth, or a combination of the two. Each fund is managed by professional manager(s) who determine the investments that are most likely to achieve the fund's objectives. Investing in a mutual fund is buying its shares. Each share represents a proportional ownership in all of the fund's invested assets. Open-end fund share prices are determined by their net asset value (NAV). The NAV is calculated by dividing the value of fund's assets less its liabilities by the number of out-standing shares. Mutual fund distributes its earnings to investors in proportion to the number of shares an investor owns as of a record dividend date.

Hedge funds are unregistered, private investment pools bound by the investment agreement investors sign with the sponsors of the hedge funds. With the exception of anti-fraud standards, they are exempt from SEC regulation. The sponsors of a hedge fund generally are not subject to any limitations in portfolio selection, and are not required to disclose information about the hedge fund's holdings and performance, even though there has been drive for disclosure on strategies and portfolios. The typical fee structure for a hedge fund is that the hedge fund manager takes a fee of 1–2% of net assets, plus 20% incentive fees. Some have front-end charges as well. Most hedge funds impose a high minimum investment; a minimum investment of $250,000 or $500,000 is typical, though some have lower minimums and some have higher requirements.

Under the National Securities Markets Improvement Act of 1996, hedge funds can accept investment[2] from an unlimited number of qualified individuals who hold at least $5 million in investments or institutions with $25 million in investments, in addition to its 100 or fewer other non-qualified investors. However, it is prohibited from making a public offering of its securities. This is intended to limit participation in hedge funds and other types of high risk and high leverage pools to highly sophisticated investors.

ORGANIZATION AND OPERATION OF A MUTUAL FUND

Money management operations, especially mutual fund, must comply with a large number of federal laws and regulations. The SEC under the Investment Company Act of 1940 (ICA) and Investment Advisers Act of 1940 (IAA) regulates mutual funds. Fund companies offering their shares to the public must register them pursuant to the Securities Act of 1933 and provide notice filings to states in which they intend to offer their shares. Funds selling to the public are subject to the regulation as broker–dealer under the Securities Exchange Act of 1934. Plus, the Internal Revenue Code of 1986 grants pass-through tax treatment to mutual funds, but only if they follow certain operational requirements.

Mutual funds have several unique features. First, almost all mutual funds are externally managed, and all activities are carried out by third parties such as investment managers, broker–dealers, and banks. Second, mutual funds continuously offer new shares to the public, except when the funds are closed to new investments. Mutual funds also stand ready to redeem outstanding shares upon request at the net asset value. Third, government imposes strict requirements on the structure and operations of investment companies and imposes special responsibilities on their independent directors.

Setting up a mutual fund operation is a costly process. Legal fees generally run to $100,000 or more preparing the federal registration statement, contracts, and corporate documents. Printing and other expenses add up to another large sum. In addition, the ICA requires that a new fund must have assets of at least $100,000 before distributing shares to the public. The adviser or sponsor, in the form of an initial investment, typically contributes this initial capital. In addition to setting up expenses, the ongoing operation is also costly. There are expenses for management, transfer agent, custodian, accounting, and other business activities. To be viable, a fund needs to reach $50 million to $100 million in assets within a relatively short time after start up.

The structure of a typical mutual fund covers Directors/Trustees, Investment Adviser, Administrator, Principal Underwriter, Custodian, Transfer Agent, and Shareholders (see Figure 14.1). The directors or trustees[3] of an investment company must perform their responsibilities with care expected of a "prudent person." They are expected to evaluate the performance of the investment adviser, principal underwriter, and other parties that provide services to the fund. The ICA requires that at least 40% of the fund's board of directors be "independent directors." Independent directors serve as watchdogs for shareholder interests and provide a check on the adviser and other persons affiliated with the fund. Investment advisory and distribution contracts must be approved by a majority of a fund's independent directors.

Investment advisers are responsible for making portfolio selections in accordance with the objectives and policies set forth in the prospectus. The adviser carries out these responsibilities pursuant to a written contract with the fund. Most advisory contracts provide for an annual fee based on a percentage of the fund's average net assets during the year, generally between 0.5% and 1.5% (the fee is much lower for index

FIGURE 14.1 Structure of a Mutual Fund

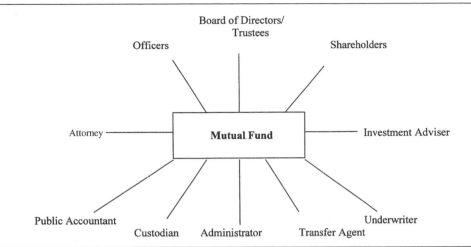

Source: Adapted from *Organization and Operation of a Mutual Fund,* Investment Company Institute, 1997.

funds). The adviser owes the fund a fiduciary duty under the IAA. An administrator is the adviser or an affiliated entity that provides administrative services, including assuring compliance with applicable regulation. Fund administrators typically pay for office space, equipment, personnel, and accounting service. Other responsibilities cover filing SEC, tax, and shareholder reports.

Mutual funds generally distribute their shares through principal underwriter or direct marketing.[4] The SEC under the 1934 act regulates principal underwriters as broker–dealers. Most principal underwriters are also members of the NASD and therefore are subject to its rules governing mutual fund sales practices.

Most funds use bank custodians. The SEC requires mutual fund custodians to protect the funds by segregating their portfolio securities from the rest of the bank's assets. Fund transfer agents maintain records of shareholder accounts. Transfer agents typically serve as dividend disbursing agents as well. They prepare and mail to shareholders periodic account statements, tax information, and other shareholder notices.

Mutual fund (open-end) shareholders are entitled to redeem shares based on the net asset value (NAV) of the request date. Shareholders also have certain voting rights. Although most mutual funds no longer have annual shareholder meetings, certain issues require shareholder approval. These matters include changes in the investment advisory contract or changes in investment objectives or policies deemed fundamental.

Most mutual funds continuously distribute shares to new investments. The marketing and distribution costs are covered by the so-called 12b-1 fee or a sales load. The 12b-1 fees are deducted from fund assets to pay marketing and advertising or to compensate sales professionals. The maximum 12b-1 fee is 0.75% of fund assets (some funds do not charge this fee). The fund may also charge a fee up to 0.25% of average NAV to compensate sales professionals. A sales load can take several different forms. A front-end load is one that purchasers pay when they buy the fund shares. By law, this charge may not exceed 8.5% on the initial investments. A back-end load (redemption fee) is charged when shares are redeemed and may be reduced progressively the longer the investor has held the shares. Additionally, an exchange fee, if any, is charged for transferring money from one fund to another within the same fund family.

The SEC advertising rules permit only two types of advertisements. One is the *tombstone advertisement*, which contains limited information about the fund. Another is *omitting prospectus* that may contain more information such as fund performance. However, an advertisement cannot include an account application or invite prospective investors to send money. The advertisement can only attract investor interest in requesting the full statutory prospectus. Also, the NASD requires mutual fund distributors and dealers to file all advertising and sales literature for staff review. Once cleared by the NASD, the SEC does not require additional filings.

DEVELOPMENT AND GROWTH OF MUTUAL FUNDS

The mutual fund industry traces its roots back to nineteenth century Great Britain. Most of these early British investment companies, and later their U.S. counterparts, sold a fixed number of shares whose price was determined by supply and demand, similar to today's closed-end funds. The first open-ended mutual fund, the Massachusetts Investors Trust, started in 1924. This revolutionized the mutual fund industry with a continuous offering of shares, and the shares can be sold any time back to the fund.

The 1929 stock market crash and the Great Depression prompted Congress to enact laws to regulate securities and financial markets, including mutual funds. The first was the Securities Act of 1933. It required for the first time a prospectus describing the fund. The Securities Exchange Act of 1934 made mutual fund distributions subject to SEC regulation. The other two important laws relating to mutual fund and investor protection were adopted in 1940. The ICA requires that a mutual fund price its assets based on market value every day, prohibits transactions between a fund and its manager(s), limits leverage, and requires the board to include a minimum of 40% of independent directors. The IAA requires the registration of all investment advisers to mutual funds.

Mutual fund investing began to grow in popularity in the 1940s and 1950s. The explosive growth occurred in the 1980s. In 1960, there were 160 funds and $17 billion in assets. Ten years later, there were 361 funds with total assets of $47.6 billion. By 1980, the number of funds reached 564 and total assets under management crossed over the $100 billion mark to $134.8 billion. Another milestone was reached in 1990, when the 3,105 funds managed more than $1 trillion of assets. By the end of 1996, total industry assets increased to $3.5 trillion. Total net assets increased by about $1 trillion in 1997. Table 14.3 lists the number of funds and total industry net assets.

The growth of the mutual fund industry is in part due to the introduction of new products and services. Innovations in investment and retirement vehicles also swept the industry:

- 1971: The first money market mutual funds were established.
- 1974: ERISA was enacted and IRAs were created.
- 1976: The first tax-exempt municipal bond funds were offered.
- 1978: 401(k) retirement plan was created.

In addition, mutual fund companies such as Fidelity, American Century, Dreyfus, Scudder, and USAA are not just managing money, a growing number bill themselves as

TABLE 14.3 Number of Mutual Funds and Total Industry Net Assets

Year	Number of Mutual Fund Complexes[1]	Number of Mutual Funds	Total Industry Net Assets ($ billion)
1960		160	17
1970		361	47.6
1980	123	564	134.8
1981	134	665	241.4
1982	150	857	296.7
1983	164	1,026	292.9
1984	189	1,241	370.6
1985	217	1,528	495.5
1986	261	1,840	716.2
1987	314	2,317	769.9
1988	349	2,715	810.3
1989	357	2,917	982.0
1990	361	3,105	1,066.8
1991	361	3,427	1,395.5
1992	364	3,850	1,646.3
1993	375	4,558	2,075.4
1994	398	5,357	2,161.5
1995	401	5,761	2,820.3
1996	417	6,293	3,539.2
1997	424	6,778	4,489.9

[1] A fund complex is a group of funds under substantially common management, composed of one or more families of funds.

Source: Adapted from *Mutual Fund Fact Book 1996, Mutual Fund Fact Book 1997, Mutual Fund Fact Book 1998*, and *Statistical Releases* March 1998, Investment Company Institute.

brokers. They are now selling stocks and other investment products, as well as basic automatic bill payment and ATM/debit card withdraws from money market funds.

The enormous growth and diversity of the fund industry have led to the development of new fund categories or investment objectives. Today's mutual fund menu runs from aggressive growth to global bond to niche funds that specialize in one segment of the securities markets (see Table 14.4).

Furthermore, in recent years the U.S. economy expanded at a healthy pace, job growth was modestly strong, inflation remained subdue, and corporate earnings advanced further. As a result, the interest-rate environment has been favorable and stock prices have moved higher. Assets of mutual funds have increased steadily, as documented in Table 14.3. The growth in mutual fund assets is split between performance and new investments. Table 14.5 lists the performance and new cash flow of mutual fund asset growth.

An increasing proportion of U.S. mutual fund assets is being invested overseas. U.S. investors have increased holdings of international and global equity and bond funds, from $230 billion in 1995 to $321 billion in 1996. The recent financial crises in Asia and their contagion effects on other markets will certainly slow this growth or lower the international exposure.

Mutual funds are also growing in many other parts of the world. Merrill Lynch's purchase of Mercury Asset Management signifies the importance of the global asset

TABLE 14.4   Types of Mutual Funds

Stock Funds
Aggressive Growth
Growth
Growth and Income
Precious Metals/Gold
International
Global Equity
Income—Equity

Bond and Income Funds
Flexible Portfolio
Balanced
Income—Mixed
Income—Bond
U.S. Government Income
GNMA
Global Bond
Corporate Bond
High-Yield Bond
National Municipal Bond—Long Term
State Municipal Bond—Long Term

Money Market Funds
Taxable Money Market
Tax-Exempt Money Market-National
Tax-Exempt Money Market-State

Source: Adapted from *Mutual Fund Fact Book 1997,* Investment Company Institute, 1997.

management markets. Worldwide assets in mutual funds have grown from $2.853 trillion at yearend 1991 to $7.159 trillion at yearend 1997. The number of open-end investment companies increased from 12,586 at yearend 1991 to 34,591 at yearend 1997. The growth in mutual fund assets worldwide can be attributed to several factors. First, the securities markets of many developed countries have benefited from favorable economic conditions in recent years. At the same time, emerging markets have

TABLE 14.5   Components of Mutual Fund Asset Growth ($ trillion)

Year	Net New Cash Flow	Performance Component	Cash Flow to New Funds
1991	1.1292	0.1617	0.1046
1992	1.2784	0.2333	0.1346
1993	1.5011	0.3907	0.1836
1994	1.5896	0.3326	0.2393
1995	1.7999	0.7423	0.2782
1996	2.1128	1.0755	0.3509
1997	2.4765	1.0690	0.4033

Source: Adapted from *Mutual Fund Fact Book 1998,* Investment Company Institute, 1998, p. 106.

prospered because of new investment opportunities arising from financial reforms, privatization, and rapid economic growth. Second, mutual fund investing is popular because it provides a way of achieving the goals of a comfortable retirement and improved living standards. Third, many countries are facing the prospect of aging populations and the pressure to reduce deficits, so they are encouraging private savings such as defined-contribution retirement plans. Finally, the continued growth of the middle class worldwide is expected to lead to greater global expansion of mutual fund investing.

THE INSTITUTIONAL AND RETIREMENT MARKETS

Institutional investors[5] have increasingly turned to mutual funds as investment options. As a result, even though individuals continue to control the majority of mutual fund assets, the mutual fund industry is seeing a shift in the business toward an increasingly institutional customer base. Over the past several years, institutional assets have accounted for an increasing share of total mutual fund assets. Total institutional assets in mutual funds were $462 billion, $630 billion, $841 billion, $897 billion, $1.219 trillion, $1.575 trillion, and $2.042 trillion each year from 1991 to 1997, respectively.

The mutual fund assets held by IRAs and employer-sponsored pension plans increased to $1.24 trillion at yearend 1996, a 25% jump from $997 billion in 1995. Retirement plan holdings of mutual fund assets accounted for about 35% of all mutual fund assets during the period 1994–1996, a 10% jump from 25% in 1992 (see Table 14.6). Several factors have contributed to the growth in the retirement holdings of mutual funds. First, the overall size of the employer-sponsored pension market had expanded to $6.6 trillion at the end of 1996 from about $1.1 trillion 15 years ago. Secondly, it is in part due to the increasing popularity of defined-contribution plans. Mutual funds are attractive to employees because they offer professional money management, investment diversification, liquidity, and price transparency. Employers favor mutual-fund assets because they can partially relieve the employer from having to serve as investment adviser and they provide recordkeeping functions for the employer. At yearend 1996, the defined-contribution market was $1.8 trillion, of which $577 billion was held in mutual funds. The third contributing factor is the IRA market. The IRA market had grown to $1.3 trillion by the end of 1996.

Table 14.6 also lists various types of retirement plan assets held in mutual funds. Employer-sponsored pension plans (defined-contribution and defined-benefit) increased to $610 billion by the end of 1996. Defined-contribution plans, including

TABLE 14.6   Retirement Plan Assets Held in Mutual Funds ($ billions)

Year	IRAs	Defined-Contribution	Defined-Benefit	Retirement Assets Total	Total Mutual Fund Assets	Retirement as % of Total
1992	225.8	181.9	4.1	411.8	1,646.3	25.0%
1993	327.5	265.3	4.6	597.4	2,075.4	28.8%
1994	382.8	352.0	31.8	766.6	2,161.5	35.4%
1995	495.4	468.6	32.9	996.9	2,820.4	35.3%
1996	632.2	576.9	33.3	1,242.5	3,539.2	35.1%

Source: Adapted from Retirement Plan Holdings of Mutual Funds, Investment Company Institute, 1997.

401(k)s, 403(b)s, and 457 plans, account for almost all of the employer-sponsored assets held in mutual funds. Defined-benefit plans held only insignificant amounts. IRA holdings of mutual funds grew to $632 billion at the end of 1996. Although new contributions to IRAs have been slow since the passage of the Tax Reform Act of 1986, the Taxpayer Relief Act of 1997 is expected to provide a boost. Qualified investors can invest as much as $2,000 annually to Roth IRA and watch the sum grow, tax free. Americans were expected to stash $40 billion in new IRAs during 1998.

MUTUAL FUND REGULATION

The investment management industry is highly regulated. Federal securities laws that govern the industry include the Investment Company Act of 1940, the Investment Advisers Act of 1940, the Securities Act of 1933, and the Securities Exchange Act of 1934. Other regulations include the Internal Revenue Code of 1986, compliance with state notice filing requirements, and anti-fraud statutes.

Investment Company Act of 1940 (ICA)

Mutual funds are a class of investment companies defined in the ICA as *management companies*, which are subclassified as either diversified or nondiversified. A diversified company has at least 75% of its total assets in cash and cash items, government securities, securities of other investment companies, and other securities. The investment in each security is limited to an amount not greater in value than 5% of the fund's assets and not more than 10% of the outstanding voting securities of such issuer. The ICA also regulates the ability of mutual funds to employ certain investment techniques such as repos, futures, options, and swaps. Under the ICA, certain fund policies may not be changed without a shareholder approval. The act also imposes specific prohibitions against certain transactions between a fund and its principal underwriter, investment adviser, or other affiliated persons. As such, a mutual fund's principal underwriter or an affiliated person may not knowingly sell to or purchase from the fund any security or other property, nor may either borrow any money or other property from the fund.

The ICA requires all funds to safeguard their assets by placing them in the hands of a custodian and by providing fidelity bonding of officers and employees of the fund. The act also requires daily valuation of the securities held in a mutual fund portfolio. The ICA requires all mutual funds to maintain detailed books and records regarding the securities owned by the fund and the fund's outstanding shares, and to file semiannual reports with the SEC and send such reports to shareholders. Independent accountants must certify the financial statements in a fund's annual report.

Mutual funds are subclassified as closed-end and open-end investment companies. Open-end funds redeem shares at any time upon shareholder request. The funds are required to pay redeeming shareholders at net asset value within seven days of receiving such request. Closed-end funds, in contrast, do not redeem their shares. Shares of closed-end funds are typically listed and traded on stock exchanges.

Another important regulatory issue is ICA's prohibition of interdealing by investment banking houses. Under the ICA, underwriters are prohibited from feeding affiliated funds during a public offering in which they participate, subject to special exemptions. The purpose was to prevent dumping any unmarketable securities that they have underwritten to their kindred funds. The exemptions cover municipal bond issues and public registered stock issues. A fund group can purchase up to 4% of such securities underwritten by its Wall Street parent. The explosive growth of mutual funds has made investment companies significant purchasers in syndicated offerings. This has put pressure on the old regulation. In 1996, the SEC proposed rule changes to lift the cap to 10% of a domestic issue or a foreign security in an acceptable market abroad. Wall Street firms are lobbying to remove the cap limitation and widen the exemptions to include Rule 144A private placements.

Investment Advisers Act of 1940 (IAA)

The IAA regulates the activities of investment advisers, including advisers to investment companies and private money managers. The IAA regulation covers any person, absent exclusion or an exemption, engaging in the business of providing advice or issuing reports about securities to clients for compensation. The persons excluded from the definition of investment adviser are:

- U.S. banks and bank holding companies
- Instrumentalities of the U.S. or any state
- Government securities advisers
- Publishers of newspapers and magazines of general and regular circulation
- Lawyers, accountants, teachers, and engineers, provided that the advice is solely incidental

Under the Investment Advisers Supervision Coordination Act of 1997 (IASCA), an investment adviser has to register with the SEC if it:

- Has more than $25 million in client assets under management, or
- Advises registered investment companies, or
- Is not regulated or required to be regulated by the state in which it maintains its principal office, or
- Is exempted from the prohibition of registration by the SEC

Any investment adviser that advises a registered investment company is required to register with the SEC. The same requirement applies for advisers that perform contractual subadvisory services to a registered investment company. Investment advisers that do not advise a registered investment company may rely on existing exemption such as Federal de Minimis Exemption from SEC registration. Such exemption applies to an investment adviser who had fewer than 15 clients during the past 12 months, does not hold himself out to the public as investment adviser, and does not advise any registered investment company. The IASCA defines the term *assets under management* to include only securities portfolio for which an investment adviser provides continuous and regular supervisory or management services. Because the assets under management for some advisers might fluctuate above and below $25 million, causing needless SEC and state registrations and withdraws, the SEC has raised the threshold for mandatory SEC registration to $30 million. When assets under management dip below $25 million, the adviser must withdraw from SEC registration.

Investment advisers that are not regulated or required to be regulated by the state in which they have their principal office must register with the SEC, even if they do not have $25 million under management. The SEC retains the regulatory responsibility with respect to a small advisory firm only if its principal office is in a state that has not enacted an investment adviser statute or the adviser is a foreign adviser doing business in the United States.

Pursuant to ERISA Section 3(38)(B), an investment manager must be registered with the SEC as an investment adviser. So those advisers who would no longer be eligible for continued registration with the SEC would become ineligible to act as investment managers under ERISA after 1996 NSMIA. To address this concern, Congress on October 30, 1997, amended ERISA to permit non–SEC-registered investment advisers to act as fiduciaries under ERISA.

The IAA also establishes requirements governing the operation of a registered adviser and the relationship between the adviser and its clients. The most important requirements include recordkeeping, brochure rule, advisory contacts and performance fees, conflicts and anti-fraud provisions, and duty to supervise (Chapter 16 provides a detailed coverage on this). Regulation on performance fees is briefly discussed here. Section 205 of the IAA generally prohibits an investment adviser from sharing in profits that its clients earn on their assets under management of the adviser. Rule 205–3 under the IAA permits investment advisers to charge certain clients performance fees. Effective August 20, 1998, to be eligible to enter into a performance fee arrangement, a client would be required to have assets under management with the adviser of at least $750,000 or net worth of more than $1.5 million.

If an investment adviser is not registered under the IAA because it has less than $25 million in assets under management and does not advise a registered investment company, then it may be required to register under state law. State-registered investment advisers whose assets under management grow to $30 million are required to register with the SEC. States remain authorized to enforce actions against SEC-registered investment advisers and associated persons under their anti-fraud laws. States also retain the authority to receive copies of documents filed with the SEC for notice purposes or to impose fees on investment advisers.

Generally, a state is free to regulate any investment adviser who is not SEC-registered and either has a place of business in the state or has clients who are residents of the state. States may not, however, require registration of an investment adviser who does not have a place of business in the state and who had fewer than six resident clients during the preceding twelve months (called National de Minimis Exemption).

The Securities Act of 1933

The 1933 act requires that all prospective investors receive a current prospectus describing the fund, and that the fund provides, upon request, a Statement of Additional Information.

Mutual funds are subject to special SEC registration rules because they continuously offer new shares to the public. In order to facilitate the continuous offering of shares, the act permits a mutual fund to maintain an "evergreen" prospectus (i.e., updated at regular intervals and whenever material changes occur) and register an indefinite number of shares. After the end of each fiscal year, mutual funds pay a registration fee to the SEC based on the shares actually sold. Mutual funds are permitted to net redemption against sales when calculating their SEC registration fees.

The Securities Exchange Act of 1934

The 1934 act regulates broker–dealers, including principal underwriters and others who sell mutual fund shares, and requires their registration with the SEC. The 1934 act requires broker–dealers to meet financial responsibility requirements; to maintain extensive books and records reflecting their own financial position and customer transactions; to segregate customer securities in custodial accounts; and to file detailed annual financial reports with the SEC and their industry self-regulatory organization. In addition, all sales and research personnel must demonstrate their qualifications by passing an examination administered by the NASD. A mutual fund's principal underwriter is required to have a registered principal. This officer must take special qualification examinations administered by the NASD.

Internal Revenue Code of 1986 and State Laws

The Internal Revenue Code of 1986 provides mutual fund entity-level tax exemption if it (1) satisfies various tests, such as those relating to asset diversification and sources of income, for qualification as a regulated investment company (RIC) and (2) meets certain income distribution requirements. One important consequence of the RIC status is that a mutual fund is relieved of entity-level tax to the extent that it distributes substantially all of its income to its shareholders. The mutual fund shareholder reports on his or her tax return the dividends received from the fund.

Another important consequence of the RIC status is that the "character" of the mutual fund's income often flows through to its shareholders. The types of income that retain their character when flowed through a mutual fund include long-term capital gains (paid out as a capital gain dividend) and municipal bond income exempt from federal taxes (the exempt-interest dividend). In addition, all local governments recognize that the character of federal obligation interest, which is exempt from state and local taxation, can flow through a mutual fund to its shareholders.

State registration of mutual fund shares is not required. A state in which a fund intends to sell its shares, however, may require a notice filing. In addition, mutual funds must pay a fee to each state in which they intend to offer their shares. Mutual funds must also comply with any state anti-fraud provisions. Once the notice filing requirements are satisfied, a mutual fund may sell its shares in a state.

Most states have adopted securities laws that require the registration of broker–dealers that offer securities in those states. In addition, investment advisers to mutual funds may be required to make a notice filing and pay a fee in states in which they do business.

HEDGE FUNDS

A hedge fund is a private investment fund that employs investment strategies in various types of securities in various markets and whose offering memorandum allows for the fund to take both long and short positions, and use leverage and derivatives. The fund is usually organized as a limited partnership, affording limited partners (LPs) limited liability. Investors in a hedge fund make their investment by contributing capital and are admitted as LPs. The general partner (GP) of the hedge fund generally has discretion over investment strategies. The GP usually receives a fixed management fee of 1% to 2% of the assets under management and an incentive fee. The incentive fee is usually 20%, even though variations range from 10% (e.g., F-500 Capital Management) to 50% (e.g., SAC Capital Management). The GP typically has a large investment in the fund.

The first hedge fund, operated by Alfred W. Jones, started trading in New York on January 1, 1949. Jones used a private partnership structure for operational flexibility. Jones took long and short positions and used leverage. It is this ability to go both long and short in equity and other markets that has given this type of partnership the name *hedge fund*. The success of Jones led to a continuing growth of hedge funds throughout the 1960s. The activities of such funds expanded during the 1970s, 1980s, and 1990s. Top Wall Street firms such as Bear Stearns, Paine Webber and Merrill Lynch have all entered into the business. Plus, many of the brightest from Wall Street have started their own hedge funds. Currently, there are estimated to be more than 3,000 hedge funds managing more than $370 billion. While the number and size of hedge funds are small relative to mutual funds, their growth reflects the importance of this alternative investment category for institutional and wealthy individual investors. Investment banks and institutional money managers are targeting the hedge fund business as a fee-rich growth area that can help retain promising talents. The ease of the restrictions on the number of limited partners a hedge fund can have without being obligated to register with the SEC has provided a boost.

Hedge funds now operate in foreign currency, government securities, and commodities transactions, as well as merger and acquisition activities. Recently, hedge funds have received significant attention from the news media and governments, getting blamed for causing the volatility in the Asian financial system. The Malaysian prime minister singled out George Soros for its financial market crisis.

Hedge Fund Structure

Hedge funds are structured as limited partnerships to avoid the application of most securities laws. Offshore hedge funds are organized outside of the United States and are offered to non–U.S. residents. A typical hedge fund structure is depicted in Figure 14.2. There are two types of partners in a hedge fund, a GP and LPs. The GP is the entity who started the hedge fund. The GP handles all trading and day-to-day operations. The LPs contribute most of the capital but are not involved in trading or day-to-day operations. The typical entity of a GP is the limited liability partnership (LLP). The LLP is preferred because the GP of a limited partnership is liable beyond the extent of his or her investment in a limited partnership. The GP often serves as the fund manager. Sometimes the GP relies on advice by an investment adviser to identify investment opportunities.

The GP and LPs typically sign a partnership agreement. The partnership agreement sets forth some of the following items:

- Investment objectives, strategies, and risk factors
- When partners can invest, increase investments, and withdraw from the fund
- Details of management fees and incentive fees
- Details of how full withdraws will be handled

The majority of U.S. hedge funds charge the standard "one-and-twenty"—1% management fee and 20% incentive fees. The 1% fee is usually charged in 0.25% increments quarterly, in advance. There are variations in incentive fees. Most funds observe a "high-water mark." If in a given performance fee period a fund loses money, the investors will not be charged in later periods until the losses have been recovered. Another variation is the *preferred return*. A fund will not collect an incentive fee until a certain set rate of return has been achieved. Furthermore, most funds require a minimum duration of investments into the funds, known as a *lockup period*. The common lockup period is one year, even though a three-year lockup is not unheard of.

Prime brokerage is a suite of services providing hedge funds with custody, clearance, financing, and securities lending. These services make it possible with multiple brokers while maintaining one brokerage account. A prime broker acts as the back office for the fund by providing the operational services necessary for the money manager to effectively manage a business. This enables the GP to focus on investment strategies rather than on operational issues. The services a good prime broker provides include:

- Centralized custody
- Clearance
- Securities lending
- Competitive financing rates
- One debit balance/one credit balance
- Real time, daily, monthly, and annual portfolio accounting
- Position and balance validation
- Electronic trade download
- Wash sale reports
- Layering reports
- Office facilities in selected markets

FIGURE 14.2   Hedge Fund Structure

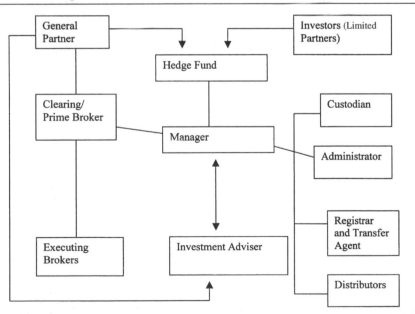

Ownership/Shareholding ⟶; Contractual relationship ⟶.
Source: Adapted from Bekier (1997), Section 2.3, p. 1, and Info-Web Technologies (1998).

Management Style

One of the common misconceptions about hedge funds is that, contrary to their name, they all use global macro strategies and place large bets on stocks, currencies, bonds, commodities, and derivatives, while using lots of leverage. In reality, only funds employing emerging markets or global macro styles like Quantum, Tiger, and Strome post a high degree of risk to investors. Most hedge funds use derivatives for hedging, not for speculating. The risk to a large extent depends on the specific strategy pursued by the fund. As listed in Table 14.7, market-neutral strategy has very minimum risk, while emerging markets and macro styles post very high risks. Very few funds use only one strategy, and some tend to change their investment styles over time. Even with the same investment style classification, there is sometimes considerable variation in risks. This can be largely explained by the differing liquidity of the assets the fund has invested in. For example, David Askin's funds (Granite Partners, Granite Corp, and Quartz Hedge Fund) were classified as market neutral. However, Askin's investment proved to be extremely risky, as the market for mortgage-backed securities became very thin, which eventually caused the collapse of David Askin's highly leveraged mortgage-backed securities hedge funds. Such liquidity risk is especially damaging in emerging markets. In countries such as Russia and parts of Latin America, it is often difficult or impossible to sell shares in a falling market because stock markets are underdeveloped and riddled with corrupt practices.

Hedge funds tend to be small enterprises; the management and skills of one or a few people are often considered the key competitive edge of a hedge fund. Hence, they are affected by management changes. In addition, structural breaks represent a danger for hedge funds that rely heavily on technically oriented trading programs and econometric models. A structural market break can lead to major losses. For example, convergence trading relies on the historical relationships between securities or between maturity segments to profit from the observed "out-of-line" relationships. However, the anticipated convergence will not take place if there are structural shifts in the relationships.

Hedge Fund Performance

Hedge funds are extremely flexible in their investment options because they use financial instruments generally beyond the reach of mutual funds, which are subject to SEC regulation and disclosure requirements that largely prevent them from using short sale, leverage, concentrated investments, and derivatives. This flexibility, which includes use of hedging strategies to protect downside risk, gives hedge funds the ability to better manage investment risks. Several studies show that hedge funds outperformed mutual funds in returns with lower risks. For example, Van Hedge Fund Advisors reached this conclusion after examining the performances of more than 1,600 hedge funds and mutual funds over a five-year period, 1991–1995. Hennessee Hedge Fund Advisory Group compared a hedge fund index to the S&P 500 and the Lipper Mutual Fund Index over a 10-year period (1987–1996), and found that hedge funds provided higher returns and were less volatile than were the S&P 500 and the Lipper Mutual Fund Index. During this 10-year period, the cumulative return of the hedge fund index is 477%. The total return of S&P 500 is at 414%, 60% behind. The average mutual fund lagged far behind, at 365%.

TABLE 14.7   Hedge Fund Investment Styles

Style	Definition	Holding period	Expected volatility
Emerging markets	Invest in emerging markets. Shorting is not permitted in some markets, so managers must resort to other alternatives to hedge.	Short/medium term	Very high
Short only	Go only short on securities.	Medium	Very high
Macro	Design strategies to profit from major currency or interest rate shifts.	Medium	Very high
Sector play	Invest in a specific sector of the market.	Medium	High
Distressed	Invest primarily in securities of companies in bankruptcy or reorganization.	Medium/long	Moderate
Growth	The dominant theme involves high-growth firms.	Medium/long	Moderate
Risk arbitrage	Simultaneously long the target and short the acquirer.	Medium	Moderate
Convertible arbitrage	Go long on convertible securities and short the underlying equities.	Medium	Low
High yield	Invest mainly in noninvestment securities.	Medium	Moderate
Event driven	Play on anticipated event.	Medium	Moderate
Value	The dominant theme is intrinsic value: asset, cash flow, book value, and out-of-favor stock.	Long	Low/Moderate
Opportunistic	Use momentum trading with short-term horizon.	Short	Low/Moderate
Market neutral	Combine positions to create a zero-beta portfolio.	Short/medium	Low
Convergence	Exploit temporary out-of-line relationships, take profits when relationship among various securities return to historical norm.	Short/medium	Low

Source: Adapted from Van Hedge Fund Advisors, 1998; Hennessee Hedge Fund Global Statistics, 1997.

The strong results of the hedge funds can be linked to performance incentives, in addition to investment flexibility. Unlike mutual funds, the hedge fund GP is usually heavily invested in a significant portion of the fund and shares the rewards as well as risks with the LPs. The incentive fee remunerates the hedge fund managers in accordance with the performance. Mutual funds pay managers a fixed percentage of the amount of money attracted, regardless of performance. This incentive fee structure tends to attract many of Wall Street's best practitioners to the hedge fund industry.

SUMMARY

Increasingly, investment bankers view money management as an integral part of the investment banking business. Fund management provides synergies to securities underwriting and generates a stable source of fee income. It is one of the most attractive segments of the financial services industry. This chapter has described in detail two types of money management operations, mutual funds and hedge funds. The coverage also includes the growing importance of the institutional market for Wall Street's asset management business and a brief description of the changing regulatory environment.

SELECT BIBLIOGRAPHY

Bekier, M. "A definition and profile of hedge funds." *AIMA*, 1997.

Curtis, C. "Are banks making it in the fund business?" *ABA Banking Journal* (October 1997):pp. 57–64.

Grerend, W., W. Crerend, and R. Jaeger. *Fundamentals of Hedge Fund Investing: A Professional Investor's Guide*, New York: McGraw-Hill, 1998.

Harman, D. K. *How to Run Your Own Money Management Business*. Burr Ridge, IL: Irwin Professional Publishing, 1995.

Info-Web Technologies. "*What is a hedge fund?*" 1998.

Investment Company Institute. *Mutual Fund Fact Book*. 1996 Edition. Washington, DC: Investment Company Institute, 1996.

Investment Company Institute. *Mutual Fund Fact Book*. 1997 Edition. Washington, DC: Investment Company Institute, 1997.

Investment Company Institute. *Mutual Fund Fact Book*. 1998 Edition. Washington, DC: Investment Company Institute, 1998.

Lederman, J., and R. Klein, eds. *Hedge Funds*. Burr Ridge, IL: Irwin Professional Publishing, 1995.

Reid, B., and J. Crumrine. *Retirement Plan Holdings of Mutual Funds 1996*. Washington, DC: Investment Company Institute, 1997.

Vince, R. *Portfolio Management Formulas*. New York: Wiley, 1990.

Vince, R. *The New Money Management*. New York: Wiley, 1995.

15

Clearing and Settlement

Timely and reliable clearance and settlement are the foundation for a safe and efficient trading environment. Automated post-trade procedures result in fewer inaccuracies, lower transaction fees and operational and fail costs. Automation and the capacity of real-time settlement are essential in meeting the complex requirements of substantial increase in transactions and the emphasis on risk reduction. This chapter describes the post-trade process that begins from a trade ticket to the back office and to clearing corporations. The major clearing corporations covered in this chapter include Government Securities Clearing Corporation, National Securities Clearing Corporation, International Securities Clearing Corporation, Mortgage-Backed Securities Clearing Corporation, Cedel Bank, and Euroclear. This chapter also lists top-rated global custodians and the top-rated agent banks in emerging markets.

INTRODUCTION

Clearing is processing a trade and establishing what the parties to the trade owe each other. Settlement is the transfer of money and securities between the parties so the transaction is completed. Clearing and settlement are usually referred to as back-office operations. Most Wall Street firms hire a clearing bank to do receiving and delivering of money and securities for them. Hence, one of the main functions of a dealer's back office is to give accurate instructions to the clearing bank to effect the trade. A securities firm's money and securities accounts at its clearing bank together make up its clearing account. Securities in the clearing account are referred to as its box position.

The significance of back-office operations is clearly manifested by the snafu that occurred at the Bank of New York (BONY) in November 1985. During a computer malfunction, BONY could accept deliveries of securities but it could not make them. BONY had to borrow $22.5 billion from the New York Fed to cover the shortfall created by this situation.

The first step in the clearing and settlement process involves conveying the details on the trade ticket to the back office. The second step is to compare and match between the purchaser and the seller to ensure that they agree on what is to be transacted and on what terms. The final phase is to deliver what has been promised in the trade.

Every trade ticket must contain certain basic information. The trader must write down on the ticket whether the order is to buy or to sell, the quantity of the transaction, a description of the security to be transacted, the account or the name of the counterparty, and the price. The time of the transaction is stamped, as well. The ticket is then sent to the back office for processing. The information enables back-office people to know the details of the trade. The customer's name and account are necessary for processing and for satisfying certain rules and regulations.

The ticket is often assigned a code that designates the details of the trade. Each trade must undergo a series of computations, known as *figuration*. Figuration includes how much the selling firm receives and how much the buying firm pays. In fixed-income transactions, figuration has to include accrued interest as well. *Comparison* then takes place to match against the opposing firm's records. A *confirmation* is typically prepared the night the trade is processed and is sent out the next morning. Once the trade has been compared and agreed to, securities are delivered and payments are made on settlement date. In addition, once the trade has been processed, it must be entered on the firm's record, or *booked*. Part of the booking process is the recording of fees and commissions due to the firm.

The following is a review of the clearance and settlement process for several major clearing corporations.

GOVERNMENT SECURITIES

The Treasury offers bills, notes, and bonds only in book-entry form. All Treasury securities held in physical form by depository institutions—whether owned by them or held on behalf of customers—are eligible for conversion to book entry and for transfer by wire.

In the 1920s, Treasury securities were transferable by telegraph among banks in different Reserve districts. Under the system, the sender of a security, usually a commercial bank, delivered certificates to the local Federal Reserve office. That office retired the securities and sent a telegram to another Reserve office located near the institution receiving the security. The Reserve office receiving the telegram issued identical physical securities to the receiving bank to which they were being transferred, or they were deposited in that bank's safekeeping account at the Federal Reserve. The difficulties involved in making actual deliveries of physical securities to and from the Federal Reserve Bank in New York City (and among the banks and dealers in the city) led to the establishment of New York's *Government Securities Clearing Arrangement* (GSCA) in 1965. The GSCA offered the telegraphic transfer of securities during the day with a net settlement in physical securities at the end of the day. In 1968, a Treasury regulation authorized the first book-entry procedures to eliminate paper government securities. Under these procedures, government securities were issued and transferred electronically on the records of a Reserve Bank. By the end of 1977, it was possible to eliminate the GSCA due to the widespread use of book-entry. As part of the program to expand the use of book-entry, the Treasury began offering new bills exclusively in book-entry form in 1979. In August 1986, the Treasury began marketing all new notes and bonds only in book-entry form.

Fedwire

Fedwire is an electronic transfer system that enables financial institutions to transfer funds and book-entry securities. The system connects Federal Reserve Banks and branches, the Treasury and other government agencies, and depository institutions. All Fedwire transfers are completed on the day they are initiated. An important feature of Fedwire transfers is that they are settled on a bilateral, trade-for-trade basis (*gross settlement*).[1]

The Fedwire works as follows. Suppose a customer asks a bank to transfer funds. If the bank of the sender and that of the receiver are in different Federal Reserve districts, the sending bank debits the sender's account and asks its local Reserve Bank to send a transfer order to the Reserve Bank serving the receiver's bank. The two Reserve Banks settle with each other through the interdistrict *Settlement Fund*, a bookkeeping system that records Federal Reserve interdistrict transactions. Finally, the receiving bank notifies the recipient of the transfer and credits its account. The funds are available immediately. Once the transfer is received, it is final and cannot be reversed. If the sending and receiving banks are in the same Federal Reserve district, the transaction is similar, but all of the processing and accounting are done by one Reserve Bank.

Now for a securities transaction: Suppose GS Securities purchases $50 million of Treasury bills from BA Securities, and GS uses Chase as its clearing bank and BA uses BONY. Chase increases GS securities account by $50 million and decreases its funds by the same amount in payment. At the other end, BONY decreases the BA securities account by $50 million and increases its funds account by $50 million. On Fedwire, the securities move from BONY to Chase by book-entry and payment moves in the opposite direction. Because funds and securities are transferred at the same time on Fedwire, such a system is called delivery versus payment (DVP).

Government Securities Clearing Corporation (GSCC)

GSCC provides comparison, netting, and settlement for government securities. Each day, GSCC settles government securities with an average value of more than $450 billion. Annually, the total volume amounts to more than $110 trillion in trades processed. In the government securities marketplace, the services provided by GSCC include:

- Trade comparison
- Netting and settlement
- Risk management
- Repurchase agreement
- Treasury auction takedown
- Yield to price processing

GSCC *comparison system* automatically matches the buy and sell of a cash transaction, or the repo and reverse sides of a repurchase agreement. The comparison system runs in real time, so results can be obtained through a GSCC terminal within seconds of trade input, or after end-of-day processing.

The *netting and settlement* services provide centralized and automated clearance and guaranteed settlement of eligible treasuries and book-entry non–mortgage-backed securities. Through netting, GSCC establishes a single net position for each participant each day in a given security. This netting includes all cash buy/sell, repo/reverse, and Treasury auction purchases. GSCC becomes the legal counterparty and guarantees the settlement of all trades entering its net. Settlement is guaranteed when GSCC makes netting results available to participants, usually before 12:00 A.M. on T+1. Obligations are settled using the Fedwire, which ensures DVP. As such, GSCC's netting system reduces the number of securities movements and the daylight overdraft charges.

Risk management is an integral part of all GSCC's services to participants. It is the foundation for GSCC's ability to guarantee settlement, as well as to protect itself and its participants. The first measure in the risk-management strategy is to maintain strict membership standards. Second, GSCC minimizes risk to participants by guaranteeing settlement of all trades entering its net. GSCC also maintains a clearing fund that ensures sufficient liquidity to guarantee orderly settlement. Finally, GSCC has adopted a loss allocation procedure to ensure that a systemic failure of the settlement process never occurs. If a firm were to default, GSCC would liquidate that member's positions. If these funds were insufficient, GSCC would allocate the remaining liabilities pro rata among participants who most recently traded with the failed firm.

GSCC also provides services for repos, covering blind-brokered repos, *collateral substitutions*, and *repo-to-maturity*. GSCC began accepting brokered repos executed on an anonymous basis in August 1996. For repo collateral substitutions, GSCC allows participants to submit details regarding rights of substitution and to submit their "intent to substitute" notifications for collateral substitutions online. Later in November 1996, GSCC implemented repo-to-maturity processing, which enables participants to submit repos where the repo close date is equal to the maturity date of the collateral.

Additionally, GSCC's *yield-to-price* service compares WI trades on their submission date, which eliminates the need for a second submission when the coupon is announced. Compared trades of netting members receive a guarantee on the original trade date. On the auction date, the trades are converted to final money trades.[2] The night before the issue date, the net positions are replaced with GSCC settlement obligations. Treasury auction takedown reduces settlement risk and costs for participant's purchases at the auction. The service nets Treasury auction purchases along with WI trades, thereby reducing securities movements and associated costs.

CORPORATE SECURITIES

National Securities Clearing Corporation (NSCC) clears and settles about 99% of all U.S. corporate stock and bond trading and most mutual fund transactions. NSCC provides three elements in the clearing and settlement process. First, it ensures that it has adequate systems capacity to handle average trading volume and the unpredictable spikes as well. The second key element is that NSCC guarantees a trade once it enters its system, as compared. This guarantee eliminates the risk of the counterparty becoming insolvent. Third, NSCC's *continuous net settlement* (CNS) nets the total number of financial obligations requiring settlement. This is accomplished by netting the total received and delivered for a given security into one net position for each firm. This CNS can reduce the total settlement volume by as much as 95%.

The Clearing and Settlement Cycle

The three-day cycle begins with the trade date, T. On the trade date, firms record and transmit all trade details via computers. NSCC's guarantee of settlement begins at midnight on the day the trade is reported back to participants as compared. From this point on, firms are dealing with the NSCC rather than with another firm. Net sellers have the obligation to deliver the securities to (and net buyers to receive from) the NSCC.

On T+1, NSCC transmits to participants computerized reports, known as contracts. These contracts show every trade reported to the NSCC on trade date, and confirm that these transactions have been compared and are ready for settlement in CNS. Transactions that fail to match are reported back to the participating firms for corrections. These firms then make corrections and retransmit the information to the NSCC.

On the morning of T+2, CNS summarizes settlement information on trades that have been matched the day before. NSCC then sends the information on the balance of shares and payments due or owed to participants.

T+3 is the settlement date. NSCC completes the settlement of matched trades by delivering securities to net buyers and payments to net sellers. Securities deliveries are via book-entry movement at the Depositary Trust Corporation (DTC). In money settlement, NSCC centralizes and nets credit and debit obligations for each participant. Each firm daily makes payment to or collects from NSCC to bring the account balance to zero.

Physical Settlement

Securities not eligible for depository processing through DTC can be settled via NSCC's physical securities processing system, *balance order system (BOS)*. The BOS nets each participant's receive and deliver to one position per issue every day. In addition, NSCC also provides the following services for physical settlement:

- *Envelope settlement service* (ESS) standardizes and controls participant-to-participant physical delivery of securities in New York City and Jersey City. Intercity ESS performs this same function between New York and NSCC branch cities.
- *Direct clearing* allows regional participants without a New York office to settle physical securities using NSCC's ESS.
- *Funds-only settlement service* centralizes the routing of envelopes containing money-only charges among full-service NSCC participants in New York City and Jersey City.
- *Dividend settlement service* is a claims-processing system that facilitates the efficient collection of cash dividends and registered bond interests.
- *National transfer service* handles securities resulting from trading activities, as well as legal and accommodation transfers within a network of cities throughout the United States and Canada.

Unsettled Fails

NSCC provides a *reconfiguration and pricing service* (RECAPS) that reconfirms and reprices aged securities transactions that have failed previously to settle. Unsettled fails previously compared in RECAPS are submitted with a special indicator. RECAPS provides reject (reject the trade) and DK (don't know; means one party does not have knowledge of a trade) capabilities for advisories received and requires participants to respond to all open fails submitted by contra party. The RECAPS system also provides participants and regulators with a report that summarizes the overall activity for a participant during the RECAPS cycle.

The RECAPS cycle begins on Tuesday. Participants submit CUSIP files for all fails. Three days later, Friday, participants must review fail files and submit all open-aged fails for eligible products. On Sunday, NSCC distributes contracts, CNS and non-CNS compared trade summaries, and balance orders. On Monday, participants must take supplemental action for uncompared items and as-of fails. Participating firms could choose to DK or reject an advisory. Finally, on Tuesday, the last day of the RECAPS cycle, all fails compared in RECAPS will settle. NSCC will send an activity report to participants and NASD.

NSCC Guarantee

NSCC performs match/record trades executed between dealers, accounts for them, and settles the associated securities and money obligations. Most of the transactions are netted, the movement of securities occurs at the DTC, and money is settled directly with the NSCC. The netting approach to settlement can best be explained by an example. Assume the following:

1. Firm A sells 800 shares to Firm B.
2. Firm B sells 800 shares to Firm C.
3. Firm C sells 800 shares to Firm D.

NSCC's multilateral netting system nets out Firm B and Firm C and would instruct Firm A to deliver shares to Firm D. The NSCC guarantees the members that if one side failed, the other firm would still deliver to or receive from NSCC, which would be the contra side of the trade.

NSCC has risk in that one of the two sides to a trade might be unable to complete the transaction. The multilateral netting system rolls obligations forward. A participant may, without penalty, fail to make delivery of the required securities on the settlement date. If this happens, the participant will be subject to a mark-to-market charge (credit) as well as the potential to be bought in by the failing to receive side. The NSCC will go out into the market to purchase the amount of securities and complete the delivery obligation. The difference between the price NSCC has to pay and the original contract price agreed upon by the two parties is the risk exposure the NSCC is subject to. Alternatively, if the receiver of securities is unable to pay for the securities delivered, the NSCC would sell the securities in the market. The difference between the amount of proceeds from the sale and the original contract price is the risk to which the NSCC is subject. Another risk is that payment for corporate securities does not take place simultaneously with its crediting on the books of the depository.[3] This is because corporate securities deliveries are credited to a member's account at DTC prior to receipt of payment.

To protect such risk, the NSCC sets collateralization requirements and also supplements them for any unusual risks. The collateralization will be adjusted upward if a firm's financial condition begins to deteriorate or the potential for such event is present. The NSCC has maintained collateral from its members in excess of $700 million, known as *clearing funds, participant funds,* or *guarantee funds*.

MORTGAGE-BACKED SECURITIES

The settlement cycle in the MBS market is much longer than it is in other securities markets—generally 45 to 90 days, compared to 1 (treasuries) and 3 (corporate) days.

The value of transaction per trade is larger in size, typically $10 million or more. Another unique characteristic is that the seller of TBA mortgage-backeds is permitted to deliver securities that vary by a certain percentage from the originally agreed-on face value. The Mortgage-Backed Securities Clearing Corporation (MBSCC) provides automated trade comparison/confirmation, net settlement, and pool notification services to ensure timely and accurate settlement.

Pool Notification

MBSCC offers a real-time *electronic pool notification* (EPN) system that enables market participants to transmit MBS pool information more quickly, efficiently, and reliably. Before the EPN, MBS market participants relied on phone and fax to exchange this information. Since the introduction of EPN in the early 1990s, successful delivery of pool information is denoted by EPN time-stamp and is independent of the recipient's retrieval of the message. The MBSCC has indicated that, as a result, the fail costs are dramatically reduced.

Users acting as principal to the underlying trade maintain *direct accounts*, while *omnibus users* (such as investment advisers and correspondent clearing organizations) process information on behalf of others in a fully disclosed capacity. EPN messages consist of terms of the trade and the specifics of the securities intended for delivery on settlement date. The codes used in EPN are the same as those in the MBSCC clearing system. EPN users may exchange three message types: original notification (ON), don't know (DK), and cancel (CX).

Clearing and Settlement

MBSCC provides two types of accounts for clearing services. First, in the dealer-to-dealer comparison system, both parties to the trade submit trade terms as principals. Second, the broker–dealer system is a three-sided trade input system that compares interdealer broker give-up trades.

MBSCC operates two settlement systems, *trade-for-trade* and *settlement balance order* (SBO). The SBO settlement system performs the pair-off process that has eliminated the need to settle more than 90% of all trades submitted for netting. Trades that cannot be paired off become SBO settlement obligations. All SBO transactions are settled in accordance with the PSA guidelines. One of the guidelines is that settlement must occur in $1 million face value increments. Secondly, the *delivery variance* permits an under- or overdelivery tolerance of 0.01% per million traded. As such, MBSCC performs postclearance cash adjustment to reconcile actual-to-original face value at the uniform price.

Trades that are SBO ineligible or for which SBO is not desired are entered into the trade-for-trade system for individual settlement.

INTERNATIONAL TRANSACTIONS

Securities markets have integrated globally. Two convergent forces are driving this trend. Investors are acquiring international securities for higher yields and diversification. Companies now raise funds throughout the world. Over the last 10 years or so, cross-border investing has increased dramatically. Non-U.S. securities acquired by U.S. investors soared from $19 billion to $383 billion, and investors outside the United States hold U.S. securities worth about $360 billion. On top of the cross-border holdings, every day a huge volume of transactions takes place. Reliable clearance and settlement are the backbone of such integration and expansion. This section reviews the services provided by the International Securities Clearing Corporation, Euroclear, and Cedel Bank.

International Securities Clearing Corporation (ISCC)

ISCC's *global clearing network* (GCN) clears and settles foreign transactions. The GCN offers global access, standardized communication, timely settlement, local expertise, accurate reporting, and book-entry movement. When a new member joins GCN, ISCC provides the necessary software and training and support for its usage. Once training is completed, all member-firm cross-border transactions can be cleared and settled through GCN.

The first step in the process is that members transmit instructions to ISCC in one of three ways: SWIFT network, CPU connection using the ISO/SWIFT format, or NSCC software. In the next step, ISCC collects and processes those instructions and delivers them to the relevant countries for processing, clearance, and settlement. Then GCN's local partner in the foreign country sends back statements detailing pending trades, settled transactions and fails, and securities and cash positions.

In conjunction with the clearance and settlement services, ISCC offers several other services as well. First, the *foreign securities comparison and netting system* automates the comparison and netting of non-U.S. transactions executed by members of NSCC. This system allows non-U.S. equity transactions to be processed in NSCC's OTC comparison system.

Second, the *Canadian depository for securities link* provides book-entry clearance and settlement to Canadian participants that trade equities and corporate bonds with U.S. counterparts. In addition, NSCC offers *London link for UK securities*, which enables U.S. broker–dealers to compare and settle UK equities transactions with LSE members and other ISCC members.

Euroclear

The Euroclear system is the world's largest clearance and settlement system for internationally traded securities. Settlement is delivery-versus-payment in book-entry form. More than 100,000 securities are accepted for settlement through the Euroclear system, the majority of which are domestic securities from more than 40 countries. The annual turnover value within the Euroclear system was $21.9 trillion, $25.0 trillion, $34.6 trillion, and $38.1 trillion over the period 1994 to 1997. During the first six months of 1998, the system settled $22.0 trillion of transactions ($18.4 trillion during the same period in 1997).

Most trades are settled in an overnight batch-processing cycle. A daylight processing cycle is also available, and is often used to facilitate settlement repairs from the previous overnight settlement process. The settlement processing options include:

- Priority codes to manage the processing sequence of instructions for securities deliveries

- Linked settlement instructions to increase settlement efficiency of back-to-back trades or to segregate client settlement activity
- Express processing so participants can submit urgent, postdeadline, cross-border settlement instructions for certain securities

These options are communicated with Euroclear Operations Center (EOC) in Brussels via EUCLID network, SWIFT, or telex. The EUCLID network is a Euroclear proprietary communications infrastructure that provides a two-way communications channel for quick, easy, and cost-effective access to Euroclear services. The EUCLID network also provides:

- A vehicle to input instructions for all Euroclear services
- Immediate validation of instructions
- A comprehensive range of reports
- User-friendly functions for managing information
- Easy inquiry of information databases
- Flexibility to access the network in different modes

High-volume users can access EOC via automated EUCLID *file transfer,* which provides a direct link between EUCLID and the participant's own computer system. The EUCLID *server* allows participants to move toward a real-time communications environment in sync with the real-time settlement processing evolution of the Euroclear system. Low-to-medium volume users can access the network via EUCLID PC, a Windows-based software application.

The SWIFT network can be used for conveying instructions to EOC and receiving Euroclear reports. For participants that do not need to invest in a network, it is also possible to communicate with EOC by telex.

Euroclear also offers a *securities lending and borrowing program* to participants to avoid costly fails, as securities may be borrowed automatically during the settlement process. This results in a high settlement efficiency of 98%. Through this program, lenders of securities can supplement their portfolio returns by lending securities for a fee to other participants that seek to avoid fails. Lenders earn competitive lending returns with no administrative burdens. They also retain most benefits of ownership when their securities are lent. In addition, Morgan Guaranty guarantees the return of lent securities (or cash equivalent). The average daily value of securities loans was $6.7 billion, $5.3 billion, $6.0 billion, and $6.7 billion each year during 1994 to 1997. The daily average for the first six months of 1998 was $7.3 billion.

Euroclear provides custody services to participants as well, including:

- Securities information
- Standardized procedures to exercise conversions or other options and offers, and to take action on elective events
- Cash management through advance notice of income and redemption proceeds
- Automatic collection and administration of income and redemption proceeds
- Simplified withholding tax treatment and procedures and extensive documentation to help participants use the system effectively

The value of securities in custody at Euroclear was $2.116 trillion in 1996. The value rose to $2.275 trillion at yearend 1997.

Cedel Bank

Cedel Bank offers against payment settlement for more than 100,000 internationally traded securities. Supporting services include automatic securities lending, flexible financing, custody, and cash management. The daily clearance and settlement value averages $60 billion, and $100 billion on peak days. Cedel uses DVP to minimize risk. On occasions when a customer cannot deliver securities at the designated time, Cedel borrows securities on the user's behalf to fulfill the settlement commitments. Likewise, Cedel lends cash to ensure smooth settlement.

Transactions are settled twice a day. All valid instructions received by 19:45 Central European Time (CET) are processed overnight to settle the next day. The overnight processing begins in the evening of the business day prior to the settlement date. Early in the morning the following reports are available to customers:

- *General report* lists settlements and new cash and securities balances.
- *Suspense report* lists outstanding unsettled transactions.
- *Portfolio report* lists the customers' securities holdings.

A second cycle takes place during the day, with all valid instructions received by 12:30 CET settled the same day. The daytime processing provides an additional interface with domestic markets and allows customers to execute same-day settlement with Cedel Bank counterparties. Transactions that failed during the overnight processing can be reconsidered for settlement in the daytime processing in addition to new or amended instructions entered before the deadline of 12:30 CET. General, portfolio, and suspense reports are available after the daytime processing.

Settlement instructions can be sent via the SWIFT network or Cedel's system, Cedcom 2000. Once an instruction is received by Cedel Bank, it is checked automatically against validation rules such as the International Securities Identification Number (ISIN) field to ensure that the instruction has been correctly inputted. Once validated, the instruction is considered to be a settlement order. If the instruction is not validated, the customer will be informed immediately so that the instruction can be rectified and a new instruction can be sent before processing deadlines.

Cedel offers a *new issues acceptance* service to lead managers, issuing and paying agents and their advisers. The lead manager or issuing and paying agent must advise Cedel Bank how the new issue will be distributed: securities may be delivered after the closing ceremony or prereleased, and distribution may be against payment or free of payment from the lead manager or issuing and paying agent's syndication account. Syndicated new issues of euro and international issues are typically distributed in the overnight processing following the closing ceremony with back valuation to closing date. Money market instruments and short- and medium-term notes are typically prereleased.

GLOBAL AND EMERGING MARKETS CUSTODIANS

With the increasing integration of the global capital markets, the business of custody is a worldwide activity. The custody industry is undergoing rapid consolidation to better service clients that are internationally invested and are increasingly active in emerging markets. Most global custodians provide services covering the global custody network, global risk management, comprehensive reporting, cash management and foreign exchange, corporate actions and tax reclaims, multicurrency portfolio valuation, fund administration services, and securities lending.

The most recent *Global Custody* survey reports the top-rated custodian on each of the following categories:

- *Experience/organization/control:* quality of personnel and the extent to which senior management maintains a focus on the business
- *Settlement:* performance on the fail rate, deadlines for notification of trade details, affirmation/prematching process, and adequacy of resources to accommodate peak volumes
- *Safekeeping:* provision of segregated accounts in local markets, effectiveness in registration of securities, corporate actions, and collection of dividends
- *Cash and foreign exchange:* the number of currencies on which clients on temporary account balances can earn interest and the rates of interest paid
- *Client service-investment managers:* consistency in meeting service expectations and the reliability of technology
- *Client service-pension funds:* providing advice, education and training, and the accessibility of bank staff to pension funds
- *Custody reporting:* assessment based on timeliness, accuracy, completeness, and ease of use
- *Valuation reporting:* valuation system built to accommodate accounting and valuation practices.
- *Network management:* the management of subcustodian networks and the overall reach of the network (number of markets serviced)
- *Securities lending:* sound collateral margin, prudent collateral management, and professional counterparty risk management
- *Offshore mutual funds:* the quality of servicing and administering offshore funds
- *Technology:* real-time processing, flexible interfaces, and user-friendly applications
- *Performance management:* providing relative performance information and explaining performance attribution in terms of asset allocation, manager selection, and security selection
- *Derivatives:* trading expertise, execution, global margin handling, and valuation and reporting.

Results of the survey arc listed in Table 15.1. Overall, the top-rated custodians include Chase Manhattan, Morgan Stanley Trust, State Street, Citibank, Bankers Trust, and Brown Brothers Harriman.

Clearing and settlement in emerging markets are often more complex than in the more established markets. The fail rates (the percentage of trades failed to settle on settlement date) in emerging markets are much higher. In 1996, the fail rate in China was more than 30%; India, more than 60%; South Africa, more than 40%; and Venezuela, more than 50%. It is important to use a knowledgeable and efficient custodian. Table 15.2 lists top-rated agent banks in each of the 48 emerging markets included in the *1996 Emerging Market Agent Bank Review*. The rating evaluates the quality of services that agent banks provide their international clients, in the areas of settlement, safekeeping, reporting, account administration, technology, and ancillary services. Overall, Citibank, Bank of Boston, Barclays Bank, Standard Chartered, and HongKong Bank are perceived to be the best service providers in emerging markets.

TABLE 15.1   Global Custodian

Area of Service	Custodian
Experience/organization/control	Chase Manhattan, State Street
Settlement	Bank of New York, Chase Manhattan
Safekeeping	Bankers Trust, Citibank, Deutsche Bank
Cash and foreign exchange	Chase Manhattan, Citibank
Client service-investment managers	Bank of New York, Brown Brothers Harriman, Chase Manhattan, Morgan Stanley Trust
Client service-pension funds	Royal Trust, State Street
Custody reporting	Morgan Stanley Trust
Valuation reporting	Northern Trust, State Street
Network management	Bank of New York, Brown Brothers Harriman
Securities lending	State Street
Offshore mutual funds	Bank of Bermuda, State Street
Technology	Chase Manhattan, Morgan Stanley Trust, State Street
Performance management	Bankers Trust, Mellon Trust
Derivatives	Bankers Trust, Chase Manhattan, Citibank

Source: Adapted from *Global Custody Survey*. Asset International, 1997.

TABLE 15.2   Emerging Market Agent Bank

Emerging Country	Bank
Argentina	Citibank, Bank of Boston
Bangladesh	Standard Chartered
Bermuda	Bank of Bermuda, Bank of NT Butterfield
Botswana	Barclays Bank, Stanbic Bank
Brazil	Citibank, Bank of Boston
Chile	Citibank
China	HongKong Bank, Standard Chartered
Columbia	Citibank
Cyprus[1]	Barclays Bank, Bank of Cyprus, Cyprus Popular
Czech Republic	Ceskoslovenska Obchodni Banka
Ecuador	Citibank, Banco de Pacifico
Egypt[1]	National Bank of Egypt, Citibank, Egyptian British Bank
Estonia[1]	Hansabank
Ghana[1]	Barclays Bank
Greece	Citibank, National Bank of Greece
Hungary	Citibank
Iceland[1]	Islandsbanki
India	HongKong Bank, Standard Chartered Bank, Deutsche Bank
Indonesia	HongKong Bank, Citibank, Standard Chartered Bank, Deutsche Bank
Israel	Bank Hapoalim, Bank Leumi, Israel Discount Bank
Jamaica[1]	Scotiabank Jamaica Trust & Merchant Bank
Jordan[1]	Arab Bank, British Bank, Citibank
Kenya[1]	Barclays Bank, Stanbic Bank
Korea	HongKong Bank, Standard Chartered, Seoulbank
Lithuania[1]	Vilniaus Bankas
Malaysia	HongKong Bank, Standard Chartered

(continues)

Mauritius[1]	HongKong Bank
Mexico	Citibank
Morocco	Banque Commercial du Maroc
Oman[1]	British Bank
Pakistan	Standard Chartered Equitor
Peru	Citibank
Philippines	HongKong Bank, Standard Chartered Equitor
Poland	Citibank, Bank Handlowy W Warszawie, Bank Polska Kasa Opieki
Romania[1]	Banca Bucaresti, Societe Generale
Russia	Citibank, Credit Suisse, Ing Bank
Slovakia[1]	Ceskolovenska Obchodni Banka
Slovenia[1]	SKB Bank
Sri Lanka	Standard Chartered Equitor, HongKong Bank
Swaziland[1]	Barclays Bank, Stanbic Bank
Taiwan	Central Trust of China, Citibank, Standard Chartered, HongKong Bank
Thailand	Standard Chartered, HongKong Bank, Citibank, Deutsche Bank
Tunisia[1]	Banque International Arable de Tunisie
Turkey	Citibank, Ottoman Bank
Uruguay[1]	Bank of Boston, Citibank, ABN-AMRO
Venezuela	Citibank
Zambia[1]	Barclays Bank, Stanbic Bank
Zimbabwe[1]	Barclays Bank, Stanbic Bank

[1]Indicates that there is not much activity in market; listed banks are ready to provide services.
Source: Adapted from *Global Custodian 1996 Emerging Market Agent Bank Review.* Asset International, 1997.

SUMMARY

This chapter discusses the post-trade procedures that ensure a safe trading environment and an efficient capital market. This chapter describes the processes of clearing and settlement for various types of securities and transactions, including government securities, corporate securities, mortgage-backed securities, and international transactions. An understanding of the back-office operations will certainly benefit front-office business.

SELECT BIBLIOGRAPHY

Asset International. *Global Custodian 1996 Emerging Markets Agent Bank Review.* Asset International, 1997.

Asset International. *Global Custody Survey.* Asset International, 1997.

Cedel Bank. *Services and Products.* 1998.

Euroclear. *Services and Products.* 1998.

Government Securities Clearing Corporation. *Services and Products.* 1998.

International Securities Clearing Corporation. *Services and Products.* 1998.

Mingle, D. L. "Behind the money market: Clearing and settling money market instruments." In *Readings on Financial Institutions and Markets*, Peter Rose, ed. Burr Ridge, IL: Irwin, 1994.

Mortgage-Backed Securities Clearing Corporation. *Services and Products.* 1998.

National Securities Clearing Corporation. *Annual Reports*. NSCC, 1998.

Stigum, M. *After the Trade*. Burr Ridge, IL:Irwin Professional Publishing, 1988.

Weiss, D. M. *After the Trade Is Made*. New York: New York Institute of Finance, 1993.

Weiss, D. M. *Global Securities Processing*. New York: New York Institute of Finance, 1998.

16

Securities Regulation and Ethics

The main objectives of securities regulation are facilitating capital formation and protecting the interest of the investing public. Registration of new securities ensures full and accurate disclosure of material information. Exemptions of registration are available when the securities are sold to certain qualified institutional investors or the amount of issuance is limited. Active secondary-market trading is key to successful primary market capital raising activities. Hence, regulating sales and trading in the secondary markets is to ensure fairness and maintain public trust. Professional investment management has become an essential part of the capital markets. Regulation of investment companies and investment advisers is in the public interest and for the protection of investors. Furthermore, integrity and professionalism are basic to success on Wall Street. This chapter provides a brief coverage on the full spectrum of these issues.

INTRODUCTION

Securities regulation provides protection for investors and ensures that the securities markets are transparent and fair. The Securities and Exchange Commission (SEC) is the regulatory agency with responsibility for administering the federal securities laws. The SEC enforces the following securities acts:[1]

- *Securities Act of 1933:* requires registration of a new security issue unless an exemption is available, also known as "truth in securities" law
- *Securities Exchange Act of 1934:* requires timely and accurate disclosure of material information, prohibits sales practice abuses and insider trading
- *Investment Company Act of 1940:* activities of "investment companies" are subject to SEC regulation
- *Investment Advisers Act of 1940:* requires registration of investment advisers and compliance with statutory standards
- *Trust Indenture Act of 1939:* the trust indenture of a debt security must conform to the statutory standards of the act

The SEC delegates significant regulatory authority to a number of securities industry self-regulatory organizations (SROs). These SROs include National Association of Securities Dealers (NASD), the New York Stock Exchange (NYSE), the American Stock Exchange (AMEX), the Chicago Board Options Exchange (CBOE), regional exchanges, and the Municipal Securities Rulemaking Board (MSRB). These SROs are responsible for establishing rules governing securities practices and markets, reviewing fair dealing by members, examining securities firms for compliance with financial requirements, surveilling the markets, taking enforcement action for proven violations, and arbitrating disputes. The SEC must approve all SRO rules and regulations before they can take effect.

The next two sections cover securities regulation in the issuance of new securities and in sales and trading in the secondary markets. Subsequent sections describe regulation of broker–dealers, investment companies, and investment advisers. The discussion naturally flows to ethics and professionalism.

ISSUANCE OF SECURITIES

The Securities Act of 1933 (*Securities Act*) governs the issuance of new securities. At the same time, the Securities Act exempts private placements and certain transactions that involve either a limited dollar amount, certain qualified investors, or are offered only on an intrastate basis. The National Securities Markets Improvement Act of 1996 (NSMIA) exempts state regulation of securities listed on the NYSE, the AMEX, the National Market System of the Nasdaq, securities sold in certain exempt offerings, and mutual funds.

Registration of Securities Offerings

The Securities Act requires issuers to register their securities offerings[2] and supply financial and other material information that will enable investors to make informed decisions. As such, the objectives are to ensure that investors are provided with material information of the offerings and to prevent misrepresentation, deceit, and other fraud in the sale of securities. The standard that must be met when registering securities is adequate and accurate disclosure of material facts concerning the issuer and the securities.

A security is registered with the SEC by filing a registration statement in triplicate (forms for registration are listed in Appendix A). Issuer's principal executive officer or officers, its financial officer, its comptroller or principal accounting officer, and the majority of its board of directors shall sign at least one copy. For a foreign issuer, its duly-authorized representative in the United States has to sign the registration statement. In the case when a foreign government issues the security, the underwriter has to sign it. At the time of filing a registration statement, the applicant must pay to the SEC a registration fee equal to 0.0278% of the aggregate offering amount (gradually reduced to 0.0067% by year 2007). The information contained or filed with any registration statement shall be made available to the public.

Information and documents required in *registration statements* are specified in Schedule A, unless the security is issued by a foreign government or political subdivision, in which case Schedule B applies. Specifically, information required in Schedule A includes:

1. The name of the issuer
2. The name of the State or other sovereign power under which the issuer is organized
3. The location of the issuer's principal business office, and if the issuer is a foreign or territorial person, the name and address of its agent in the U.S. authorized to receive notice
4. The names and addresses of the directors, the chief executive, and financial and accounting officers
5. The names and addresses of the underwriters
6. The names and addresses of all persons owning of record or beneficially more than 10% of any class of stock of the issuer, or more than 10% in the aggregate of the outstanding stock of the issuer as of a date within 20 days prior to the filing of the registration statement
7. The amount of securities of the issuer held by any person specified in (4), (5), and (6), as of a date within 20 days prior to the filing of the registration statement
8. The general character of the business
9. A statement of the capitalization of the issuer
10. A statement of the securities covered by options outstanding or to be created in connection with the security to be offered
11. The amount of capital stock of each class issued or included in the shares of stock to be offered
12. The amount of the funded debt outstanding and to be created by the security to be offered, with a brief description of such security
13. The specific purposes in detail
14. Remuneration paid, or estimated to be paid, to directors and officers
15. The estimated net proceeds from the security to be offered
16. The proposed offering price or the method by which such price is computed
17. All commissions or discounts paid or to be paid, directly or indirectly, by the issuer to the underwriters in respect of the sale of the security to be offered
18. The estimated amounts of other expenses
19. The net proceeds derived from any security sold by the issuer during the past two years, the offering price, and the names of the principal underwriters of such security
20. Any amount paid within two years preceding the filing of the registration statement or intended to be paid to any promoter and the consideration for any such payment
21. The names and addresses of the vendors and the purchase price of any property, or good will, acquired or to be acquired, which is to be defrayed in whole or in part from the proceeds of the security to be offered
22. Full particulars of the nature and extent of the interest, if any, of every director, principal executive officer, and of every stockholder holding more than 10% of any class of stock
23. The names and addresses of counsel who have passed on the legality of the issue
24. Dates of and parties to, and the general effect concisely stated of, every material contract made, not in the ordinary course of business, which contract is to be executed in whole or in part at or after the filing of the registration statement or which contract has been made within two years before such filing

25. A balance sheet as of a date not more than 90 days prior to the filing date of the registration statement showing all of the assets and liabilities of the issuer in detail
26. A profit and loss statement of the issuer showing earnings and income, the nature and source thereof, and the expenses and fixed charges in detail
27. If the proceeds or any part of the proceeds of the security are to be applied to the purchase of any business, a profit and loss statement of such business certified by an independent public or certified accountant
28. A copy of any agreement or agreements made with any underwriter, including all contracts and agreements referred to in (17) of this schedule
29. A copy of the opinion or opinions of counsel in respect to the legality of the issue
30. A copy of all material contracts referred to in (24) of this schedule
31. Unless previously filed and registered under the provisions of this title, and brought up to date, a copy of its articles of incorporation
32. A copy of the underlying agreements or indentures affecting any stock, bonds, or debentures offered or to be offered

For a security issued by a foreign government or political subdivision, the requirements are (Schedule B):

1. Name of borrowing government or subdivision
2. Specific purposes in detail and the approximate amounts to be devoted to such purpose
3. The amount of the funded debt and the estimated amount of the floating debt outstanding and to be created by the security to be offered, excluding intergovernmental debt, and a brief description of such debt
4. Whether or not the issuer or its predecessor has, within a period of 20 years prior to the filing of the registration statement, defaulted on the principal or interest of any external security
5. The receipts and the expenditures in detail for the latest fiscal year for which such information is available and the two preceding fiscal years, year by year
6. The names and addresses of the underwriters
7. The name and address of its authorized agent, if any, in the United States
8. The estimated net proceeds to be derived from the sale in the United States of the security to be offered
9. The proposed offering price in the United States to the public or the method by which such price is computed
10. All commissions paid or to be paid, directly or indirectly, by the issuer to the underwriters in respect of the sale of the security to be offered
11. The amount or estimated amounts of other expenses
12. The names and addresses of counsel who have passed upon the legality of the issue
13. A copy of any agreement or agreements made with any underwriter governing the sale of the security within the United States
14. An agreement of the issuer to furnish a copy of the opinion or opinions of counsel in respect to the legality of the issue

After the registration statement is filed with the SEC, the *waiting period* begins. During this waiting period, the SEC's Division of Corporate Finance reviews it to ensure full and accurate disclosure. The waiting period was originally 20 days. Now it is much longer. If it appears to the SEC staff that the registration statement is incomplete or inaccurate in any material respect, the Commission may issue an order refusing such statement to become effective until it has been amended in accordance with such order. Concurrent with the SEC's review, the NASD Regulation's Corporate Financing Department[3] also reviews the offering to ensure that the amount of underwriting compensation to be paid to the NASD members underwriting the issue is fair and within NASD's guidelines. After the SEC has determined that the amendments satisfy its comments and has been informed that NASD Regulation has no objections to the underwriting compensation, terms, and arrangements, the SEC issues an order allowing the registration statement to become effective (*declared effective*). At that point, sales to the public can take place.

When the issue is *in registration,* the investment bank may not provide any other information to its clients other than what is contained in the *preliminary prospectus* (*red herring*). During the waiting period, the issuing company or underwriter may not instigate publicity to promote the security. Using the red herring, the underwriters may offer the security and accept *indications of interest.* However, no sales may be made.

Once an issue has been declared effective, the security is placed and trading begins. If this is an IPO and the issue is traded on Nasdaq or an exchange, then, for 25 days after the effective date, a buyer is entitled to a prospectus. The requirement extends 90 days after the effective date if the security is not traded on Nasdaq or listed on an exchange. The *final prospectus* is similar to the red herring. Except it will have the missing numbers for the offering price and the effective date filled in.

In order for the stock to begin trading on Nasdaq or an exchange, an issuer must sign a listing agreement and meet certain quantitative and often qualitative standards set by Nasdaq or the exchange. These include a minimum per-share bid, public float, market value of public float, company assets, and capital. In addition, a minimum number of market makers is required for trading on the Nasdaq.

The states also regulate the registration of new securities through state blue-sky laws. The National Securities Markets Improvement Act of 1996 (NSMIA) exempts from state registration securities that are listed on the Nasdaq National Market, the NYSE, or the AMEX. Unlike the SEC regulation that ensures full and accurate disclosure, some state laws deal with the merits of a security.

In addition, debt securities can be offered for public sale only under a trust indenture approved by the SEC. The Trust Indenture Act of 1939 applies to debt securities offered for public sale and issued under trust indentures with more than $7.5 million of securities outstanding at any one time. Such securities, even though they may be registered, may not be offered for public sale unless the trust indenture conforms to the statutory standards of this act. The act is aimed at safeguarding the rights and interests of the purchasers. To meet this objective, the act prohibits the indenture trustee from conflicting interests, requires the trustee to be a corporation with required capital and surplus, and requires the trustee to provide reports and notices to security holders.

EXEMPT OFFERINGS

The Securities Act provides for certain exemptions of registration; that is, under certain conditions, a company can sell its securities as a private placement. A private placement of securities is intended to be limited in frequency and scope. The principal exemptions[4] available are the traditional private placements, Rule 144A, and Regulation S safe harbors.

Private Placements

A private placement under Rule 505 and Rule 506 of Regulation D is generally limited to 35 nonaccredited investors, but there is no limit on the number of accredited investors. Accredited investors must have a net worth of $1 million, or an annual income of $200,000, or an annual family income of $300,000. A private placement memorandum must be prepared. The securities acquired are considered *restricted securities*, and they may not be freely traded until registered with the SEC.

Rule 504 of Regulation D provides exemption from SEC registration for an amount up to $1 million. However, these offerings must comply with state blue-sky laws. Under Rule 504, there are "test the waters" and SCOR offering. Massachusetts has a "test the waters" exemption, which permits a public solicitation for indications of interest, but the security must be registered with the state Securities Division before sale. A SCOR (small corporate offering registration) offering is exempt from SEC registration, but must be registered or qualified under state law. Many states allow registration on a Form U-7.

An exemption from SEC registration is also available for an *intrastate offering*, where the securities are sold only to residents of a single state and the issuer is both a resident and doing business within that state. Another type of exempt offering is under Regulation A. It allows a company to raise capital through public offering of up to $5 million per year, including no more than $1.5 million in secondary offerings.

Rule 144 governs the sale of restricted securities and *control securities.* Restricted securities are purchased in unregistered nonpublic offerings, and control securities are held by affiliates of the issuer. Generally, a one-year holding period applies when the volume of securities sold is limited to the greater of 1% of all outstanding shares or the average weekly trading volume for the preceding four weeks. If the shares have been owned for two years or more, no volume restrictions apply to nonaffiliates. Affiliates are always subject to volume restrictions. The term *affiliate* includes the chief executive officer, inside directors, holders of at least 20% of the company voting power, and holders of at least 10% of the company's voting power with at least one director on the company's board of directors.

Rule 144A

Rule 144A addresses private sales of restricted securities among qualified institutional buyers (QIBs). Rule 144A states four conditions that the securities and the transaction must satisfy. First, the securities must be sold to QIBs. Second, the seller or any other person acting on behalf of the seller must take reasonable steps to ensure that the purchaser is aware that the seller may rely on the exemption of registration and associated requirements. Third, the current holder of the securities and the prospective purchaser have the right to obtain certain basic information from the issuer if the issuer is not subject to reporting requirements. Finally, the securities, when issued, are not of the same class as securities listed on a national exchange or quoted in a U.S. automated interdealer quotation system, and the issuer is not an open-end investment company or a unit investment trust.

A QIB sometimes is called a sophisticated investor and is an entity acting for its own account or the accounts of other QIBs that in aggregate owns and invests on a discretionary basis at least $100 million in securities of issuers not affiliated with the entity. For a registered dealer, the qualification is at least $10 million of securities. A QIB also includes:

- A registered dealer acting in a riskless principal transaction on behalf of a QIB
- Any investment company registered under the Investment Company Act that is part of investment companies that together own at least $100 million of such securities
- Any entity, all of whose equity owners are QIBs
- Any bank or S&L or similar institution that in aggregate with other QIBs owns and invests at least $100 million in such securities and that has a net worth of at least $25 million

Regulation S

Regulation S under the Securities Act was adopted in 1990 in order to provide companies with clear guidelines as to the circumstances under which Regulation S securities sold overseas are not subject to the SEC registration. The provisions of Regulation S require that such securities not be advertised in the United States, and there is a restricted period during which Regulation S securities cannot be resold in the United States.

Regulation S establishes *issuer safe harbor* and *resale safe harbor*. Issuer safe harbor deals with offers and sales by issuers, underwriters, and other persons involved in the distribution process pursuant to a contract. The resale safe harbor applies to resales by persons other than the issuer, distributors and their respective affiliates. Two general conditions must be satisfied to take advantage of the issuer and resale safe harbors. The first condition is that any offer or sale must be made in an offshore transaction. The second general condition is that no direct selling efforts may be made in the United States.

To qualify for the issuer safe harbor, the issuer's offer or sales must be made in an offshore transaction and the offer must not be made to a person in the United States. In accordance, compliance must be made with regard to (1) reasonable belief that the buyer is outside the United States at the time of the transaction and (2) submission of evidence that the sale is made through an established exchange or through a designated offshore securities market. For resale safe harbor, Regulation S permits resale in an offshore transaction without any directed sales effort into the United States. Also, after the expiration of the restricted period, the securities can be resold into the United States provided that such sales are made in compliance with the U.S. securities laws.

Since its adoption in 1990, the SEC has identified abusive practices in offshore Regulation S securities transactions. In an effort to address these abuses, the SEC has adopted a rule requiring U.S. reporting companies to disclose on Form 8-K offshore sales of equity securities in reliance upon Regulation S within 15 days of sale. A new SEC proposal would require Regulation S sales to be reported by the issuer on Form 10-Q instead of Form 8-K as currently required. The SEC has also proposed to amend Rule 903 of Regulation S. The amendments will lengthen to two years the restricted period. This represents an increase from the current 40-day holding period applicable to reporting issuers and the one-year holding period applicable to nonreporting issuers. The SEC has also proposed to add a new Rule 905 that would classify as restricted securities covered equity securities placed offshore under the issuer safe harbor. This would prohibit unregistered public resales into the United States for at least one year.

SECONDARY TRADING

The Securities Exchange Act of 1934 (*Exchange Act*) governs the secondary market trading. The Exchange Act seeks to ensure fair and orderly securities markets by requiring timely and accurate disclosure of material information, by prohibiting certain types of activities, and by requiring compliance with rules regarding the operation of the markets and participants. The following discussion covers corporate reporting, insider trading, and Regulation M (trading practices in connection with securities offerings).

Corporate Reporting

Following the registration of their securities, companies must file annual and other periodic reports with the SEC. These filings are available through EDGAR as well as on the SEC's Web site. Appendix B lists forms prescribed under the Exchange Act.

The first reporting requirement is the Form 10-K, which is an annual report to stockholders. It discloses in detail information about the company's activities and results of operations. It contains the company's annual financial reports. The report is due within 90 days of the yearend. Also, a quarterly report on Form 10-Q is required for each of the first three quarters of the fiscal year. It includes condensed financial data and information on significant events. The report must be filed within 45 days of quarter-end. In addition, a Form 8-K that reports any significant events is due within 15 days of the event. The types of information generally considered material include financial results, new products, acquisitions or dispositions of assets, and changes in dividends, management, or corporate control.

Under the SEC rules, all proposed proxy material must be filed in advance for examination to ensure compliance with disclosure requirements. Proxy solicitations must make public all material facts concerning matters on which security holders are asked to vote. Plus, the Williams Act requires reporting and disclosure when control of a company is sought through a tender offer or other planned stock acquisition of more than 5%. This disclosure is also required of anyone soliciting shareholders to accept or reject a tender offer.

Insider Trading

There are two types of *insider trading*. One is the legal trading by insiders, corporate officers and directors, and beneficial owners of more than 10% of registered equity shares. Such insiders must file an initial report on their holdings with the SEC. Thereafter, they must file reports during the month when there are changes in their holdings.

The illegal *insider trading* is trading on material nonpublic information. State law plays a limited role in regulating insider trading. The one limited way is through rules against fraud and deceit. Many states have adopted what is known as *special facts doctrine* and some states have expended the doctrine into the *Kansas rule*. Both are very limited in regulating insider trading. Both theories apply only where there is an existing shareholder trading with an insider. Also, both rules require privity or face-to-face transactions. Therefore, state law mostly comes into play with stock transactions in closely held companies.

Primarily, Rule 10b-5 of the Exchange Act governs such insider trading. Under Rule 10b-5,

> *It shall be unlawful for any person, directly or indirectly, by the use of any means or instrumentality of interstate commerce, or of the mails, or of any facility of any national securities exchange, (a) to employ any device, scheme, or artifice to defraud, (b) to make any untrue statement of a material fact or to omit to state a material fact necessary in order to make the statements made, in the light of the circumstances under which they were made, not misleading, or (c) to engage in any act, practice, or course of business which operates or would operate as a fraud or deceit upon any person, in connection with the purchase or sale of any security.*

Five elements must be proved to impose criminal or civil liability under Rule 10b-5:

1. *Misinformation:* The defendant must misrepresent a fact or not disclose a fact.
2. *Material and nonpublic:* The fact must be material and nonpublic.
3. *Knowledge:* The defendant must know that he or she made a misrepresentation and intended for the plaintiff to rely on it.
4. *Reliance:* The plaintiff must rely on the information in the transactions.
5. *Causation and injury:* The plaintiff must show that his or her trades relied on such information, such misinformation caused losses, and the plaintiff suffered damages.

However, Rule 10b-5 liability cannot be imposed on everyone who trades on the basis of material nonpublic information. As an example, a person with no fiduciary responsibility to the shareholders of the company in whose stock he or she trades does not violate Rule 10b-5 so long as the person is not a "tippee" or "misappropriator." Rule 10b-5 liability can generally be imposed on four types of groups:

1. *Insiders and constructive insiders:* Corporate insiders and constructive insiders (attorneys, investment bankers and accountants hired by the company) have an abstain-or-disclose duty while in possession of material nonpublic information. It is a violation of regulation if they trade on such information.
2. *Tippers:* An insider or constructive insider who never trades may be in violation for tipping the material nonpublic information to someone who trades based on such information.
3. *Tippees and subtippees:* A tippee or a tippee of the tippee can be liable for trading on such nonpublic material information.
4. *Misappropriators:* Under the misappropriation theory, an outsider can be criminally liable if he or she breaches a duty arising from a relationship of trust and confidence and uses that information in securities transactions, regardless of whether that person owed any fiduciary responsibility to the shareholders of the traded stock.

The misappropriation theory is an important weapon in SEC's fight against insider trading. As in the case *United States v. O'Hagan*, an attorney hired by an acquirer is criminally liable if the attorney trades on the target's stocks while in possession of confidential information that the firm's client was planning to launch a tender offer for another company. The attorney would not have been liable without the misappropriation theory. In the case of *O'Hagan*, he was not an insider or constructive insider of the target company, and he was not a tippee of an insider or constructive insider of the target. He learned of the tender offer from the acquirer, the company to which he was a constructive insider. The misappropriation theory extends Rule 10b-5 to cover this situation. The misappropriation theory also extends liability to the tippers and tippees of the person who misappropriated the information.

In addition, Rule 14e-3 prohibits trading during the course of a tender offer by anyone, other than the bidder, who has material nonpublic information about the offers that was knowingly obtained either from the bidder or the target. Thus, Rule 14e-3 provides that the misappropriation theory may be used to hold a person liable for securities fraud involving tender offers.

Regulation M

Regulation M became effective on March 4, 1997. It governs trading practices during securities distributions. The new Regulation M replaces the former "anti-manipulation" rules. Regulation M significantly reduces the trading restrictions during a distribution by narrowing the basic coverage of the restrictions, expanding old exemptions, and adding new exemptions. Significant changes from the previous trading practices rules are outlined in the following paragraphs.

The first significant change is the deregulation of brokerage firm trading in actively traded securities. Underwriters, prospective underwriters, and their affiliated purchasers are generally no longer subject to any trading restrictions during the distribution of *actively traded securities*. Actively traded securities are securities with a public float of $150 million and an average daily trading volume (ADTV) value of at least $1 million. Another exemption is called the *De Minimis* exemption. Inadvertent purchases by an underwriter, prospective underwriter or affiliated purchaser of less than 2% of the ADTV of the security being distributed are exempt from the trading restrictions. Basket transactions are also exempt. The exemption applies to basket securities containing a covered security where the basket contains at least 20 securities and the covered security is no more than 5% of the basket value.

Second, Regulation M provides several new exemptions or exclusions from the trading restrictions. Restrictions on trading in derivatives such as options, warrants and convertible securities are eliminated when the offering involves only a distribution of the underlying securities. New exemptions are provided for trading in investment-grade asset-backed securities, Rule 144As, odd-lot transactions, and distribution pursuant to dividend reinvestment plans and employee plans.

Third, the restricted periods are shortened. Regulation M limits buying and soliciting of purchases by issuers, selling shareholders, and their affiliated purchasers during the restricted period. The restricted period starts either one business day or five business days[5] prior to the day of pricing and runs through the end of the distribution. The one-business-day restricted period applies to offered securities with ADTV of $100,000 or more and a public float of $25 million. Offered securities that do not meet these qualifications are subject to a restricted period of five business days.

In addition, Regulation M permits broker–dealers to engage in passive market-making transactions in all Nasdaq securities. Passive market making is disallowed only when

Nasdaq securities are distributed in an "at the market" or best-efforts offering. Regulation M also provides that a stabilizing bid can be maintained, reduced, or raised to follow the independent market as long as the bid does not exceed the lower of the offering price or the stabilizing bid for the security in the principal market. Finally, Regulation M reduces the period during which short sales that are covered by securities purchased in an offering are prohibited. Short sales are prohibited during the period starting five business days prior to pricing. This is in contrast to the former rule, which prohibited such short sales starting at the filing date of the registration statement.

BROKER–DEALER REGISTRATION AND REGULATION

The registration of brokers and dealers engaged in soliciting and executing securities transactions is an important part of the regulatory plan of the Exchange Act. Under the Exchange Act, there is a high degree of industry self-regulation as well. Each exchange is responsible for setting standards of qualification and monitoring the conduct of its members. The NASD performs this function with respect to broker–dealers in the OTC market. Every registered broker–dealer must be a member of the NASD, except for certain exchange members who carry no customer accounts and conduct all of their business on the exchange. Thus, all U.S. broker–dealer registrants file one application for registration on Form BD with the NASD, which in turn passes over the application to the SEC for review. Foreign applicants are required to forward certain application materials such as Forms 9M and 10M directly to the SEC, as well as to the NASD.

Form BD requires detailed information regarding the broker–dealer applicant, its principals, and controlling persons. Form BD must be amended whenever there is any material change in the information included in the form. In addition to Form BD, the NASD requires additional materials before it will grant membership approval. These additional documents generally include a statement of financial condition, a copy of the applicant's written supervisory procedures, evidence of fidelity bonding, fingerprint cards and Form F-4 registration applications, a membership fee, and a clearing agreement.

A fidelity bond is to cover the loss, theft, forgery, and misplacement of securities by its personnel. The bond must be 120% of the applicable minimum net capital requirement, subject to an overriding minimum of $25,000. A Form U-4 must be submitted for each candidate who applies for registration as a principal or a representative. For purposes of the NASD registration, a principal is any person actively engaged in the management and supervision of the business. Any employee engaged in the member's investment banking or securities business must qualify and register as a representative. Furthermore, all registered broker–dealers are required to become members of the Securities Investor Protection Corporation (SIPC) and pay annual assessments. The SIPC insurance fund provides each customer with coverage up to $100,000 for cash owed and $500,000 for securities owed by a financially distressed broker–dealer.

All registered broker–dealers are subject to rules of the SEC and the NASD. Major procedural rules include recordkeeping, net capital rule, periodic financial reporting, and continuing education. First, recordkeeping covers basic record creation, maintenance, and preservation. The SEC and the NASD periodically conduct inspections to monitor compliance with the recordkeeping and other internal operating procedures. Second, the net capital rule specifies that the "aggregate indebtedness" may not exceed 800% of "net capital" in the first year of operation and 1,500% thereafter. Aggregate indebtedness includes all liabilities, except for certain subordinated collaterialized debt. The net capital requirements are determined by the broker-dealer's activities; the less contact it has with customer funds and securities, the lower the requirements. For example, the minimum net capital requirement is $5,000 for an introducing broker-dealer that does not hold customer securities and funds. Broker–dealers who are engaged only in riskless principal transactions would be subject to the same minimum requirements. In contrast, introducing broker–dealer that receives funds and securities are subject to a $50,000 minimum requirement. A broker–dealer that provides clearing services to customer transactions but does not hold funds and securities beyond settlement is required to maintain $250,000 in net capital. The maximum requirement of net capital is $1,000,000 for broker–dealers engaged in substantial market-making activities.

Third, all broker–dealers are required to file with the SEC annual financial statements, and copies of these statements must be furnished to the NASD. Finally, the NASD and the SEC introduced continuing education program requirements in 1995. The *Regulatory Element* of continuing education requires individual registered persons to complete NASD administered continuing education sessions within 120 days of the anniversary of the second, fifth, and tenth years of registration. The *Firm Element* requires NASD member broker–dealers to implement, maintain, and administer internal continuing training programs for all covered registered persons.

In addition to the requirements by the SEC and the NASD, practically every state has its own securities law requiring registration of broker-dealers before a broker–dealer conducts its business in the state. Generally, state broker–dealer requirements are no more onerous than the SEC and the NASD requirements. However, associated persons of a broker–dealer may have to take a Series 63 examination in order to qualify in certain states, such as New York.

INVESTMENT COMPANY AND INVESTMENT ADVISERS

The Investment Company Act of 1940 (ICA) governs the regulation of investment companies, while the Investment Advisers Act of 1940 (IAA) regulates the activities of investment advisers including advisers to registered investment companies, private money managers, and most financial planners.

Activities of companies engaged primarily in investing, reinvesting, and trading in securities, and whose own securities are offered to the investing public, are subject to the regulation of ICA. There are three classifications for such investment companies: face-amount certificate company, unit investment trust, and management company. A *face-amount certificate company* is an investment company that is engaged in the business of face-amount certificates of the installment type. A *unit investment trust* is an investment company that is organized under a trust indenture, does not have a board of directors, and issues only redeemable securities. A *management company* is any investment company other than a face-amount certificate company or a unit investment trust.

Every registered investment company is subject to SEC registration requirements. The registration statement must include the following information and documents:

- The policy in respect of types of activities that the registrant proposes to operate, lending and borrowing money, engaging in the business of underwriting securities, concentrating investment in a particular industry or industries, trading of real estate or commodities, and portfolio turnover

- Investment and other important fundamental policies, which are changeable only if authorized by a shareholder vote
- The name and address of each affiliated person of the registrant, and a brief statement of the business experience for the preceding five years of each officer and director of the registrant
- The information and documents that would be required to be filed in order to register under the Securities Act and Exchange Act, and all securities that the registrant has outstanding or proposes to issue

In addition to the registration requirement, the ICA bars persons guilty of securities fraud from serving as officers or directors and requires that management contracts and any other material changes are submitted to shareholders for their approval. Under the ICA, it is unlawful for any registered investment company to purchase any security on margin or to effect a short sale of any security. The ICA also prevents underwriters, investment bankers, or brokers from constituting more than a minority of the directors of an investment company. In addition, the ICA forbids investment companies to issue senior securities except under specified conditions and upon specified terms.

Other provisions of the ICA involve advisory fees, sales and repurchases of securities issued by the investment companies, exchange offers, and other activities of the investment companies.

Investment Advisers Act of 1940

The IAA regulates the activities of investment advisers, including advisers to investment companies, private money managers, and most financial planners. Registration is required of any person, absent an exclusion or an exemption, engaging in the business of providing advise or issuing reports about securities to clients for compensation. The persons excluded from the definition of investment adviser are:

- U.S. banks and bank holding companies
- Instrumentalities of the United States or any state
- Government securities advisers
- Publishers of bona fide newspapers and magazines of general and regular circulation
- Lawyers, accountants, teachers, and engineers, provided that the advise is solely incidental

There are five statutory exemptions available as well: instrastate advisers, insurance company advisers, private investment advisers, charitable organization advisers, and church employee pension plans. The private adviser exemption is the one most often used by advisers to avoid registration. Private investment advisers are investment advisers who had fewer than 15 clients during the past 12 months, do not hold themselves out to the public as investment advisers, and do not advise any registered investment company. In addition, under the 1996 NSMIA, an adviser that has less than $25 million of assets under management and is not an adviser to a registered investment company may register with the state, and need not register with the SEC.

An investment adviser registers with the SEC by filing a Form ADV. The information required to be disclosed on Form ADV consists of two parts. Part I requires information on the adviser's jurisdiction of incorporation and principal place of business, the ownership and control of the adviser, how the operations are financed, detailed employment histories and educational backgrounds of key personnel, and whether an adviser or an affiliate has been involved in any material civil or criminal or administrative legal proceedings. Part II requires detailed disclosures on the operations and business practices of the investment adviser, and is usually provided to clients. Generally, an adviser's registration becomes effective 45 days after Form ADV is filed with the SEC. After registration, information contained in Form ADV must be kept current through the filing of amendments.

The IAA also establishes requirements governing the operation of a registered adviser and the relationship between the adviser and its clients. The most important requirements include recordkeeping, brochure rule, advisory contacts and performance fees, conflicts and anti-fraud provisions, and duty to supervise. Each of these requirements is briefly explained as follows:

- The IAA requires investment advisers to maintain books and records. Registered investment advisers are required to keep business and financial records and proprietary trading records. All these records are subject to inspection by the SEC at any time.
- The brochure rule requires an adviser to provide each client with a written statement concerning the adviser, its operations, and its principals.
- The IAA requires that any contract for advisory services contain a provision prohibiting the adviser from assigning the contract without the consent of the client (assignment of contracts). The IAA prohibits, with certain exceptions, performance-based compensation (performance fees). There are three exceptions. First, an adviser may charge a *fulcrum fee*, based on the total value of client funds under management over a specified period. Second, a registered investment adviser may charge a performance fee if the client meets an eligibility requirement and the fee formula includes realized losses as well. The third exemption is provided under the NSMIA that an investment adviser is permitted to charge performance fees to persons who are not U.S. residents and to private investment funds that are restricted to qualified purchasers.[6]
- The IAA requires investment advisers to conform to the statutory requirements that prohibit violation of the fiduciary duties on an investment adviser to its clients. The IAA requires an adviser to disclose to clients material facts concerning any conflict of interest.
- Under the IAA, an investment adviser is required to use reasonable efforts to supervise the activities of its employees, agents, and associated persons to prevent violations of related statutes.

If an investment adviser is not registered under the IAA because it has less than $25 million in assets under management and does not advise a registered investment company, then it may be required to register under state law. The NSMIA provides that state registration and other requirements will not apply to any person registered under the IAA or is a supervised person of a registered adviser.

ETHICS

On Wall Street, your word is your bond. Integrity and high ethical standards are basic to success. Without strict regulatory compliance and high ethical standards, any success will eventually fade away. To abide by the highest professional standards is an obligation to all securities industry professionals. Anything less would be a betrayal of the professional obligation.

The SEC enforces securities regulation. There are, however, gray areas in which integrity and ethics is the guiding principle. Successful capital market professionals use reasonable care and practice in a professional and ethical manner. The basics of professional conduct are to maintain knowledge of and comply with all applicable laws and rules. Furthermore, anyone in the securities business shall not knowingly participate in or assist any violation of such laws or rules. Members of the markets shall not engage in any professional conduct involving dishonesty, fraud, deceit, or misrepresentation.

Securities firms should emphasize the high value of their reputation and interest in contributing to enhanced investor protection and the integrity of the securities industry. Firms should insist on compliance and professionalism throughout the firm with senior management leading by example. Special emphasis is that compliance with laws, rules and ethical standards is expected of every employee. Compliance record is made part of performance evaluations. To achieve this, firms should provide vehicles and resources for the transmission of compliance and regulatory information to all employees. In addition, input by compliance professionals is an integral component of decisions relating to hiring and training.

As an employee, there are certain responsibilities to your employer. An employee shall not undertake any independent practice that could result in compensation or other benefit in competition with the employer unless written consent is obtained from both employer and client. When called for, the employee should disclose to the employer all matters, including beneficial ownership of securities or other investments, that could be expected to interfere with his duty or ability to make unbiased and objective recommendations.

When dealing with clients, securities markets professionals should put the customer first and use particular care in determining applicable fiduciary duty and shall comply with such duty. Customers expect fair dealing, preservation of confidentiality, and trust. Misrepresentation of any kind, including qualifications, credentials, and capabilities, is a violation of integrity.

The code of ethics and standards of professional conduct have been put into practice at most investment banks. For example, the business principles of Goldman Sachs are:

1. Our clients' interests always come first. Our experience shows that if we serve our clients well, our own success will follow.
2. Our assets are our people, capital and reputation. If any of these is ever diminished, the last is the most difficult to restore. We are dedicated to complying fully with the letter and spirit of the laws, rules and ethical principles that govern us. Our continued success depends upon unswerving adherence to this standard.
3. We take great pride in the professional quality of our work. We have an uncompromising determination to achieve excellence in everything we undertake. Though we may be involved in a wide variety and heavy volume of activity, we would, if it came to a choice, rather be best than biggest.
4. We stress creativity and imagination in everything we do. While recognizing that the old way may still be the best way, we constantly strive to find a better solution to a client's problems. We pride ourselves on having pioneered many of the practices and techniques that have become standard in the industry.

5. We make an unusual effort to identify and recruit the very best person for every job. Although our activities are measured in billions of dollars, we select our people one by one. In a service business, we know that without the best people, we cannot be the best firm.

6. We offer our people the opportunity to move ahead more rapidly than is possible at most other places. We have yet to find the limits to the responsibility that our best people are able to assume. Advancement depends solely on ability, performance and contribution to the firm's success, without regard to race, color, religion, sex, age, national origin, disability, sexual orientation, or any other impermissible criterion or circumstance.

7. We stress teamwork in everything we do. While individual creativity is always encouraged, we have found that team effort often produces the best results. We have no room for those who put their personal interests ahead of the interests of the firm and its clients.

8. The dedication of our people to the firm and the intense effort they give their jobs are greater than one finds in most other organizations. We think that this is an important part of our success.

9. Our profits are a key to our success. They replenish our capital and attract and keep our best people. It is our practice to share our profits generously with all who helped create them. Profitability is crucial to our future.

10. We consider our size an asset that we try hard to preserve. We want to be big enough to undertake the largest project that any of our clients could contemplate, yet small enough to maintain the loyalty, the intimacy and the esprit de corps that we all treasure and that contribute greatly to our success.

11. We constantly strive to anticipate the rapidly changing needs of our clients and to develop new services to meet those needs. We know that the world of finance will not stand still and that complacency can lead to extinction.

12. We regularly receive confidential information as part of our normal client relationships. To breach a confidence or to use confidential information improperly or carelessly would be unthinkable.

13. Our business is highly competitive, and we aggressively seek to expand our client relationships. However, we must always be fair competitors and must never denigrate other firms.

14. Integrity and honesty are at the heart of our business. We expect our people to maintain high ethical standards in everything they do, both in their work for the firm and in their personal lives.

SUMMARY

This chapter provides an overview of major regulatory issues and ethics in the securities markets. The coverage starts with the process of bringing new securities to the marketplace, and then to the trading practices in the exchanges or the OTC markets. Subsequent sections cover exempt offerings and restrictions of trading on these restricted securities. Another subject is regulation of the money management operations. Finally, maintaining the highest professional standards is an obligation for all market professionals.

SELECT BIBLIOGRAPHY

Association for Investment Management and Research. *Code of Ethics & Standards of Practice*. 1997.

Astarita, M. J. *Introduction to Securities Laws*. New York: Mark J. Astarita, Esq., 1997.

Coudert Brothers. *Introduction to U.S. Broker-Dealer Registration and Regulation*. 1997.

Coudert Brothers. *Introduction to U.S. Regulation of Investment Advisers*. 1997.

Equity Analytics. *Initial Public Offerings of Securities*. 1997.

NASD. *Securities Regulation in the United States*. 1997.

North American Securities Administrators Association. *1997 Conference on Federal-State Securities Regulation: Final Report*. 1997.

Perkins C. *Regulation M: The New Trading Practices Rules*. 1997.

Securities and Exchange Commission. *1996 Annual Report: Regulation of the Securities Market*. 1997.

Securities and Exchange Commission. *The U.S. Securities and Exchange Commission: What It Is, What It Does*. 1997.

Securities and Exchange Commission. *The Work of the SEC*. June 1997.

Shearman and Sterling. *The National Securities Markets Improvement Act of 1996: An Overview*. 1997.

Skousen, K. F. *An Introduction to the SEC*. Cincinnati, OH: Southwestern Publishing, 1991.

University of Cincinnati College of Law. *Securities Lawyer's Deskbook*. 1997.

APPENDIX A   Selected Forms Prescribed Under the 1933 Act

A. Forms for Registration Statements

Form SB-1 – Optional Form for the Registration of Securities to Be Sold to the Public by Certain Small Business Issuers

Form SB-2 – Optional Form for the Registration of Securities to Be Sold to the Public by Small Business Issuers

Form S-1 – Registration Statement under the Securities Act of 1933

Form S-2 – for Registration under the Securities Act of 1933 of Securities of Certain Issuers

Form S-3 – for Registration under the Securities Act of 1933 of Securities of Certain Issuers Offered pursuant to Certain Types of Transactions

Form S-4 – for the Registration of Securities Issued in Business Combination Transactions

Form S-6 – for Unit Investment Trusts Registered on Form N-8B-2

Form S-8 – for Registration under the Securities Act of 1933 of Securities to Be Offered to Employees pursuant to Employee Benefit Plans

Form S-11 – for Registration under the Securities Act of 1933 of Securities of Certain Real Estate Companies

Form S-20 – for Standardized Options

B. Forms for the Use of Foreign Issuers

Form F-1 – Registration Statement under the Securities Act of 1933 for Securities of Certain Foreign Private Issuers

Form F-2 – for Registration under the Securities Act of 1933 for Securities of Certain Foreign Private Issuers

Form F-3 – for Registration under the Securities Act of 1933 of Securities of Certain Foreign Private Issuers Offered pursuant to Certain Types of Transactions

Form F-4 – for Registration of Securities of Foreign Private Issuers Issued in Certain Business Combination Transactions

Form F-6 – for Registration under the Securities Act of 1933 of Depositary Shares Evidenced by American Depositary Receipts

Form F-7 – for Registration under the Securities Act of 1933 of Securities of Certain Canadian Issuers Offered for Cash Upon the Exercise of Rights Granted to Existing Securityholders

Form F-8 – for Registration under the Securities Act of 1933 of Securities of Certain Canadian Issuers to Be Issued in Exchange Offers or a Business Combination

Form F-9 – for Registration under the Securities Act of 1933 of Certain Investment Grade Debt or Investment Grade Preferred Securities of Certain Canadian Issuers

Form F-10 – for Registration under the Securities Act of 1933 of Securities of Certain Canadian Issuers

Form F-80 – for Registration under the Securities Act of 1933 of Securities of Certain Canadian Issuers to Be Issued in Exchange Offers or a Business Combination

C. Forms Pertaining to Exemptions

Form 1-A – Offering Statement under Regulation A

Form 2-A – Report pursuant to Rule 257 of Regulation A

Form 144 – for Notice of Proposed Sale of Securities pursuant to Rule 144

(continues)

APPENDIX A   *(continued)*

C. Forms Pertaining to Exemptions

Form 1-E – Notification under Regulation E

Form 2-E – Report of Sales pursuant to Rule 609 of Regulation E

Form 1-F – Notification under Regulation F

Form D – Notice of Sales of Securities under Regulation D and Section 4(6) of the Securities Act of 1933

Form 701 – Report of Sales Securities pursuant to a Compensatory Benefit Plan or Contract Relating to Compensation

APPENDIX B   Forms Prescribed Under the Securities Exchange Act of 1934

A. Forms for Registration or Exemption of, and Notification of Action Taken by, National Securities Exchanges

Form 1, for Application for, or Exemption from, Registration as a National Securities Exchange

Form 1-A, for Amendments to Form 1

Form 25, for Notification of Removal from Listing and Registration of Matured, Redeemed or Retired Securities

Form 26, for Notification of the Admission to Trading of a Substituted or Additional Class of Security under Rule 12a-5

B. Forms for Reports to Be Filed by Officers, Directors, and Securityholders

Form 3, Initial Statement of Beneficial Ownership of Securities

Form 4, Statement of Changes in Beneficial Ownership of Securities

Form 5, Annual Statement of Beneficial Ownership of Securities

C. Forms for Applications for Registration of Securities on National Securities Exchanges and Similar Matters

Form 8-A, for Registration of Certain Classes of Securities pursuant to Section 12(b) or (g) of the Securities Exchange Act of 1934

Form 8-B, for Registration of Securities of Certain Successor Issuers pursuant to Section 12(b) or (g) of the Securities Exchange Act of 1934

Form 10 and Form 10-SB, General Form for Registration of Securities pursuant to Section 12(b) or (g) of the Securities Exchange Act of 1934

Form 10-SB, Optional Form for the Registration of Securities of a Small Business Issuer

Form 18, for Foreign Governments and Political Subdivisions Thereof

Form 20-F, Registration of Securities of Foreign Private Issuers pursuant to Section 12(b) or (g) and Annual and Transition Reports pursuant to Sections 13 and 15(d)

(continues)

APPENDIX B   *(continued)*

C. Forms for Applications for Registration of Securities on National Securities Exchanges and Similar Matters

Form 40-F, for Registration of Securities of Certain Canadian Issuers Pursuant to Section 12(b) or (g) and for Reports pursuant to Section 15(d) and Rule 15d-4

Form F-X, for Appointment of Agent for Service of Process by Issuers Registering Securities on Form F-8, F-9, F-10 or F-80, or Registering Securities or Filing Periodic Reports on Form 40-F

D. Forms for Annual and Other Reports of Issuers Required under Sections 13 and 15(d) of the Securities Exchange Act of 1934

Form 6-K, Report of Foreign Issuer pursuant to Rules 13a-16 and 15d-16 under the Securities Exchange Act of 1934

Form 8-K, for Current Reports

Form 10-Q and Form 10-QSB, for Quarterly and Transition Reports under Section 13 or 15(d) of the Securities Exchange Act of 1934

Form 10-QSB, Optional Form for Quarterly and Transition Reports of Small Business Issuers under Section 13 or 15(d) of the Securities Exchange Act of 1934

Form 10-K, for Annual and Transition Reports pursuant to Sections 13 or 15(d) of the Securities Exchange Act of 1934

Form 10-KSB, Optional Form for Annual and Transition Reports of Small Business Issuers under Sections 13 or 15(d) of the Securities Exchange Act of 1934

Form 10-C, for Report by Issuers of Securities Quoted on Nasdaq Interdealer Quotation System, pursuant to Section 13 or 15(d) of the Act

Form 11-K, for Annual Reports of Employee Stock Purchase, Savings and Similar Plans pursuant to Section 15(d) of the Securities Exchange Act of 1934

Form 18-K, Annual Report for Foreign Governments and Political Subdivisions Thereof

Form 12b-25, Notification of Late Filing

Form 15, Certification of Termination of Registration of a Class of Security under Section 12(g) or Notice of Suspension of Duty to File Reports pursuant to Sections 13 and 15(d) of the Act

Form 13F, Report of Institutional Investment Manager pursuant to Section 13(f) of the Securities Exchange Act of 1934

Form 13F-E, for Filing of Form 13F Reports on Magnetic Tape

Form 17-H, Risk Assessment Report for Brokers and Dealers pursuant to Section 17(h) of the Securities Exchange Act of 1934 and Rules thereunder

Form N-SAR, Semi-Annual Report of Registered Investment Companies

Form SE, Form for Submission of Paper Format Exhibits by Electronic Filers

Form ET, Transmittal Form for Electronic Format Documents on Magnetic Tape or Diskette to Be Filed on the EDGAR System

Form ID, Uniform Application for Access Codes to File on EDGAR

Form TH, Notification of Reliance on Temporary Hardship Exemption

(continues)

APPENDIX B *(continued)*

E. Forms for Registration of Brokers and Dealers Transacting Business on Over-the-Counter Markets

Form BD, for Application for Registration as a Broker and Dealer or to Amend or Supplement Such an Application

Form BDW, Notice of Withdrawal from Registration as Broker–Dealer pursuant to Rules 15b6-1, 15Bc3-1, or 15Cc1-1

Form 7-M, Consent to Service of Process by an Individual Nonresident Broker–Dealer

Form 8-M, Consent to Service of Process by a Corporation Which Is a Nonresident Broker–Dealer

Form 9-M, Consent to Service of Process by a Partnership Nonresident Broker–Dealer

Form 10-M, Consent to Service of Process by a Nonresident General Partner of a Broker–Dealer Firm

F. Forms for Reports to Be Made by Certain Exchange Members, Brokers, and Dealers

Form X-17A-5, Information Required of Certain Brokers and Dealers pursuant to Section 17 of the Securities Exchange Act of 1934 and Rules 17a-5, 17a-10 and 17a-11

Form X-17A-19, Report by National Securities Exchanges and Registered National Securities Associations of Changes in the Membership Status of Any of Their Members

Form 17A-23, Information Required of Certain Broker and Dealer Sponsors of Broker-Dealer Trading Systems pursuant to Section 17 of the Securities Exchange Act of 1934 and Rule 17a-23

G. Forms for Self-Regulatory Organization Rule Changes and Forms for Registration of and Reporting by National Securities Associations and Affiliated Securities Associations

Form X-15AA-1, for Application for Registration as a National Securities Association or Affiliated Securities Association

Form X-15AJ-1, for Amendatory and/or Supplementary Statements to Registration Statement of a National Securities Association or an Affiliated Securities Association

Form X-15AJ-2, for Annual Consolidated Supplement of a National Securities Association or an Affiliated Securities Association

Form 19b-4, for Filings with Respect to Proposed Rule Changes by All Self-Regulatory Organizations

H. Forms for Registration of, and Reporting by, Securities Information Processors

Form SIP, for Application for Registration as a Securities Information Processor or to Amend Such an Application or Registration

I. Forms for Registration of Municipal Securities Dealers

Form MSD, Application for Registration as a Municipal Securities Dealer pursuant to Rule 15Ba-2-1 under the Securities Exchange Act of 1934 or Amendment to Such Application

Form MSDW, Notice of Withdrawal from Registration as a Municipal Securities Dealer pursuant to Rule 15Bc3-1

J. Forms for Reporting and Inquiry with Respect to Missing, Lost, Stolen, or Counterfeit Securities

Form X-17F-1a, Report for Missing, Lost, Stolen or Counterfeit Securities

17

Investment Banking Trends and Section 20

Wall Street firms are operating in a rapidly changing environment. They are facing increasing competition from home and abroad. Those firms that want to control their own destinies must have leading market positions in all of their businesses, balanced earnings stream, broad-based customer access, and a global presence. This concluding chapter discusses the future trends of the investment banking business and the crumbling Glass–Steagall Act, which separated commercial and investment banking activities. The Federal Reserve Board has raised the amount of ineligible revenue that a Section 20 subsidiary is permitted to earn from securities underwriting and dealing to 25% of its total revenue. Most large commercial banks would now be permitted to operate very large securities subsidiaries, which might eventually threaten top Wall Street firms.

FUTURE TRENDS

The business of investment banking is undergoing radical reshaping. It is trending toward globalization and one-stop shopping, and consolidation is the wave of the future.

Globalization

Companies around the world are increasingly tapping international markets to enhance their global presence and raise capital abroad. At the same time, investors are looking across their national borders to take advantage of new opportunities for capital growth and to add an element of diversification by investing in international securities. With the increasing integration of the global capital markets, the business of investment banking is a worldwide activity. To maintain growth and profitability, and because the U.S. market is mature and, to some extent, overbanked, all major investment banks have expanded abroad. Wall Street's international expansion came as U.S.-based corporate clients rapidly increased their global production and sales. Foreign companies likewise raised substantial amounts of capital worldwide using U.S. investment banks to play key management roles in the underwriting deals. Total U.S. underwriting of non–U.S.-based companies soared from $18 billion to $76 billion between 1990 and 1997. Meanwhile, investors both home and abroad are going global with their portfolios. The Securities Industry Association reported that the dollar volume of foreign transactions in U.S. securities jumped from $4.2 trillion to $9.2 trillion between 1990 and 1996. During the same period, U.S. activity in foreign securities soared from $906 billion to $3.3 trillion.

Merrill Lynch is by far the most aggressive in pursuing a global presence. Merrill has already purchased British brokerage firm Smith New Court, Spain's FG Inversiones, Australia's McIntoch Securities, and stakes in securities firms in India, Thailand, South Africa, Indonesia and Italy. In addition, Merrill has recently acquired British money manager Mercury Asset Management and launched a retail business in Japan. Now it has offices in 43 countries. In the domestic arena, investment banks, brokerage houses, mutual funds, and other arms of the financial world are gradually leaning toward combinations. Recent headline mergers include SBC Warburg Dillon Read, Bankers Trust Alex. Brown, Morgan Stanley Dean Witter, and Salomon Smith Barney. The consolidation trend is expected to continue.

In investment banking business, Wall Street firms are at the heart of global financial markets, and most large firms earn between one-quarter and one-half of their revenues overseas. Major Wall Street firms (Table 17.1) ranked high in the global markets in both underwriting and trading (Table 17.2)

One-Stop Shopping

This trend of moving toward one-stop shopping will eventually unite the businesses of banking, insurance, securities, and fund management. The driving force is that corporate clients want their financial advisers to be able to address any capital need they might have, regardless of what type of instrument it might be. The Financial Services Act of 1998, still in legislative process in Congress, will provide the legal infrastructure for a financial services supermarket. Wall Street firms have been aggressively expanding the menu of services they provide, adding money lending, retail and institutional fund management, and trust services. In addition, investment bankers, including AG Edwards, Merrill Lynch, and Travelers Group, have applied for thrift charters. Morgan

---

TABLE 17.1   Largest U.S. Investment Banks

Investment Bank
Morgan Stanley Dean Witter
Merrill Lynch
Goldman Sachs
Salomon Smith Barney
Lehman Brothers
Bear Stearns
Credit Suisse First Boston
Paine Webber
Donaldson, Lufkin & Jenrette

Source: Adapted from Securities Industry Association Yearbook, 1997; and *Wall Street Journal*, various issues.

TABLE 17.2   *Euromoney* **Ranking in Underwriting and Trading**

Underwriting Ranking			Trading Ranking		
1997	1996	Company	1997	1996	Company
1	2	Merrill Lynch	1	***	SBC Warburg Dillon Read
2	1	Goldman Sachs	2	2	Merrill Lynch
3	4	Morgan Stanley Dean Witter	3	6	Deutsche Morgan Grenfell
4	5	J.P. Morgan	4	1	J.P. Morgan
5	*	SBC Warburg Dillon Read	5	7	Goldman Sachs
6	6	Credit Suisse First Boston	6	4	Morgan Stanley Dean Witter
7	7	Deutsche Morgan Grenfell	7	12	Union Bank of Switzerland
8	8	Union Bank of Switzerland	8	8	Citicorp
9	9	ABN Amro Hoare Govett	9	13	NatWest Group
10	10	Lehman Brothers	10	9	HSBC Group
11	56	Credito Italiano	11	10	Credit Suisse First Boston
12	**	Salomon Smith Barney	12	5	Chase Manhattan
13	11	Nomura Securities	13	14	ABN Amro Hoare Govett
14	14	HSBC Group	14	21	Dresdner Kleinwort Benson
15	22	Banque Paribas	15	11	Barclays Capital

* SBC Warburg ranked 3 in 1996.
** Salomon ranked 15 and Smith Barney 45 in 1996.
*** SBC Warburg ranked 3.
Source: Adapted from *Euromoney*, January 1998.

Stanley Dean Witter acquired Union Federal Savings & Loan in July 1996. In April 1998, the announcement of Citicorp's plan to merge with Travelers Group fastened the convergence trend where a financial services supermarket would offer a vast array of products and services including savings and checking accounts, credit cards, mortgages, stock and bond underwriting, homeowners, auto, and life insurance, asset management, mergers and acquisitions advice, commercial loans, and derivative securities and foreign exchange trading. The development has resulted in the observation that many investment banks, such as Merrill Lynch, Lehman Brothers, Morgan Stanley Dean Witter, Paine Webber, Bear Stearns, and DLJ, derive 20% or less of revenues from the conventional investment banking activities such as underwriting and M&As. Even a boutique like Hambrecht & Quist receives more than half of its revenues from other sources such as commissions, principal transactions, and interest and others.

Commercial banks, of course, have made progress at building up their debt-underwriting capabilities, but the ability to underwrite stocks was still missing. A select number of banks have built an equity shop through Section 20 subsidiaries, but when the Fed raised the revenue limit to 25%, that changed the buy-versus-build equation. Facing the pressure to provide one-stop shopping, it did not take long for bankers to seize the opportunity of a higher 25% ineligible revenue cap to join forces or to apply for Section 20 subsidiaries, while investment banking firms are expanding into money lending and applying for thrift charters. Bankers Trust acted first and paid $1.7 billion to acquire Alex. Brown & Sons. A wave of deals quickly followed:

- NationsBank acquired Montgomery Securities for $1.2 billion.
- BankAmerica acquired Robertson Stephens for $540 million.

TABLE 17.3   Links between Underwriters and Retail Brokerages

Investment Bank	Retail Link-up
Bankers Trust	Bought Alex. Brown
Donaldson, Lufkin & Jenrette	Selling IPOs through own online broker
Salomon Brothers	IPO distribution through Fidelity
Credit Suisse First Boston	IPO distribution through Schwab
J.P. Morgan	IPO distribution through Schwab
Hambrecht & Quist	IPO distribution through Schwab

Source: Adapted from Wall Street Journal (September 9, 1997), C1 & C24.

- CIBC bought Oppenheimer for $525 million.
- SBC Warburg purchased Dillon Read for $600 million.
- First Union linked up with Wheat First Butcher Singer Securities for $470 million.
- ING Barings made a $500 million bid for Furman Selz.
- U.S. Bancorp took over of Piper Jaffray for $730 million.
- Fleet Financial acquired Quick & Reilly for $1.6 billion.

Major Wall Street firms are also buying into the money management business. Merrill Lynch, Goldman Sachs, J.P. Morgan, Salomon Smith Barney, and Morgan Stanley Dean Witter are among the major buyers of fund companies. Commercial banks are also expanding into the fund business. Recent acquirers include State Street, PNC Bank Corp., Northern Trust, Banc One, Fleet Financial, Mellon Bank, CIBC Wood Gundy, and ING Barings.

Another important development toward full service is that, to better support the primary market underwriting business, many investment banks have joined forces with retail brokerages to sell stock to small investors. This is aimed at getting access to individual investors and the money they are salting away for the future amid a continuing boom in mutual fund sales. The merger of the premier investment banking house, Morgan Stanley, with the third largest retail brokerage firm, Dean Witter Discover, exemplifies this development. Several other investment bankers have merged with or forged alliances with retail firms. Table 17.3 lists those recent linkups.

In summary, the lines are blurring between banking and brokerage and between money management and money lending. In addition, financial service firms are more global than ever.

SECTION 20 SUBSIDIARIES

Beginning in 1987, the Fed has granted banks expanded powers with respect to securities activities as long as such ineligible activities contribute only 5% of the subsidiary's gross income. The percentage of ineligible revenues was later lifted to 10%. Effective March 6, 1997, the Fed increased the amount a Section 20 subsidiary may derive from underwriting and dealing in securities, from 10% to 25% of its total revenue. The Fed tracks the ineligible revenues on an eight-quarter moving average. Banks generally monitor the percentage daily. As of February 11, 1998, there were 45 of these Section

20 subsidiaries in existence (Table 17.4). Twenty-nine of these subsidiaries are autho-rized to underwrite both corporate debt and equity (Tier II authority). Fourteen such bank subsidiaries are authorized to underwrite in certain municipal revenue bonds, mortgage related securities, commercial paper, and asset-backed securities (Tier I authority), and an additional two are authorized to underwrite corporate debt but not equity (BZW Securities and First of America Securities).

TABLE 17.4　Section 20 Subsidiaries[1] (As of February 11, 1998)

Parent Organization	Section 20 subsidiary	Order Initial
Boston District		
Fleet Financial Group Inc.[2]	Fleet Securities Inc.	10/88
Bank of Boston Corporation[2]	BancBoston Securities Inc.	11/96
New York District		
Banco Santander, S.A.[2]	Santander Investment Securities Inc.	03/95
The Bank of New York Company Inc.[2]	BNY Capital Markets, Inc.	06/96
The Bank of Nova Scotia[2]	Scotia Capital Markets (USA) Inc.	04/90
Bankers Trust N.Y. Corp.[2]	BT Alex. Brown Inc.	04/87
Barclays Bank PLC[3]	BZW Securities, Inc.	01/90
Canadian Imperial Bank of Commerce[2]	CIBC Oppenheimer Corp.	01/90
Chase Manhattan Corp.[2]	Chase Securities Inc.	05/87
Citicorp[2]	Citicorp Securities Inc.	04/87
Deutsche Bank AG[2]	Deutsche Morgan Grenfell Inc.	12/92
Dresdner Bank AG[2]	Dresdner Kleinwort Benson	07/96
HSBC Holdings PLC[2]	HSBC Securities, Inc.	02/96
J.P. Morgan & Co., Inc.[2]	J.P. Morgan Securities Inc.	04/87
National Westminster Bank Plc	Greenwich Capital Markets Inc.	09/96
The Royal Bank of Canada[2]	RBC Dominion Securities Inc.	01/90
Saban/Republic New York Corp.[2]	Republic N.Y. Securities Corp.	01/94
Swiss Bank Corporation[2]	SBC Warburg Inc.	12/94
The Toronto-Dominion Bank[2]	Toronto Dominion Securities (USA)	05/90
Philadelphia District		
CoreStates Financial Corporation	CoreStates Securities Corporation	08/97
Cleveland District		
Banc One Corp.[2]	Banc One Capital Corp.	07/90
Huntington Bancshares, Inc.	Huntington Capital Corp.	12/92
KeyCorp[2]	Key Capital Markets, Inc.	02/96
Mellon Bank Corporation	Mellon Financial Markets, Inc.	04/95
National City Corporation[2]	NatCity Investments, Inc.	02/94
PNC Bank Corp.	PNC Capital Markets, Inc.	07/87
Richmond District		
Allied Irish Bank PLC[2]	Hopper Soliday & Co., Inc.	05/97
BB&T Corporation[2]	Craigie Incorporated	09/97
Crestar Financial Corporation	Crestar Securities Corp.	04/97
First Union Corp.[2]	First Union Capital Markets Corp.	08/89
NationsBank Corp.[2]	NationsBanc Montgomery Securities	05/89

(continues)

Atlanta District		
SouthTrust Corp.	SouthTrust Securities, Inc.	07/89
SunTrust Banks, Inc.	SunTrust Equitable Securities Corp.	08/94
Chicago District		
ABN AMRO Bank N.V.[2]	ABN AMRO Chicago Corp.	06/90
Bankmont Financial Corp.[2,4]	Nesbitt Burns Securities, Inc	05/88
(The Bank of Montreal).	Nesbitt Burns Chicago, Inc.	02/96
First of America Bank Corp.[3]	First of America Securities, Inc.	10/94
First Chicago NBD Corp.[2]	First Chicago Capital Markets, Inc.	08/88
Minneapolis District		
Norwest Corp	Norwest Investment Services	12/89
U.S. Bancorp	U.S. Bancorp Investments Inc.	11/97
Kansas City District		
BOK Financial Corporation	Alliance Securities Corp.	04/97
San Francisco District		
BankAmerica Corp.[2]	BancAmerica Robertson Stephens	03/92
Dai-Ichi Kangyo Bank Ltd.	DKB Securities (USA) Corp.	01/91
First Security Corporation	First Security Capital Markets Inc.	12/97
The Sanwa Bank Ltd.	Sanwa Securities (USA) Co., L.P.	05/90

[1] Authorized to underwrite and deal in certain municipal revenue bonds, mortgage-related securities, commercial paper and asset-backed securities (Tier I authority).
[2] Also has corporate debt and equity underwriting and dealing powers (Tier II authority).
[3] Also has corporate debt securities powers.
[4] Currently has two Section 20 subsidiaries. Nesbitt Thomas Securities, Inc. was initially granted Section 20 status in May 1988. The company was then acquired by Bank of Montreal in 1995, and renamed Nesbitt Burns Securities Inc.

Section 20 Application

Banks wishing to underwrite and deal in ineligible securities must obtain approval from the Federal Reserve Board to set up so-called Section 20 subsidiaries. The application guidelines are as follows:

1. Indicate the capital position of the notificant organization on a consolidated basis as of the most recent fiscal quarter, and discuss why the notificant organization should be viewed to be "strongly capitalized," the standard for bank holding companies that underwrite and deal in bank-ineligible securities.
2. If the notificant has subsidiaries that are in less-than-satisfactory financial condition or a U.S. bank subsidiary that is less than "well-capitalized," discuss how such circumstances are consistent with approval and demonstrate how the proposed transaction would not divert financial or managerial resources from the efforts to improve the condition of those subsidiaries.
3. Provide a copy of notificant's business plan for the proposed activities. The business plan should cover at least one full year of operations for the proposed Section 20 company. The recommended format is provided in the Appendix.
4. To the extent not covered by (3), provide the following: describe how the proposed Section 20 company is currently funded and how it will be funded in the

future; provide a detailed discussion of the proposed management of the Section 20 subsidiary, and indicate the expertise available for all of the proposed activities; describe separately the risk management and internal control systems that will be in place with respect to the proposed activities.

5. If the notificant is acquiring a going concern (the proposed Section 20 company), provide the most recent two years' financial statements. To the extent possible, indicate how much "ineligible" revenue the subsidiary generated over that period. If future revenues of the underwriting subsidiary are expected to be substantially different from historical levels, identify the changes that will be made to ensure compliance with the 25% revenue limit.

Firewalls

The firewalls apply to bank holding companies engaged in securities underwriting and dealing activities through their Section 20 affiliates. The current operating standards cover the following areas:

- Capital requirements for bank holding company and Section 20 subsidiary
- Internal controls
- Interlocks restriction
- Customer disclosure
- Credit for clearing purposes
- Funding of securities purchases from a Section 20 affiliate
- Reporting requirement
- Application of Sections 23A and 23B to foreign banks

One important objective of the firewalls is to prevent the securities subsidiaries from funding their activities through the bank. This is the main reason why the matched books are so important to Section 20 companies. Matched books are essentially a self-funding mechanism and can be used to raise the eligible revenues. Some bankers estimate that billions of dollars in matched books exist primarily to meet the revenue cap, especially before the lifting of ineligible revenue to 25% from 10%. Banks have also moved fee-generating businesses into their Section 20 subsidiaries to better manage the ineligible-revenue test.

The interlocks restriction provides that directors, officers or employees of a bank may not serve as a majority of the board of directors or as the chief executive officer of an affiliated Section 20 company (and vice versa). As such, employees can work in both organizations and some directors can serve jointly as long as they are only a minority of either organization's board. A shared chief executive officer is still prohibited. Given the convergence of commercial and investment banking, it makes sense to exploit the natural synergies such as credit evaluation and cross marketing of products. Banks or thrifts are permitted to act as an agent for or engage in marketing activities on behalf of an affiliated Section 20 company. However, securities law limits the advantage of such cross marketing. A bank employee cannot pitch some securities business without being registered by the NASD, and you cannot be registered as an employee of the bank.

The firewalls also restrict purchases or sales of financial assets between a bank and an affiliated Section 20 company. The permitted transactions include U.S. Treasury securities, direct obligations of the Canadian federal government at market terms, and "assets having a readily identifiable and publicly available market quotation and purchased at that market quotation." The same standard applies to interaffiliate funding under Sections 23A and 23B of the Federal Reserve Act. In addition, the Fed has proposed to exempt any transaction involving the underwriting or dealing of mortgage-backed securities from the Board's appraisal requirements.

Section 20 subsidiaries are generally permitted to underwrite and deal in municipal revenue bonds, mortgage-related securities, commercial paper, asset-backeds, corporate debt, and corporate equity. But the firewalls prohibit a Section 20 company from underwriting or dealing in bank-ineligible securities issued by an affiliate unless the securities are: (1) rated by an unaffiliated, nationally recognized statistical rating organization; or (2) issued or guaranteed by FNMA, FHLMC, or GNMA. To engage in such nonpermitted transactions, the Section 20 company has to request a relief. For example, on April 16, 1997, the Fed granted a one-time relief to permit Deutsche Bank's Section 20 subsidiary Deutsche Morgan Grenfell to participate in the underwriting syndicate in connection with a proposed offering in the U.S. of subscription rights to purchase certain convertible notes of Daimler-Benz Aktiengesellschaft. On May 19, 1997, the Federal Reserve Board granted a one-time relief from Section 20 firewalls to permit ABN AMRO's Section 20 subsidiary, ABN AMRO Chicago Corporation, to underwrite the initial public offering of ADRs of ABN AMRO Holding.

SUMMARY

The business of investment banking is trending toward one-stop shopping and globalization. This trend is the driving force behind the wave of consolidation. This concluding chapter discusses the trends and the repeal of the Glass–Steagall Act. The financial services one-stop shop will become reality if the Financial Services Act of 1998 (known as H.R.10) is passed and signed into law.

SELECT BIBLIOGRAPHY

Benston, G. J. "The origins and justification for the Glass–Steagall Act." In *Universal Banking: Financial System Design Reconsidered*. Burr Ridge, IL: Irwin, 1996, pp.31–69.

Cearier, M. "Chipping at the firewalls." *Euromoney* (December 1996): 52–55.

Federal Reserve Bank of New York. "4(c)(8) Notices for 1987 and 1989 Securities Power." August 28, 1997.

Johnson, H. J. *The Banker's Guide to Investment Banking*. Chicago, IL: Irwin Professional Publishing, 1996.

Kuhn, R. L. *Investment Banking*. New York: Harper & Row, 1990.

Mester, L. J. "Repealing Glass–Steagall: The past points the way to the future." *Business Review*, Federal Reserve Bank of Philadelphia, July/August 1996.

Puri, M. "Commercial banks in investment banking: Conflict of interest or certification role?" *Journal of Financial Economics* (March 1996): pp. 373–402.

Securities Industry Association. *Fact Book*, 1997.

APPENDIX   Recommended Format for Section 20 Application

Balance Sheet

	Actual	Pro Forma at Consummation	PROJECTIONS (yearend) Year 1	Year 2

Assets

Cash
Securities held at market value:
  Eligible Securities:
    U.S. government & agencies
    Municipal bonds
    Mortgage-backed securities
  Ineligible Securities:
    Commercial paper
    Municipal bonds
    Mortgage backed securities
    Corporate debt obligations
    Other debt obligations
    Preferred stock
    Common stock
Money market securities
Securities purchased under repos
Receivables from brokers, dealers,
  and banks
Receivables from customers
Receivables from affiliates
Other assets
  TOTAL ASSETS

Liabilities & Equity

Short-term borrowings
Securities sold under repos
Securities sold, not yet purchased
Payables to brokers, dealers, banks
Payables to customers
Payables to affiliates
Other liabilities
  Total liabilities

Common stock
Paid-in capital
Retained earnings

  Total shareholder equity

TOTAL LIABILITIES & EQUITY

(continues)

APPENDIX   *(continued)*

Net Capital Analysis—Section 20 Subsidiary		Pro Forma at	PROJECTIONS (yearend)	
	Actual	Consummation	Year 1	Year 2
Ownership equity:				
Common stock				
Paid-in-capital				
Retained earnings				
LESS: nonallowable capital				
Total Ownership Equity				
Allowable subordinated debt				
Other allowable credits				
LESS: other deductions				
Total SEC Capital (Equity & Sub Debt)				
Deductions and/or charges:				
Nonallowable assets:				
Nonmarketable securities				
Additional charges for security accounts				
Additional charges for commodity accounts				
Aged fail-to-deliver				
Other aged items				
Futures and commodity related charges				
Other deductions				
Total Deductions				
SEC adjusted net capital before haircuts				
LESS: Haircuts on securities				
SEC Net Capital				
Net Capital Requirement				
Excess Net Capital				
Liquid Capital Ratio				

(continues)

APPENDIX *(continued)*

Net Income—Section 20 Subsidiary (Include eligible/ineligible analysis)				
	Actual	Pro Forma at Consummation	PROJECTIONS (yearend) Year 1	Year 2

Revenues

Bank-eligible revenues
   U.S. government & agencies
      Underwriting
      Secondary dealing
      Interest income
   Municipal bonds
      Underwriting
      Secondary dealing
      Interest income
   Mortgage-backed securities
      Underwriting
      Secondary dealing
      Interest income
   Advisory fees
   Brokerage commissions
   Corporate finance fees
   Private placement fees
   Research & consulting fees
   Other dealing or trading
   Other interest income & dividends
   Intercompany expense reimbursement
   Other revenues

Bank-ineligible revenues
   Commercial paper
      Underwriting
      Secondary dealing
      Interest income
   Municipal bonds
      Underwriting
      Secondary dealing
      Interest income
   Mortgage-backed securities
      Underwriting
      Secondary dealing
      Interest income
   Consumer receivable related securities
      Underwriting
      Secondary dealing
      Interest income
   Corporate debt securities
      Underwriting
      Secondary dealing
      Interest income
   Other debt securities
      Underwriting
      Secondary dealing
      Interest income

(continues)

APPENDIX *(continued)*

	Actual	Pro Forma at Consummation	PROJECTIONS (yearend) Year 1	Year 2
Equity securities				
Underwriting				
Secondary dealing				
Dividend income				
Fund distribution & related adv/adm fees				
Other incidental activity income				
Neutral Revenues				
Securities associated with affiliated interests				
Underwriting				
Secondary dealing				
Interest income				
Total Revenues				
Ineligible Revenue Ratio				
Expenses				
Interest expense on repos				
Other interest expense				
Floor brokerage & commissions paid				
Salaries & employee benefits				
Occupancy & equipment				
Communications & data processing				
Other expenses				
Total Expenses				
Income Before Taxes				
Income Taxes				
NET INCOME/(LOSS)				
RETAINED EARNINGS, beginning of period				
Dividend paid				
Current income/(loss)				
RETAINED EARNINGS, end period				

Source: Adapted from Federal Reserve Bank of New York, format date: 8/29/97.

Chapter Notes

CHAPTER 2

1. The address is 1655 North Fort Myer Drive, Suite 700, Arlington, Virginia 22209; (703) 528–4370.

2. International Venture Capital Institute, Inc.; P.O. Box 1333, Stamford, Connecticut 06904.

3. The telephone number is 800-292-1993, fax number is 503-221-9987, and the e-mail address is *avce@aol.com.*

4. Generally, the miscellaneous investment expenses are deductible only if they exceed 2% of the taxpayer's adjusted gross income, regardless of whether the fund has a profit or loss in the year.

5. A detailed description of exempt offerings is covered in Chapter 4.

6. ERISA regulates corporate pension plans. First, ERISA establishes the minimum contributions a plan sponsor must make to satisfy the actuarially projected benefits payments. Second, ERISA establishes fiduciary standards for pension fund trustees, managers, or advisors. The minimum vesting standards are established as well. Finally, ERISA created the Pension Benefits Guaranty Corporation (PBGC) to insure vested benefits.

7. An ERISA plan is a pension or profit sharing plan sponsored by a U.S. employer other than a government entity. ERISA type entities include ERISA plans, public retirement plans, foreign retirement plans, and individual retirement accounts.

8. A venture capital fund is a venture capital operating company only if at least 50% of its investments are in portfolio companies engaged in the production or sale of a product or service and the fund has direct contractual rights to influence the conduct of portfolio company's management. Additionally, the fund actively exercises such rights to at least one portfolio company.

9. The SEC has adopted new rules to reallocate regulatory responsibilities for investment advisors between the SEC and the states. The new rules took effect on July 8, 1997. Generally, the new rules provide for SEC regulation of advisors with $25 million or more of asset under management and state regulation of advisors with less than $25 million under management.

10. The SEC amended Rule 144 in the belief that the shorter holding periods will lower funding costs for companies, especially small businesses, by reducing the liquidity discount associated with privately placed securities.

CHAPTER 3

1. Mergers are often categorized as horizontal, vertical, or conglomerate. A horizontal merger is between two firms in the same line of business. A vertical merger is one in which the buyer expands to the source of materials or to the direction of ultimate consumers. Finally, a conglomerate merger involves companies in unrelated industries.

2. Worldwide transaction volume was $1.1 trillion in 1996 and $1.6 trillion in 1997.

3. There are three types of synergies: economies of scale (horizontal merger), economies of scope (conglomerate merger), and economies of vertical integration (vertical integration).

4. The financial synergy is still subject to debate. Some argue that the lower probability of bankruptcy benefits bondholders at the expense of shareholders.

5. See Lee and Liaw (1994) for theoretical proof.

6. Top M&A law firms include Sullivan & Cromwell; Cravath, Swaine, & Moore; Shearman & Sterling; Skadden, Arps, Slate, Meagher & Flom; and Epstein, Becker & Green.

7. The IRS is seeking to reduce the cost advantage of using in-house staff, citing a 1973 ruling that holds that compensation to employees working on mergers is not currently deductible but must be capitalized.

8. The average fees have slid from 2% in the 1980s to 1% or less in the 1990s. As an example, investment bankers took in $138 million when Canada's Campeau Corp. took over Federated Department Store for $6.5 billion in 1988. Early in 1996, investment bankers earned only $21 million for the $4.2 billion acquisition of National Medical Care by Fresenius (Germany).

9. A management-led LBO is called management buyout. If an outside management team that is not associated with the bought company leads the buyout, it is called management buy-in.

10. This is based on a J.P. Morgan study, as reported in Lipin (1996).

11. Returns on stock-for-stock deals over five years have been well below the returns on cash acquisitions.

12. See Chapter 6 for detailed discussion on securitization.

13. Chapter 12 of Ernst & Young (1994).

14. SEC permits passive investors and insitutional investors to report their beneficial ownership on the short-form Schedule 13G, in lieu of schedule 13D.

15. KKR declined the special committee's offer of more than $600 million break fees during the drama of the RJR Nabisco bidding process (Burrough and Helgar 1990).

CHAPTER 4

1. See Perlmuth (1995) and Raghavan (1996).

2. Under the National Securities Markets Improvement Act of 1996, blue-sky registration and review are eliminated. The act prohibits states from reviewing or requiring the registration of securities issued by registered investment companies, listed securities, securities sold to qualified purchasers, and securities sold in certain offerings exempt from registration under the Securities Act.

3. Certain types of businesses may use other forms instead. Form S-4 is used for a company that is involved in a merger or acquisition. Form S-6 is used to register unit investment trusts. Form S-8 is primarily for employee stock options plan or other employee benefits plan. Form S-11 is used for registering securities for real estate companies and investment trusts.

4. This is typically conducted by counsels of underwriter, issuer, and so on. A formal meeting may not be necessary. Rather, they just need to satisfy for themselves that everything told by the management is correct.

5. There was an incident in the early 1980s. The IPO team included a major underwriter, accounting firm, and law firm. The offering raised $20 million. However, it turned out that the company they were dealing with never existed. It seems that a small group of "corporate officers" fabricated records and related materials. For a year or so, they created a continuing stream of operations and financial records. The underwriter, accountant, and attorney had never visited the office of the issuer. This is reported in Arkebauer (1994).

6. The underwriting agreements sometimes give the manager the right of first refusal. There are several reasons why companies change underwriters in followup stock sales. Pricing is one. Some companies that start with a small IPO underwriter outgrow them. They often seek broader market distribution in add-on offerings. And more and more bankers are jumping ship and taking business with them.

7. This example is documented in Block (1989), Chapter 14.

8. The holding period requirement for U.S. investors is one year. The exception is SEC Rule 144A, which permits large institutions to trade securities acquired in a private placement among themselves without having to register these securities with the SEC.

CHAPTER 5

1. The figures are obtained from The Bond Market Association.

2. Seven-year notes have not been issued since April 1993.

3. A noncompetitive bid indicates the amount of purchase without specifying the yield. The yield applied to noncompetitive bids is the average of the accepted competitive bids.

4. Based on a report compiled by Sundaresan (1997), Chapter 3.

5. Based on a report compiled by Sundaresan (1997), Chapter 3.

6. The discussion here is taken from Liaw (1997).

7. The most recently issued treasury in its maturity segment is referred to as the on-the-run issue.

8. Data are on nonconvertible debt and are obtained from publications by PSA Research, February 1998.

CHAPTER 6

1. A large portion of the reduction is captured by the end users, the investors and the borrowers. For example, MBS programs have probably knocked down 100 basis points off the cost of mortgages.

2. The issue could be subject to downgrade if the third party guarantor is downgraded. A case in point is the downgrade of Citibank Mortgage Securities when the Citibank was downgraded in 1990.

3. The Federal Housing Administration experience is no longer in use.

4. The example is obtained from E. Block, *Inside Investment Banking*, Chicago: Irwin Professional Publishing, 1989, p. 133.

5. The following discussion is drawn from Deloitte & Touche (1996), Grant Thornton (1997), and Milbank, Tweed, Hadley, and McCloy (1997).

CHAPTER 7

1. This chapter focuses on ADRs. Building on similar concepts, investment banks have helped companies in a variety of countries issue European Depositary Receipts (EDRs) and Global Depositary Receipts (GDRs) to investors in the Euromarkets and elsewhere.

2. As reported in Brancato (1996), Introduction section and Chapter 1.

3. Form 20-F is similar to a 10-K.

4. The ADR, GDR, and EDR programs totaled more than 2,100 as of April 1997.

5. Holders of ADRs are counted as holders of the underlying security for this purpose.

6. A statutory underwriter is a person who took the securities from the foreign issuer with a view toward distribution, causing resale of the securities and possibly the original sale of securities by issuer, which is in violation of Sections 5 and 12(1) of the Securities Act.

7. ADRs can be registered on the form used to register the underlying securities if the information required of Form F-6 is supplied and the legal entity created by the agreement for the issuance of the ADRs also signs the registration statement.

8. Form F-4 is used to register securities of foreign issuers issued in acquisitions or exchange offers.

9. *Pension and Investment*, February 4, 1991.

CHAPTER 8

1. First transfers were to Eurobank in Paris and the Moscow Narodny Bank in London.

2. This takes leap years into account.

3. The SEAQ is modeled after Nasdaq system.

4. Less common are offers by way of tender. Shares are offered and underwritten at a minimum price. Investors may subscribe at a price at or above the minimum. A "striking price" for all investors is determined based on all subscriptions submitted. This method is used when it is difficult to establish a fair value for the company.

5. The conditions for listing medium-term note programs are similar to those for eurobonds. The listing is for one year and must be renewed on an annual basis.

6. "Order collector" refers to nonmember institutions that are authorized by SICOVAM S.A. to hold securities accounts in their own name and in the names of their clients. Members may act as order collectors for trades they do not execute themselves.

7. Options and futures are traded through DTB (Deutsche Terminbörse).

CHAPTER 9

1. Yamaichi Securities was founded in 1897. It was the largest securities company until 1965 when large losses from an extended market downturn threatened to swamp it. The Bank of Japan came to the rescue. Yamaichi again fell on hard times in the early 1990s. Then a racketeering scandal in 1996 engulfed Yamaichi and other three large securities companies. Yamaichi's trouble deepened when it was unable to borrow sufficient operating funds on November 21, 1997, when its credit rating was slashed to "junk" by two U.S. rating companies.

2. Traditionally, Japanese financial institutions have seen themselves as part of a convoy in which the strong support the weak for the good of the system. Recent failures of Yamaichi, Sanyo, and Kokkaido Takushoku showed signs of a weakening convoy mindset.

3. This modeled after U.S. Securities Act of 1933 and Securities and Exchange Act of 1934.

4. This practice is different from the U.S. government securities market. In the U.S., the treasury sets the coupon rate after it has received all competitive bids.

5. The amount represented 10 issues that would not have been allowed if the rating requirement had remained in effect.

6. These listed fees here are lower than for Japanese companies, for the purpose of encouraging foreign listing.

7. Loan transactions are transactions in which a securities firm borrows money or stocks needed for margin transaction from a securities finance company.

8. These big companies include well-known names such as Kirin Brewery, Fuji Photo, Sony, Nippon Steel, Hitachi, Nissan Motor, Cannon, Bank of Tokyo–Mitsubishi, Industrial Bank of Japan, and Tokyo Electric power.

CHAPTER 10

1. The classification of regions and countries in each region are taken from Emerging Markets Traders Association's survey list.

2. The name change was made in May 1997.

3. Named after former Treasury Secretary Nicholas Brady.

4. See Eng and Lees (1997) for details.

5. This is according to a recent poll by *Euromoney*, May 1997.

6. S&P and Moody's often have different ratings for a given country issue in emerging debt, due to problems of analysis.

7. Market impact is the difference between the price at which a stock trade is executed and the average of that stock's high, low, opening and closing of the day.

8. Privatization proceeds cannot be taken into account when calculating the deficit, but they can be used to reduce governments' financial debt.

9. Trax is owned by the International Securities Association and linked to Euromarkets.

10. The derivative transaction behind the notes was the sale to YPF of WTI Asian style oil put options designed to make up any shortfall from the barrels committed to the structure.

11. For a more complete discussion on the default swaps, see *Financial Engineering* chapter.

CHAPTER 11

1. This is taken from Jack D. Schwager's *The New Market Wizards*, New York: Harper Business, 1992, p. xv.

2. This is generally not understood. When you lose 50% of your equity, your capital base is only half of what you started with. You need to double in order to bring the equity back to the initial level. For example, you lose $50 on $100 equity. The new balance is $50. A 100% gain on the new capital base, $50, will bring the amount back to $100.

3. These are reported in the August 29, 1994, issue of *Business Week* and November 1996 issue of *Institutional Investor*.

4. The repo was done with an Italian bank or a foreign bank branch licensed in Italy with back office capability to routinely file for the withholding tax rebate. LTCM got a below-market repo rate that was nearly equivalent to the value of the withholding tax. In addition, cash lenders do not require a haircut on the collateral in Italy.

5. Marcia Stigum spotted the arbitrage opportunity and reported it in her book on money markets.

6. A more detailed description of the covered interest arbitrage strategy can be found in Stigum and Robinson (1997).

7. The 12-day, 26-day, and 9-day EMAs are commonly used in MACD.

CHAPTER 12

1. The Federal Reserve Bank of New York; and Muehring, Kevin, The Fed's repo man, *Institutional Investor* (April 1997): 45–48.

2. Some market participants call it letter repo or a due bill.

3. The financing is usually done with the same dealer. A different dealer is used here for illustrative purpose only.

4. A roll is when a dealer purchases from a customer the outstanding Treasury for next day settlement and simultaneously sells to the same customer the same amount of the recently announced new issue for forward settlement. The forward, known as when-issued sale, settles on the new issue settlement date. The roll is the spread between the yield on the to-be-auctioned new security and that on the outstanding issue.

5. These are estimates based on data from June 1992 through January 1995 by Frank Keane (1995).

6. Other factors include the size of its coupon, whether or not it is deliverable into a futures contract, whether it is a benchmark issue, and tax consideration.

7. This was reported in Darrell Duffie (1996).

8. See, for example, Duffie (1996) and Rogg (1991).

9. Patriot Secs. is a wholly-owned subsidiary of Liberty Brokerage Inc.

10. A division of Cantor Fitzgerald Secs.

11. In a reverse, a dealer usually first looks into in-house customer accounts to see if the securities are available. If not, the next step is the dealer will talk to other dealers for the collateral. Brokers are the last resort. Brokers usually try to find specific issues from regional banks or S&Ls. In doing so, brokers are providing a real service to the dealer. When a portfolio manager does a reverse, it is frequently part of an arbitrage. Typically, the broker points out an arbitrage opportunity to a manager and provides one-stop shopping.

12. The complete guidelines are available at The Bond Market Association, 40 Broad Street, New York, NY 10004-2373.

13. Reversals can be done at any time during the day prior to the closing of the Fed, but 3:15 P.M. to 3:30 P.M. is reserved exclusively for reversals.

CHAPTER 13

1. There are numerous types of options, including geographic options, barrier options, compound and installment options, digital options, exchange options, and Asian options.

2. According to a *Business Week* report (February 23, 1998), Dell Computer saved $1.6 billion and Microsoft reaped $600 million from the options techniques that are used in line with stock repurchase programs. Boeing, IBM, Intel, McDonald's and Maytag all have used these techniques.

3. This is the principal method individual investors use to enter the high-yield market.

4. Defaulted issues are included in the outstanding par value calculations. The rates would be slightly higher if defaulted issues were excluded from the par value outstanding.

5. The Federal Reserve Bank of New York; and Muehring, Kevin, "The Fed's repo man," *Institutional Investor* (April 1997): 45–48.

6. It is important to know that a unique feature in equity swap is that the return could be negative.

7. As reported in "Dizzying new ways to dice up debt," *Business Week*, (July 21, 1997): 102–03.

8. John D. Finnerty. "Interpreting SIGNs," *Financial Management* 22 (Summer 1993): 34–47.

CHAPTER 14

1. The list includes Merrill Lynch, Goldman Sachs, Morgan Stanley Dean Witter, Salomon Smith Barney, Donaldson Lufkin Jenrette, Lehman Brothers, BT Alex. Brown, BA Robertson Stephens, J.P. Morgan, and Credit Suisse First Boston.

2. Only qualified investors may become new investors in the fund. Even if a hedge fund has only 91 non-qualified investors, it may not add a 92nd. All non-qualified investors must have acquired at least part of their interests in the fund on or before September 1, 1996.

3. A board of director governs a mutual fund when the fund is established as a corporation. A board of trustees governs the fund when it is established as a business trust.

4. For example, in 1994 through its sales force the mutual fund industry sold $854 billion, and direct marketing took in $471 billion. In 1995, sales force contributed $820 billion new investments and direct marketing was responsible for $571 billion new cash flow.

5. Institutional investors include retirement plan sponsors, foundations, nonprofit organizations, personal trusts and estates, and corporations.

CHAPTER 15

1. Government Securities Clearing Corporation provides netting for clearance and settlement.

2. Before coupon announcement, WI trades on yields.

3. U.S. government securities are DVP (delivery versus payment).

CHAPTER 16

1. The enforcement includes amendments.

2. In addition, companies seeking to have their securities registered and listed for public trading on an exchange must file a registration statement with the exchange and the SEC. If they meet the size test, companies whose equity securities are traded OTC must file a similar registration form. The required documents are generally comparable to, but less extensive than, the disclosures required in Securities Act registration statement.

3. In 1996, NASD Regulation processed 2,718 offerings with a total value of more than $330 billion. Of the offerings reviewed, 25% did not require modification. The other 75% required either additional information or a change in compensation amount.

4. Also include securities of municipal, state, federal, and other domestic governmental agencies.

5. Previous trading practices rules required a restricted period of 2 or 5 business days prior to pricing.

6. Include natural persons with at least $5 million in investment and entities with at least $25 million in investments.

Glossary

Aftermarket   The public market for a security after the initial public offering.

Alternative investment market   A separate section on the London Stock Exchange for listing young and fast-growing companies.

American depository receipt   A registered certificate issued by an American depositary in the name of a particular foreign issuer.

Asset securitization   The process of packaging illiquid individual loans and debt instruments into liquid securities.

Back-end load   The charge when mutual fund shares are redeemed. Also called redemption fee.

Basis point   One one-hundredth of 1%.

Best efforts   An underwriting arrangement in which underwriters only agree to use their best efforts to sell the shares on the issuer's behalf.

Bid-to-cover ratio   The ratio of the bids received to the amount awarded in a Treasury auction.

Big Bang   Securities market reforms in UK that included lifting the separation of jobbers and brokers, extending dealership to banks and other financial institutions, and deregulating commissions.

Blue Sky laws   State securities laws that protect investors against fraud.

Book-entry securities   Securities that are not in physical certificate form but instead are maintained in computerized records.

Bought deal   A firm commitment by the underwriter to purchase an entire offering from the issuer.

Brady bonds   Brady bonds are created under the 1990 Brady Plan. Brady bonds are collateralized securities that have resulted from the exchange of commercial bank loans into new bonds. There are four basic types: par or discount, debt conversion, front loaded interest reduction, and interest arrears capitalization bonds.

Break fee   Payments by the target to the first accepted bidder if it is beaten out by another offer.

Bulge bracket firm   Major underwriter in a syndicate.

Call auction   In a call auction, orders are collected for execution at predetermined points in time. A clearing price is set to maximize the trading volume.

Carry   The difference between interest income and interest expense.

Chinese wall   The safeguards, also called firewalls, that separate commercial and investment banking activities.

CHIPS   Clearing House Interbank Payment System.

Clearing   The processing of a trade and the establishment of what the parties to the trade owe to each other.

Closed-end mutual fund   One type of investment company that offers a fixed number of shares and the shares are traded on exchanges.

Collared floater   A floating rate debt with a cap and floor on its interest rate.

Collateralized bond obligation   Securitized pool of junk bonds and leveraged loans. The credit ratings are generally higher than the underlying assets, because of the added credit enhancements.

Collateralized mortgage obligation   A mortgage backed security that has separate tranches with a whole range of maturities backed by one or more pools of mortgages or path-throughs.

Comfort letter   A letter from an accountant expressing negative assurance on any unaudited interim financial statements included in the prospectus.

Commercial paper   An unsecured promissory note with a maturity of no more than 270 days.

Commodity swap   In a commodity swap agreement, each counterparty promises to make a series of payments to the other, and a commodity price or index determines at least one set of the payments.

Constructive insider   Attorneys, investment bankers, and accountants hired by the company have an abstain–disclose duty while in possession of material nonpublic information.

Convertible arbitrage   Trading involves the purchase of convertible bonds or preferred stocks and then hedging that investment by selling short the underlying equity.

Cooling off period   A period following the filing of the registration statement with the SEC, prior to the issue's offering.

Coupon pass-through   The collateral holder in a repurchase transaction has to pass over to the cash borrower any coupon received from the collateral.

Coupon roll   A coupon roll trade is when a dealer purchases from a customer an on-the-run coupon security for next-day settlement and simultaneously sells to that customer the same amount of the recently announced new security for forward settlement.

Credit default swap   A synthetic instrument in which one counterparty pays a premium in return for a contingent payment triggered by the default of the reference credits.

Credit linked notes   A structured note in which the instrument has an embedded option that allows the issuer to reduce the security's payments if a key financial variable specified deteriorates.

Credit spread contract   The payoffs of the contract depend on the yield differential between a credit-sensitive instrument and the reference security.

Currency swap   In a currency swap contract, the two counterparties agree to exchange certain amounts of currencies on scheduled dates.

Custodian   A bank that holds securities in custody for a customer.

Customer repo   The Fed buys collateral on behalf of a customer.

Delivery versus payment   Funds and securities are transferred at the same time.

Diet   Japanese legislature.

Digital option   A type of option that pays either a large lump sum or nothing.

Direct offering   Issuing companies bypass the underwriters and brokerages, and market the securities directly to investors.

DK   Don't know, indicating one party lacks knowledge of a trade or receives conflicting instructions from a counterparty.

Drag-along agreement   When a venture capitalist is the majority shareholder, it frequently insists on the right to find buyers for all or part of the portfolio company.

DTC   Depositary Trust Company.

Dual-currency bond   A debt security that pays interest in one currency and the bond is redeemed in another currency.

Due diligence   Obligation of the underwriter to investigate and assure that there are no misstatements or omissions in the registration statement.

EDGAR   SEC's Electronic Data Gathering, Analysis, and Retrieval.

Effective date   Date when an offering is declared effective by the SEC. The issue can now be sold to the public.

EMCC   Emerging Markets Clearing Corporation.

Emerging market   The securities markets of developing countries and the use they make of international capital markets.

EMTA   Emerging Markets Traders Association.

Equity kicker   Bridge financing often includes an equity kicker in the form of a warrant to purchase equity securities at a discount. The size of the warrant is tied to the length of time the bridge financing is in place.

Equity swap   An equity swap involves an investor receiving capital gains plus dividends in a target market and in turn paying to the swap dealer LIBOR and any decrease in the market index.

Equity takedown   An investment banker commits to buy a large block of stock at a discount from the issuing company after the market closes, and then seeks to redistribute these shares to clients before market opens the next day.

ERISA   Employee Retirement Income Security Act of 1974.

Euro median-term note   Euro issues that offer tranches tailored to investor requirements.

Euro straight   Eurobonds that pay fixed-rate coupons.

Eurobonds   Eurobonds are denominated in a currency different from the currency of the country in which they are issued.

Eurocommercial paper   A short-term bearer, unsecured zero-coupon security with a maturity range of 7 to 365 days.

Euromarket   The global market, trading around the clock in all major financial centers throughout the world.

European Monetary Union   The union is based on the 1991 Maastricht Treaty. The European Monetary Union (EMU) is scheduled to go into effect in January 1999 when the euro becomes a currency of the euroland.

Exempt securities   Securities that are exempt from SEC registration requirements.

Fallen angel   A bond that was rated investment grade at issue but was downgraded to junk status after its issuer's financial status deteriorated.

Fedwire   A Federal Reserve communications and settlement system that enables financial institutions to transfer funds and book-entry securities.

Filing date   The day the underwriter turns in the registration statement with the SEC.

Financial buyer   A buyer of a target company for financial gains, not for strategic or consolidating purposes.

Firm commitment   A type of underwriting agreement in which investment bankers risk their own capital by purchasing the whole block of new securities from the issuer and then resell them to the public.

First-price auction   A Treasury auction technique in which each accepted bidder pays his bid price for the security awarded.

Flex repo   A term repurchase agreement lasting for several years that provides for principal drawdowns prior to its final maturity.

Floater   A security with the interest rate tied to LIBOR or T-bill rate.

Floating-rate note   A Eurobond that pays a variable-rate coupon.

Flotation cost   The total costs of issuing securities.

Front-end load   A front-end load is one that purchasers of mutual funds pay when they buy the fund shares.

Glass–Steagall Act   The 1933 act separates commercial and investment banking activities.

Global depositary receipt   The underlying shares are held with a local custodian, and the depositary issues certificates—global depositary receipts—to foreign markets.

Good delivery   Delivery of the correct security in an acceptable form.

Green shoe option   An option allowing investment bankers to purchase up to a specified number of additional shares from the issuer in the event they sell more than agreed in the underwriting agreement. Also called over-allotment option.

Gross settlement   Transactions are settled on a bilateral, trade-for-trade basis.

Gross spread   The difference between the price offered to the public and the price the underwriter pays to the issuer.

GSCA   Government Securities Clearing Arrangement.

GSCC   Government Securities Clearing Corporation.

Haircut   A margin required when borrowing money in the repo market.

Hedge fund   A private investment fund that employs investment strategies in various types of securities in various markets and whose offering memorandum allows for the fund to take both long and short positions, and use leverage and derivatives.

Hit   A trader who agrees to sell at the bid price quoted by another dealer is said to hit that bid.

IBFs   International Banking Facilities.

Impact day   In the United Kingdom, this is the day when details of a new issue are published and when the underwriting or placing agreements become effective.

Indenture   A bond contract that sets forth the legal obligations of the issuer and names a trustee representing the interests of the bondholders.

Index arbitrage   An index arbitrage trades in the cash and futures markets when the differences between the theoretical futures price and the actual futures price are sufficiently large to generate arbitrage profits.

Indexed repo   A term repo with interest rate reset periodically based on a certain benchmark.

Initial public offering   A company's first equity issue in the public markets. Also called an IPO.

Insider trading   Trading based on nonpublic information.

Interest-only class   A stripped mortgage-backed security that receives all interest payments from the underlying mortgages.

Interest-rate swap   A contract between two parties in which each party agrees to make a series of interest payments to the other on scheduled dates.

Intrastate offering   An exempt offering where the securities are sold only to residents of a single state and the issuer is both a resident and doing business within that state.

Inverse floater   A floating-rate security whose interest rate moves inversely with a specified reference rate.

Investment adviser   An investment adviser is a person who engages in the business of providing advice or issuing reports about securities to clients for compensation.

Investment Advisers Act   The 1940 act requires registration of investment advisers and compliance with statutory standards.

Investment banking   Underwriting and distribution of new issues of securities, and mergers and acquisitions.

Investment Company Act   The 1940 act governs the activities of investment companies.

ISCC   International Securities Clearing Corporation.

ISMA   International Securities Market Association.

Junk bonds   High-yield debt instruments with credit ratings below investment grade.

Lehman 5–4–3–2–1 formula   One fee scale in the M&A market. Under this formula, 5% is paid on the first $1 million of sale price, 4% on the next $1 million, 3% on the next $1 million, 2% on the next $1 million, and 1% on the amount in excess of $4 million.

Letter repo   A term used to describe repo transactions when collateral is not delivered to the investor.

LIBID   London InterBank Bid, which is the rate London banks offer to borrow from each other.

LIBOR   London Interbank Offered Rate.

LIMEAN   The midpoint between LIBOR and LIBID.

Long bond   The 30-year Treasury bond.

Managing underwriter   The lead investment bank of an underwriting syndicate.

Market impact   Market impact is the difference between the price at which a stock trade is executed and the average of that stock's high, low, opening, and closing of the day.

Matched book   In a matched book operation, the quantities of securities reversed in and repoed out are the same.

Merchant banking   An investment bank commits its own capital on a long-term basis by taking an equity interest or creditor position in companies.

MBSCC   Mortgage Backed Securities Clearing Corporation.

Misappropriators   Under the misappropriation theory, an outsider can be criminally liable if he breaches a duty arising from a relationship of trust and confidence and uses that information in securities transactions, regardless of whether he owed any fiduciary responsibility to the shareholders of the traded stock.

Mortgage pass-through   Securities backed by pools of mortgage obligations in which payments of the underlying mortgages are passed over to the security holders.

MSRB   Municipal Securities Rulemaking Board.

Mutual fund   An investment management company that pools together from investors who have similar investment objectives.

NASD   National Association of Securities Dealers.

Net settlement   A clearing corporation establishes a single net position for each participant each day in a given security.

Nondeliverable forward   An NDF contract is an agreement in which the returns for a specified notional investment in an indexed asset are settled for cash in the reference currency.

Note Issuance Facilities   Corporate customer has the choice of drawing down a loan at an agreed formula based on LIBOR or selling Euro-CP through banks.

NSCC   National Securities Clearing Corporation.

NSMIA   National Securities Markets Improvement Act of 1996.

Official statement   An underwriter of municipal securities must deliver an official statement in connection with the issue. An official statement describes the issue, the issuer, and the legal opinions.

Open-end mutual fund   A type of mutual fund structure that continuously offers new shares to the public and accepts redemption based on the net asset value of the fund.

Open repo   An arrangement in a repurchase transaction in which the repo is rolled over until terminated by either party.

Pacman strategy   The counterattack by the acquisition target to tender the acquirer's shares.

Pari passu   New shares issued that rank equally with the old shares.

Phantom stock   An employer's stock that is credited to selected employees as nonqualified deferred compensation benefits tied primarily to the success of the corporate employer. Each year, the employee is vested with a specified number of shares in the account. The employee is entitled to the value of the vested shares.

Poison pill   A right distributed to shareholders that allows them to buy additional shares triggered by certain events.

Poison shares   Preferred stock with super voting right, triggered by unwanted takeover attack.

Pooling of interest   The most popular method companies use in big stock mergers. Poolings let companies simply combine their assets that do not create goodwill charges.

Portfolio company   A company in which a venture capital has invested.

Preliminary prospectus   The preliminary prospectus is filed with the SEC and provided by underwriters to prospective purchasers. It does not disclose the offering price, underwriting spread, or net proceeds. Also known as red herring.

Prepayment   Homeowners have the option to pay off the principal outstanding and not make any more mortgage payments.

Primary dealers   Banks and securities broker–dealers that bid at the auction and trade government securities with the Federal Reserve Bank of New York.

Primary offering   An offering of a company of unissued securities.

Principal-only class   A stripped mortgage backed security that receives all principal payments from the underlying mortgages.

Private placement   The sale of new securities to a few qualified investors instead of through a public offering. Privately placed securities do not have to be registered with the SEC.

Prospectus   Part I of the registration statement is the prospectus that contains detailed information on the issue and on the issuer's condition and prospects. This is distributed to the public as an offering document. Before the final prospectus is completed, securities firms generally distribute the preliminary prospectus, also called the red herring, to perspective investors.

Qualified institutional buyer   An institution that has at least $100 million of securities under investment. For registered dealers, the requirements are $10 million.

Quiet period   The period that begins with the signing of the letter of intent and ends 25 days after the effective date if the security is listed on an exchange or quoted on Nasdaq. During this period, the company is subject to SEC guidelines on publication of information outside of the prospectus.

Real estate swap   The property owner agrees to pay the counterparty who wants to get into the real estate market a rate of return linked to the performance of the real estate market. In exchange, the counterparty pays the property owner another type of return.

Red herring   The preliminary prospectus.

Registration statement   The document companies use to register with the SEC new issues of securities. Disclosed in the registration statement are various kinds of important information for investors when making investment decisions, including the business of the issuer, purpose of funds, description of the security, risk factors, and the background of management.

Regulation M   This piece of regulation, which took effect in March 1997, governs trading practices during securities distribution.

Repurchase agreement   A financing tool in which a dealer sells the collateral for cash and simultaneously contracts to repurchase the same securities at a future date and at a higher price that reflects the financing rate.

Restricted securities   Securities purchased in a private placement directly from an issuer are subject to a one-year holding period restriction. Restricted securities frequently will have a legend printed on the back of the certificate stating that the shares cannot be sold or disposed of without either registration under the Securities Act of 1933 or an exemption from such registration.

Risk arbitrage   In the merger and acquisition market, risk arbitrageurs long the target stocks while shorting the acquirer's at the same time.

Rule 144   It governs the sale of restricted securities acquired in a private placement.

Rule 144A   This rule addresses private sales of restricted securities among qualified institutional buyers.

Samurai bond   Yen denominated bonds issued in the Japanese market.

SCOR   A Small Corporate Offering Registration offering is exempt from SEC registration.

SEC   Securities and Exchange Commission.

Second-price auction   A Treasury auction technique in which all accepted bids pay the same price, the lowest price (highest yield) accepted. This is also called Dutch auction.

Secondary offering   A public offering of shares owned by existing shareholders.

Section 20 subsidiary   The Federal Reserve Board grants commercial banks expanded powers with respect to securities activities through reinterpretation of Section 20 of the Glass–Steagall Act. A commercial bank's subsidiary that is permitted to operate securities underwriting and dealing is called a Section 20 subsidiary.

Securities Act   The 1933 act requires registration of a new security issue unless an exemption is available, also known as "truth in securities" law.

Securities Exchange Act   This 1934 act requires timely and accurate disclosure of material information, and prohibits sales practice abuses and insider trading.

Settlement   The transfer of money and securities between parties to the trade so the transaction is complete.

Settlement fail   Trades fail to settle on settlement dates.

Shelf registration   An issuer files a single registration document indicating that it intends to sell a certain amount of securities at one or more times within the next two years. This is Rule 415.

Shell   An inactive public company with securities traded in the marketplace. It can be used as a back-door way of becoming a public company.

Short sale   The sale of securities not owned by the seller in the expectation of falling price or as part of an arbitrage.

Short squeeze   In a short squeeze, traders and arbitrageurs who short ahead of the auction are forced to pay a sharply higher price to buy or accept a special repo rate to reverse in securities in order to make good delivery.

SIPC   Securities Investor Protection Corporation.

Special   When government securities trade at a lower rate than the general collateral in the repo market, these securities are called on special.

SRO   Self-Regulatory Organization.

Stabilization   Upon release of a new issue, the managing underwriter is allowed to bid for the securities in the aftermarket to provide price support.

Step-up callable note   A debt security that pays a higher and higher coupon if it is not called.

Stop yield   The highest yield that is accepted at the Treasury securities auction.

Stripped mortgage-backed securities   A type of mortgage pass-through that divides the cash flow from the underlying collateral on a pro rata basis across the security holders.

Structured arbitrage   Trades that exploit opportunities through the recombination and restructuring of securities. Also called primary market arbitrage.

Structured note Structured notes are debt securities, with interest and, at times, principal payments, depending on formulas and terms specific to the security.

Substitution In a repurchase transaction, the party that repos out securities generally has the right to make collateral substitution. There are two exceptions: reverse to cover short and reverse to maturity.

System repo The Fed's purchase of collateral for its own account.

T+1 Settlement is one business day after the trade date. This is a practice used in the government securities markets. In corporate securities markets, the current practice is T+3 in the United States.

Tail The tail of an auction is the difference between the average yield of all accepted bids and the stop yield.

Take A trader who agrees to buy at the dealer's offered price is said to take that offer.

Take along When the venture capitalist is a minority investor, it would want to have the right to sell alongside management and other shareholders.

Tombstone A boxed-in ad that appears in financial sections of newspapers or magazines and announces the particulars of a new security issue.

Total return swap In a total return swap, the counterparty exchanges the returns of the underlying assets for a floating rate of interest.

Treasury auction This is the method used to issue government securities. Currently, there are two techniques used in the auction: first price and second price.

Triparty repo A custodian bank maintains accounts for both parties in a repo transaction and, hence, the actual delivery of securities and cash can be reduced to just credit and debit transfers within the bank.

Underwriter spread The difference between the price the underwriters pay the issuer and the price they receive from resale of the securities.

Underwriting agreement The contract that establishes the relationship between the corporate issuer and the underwriting syndicate. It includes the type of underwriting, the underwriting spread, the offering price, and the number of shares.

Underwriting syndicate Each member in the underwriting syndicate is committed to buying a portion of the securities. There is also the selling group, which helps sell the issue but accepts no risk.

Waiting period The period that begins with the filing of the registration statement with the SEC and lasts until the offering is declared effective.

When-issued trading The when-issued (WI) trades of Treasury securities begin right after the auction announcement and last until the new issue settlement date.

White knight A common technique used in defending a hostile bidder. A white knight is a more compatible buyer that will pay a higher price on a friendly basis than the hostile bidder.

Yield burning Dealers sell Treasury securities to the escrow account of a municipality at inflated prices, thereby lowering yield.

Yield curve arbitrage A yield curve arbitrage involves trading bonds of different maturities on the yield curve.

Index

About the Author

K. Thomas Liaw, Ph.D., is a finance professor at St. John's University. He has a consulting practice in private equity and securities business. He has also been invited to speak on various subjects of capital markets at executive business conferences and securities firms. Professor Liaw has published articles in the areas of Treasury coupon rolls, repurchase agreements, mergers and acquisitions, and market risks. His principal areas of teaching and research include capital markets, trading, risk management, and investment banking. His most recent book publication is *Foreign Participation in China's Banking and Securities Markets*. He has also co-chaired an annual *Economics and Business Conference* and co-edited several books on emerging markets. Professor Liaw holds his Ph.D. from Northwestern University.